A COMMON CULTURAL HERITAGE

STUDIES ON MESOPOTAMIA AND THE BIBLICAL WORLD IN HONOR OF BARRY L. EICHLER

Barry L. Eichler

A COMMON CULTURAL HERITAGE

STUDIES ON MESOPOTAMIA AND THE BIBLICAL WORLD

IN HONOR OF
BARRY L. EICHLER

edited by
Grant Frame,
Erle Leichty,
Karen Sonik,
Jeffrey Tigay,
Steve Tinney

CDL Press
Bethesda, Maryland
2011

LIBRARY OF CONGRESS CATALOGING-IN-PUBLICATION DATA

A common cultural heritage : studies on Mesopotamia and the biblical world in honor of Barry l. Eichler / edited by Grant Frame ... [et al.].
p. cm.
ISBN 978-1-934309-37-7 (alk. paper)
1. Bible. O.T.—Criticism, interpretation, etc. 2. Middle Eastern literature—History and criticism. I. Frame, Grant. II. Eichler, Barry L. III. Title: Studies on Mesopotamia and the Biblical World in Honor of Barry L. Eichler. IV. Title.

BS1171.3.C65 2011
221.9--dc23 2011034292

The tablet on the cover is the laws of Lipit-Ishtar (UM 29-16-55 + UM 29-16-249 + N 1791); courtesy of the University of Pennsylvania Museum of Archaeology and Anthropology. The Cairo Genizah fragment containing Genesis 10:14-12:15 with Masorah magna and parva (Halper 002) is courtesy of the Library at the Herbert D. Katz Center for Advanced Judaic Studies, University of Pennsylvania.

ISBN 978–1934309–377

CONTENTS

PREFACE

Barry Eichler's scholarship covers a range of fields that in our age of specialization are generally separated because any one of them is a full-time pursuit: Sumerian and Akkadian language and literature, biblical studies, and Jewish law and ethics. This range is evident in his book and articles about the legal documents from Nuzi, such as his retrospective study of "Nuzi and the Bible," in which he surveys, corrects, and updates a generation's worth of influential scholarship about those documents and the light they shed on the Bible; his masterful comparative survey of "Law and Morality in Ancient Near Eastern Thought" and—in contrast to these broad studies of concepts and legal institutions—his subtle word-studies, which juxtapose terms in Sumerian, Akkadian, Ugaritic, Egyptian, Coptic, Hebrew, Aramaic, and Arabic and draw on archaeological and artistic evidence, all in mutual illumination. His major research interests focus on the cultural interrelationships between Mesopotamia and Israel, particularly in the areas of law, religion, and historiography. He views his subject matter through philological, literary-critical, anthropological, and jurisprudential lenses simultaneously, a combination brilliantly illustrated by his masterful multidisciplinary study "On Reading Genesis 12:10–20." His publications are original, thoughtful, profound, insightful, and methodologically sophisticated, but at the same time unpretentious. Barry's peers know him as a brilliant scholar and a profound thinker. His students know him as a devoted, conscientious, and quietly inspiring teacher. He is one of the fairest, most modest, selfless and compassionate persons any of us know.

It was inconceivable that Barry's retirement from the University of Pennsylvania—though not from the academic and scholarly life that is an innate part of him—should pass unmarked by some small token of appreciation by his many colleagues, students, and friends. Thus, on

March 30, 2009, the conference "Tablet and Torah: Mesopotamia and the Biblical World," reflecting his major research interests, was held at the University Museum. Fifteen individuals who had been either his student or his one-time classmate presented papers in his honor. These papers, along with three others, are published here. It is a great pleasure for us to dedicate this volume to him. The title of the volume is taken from Barry's article "The Study of Bible in Light of Our Knowledge of the Ancient Near East" in *Modern Scholarship in the Study of the Torah: Contributions and Limitations*, ed. S. Carmy, p. 81, and reflects one of the ideas that animates his own scholarship and teaching.

Generous support for the conference and the publication of this volume came from a number of places in the University of Pennsylvania's academic community: the Center for Ancient Studies, the Department of Near Eastern Languages and Civilizations, the Jewish Studies Program, Penn Hillel, the University of Pennsylvania Museum of Archaeology and Anthropology, and, in particular, a Mellon Grant for Cross Cultural Studies administered by the School of Arts and Sciences.

Our appreciation must be expressed to several people for their help in the preparation of this manuscript: Jonathan Ben-Dov, Erik Hermans, Shalom Holtz, and Ariel Smith. The photograph of Barry on p. ii was kindly supplied by Yeshiva University's Bernard Revel Graduate School of Jewish Studies.

Grant Frame
Erle Leichty
Karen Sonik
Jeffrey Tigay
Steve Tinney

FOREWORD

When E.A. Speiser died prematurely in 1965 his colleague, S.N. Kramer, who was nearing retirement age, arranged the appointment of Åke W. Sjöberg to Speiser's open faculty position. Three years later, in 1968, I was invited to join the Penn faculty to resurrect Speiser's Assyriological program. Before I was able to start at Penn, M. Greenberg left for Jerusalem and Hebrew University, thus leaving a broken Bible program as well. Soon after I arrived at Penn I was informed by Åke, whom I knew from our days together at the Oriental Institute, that we had a third Assyriological colleague, Barry L. Eichler. Barry was an Instructor of Assyriology in our department, at that time, Oriental Studies. He was on leave that academic year (1968–69) and was spending his leave at Yale while preparing his dissertation for publication.

Speiser had spent the last few months of his life taking care of his advanced graduate students, managing to place nearly all of them, both recent graduates and a handful of all but dissertation students. Barry L. Eichler was his legacy to Penn.

When Barry returned to Penn after his year's leave I had the opportunity to discuss the Penn Assyriological and Bible programs with him at length. I was delighted to find that we entertained complete agreement on what these programs should look like. I was even more delighted to learn that Barry's research and teaching interests were wholly complementary and non-conflicting with those of Åke and mine. Åke was immersed in the third millennium BCE and Sumerian literature, Barry was anchored in the second millennium BCE with special interests in Mari, Nuzi, legal and literary texts, while I was involved with first-millennium BCE texts, especially historical, divinatory, and economic documents.

We were all trained philologists. The first order of business was fixing the Ancient Near East and Bible programs. For Bible we hired J. Tigay, a recent Yale Ph.D. in Bible and Assyriology. Since we had inherited J. Muhly, who did Hittite, J. Pritchard in Biblical Archaeology, and R. Dyson in Near Eastern Archaeology, we had a potentially very strong program. We managed later to add I. Winter in the Art History program. Our only problem was the fact that Muhly, Eichler, and Tigay were untenured, but that problem was resolved over the next few years.

At that time the Museum was building a new, academic wing and the design had been drawn up with only S. N. Kramer in mind, so there were two adjacent, interconnecting offices and the tablet room. When we moved into the new wing Åke took one office and Barry and I doubled up in the other, a situation that remained until my retirement.

Åke, Barry, and I had radically different teaching methods, but we all communicated well with each other and with our students. I believe our students profited from our different styles. Barry taught beginning Akkadian, advanced courses in his primary interests, and occasional courses in Bible. Åke taught Sumerian and Muhly taught Hittite and history. I taught second-year Akkadian, history, and advanced courses in first-millennium Akkadian.

It was quickly apparent that Barry was the best teacher in our Ancient Near Eastern group. He taught both undergraduates and graduates at all levels. He was always thoroughly prepared and he had endless patience. Barry refused to accept that some students were not going to do well. If a student was not performing up to snuff, Barry assumed that problem lay in his teaching, not in the student. I watched him spend extraordinary quantities of time tutoring lagging students until they grasped what he was trying to communicate to them. He did everything possible to prevent any student from doing poorly in any of his courses.

Barry also was the most conscientious administrator in our program. I regret to say that Åke and I, and to some extent the rest of our group, took advantage of him and let him take care of the petty tasks of teaching, such as checking the course roster every term and filling out much of the minor paper work in both the department and the Museum. We are both very grateful for all of the help he gave us over the years.

I could not have asked for a better colleague in my years at Penn than Barry L. Eichler. I think it is very appropriate that we honor his retirement with this small volume written by his former students and one-time classmates.

Erle Leichty
Clark Professor of Assyriology Emeritus

ABBREVIATIONS

AASOR	Annual of the American Schools of Oriental Research
ABAW	Abhandlungen der Bayerischen Akademie der Wissenschaften
AbB	Altbabylonische Briefe in Umschrift und Übersetzung
ABCD	F. Rochberg-Halton. *Aspects of Babylonian Celestial Divination: The Lunar Eclipse Tablets of Enūma Anu Enlil*. Archiv für Orientforschung Beiheft 22. Horn: Ferdinand Berger und Söhne, 1988
ABL	R. F. Harper. *Assyrian and Babylonian Letters Belonging to the Kouyunjik Collections of the British Museum*. 14 vols. Chicago: University of Chicago Press, 1892–1914
ACh	Ch. Virolleaud. *L'astrologie chaldéenne: Le Livre intitulé "Enuma (Anu) ^{ilu}Bêl"*. Paris: H. Welter, 1908–1912
AfO	*Archiv für Orientforschung*
AHw	W. von Soden. *Akkadisches Handwörterbuch*. Wiesbaden: Harrassowitz, 1959–1981
AJA	*American Journal of Archaeology*
AMD	Ancient Magic and Divination
ANEP	J. B. Pritchard, ed. *Ancient Near East in Pictures Relating to the Old Testament*. Princeton: Princeton University Press, 1954
ANET	J. B. Pritchard, ed. *Ancient Near Eastern Texts Relating to the Old Testament*. 3rd edition with Supplement. Princeton: Princeton University Press, 1969
AnOr	Analecta Orientalia
AO	*Der Alte Orient*
AO	Antiquités Orientales, Louvre (Paris), museum siglum
AOAT	Alter Orient und Altes Testament
AOS	American Oriental Series
ARE	J. H. Breasted. *Ancient Records of Egypt: Historical Documents from the Earliest Times to the Persian Conquest*. 5 vols.

	Chicago: University of Chicago Press, 1906–1907
ARM	Archives royales de Mari
ArOr	*Archiv Orientálni*
AS	Assyriological Studies
ASJ	*Acta Sumerologica*
BAP	B. Meissner. *Beiträge zum altbabylonischen Privatrecht* Leipzig: J. C. Hinrichs, 1893
BASOR	*Bulletin of the American Schools of Oriental Research*
BBSt	L. W. King, ed. *Babylonian Boundary-Stones and Memorial-Tablets in the British Museum.* 2 vols. London: British Museum, 1912
BDB	F. Brown, S. R. Driver, and C. A. Briggs. *A Hebrew and English Lexicon of the Old Testament with an Appendix Containing the Biblical Aramaic.* Corrected Edition. Oxford: Clarendon Press, 1951
BE	The Babylonian Expedition of the University of Pennsylvania
BiAr	*Biblical Archaeologist*
BM	British Museum siglum
BWL	W. G. Lambert. *Babylonian Wisdom Literature*. Oxford: Clarendon Press, 1960; Winona Lake, Ind.: Eisenbrauns, 1996
BZAW	Beihefte zur Zeitschrift für die alttestamentliche Wissenschaft
CAD	A. L. Oppenheim et al., eds. *The Assyrian Dictionary of the Oriental Institute of the University of Chicago*. Chicago: Oriental Institute of the University of Chicago, 1956–
Camb.	J. N. Strassmaier. *Inschriften von Cambyses, König von Babylon (529-521 v. Chr.).* Babylonische Texte 9. Leipzig: E. Pfeiffer, 1890
CBQ	*Catholic Biblical Quarterly*
CBS	Babylonian Section, University of Pennsylvania Museum of Archaeology and Anthropology (Philadelphia), museum siglum
CIS	*Corpus inscriptionum semiticarum.* Paris: E. Reipublicae Typographico, 1881-
COS	William W. Hallo et al., eds. *The Context of Scripture.* 3 vols. Leiden: Brill, 1997-2002

CRRAI Compte rendu de la Rencontre Assyriologique Internationale

CT Cuneiform Texts from Babylonian Tablets in the British Museum

Dar. J. N. Strassmaier. *Inschriften von Darius, König von Babylon (521-485 v. Chr.).* Babylonische Texte 10. Leipzig: E. Pfeiffer, 1892

DBH M. Z. Kaddari. *A Dictionary of Biblical Hebrew (Alef-Taw).* Ramat-Gan: Bar-Ilan University Press, 2007

DCH J. A. Clines and J. Edwolde, eds. *The Dictionary of Classical Hebrew.* Sheffield: Sheffield Academic Press, 1993

EA J. A. Knudtzon. *Die El-Amarna-Tafeln.* Leipzig: J. C. Hinrichs, 1915

EN D. I. Owen, M. A. Morrison, et al. *General Studies and Excavations at Nuzi.* Winona Lake, Ind.: Eisenbrauns; Bethesda, Md.: CDL Press, 1987–

ESV English Standard Version of the Bible

ETCSL Electronic Text Corpus of Sumerian Literature

EVO *Egitto e Vicino Oriente*

FAOS Freiburger altorientalische Studien

Gesenius-Donner W. Gesenius, *Hebräisches und aramäisches Handwörterbuch.* 18th ed. Revised by H. Donner. Berlin: Springer, 1987–

H Tell Hadad excavation number

HALOT L. Koehler and W. Baumgartner. *The Hebrew and Aramaic Lexicon of the Old Testament*. Leiden: Brill, 1994–

HSM Harvard Semitic Monographs

HSS Harvard Semitic Series

HTR *Harvard Theological Review*

HUCA *Hebrew Union College Annual*

ICC International Critical Commentary

ISET S. Kramer, M. Çig, and H. Kizilyay. *Istanbul Arkeoloji Muezelerinde Bulunan Sumer edebî tablet ve parçalari* [Sumerian Literary Tablets and Fragments in the Archaeological Museum of Istanbul]. 2 vols. Ankara: Türk Tarih Kurumu Basimevi, 1969–1976

JAOS *Journal of the American Oriental Society*

JBL *Journal of Biblical Literature*

JCS *Journal of Cuneiform Studies*

JEN	E. Chiera, E. R. Lacheman, et al. *Joint Expedition with the Iraq Museum at Nuzi I-VIII.* Paris: P. Geuthner; Winona Lake, Ind.: Eisenbrauns; Bethesda: CDL Press, 1927-2003
JEOL	*Jaarbericht van het Vooraziatisch-Egyptisch-Gezelschap: Ex Oriente Lux*
JESHO	*Journal of the Economic and Social History of the Orient*
JNES	*Journal of Near Eastern Studies*
JPS	Jewish Publication Society Bible
JSOT	*Journal for the Study of the Old Testament*
KBo	Keilschrifttexte aus Boghazköi
KTU	M Dietrich, O. Loretz, J. Sanmartin et al. *Die keilalphabetischen Texte aus Ugarit*. Kevelaer: Butzon & Bercker, 1976
LAS	S. Parpola. *Letters from Assyrian Scholars to the Kings Esarhaddon and Assurbanipal.* 2 vols. AOAT 5/1-2. Kevelaer: Butzon & Bercker; Neukirchen-Vluyn: Neukirchener Verlag, 1970–1983
LH	Laws of Hammurabi
LKA	E. Ebeling. *Literarische Keilschrifttexte aus Assur.* Berlin: Akademie-Verlag, 1953
LL	Laws of Lipit-Ishtar
LU	Laws of Ur-Namma
MAH	Musée d'Art et d'Histoire (Geneva), museum siglum
MAL	Middle Assyrian Laws
MARI	*Mari Annales de Recherches Interdisciplinaires*
MSL	Materialien zum sumerischen Lexikon / Materials for the Sumerian Lexicon
N	Siglum for field registration numbers from the post World War II American excavations at Nippur
NABU	*Nouvelles Assyriologiques Brèves et Utilitaires*
Nbn	J. N. Strassmaier. *Inschriften von Nabonidus, König von Babylon (555–538 v. Chr).* Babylonische Texte 1-4. Leipzig: E. Pfeiffer, 1889
NF	Neue Folge
Ni	Siglum for items in the Nippur collection of the Arkeoloji Müzeleri (Istanbul)
NJPS	New Jewish Publication Society
NRSV	New Revised Standard Version of the Bible

N-T	Siglum (infix) for field registration numbers of inscribed objects from the post World War II American excavations at Nippur
OBO	Orbis Biblicus et Orientalis
OECT	Oxford Editions of Cuneiform Texts
OIP	Oriental Institute Publications
OrAnt	*Oriens Antiquus*
OrNS	*Orientalia* New Series
OTL	Old Testament Library
PBS	Publications of the Babylonian Section, University of Pennsylvania
PIHANS	Publications de l'Institut historique-archéologique néerlandais de Stamboul
PNA	K. Radner and H. D. Baker, eds. *The Prosopography of the Neo-Assyrian Empire.* Helsinki: The Neo-Assyrian Text Corpus Project, 1998–
PUL	Patrimoine de l'Université de Liège, collection siglum
RA	*Revue d'Assyriologie et d'Archéologie Orientale*
RB	*Révue biblique*
RBL	*Review of Biblical Literature*
RE	H. Gärtner et al. *Paulys Realencyklopädie der classischen Altertumswissenschaft.* Munich: A Druckenmüller, 1980
RIMA	Royal Inscriptions of Mesopotamia, Assyrian Periods
RlA	*Reallexikon der Assyriologie und Vorderasiatischen Archäologie*
RS	Ras Shamra Tablets, Louvre and Damascus Museum siglum
SAA	State Archives of Assyria
SAACT	State Archives of Assyria Cuneiform Texts
SAAS	State Archives of Assyria Studies
Sb	Susa collection, Louvre (Paris), museum siglum
SCCNH	Studies on the Civilization and Culture of Nuzi and the Hurrians
SCIAMVS	*Sources and Commentaries in Exact Sciences*
SJOT	*Scandinavian Journal of the Old Testament*
SLTN	S. N. Kramer. *Sumerian Literary Texts from Nippur in the Museum of the Ancient Orient at Istanbul.* New Haven: ASOR, 1944

STT	O. R. Gurney and J. J. Finkelstein. *The Sultantepe Tablets I.* London: British Institute of Archaeology at Ankara, 1957; O. R. Gurney and P. Hulin. *The Sultantepe Tablets II.* London: British Institute of Archaeology at Ankara, 1964
TAD	B. Porten and A. Yardeni. *Textbook of Aramaic Documents from Ancient Egypt*. 4 vols. Winona Lake, Ind.: Eisenbrauns, 1986–1999
TCL	Textes cunéiformes du Louvre
TDOT	*Theological Dictionary of the Old Testament*
TMH	Texte und Materialien der Frau Professor Hilprecht Collection of Babylonian Antiquities, im Eigentum der Universität Jena
TU	F. Thureau-Dangin. *Tablettes d'Uruk à l'usage des prêtres d'Anu au temps des Séleucides.* TCL 6. Paris: P. Geuthner, 1922
UE	Ur Excavations
UET	Ur Excavations, Texts
UF	*Ugarit-Forschungen*
UM	Babylonian Section, University of Pennsylvania Museum of Archaeology and Anthropology (Philadelphia), museum siglum
VAB	Vorderasiatische Bibliothek
VAS	Vorderasiatische Schriftdenkmäler der Königlichen Museen zu Berlin
VAT	Siglum for tablets in the collection of the Vorderasiatisches Museum (Berlin)
VT	*Vetus Testamentum*
YNER	Yale Near Eastern Researches
YOR	Yale Oriental Series, Researches
YOS	Yale Oriental Series, Babylonian Texts
YRL SC	Special Collections, Young Research Library, University of California at Los Angeles, collection siglum
ZA	*Zeitschrift für Assyriologie und verwandte Gebiete*
ZAW	*Zeitschrift für die alttestamentliche Wissenschaft*
ZDMG	*Zeitschrift der Deutschen Morgenländischen Gesellschaft*

THE PUBLICATIONS OF BARRY L. EICHLER

BOOKS AND EDITED VOLUMES

Indenture at Nuzi: The Personal Tidennūtu Contract and Its Mesopotamian Analogues. YNER 5. New Haven, Conn.: Yale University Press, 1973.

Kramer Anniversary Volume: Cuneiform Studies in Honor of Samuel Noah Kramer, editor. AOAT 25. Kevelaer: Butzon & Bercker; Neukirchen-Vluyn: Neukirchener Verlag, 1976.

The Sumerian Dictionary of the University Museum of the University of Pennsylvania, Volume 1/I–III: A and Volume 2: B, co-edited with Å. W. Sjöberg et al. Philadelphia, Pa.: Babylonian Section of the University Museum, 1984–98.

Judah Goldin: Studies in Midrash and Related Literature, co-edited with J. H. Tigay. Philadelphia, Pa.: Jewish Publication Society, 1988.

Tablet, Scroll and Book: Judaic Treasures. Van Pelt-Dietrich Library Exhibition Catalogue, January 20-March 18, 1994, 1–16. Philadelphia, Pa.: University of Pennsylvania, 1994.

Tehillah le-Moshe: Biblical and Judaic Studies in Honor of Moshe Greenberg, co-edited with M. Cogan and J. H. Tigay. Winona Lake, Ind.: Eisenbrauns, 1997.

"An Experienced Scribe Who Neglects Nothing": Ancient Near Eastern Studies in Honor of Jacob Klein, co-edited with Y. Sefati et al. Bethesda, Md.: CDL Press, 2005.

First-Year Akkadian: An Introduction. Forthcoming.

Inanna and Mt. Ebih. In preparation.

ARTICLES

"reṣaḥ." [English: "Homicide in Biblical and Ancient Near Eastern Law"]. *Encyclopaedia Biblica* 7 (1976): 426–31.

"šôgēg ûmēzîd." [English: "Intention in Biblical and Ancient Near Eastern Law"]. *Encyclopaedia Biblica* 7 (1976): 529–31.

"Bestiality." *Interpreter's Dictionary of the Bible Supplement* (1976): 96–97.

"Nuzi." *Interpreter's Dictionary of the Bible Supplement* (1976): 635–36.

"Another Look at the Nuzi Sistership Contracts." In *Essays on the Ancient Near East in Memory of Jacob Joel Finkelstein*, edited by M. deJong Ellis, 45–59. Connecticut Academy of Arts & Sciences, Memoir 19. Hamden, Conn.: Archon Books, 1977.

"'Please say that you are my sister': Nuzi and Biblical Studies." *Shnaton: An Annual for Biblical and Ancient Near Eastern Studies* 3 (1978–79): 108–15.

"Of Slings and Shields, Throwsticks and Javelins." *JAOS* 103 (1983): 95–102.

"Inheritance"; "Loan"; "Nuzi"; "Ownership"; "Perjury"; "Slavery"; "Stoning." *The Harper-Collins Bible Dictionary*, edited by P. J. Achtemeier et al. San Francisco, Calif.: HarperSanFrancisco, 1985; rev. ed. 1996.

"Literary Structure in the Laws of Eshnunna." In *Language, Literature and History: Philological and Historical Studies Presented to Erica Reiner*, edited by F. Rochberg-Halton, 71–84. AOS 67. New Haven, Conn.: American Oriental Society, 1987.

"Israelite Law. An Overview." In *Encyclopedia of Religion* 7, edited by M. Eliade et al., 466–69. New York, N.Y.: Macmillan, 1987.

"Nuzi and the Bible: A Retrospective." In *DUMU-E$_2$-DUB-BA-A: Studies in Honor of Åke W. Sjöberg*, edited by H. Behrens, D. Loding, and M. T. Roth, 107–19. Occasional Publications of the Samuel Noah Kramer Fund 11. Philadelphia, Pa.: Babylonian Section, University Museum, 1989.

"On Weaving Etymological and Semantic Threads: The Semitic Root *ql'*." In *Lingering over Words: Studies in Ancient Near Eastern Literature in Honor of William L. Moran*, edited by T. Abusch, J. Huehnergard, and P. Steinkeller, 163–69. HSS 37. Atlanta, Ga.: Scholars Press, 1990.

"The Mari Tablets"; "The Nuzi Tablets." *The Oxford Companion to the Bible*, edited by B. M. Metzger and M. D. Coogan. Oxford: Oxford University Press, 1993.

"mar-URU$_5$: Tempest in a Deluge." In *The Tablet and the Scroll, Near Eastern Studies in Honor of William W. Hallo*, edited by M. E. Cohen, D. C. Snell, and D. B. Weisberg, 90–94. Bethesda, Md.: CDL Press, 1993.

"The Study of Bible in Light of Our Knowledge of the Ancient Near East." In *Modern Scholarship in the Study of Torah: Contributions and Limitations*, edited by S. Carmy, 81–100. Northvale, N.J.: Jason Aronson, 1996.

"Moshe Greenberg: An Appreciation," (co-author). In *Tehillah le-Moshe: Biblical and Judaic Studies in Honor of Moshe Greenberg*, edited by M. Cogan, B. L. Eichler, and J. H. Tigay, ix–xxi. Winona Lake, Ind.: Eisenbrauns, 1997.

"On Reading Genesis 12:10–20." In *Tehillah le-Moshe: Biblical and Judaic Studies in Honor of Moshe Greenberg*, edited by M. Cogan, B. L. Eichler, and J. H. Tigay, 23–38. Winona Lake, Ind.: Eisenbrauns, 1997.

"Speiser, Ephraim Avigdor." In *The Oxford Encyclopedia of Archaeology in the Near East*, Vol. 5, edited by E. M. Meyers, 68–69. New York: Oxford University Press, 1997.

"Mesopotamian Ethics and Law Codes." In *Religions of the Ancient World: A Guide*, edited by S. I. Johnston, 516–19. Cambridge, Mass.: Harvard University Press, 2004.

"Cuneiform Studies at Penn: From Hilprecht to Leichty." In *If a Man Builds A Joyful House: Assyriological Studies in Honor of Erle Verdun Leichty*, edited by A. K. Guinan et al., 87–109. Cuneiform Monographs 31. Leiden: Brill, 2006.

"Exodus 21:22–25 Revisited: Methodological Considerations." In *Birkat Shalom: Studies in the Bible, Ancient Near Eastern Literature, and Postbiblical Judaism Presented to Shalom M. Paul on the Occasion of his Seventieth Birthday*, edited by C. Cohen, V. A. Hurowitz, A. Hurvitz, Y. Muffs, Baruch J. Schwartz, and J. H. Tigay, 11–29. Winona Lake, Ind.: Eisenbrauns, 2008.

"Law and Morality in Ancient Near Eastern Thought." In *Ethics, Politics, and Democracy: From Primordial Principles to Prospective Practices*, edited by J. V. Ciprut, 33–58. Cambridge, Mass.: MIT Press, 2008.

"Examples of Restatement in the Laws of Hammurabi." In *Mishneh Todah: Studies in Deuteronomy and Its Cultural Environment in Honor of Jeffrey H. Tigay*, edited by N. S. Fox, D. A. Glatt-Gilad, and M. J. Williams, 365–400. Winona Lake, Ind.: Eisenbrauns, 2009.

REVIEWS

Review of *Self-incrimination in Jewish Law*, by A. Kirschenbaum. *Journal of the American Academy of Religion* 41.2 (1973): 312–13.

Review of *Bernard Revel: Builder of American Jewish Orthodoxy*, by A. Rothkoff. *Tradition* 13 (1973): 212–16.

Contributing review editor to the "Survey of Recent Literature" for the *Jewish Law Annual* 1976–1987.

Review of *Studies in Biblical and Cuneiform Law*, by R. Westbrook. *Hebrew Studies* 34 (1993): 222–25.

Review of *Love and Joy: Law, Language and Religion in Ancient Israel*, by Y. Muffs. *JAOS* 117.4 (1997): 721–23.

Review of *Social Justice in Ancient Israel and the Ancient Near East*, by M. Weinfeld. *Jewish Quarterly Review* 89.1–2 (1998): 185–90.

THE KING OF JUSTICE

A RECONSIDERATION OF THE RIVER ORDEAL IN BM 456901*

JANICE BARRABEE

KOLB SOCIETY, UNIVERSITY OF PENNSYLVANIA

From the time that BM 456902 was first edited by Lambert,[1] the so-named "King of Justice" has received attention from scholars mainly due to the seemingly straightforward and descriptive account of a river ordeal inscribed upon the tablet. This unique literary text contemplating the themes of Mesopotamian kingship and the judicial system, as well as morality and social justice, demonstrates characteristics of royal inscriptions, law codes, and historical epics.[2] At the same time, it juxtaposes traditional structure and phrasing with more dramatic and realistic elements and vivid narrative characteristic of the "new style" of late Babylonian literature.[3] The text dates to the Neo-Babylonian period and was ascribed to Nebuchadnezzar II (605–562 BCE) by Lambert,[4] although others have reached the conclusion that Nabonidus (556–539 BCE) is more likely the ruler whose name appears in the lines that are now lost.[5]

---

* This article offered in honor of Prof. Barry Eichler stems from reading the "King of Justice" in his Akkadian class and my first fumbling attempts as a student to understand this text. It is the perfect vehicle to recognize his grace as a teacher of the neophyte and mentor of the more mature scholar. For the purpose of honoring my teacher, dissertation advisor, and a man I admire more than he knows, I will re-examine the lines we were reading and my interpretation and, in doing so, I hope to fulfill a promise I made to Prof. Eichler back then. It is with immense gratitude for both his example and his generosity in informing and forming my scholarship that I present this article here.

1 CT 46 45. Lambert, "Nebuchadnezzar," 1–11. For an updated edition with collations, see Schaudig, *Die Inschriften Nabonids*, 579–88. See also the translation in Foster, *Before the Muses*, 870–74, which incorporates new readings and translations.

2 See discussion in Lambert, "Nebuchadnezzar," 4; Grayson, *Babylonian Historical-Literary Texts*, 6 n. 5 and 43 n. 14; Frymer-Kensky, *Judicial Ordeal*, 462–63.

3 Foster, *Akkadian Literature*, 105–6; Lambert, "Nebuchadnezzar," 4.

4 Lambert, "Nebuchadnezzar," 2–3. See also Beaulieu, "Note on the River Ordeal," 58, and additionally, Beaulieu, *The Reign of Nabonidus*, 4–5.

5 Von Soden, Review of Grayson, *Babylonian Historical-Literary Texts*, 283;

Originally a six-column tablet, all that is preserved at this time is the bottom of columns ii and iii and the top of columns iv and v.[6] The beginning portion of the text, column i, is missing except for scattered and broken signs and fragments of words or phrases, but was most likely a preamble giving the name, titles, and epithets of the king in the manner typical of a royal inscription.[7]

The preserved text in column ii introduces the topic of moral, economic, and social corruption within the judicial system and law courts and the resulting reform.[8] Beginning with recognizable depictions of injustice, the intent is to indict the representatives and practices of the legal system, where, due to corruption at that time, the underprivileged have no course for redress.[9] The strong oppress the weak, as the latter are not equals within the legal system.[10] The rich take from the poor. Magistrates do not aid the unfortunate within the law courts.[11] In more specific terms, the text details the corruption of the judges as they sit in the court of law.[12] Bribes are accepted by the judge, but a favorable decision is not forthcoming.[13] The cases of those without means are ig-

---

von Soden, "Kyros und Nabonid," 63; Frymer-Kensky, *Judicial Ordeal*, 462; Schaudig, *Die Inschriften Nabonids*, 579–80.

6 For a possible additional fragment, see Schaudig, *Die Inschriften Nabonids*, 579.

7 See Foster, *Before the Muses*, 870. For the remnants of the column, see Schaudig, *Die Inschriften Nabonids*, 581.

8 Foster, "Social Reform," 170, 175; Silver, "Prophets and Markets Revisited," 184.

9 These expressions of social and judicial disorder are reminiscent of the language of the prologue of the Laws of Ur-Namma and the prologue and epilogue of the Code of Ḫammurabi, see Roth, *Law Collections*, 16, 76, 133. Similar statements occur in wisdom literature, such as the Babylonian Theodicy XXV 267–74, see Lambert, *BWL*, 86–87; Hallo, ed., *COS* I, 494–95, and passim in royal inscriptions. The obligation to right these wrongs and maintain social order falls under the purview of Šamaš, the god of justice, as well as the just king. It should be noted that the "King of Justice" is not advocating equality under the law, but a return to the correct moral, social, and judicial codes that reflect the unequal positions of the inhabitants of Babylonia, see Westbrook, "Social Justice in the Ancient Near East," 149–63; Irani, "Idea of Social Justice," 3.

10 Col. ii 3'–4'.

11 Col. ii 5'.

12 See a similar statement concerning a corrupt judge in the Šamaš Hymn, line 98 and the contrasting view of a benevolent and upstanding judge who is pleasing in the eyes of Šamaš, lines 99–100, Lambert, *BWL*, 132–33.

13 Col. ii 7'–8'.

nored.[14] The judge makes a mockery of a disaffected plaintiff, arriving at a decision, recording the judgment, and sealing the document; however, instead of delivering it to the petitioner, the judgment is discarded.[15] In this portion of the text, the political leaders and the juridical officials are depicted preventing the carrying out of justice and subverting the traditional channels of the judicial system.

Into this atmosphere of moral misconduct and judicial disarray enters the unnamed just king at the end of the preserved portion of column ii. According to the text, he does not neglect righteous judgment, tirelessly records beneficial judgments, improves regulations in the city of Babylon, and builds the law courts anew.[16] He puts an end to the courtroom practice of refusal to try cases and ignoring the claims of the lesser man. In opposition to the previously described corruption that pervades the legal system, the king corrects the balance, restoring social equilibrium and reinstituting law, stability, and peace to his realm in general, and specifically to the city of Babylon. At the end of this section there is a break of one line.

The preserved text resumes in the third column and continues into the fourth column with two separate vignettes depicting individual cases within the judicial system. These appear to provide examples of the new course of action initiated by the just king in order to address specific issues within the legal system. As will be demonstrated below, these cases relate to one another with regard to structure, context, and style, and support the theme of the text as a whole.

The first episode involves an individual who has received a judgment, but who returns to the courthouse for a new trial for "false and unjust purposes."[17] The justice of the king was swift. He had the head of the man cut off and sent throughout the land.[18] He had a head made in the likeness of the man and inscribed upon it: "A man whose case has

14 Col. ii 6'.

15 Col. ii 14'–17'. For comparison, see LH §5, vi 6–30 (Roth, *Law Collections*, 82), recording the punishment of a judge who has tried a case, given a verdict, written and sealed the document, but then changed his decision. Col. ii 14'–17' and the previous lines (col. ii 9'–13', which appear to relate to a specific case of usury brought before the court) provide an example of the realistic quality and narrative aspect of the "King of Justice," using a journalistic approach to furnish evidence to support the claims of corruption depicted in the text.

16 Col. ii 22'–27'.

17 Col. iii 4'–5': *a-na sur-ra-a-tú u la ki-na-a-tu*$_4$.

18 Col. iii 6'.

been judged, whose tablet of judgment has been written, but afterwards he alters the sealed tablet and returns for judgment—his head shall be cut off in a like manner."[19] The inscribed head was set up on the outer gate of the law court for all mankind to see.[20] Its presence inspired fear and caused "evil and wicked men to go into hiding."[21] Directly following this edifying example is a brief statement providing further proof of the ruler's commitment to justice. He eliminates bribes and presents from the people.[22] The deeds of the king usher in a return to tranquility and the restoration of the favor of the gods.[23]

The second episode (to which I will return in greater depth below) involves the performance of a river ordeal after one man accuses another man of murder but cannot prove his charge.[24] Based on the first law of the Code of Ḫammurabi, the accuser in an unsubstantiated allegation of murder is to be sentenced to death.[25] In this instance, however, the king sends the accuser and accused to perform the river ordeal in order to reach a verdict. The result of the ordeal is the death and mutilation of the body of one of the participants, an event that causes fear to spread throughout the land and the wicked and criminal to seek concealment. A second case in which an individual denounces another, swears an oath to the divine judge, the Šamaš, and enters a magic circle,[26] directly follows this episode.[27] These few lines are poorly preserved and occur just before the break at the end of the column. The fragmentary section appears to continue the theme of false accusation introduced by the lengthier episode depicting the river ordeal.

The concluding portion of the preserved text (column v) relates the beneficial results of the actions taken by the king, providing details of the abundance sacrificed before the gods and the reconstruction of a

---

19 Col. iii 8'–9': LÚ *šá di-in-šú di-nu* DUB-*pi* EŠ.BAR-*a-šú šaṭ-ru-ma ba-ram* ^{na_4}KIŠIB EGIR *i-ni-ma* ⸢*i*⸣*-tu-ra ana di-ni*$_7$ *ki-ma šú-a-tú* SAG.DU-*su* TA[R]-*is*.

20 Col. iii 11'–12'.

21 Col. iii 13'–14': *rag-gu u ṣe-e-nu ip-pal-su-ma* ⸢*i*⸣*-ḫu-zu šá-ḫa-tú i-mi-id*.

22 Col. iii 14'. This alludes to the bribery of judges described in col. ii 7'.

23 Col. iii 15'–20'.

24 Col. iii 21'–iv 23.

25 LH §1, see Roth, *Law Collections*, 81.

26 This refers to a place where oaths are taken, see *CAD* G, 102 s.v. *gišḫuru* 2, and references therein; Reiner, *Šurpu*, 22, III 127; Meier, "Beschwörung mittels eines Mehlkreises," 365–67; Magnetti, "'Oath-Functions' and the 'Oath Process'," 1–30.

27 Col. iv 24–25.

temple whose name is not preserved.[28] The final reconstructable lines recount the conquests of the ruler in foreign territories.[29]

Encased within the framework of the unfortunately poorly preserved preamble and epilogue, the body of the text combines both comprehensive statements and specific episodes written in a detailed narrative style. Although the incomplete nature of the tablet and the numerous breaks make it difficult to discern the structure of the text with certainty, the following outline is suggested:

I. Preamble
II. Overview of judicial corruption, king's reform, return to equilibrium
III. Individual case with resolution and return to equilibrium
IV. Individual case with resolution and return to equilibrium
V. Epilogue

The text demonstrates a thematic cohesiveness, and the conflict and resolution within the narrative of the individual cases punctuates with dramatic impact the message of the righteous and just ruler.

The River Ordeal

The most detailed and vivid of the episodes in the "King of Justice" relates to the performance of the river ordeal; it has, therefore, assumed a place of prominence in the attempts to understand the format, individual elements, and intrinsic nature of the river ordeal in ancient Mesopotamia.[30] The river ordeal refers to a trial before the divine river.[31] This judicial enactment relates to a wide variety of trial by ordeal in the ancient Near East and other cultures.[32] The trial, which often takes

---

28 Col. v 1–19.

29 Col. v 20–23.

30 Frymer-Kensky, *Judicial Ordeal*, 462–73; Bottéro, "L'ordalie," 1048–51; Lafont, "The Ordeal," 203–4; Beaulieu, "Note on the River Ordeal," 58–60; Cardascia, "L'ordalie fluviale," 175–76; Cardascia, "L'ordalie par le fleuve," 24–25 and 29; Heimpel, "River Ordeal," 8–10, 13, and 15–16.

31 For the divine river of the river ordeal, see *CAD* Ḫ, 254–55 s.v. *ḫuršānu*; *CAD* N/1, 374–75 s.v. *nāru* A 1l, esp. 2'; Bottéro, "L'ordalie," 1011–12; Cardascia, "L'ordalie fluviale," 171; Frymer-Kensky, *Judicial Ordeal*, 481–89.

32 See Klíma, "L'ordalie par le fleuve," 39–59; Laroche, "Fleuve et ordalie en Asie mineure," 179–89; Démare, "L'interprétation de Nb. 5, 31," 49–52; McCarter, "The River Ordeal in Israelite Literature," 403–12; Fishbane, "Accusations of Adultery," 25–45; Brichto, "The Case of the śōṭā," 55–70; Bartlett, *Trial by Fire and Water*.

the form of performance of a particular act, uses divine adjudication to determine the validity of a claim, the truth of an allegation, the correct judgment; in essence the decision of the deity establishes the truth of the case placed before him, leaving to the human realm the execution of justice.

Law codes, legal records, letters, and literary texts are the source of much of the information concerning the river ordeal in Mesopotamia.[33] The law codes provide context for the performance of the ordeal, but not the details of its components. The legal documents record the type of case requiring an ordeal and the outcome, but rarely furnish more than an outline of the events. The letters, particularly those to Zimri-Lim of Mari giving insight into the performance of river ordeals at Ḫit,[34] and literary texts such as the "King of Justice" are the most informative sources for details concerning the judicial procedure of the ordeal.

In general, river ordeals in Mesopotamia take place when a decision cannot be determined based on the evidence presented; when there is no definitive path to reach a verdict. Cases sent to be decided by the divine river involve accusations of witchcraft,[35] adultery (when the accused has not been caught in flagrante delicto),[36] and treason.[37] In all these instances, there is no evidence to resolve the charge. In addition, this type of accusation is fraught with difficulty and ripe for corruption and misuse. The river ordeal is employed also for disputes with no unambiguous evidence to achieve a resolution, encompassing both criminal charges,[38] for instance, accusations of murder or theft without proof, and civil litigation,[39] such as monetary or land disputes.

---

33 For overviews, discussion, and extensive documentation of all these sources, see Frymer-Kensky, *Judicial Ordeal*; Bottéro, "L'ordalie," 1048–51; Cardascia, "L'ordalie fluviale," 169–84.

34 Durand, "L'ordalie," 507–39; Bottéro, "L'ordalie," 1030–47; Dossin, "L'ordalie à Mari," 387–93; Frymer-Kensky, *Judicial Ordeal*, 162–80.

35 See, for example, LU §10 and LH §2; Roth, *Law Collections*, 18, 81; Frymer-Kensky, *Judicial Ordeal*, 138–44; von Weiher, "Bemerkungen zu §2 KH," 95–102. See also Abusch, *Mesopotamian Witchcraft*, 201–7.

36 See, for example, LU §14, LH §132, MAL §17, §22; Roth, *Law Collections*, 18, 106, 159–60; Cardascia, "L'ordalie par le fleuve," 19–36; Frymer-Kensky, *Judicial Ordeal*, 145–51, 347–60, and 501–5.

37 See, for example, Dossin, "Un cas d'ordalie," 112–18; *ABL* 965, *ABL* 390, *ABL* 896; Frymer-Kensky, *Judicial Ordeal*, 163–69 and 394–405.

38 For several examples from Nuzi, see Frymer-Kensky, *Judicial Ordeal*, 259–63, 267–69, and 277–83.

39 See, for example, San Nicolò, *Babylonische Rechtsurkunden*, no. 85; Cardascia, "L'ordalie par le fleuve," 33–34; Frymer-Kensky, *Judicial*

The specific elements of what occurs within the ordeal itself are less obvious. The ordeal takes place at a river location removed from the court.[40] The enactment of the river ordeal occurs at sunrise.[41] The presence of dignitaries, officials in charge of the performance, and guard troops is indicated.[42] These individuals act as witnesses to the event. It is clear that in certain instances the ordeal is unilateral: a single person—most often the accused—undergoes the ritual, and guilt or innocence is decided by the outcome. In other cases, the ordeal is thought to be bilateral: both parties participate, and one is declared innocent and the other guilty.[43] At times one or a series of champions may be chosen to perform the ordeal for the original litigants.[44]

As the participants face the water, our understanding of the procedure becomes less clear. The terminology varies for different periods and locations; however, certain observations can be made. The ordalists immerse themselves or are immersed in the water, often expressed with the verb *šalû*.[45] The one who passes through the ritual successfully is often described as "safe" (*šalāmu*).[46] Those who fail the ordeal may be described as "detained," "seized," or "enclosed" by the river.[47] In later

---

Ordeal, 413–15. There are several land disputes recorded from Nuzi, Frymer-Kensky, *Judicial Ordeal*, 291–311. For a land dispute from a letter to Zimri-Lim of Mari, see Durand, "L'ordalie," 527–30, No. 249; Bottéro, "L'ordalie," 1041–44; Heimpel, "River Ordeal," 10–13 and 16–17; Sasson, "Thoughts of Zimri-Lim," 113–14.

40 Frymer-Kensky, *Judicial Ordeal*, 526–27; Heimpel, "River Ordeal," 18–19.

41 Frymer-Kensky, *Judicial Ordeal*, 524–25; Cardascia, "L'ordalie par le fleuve," 24; see also Incantation to Utu A 40, Castellino, "Incantation to Utu," 8–9; Alster, "Incantation to Utu," 44 and 72. The significance of the sunrise for the performance of ritual is explored in Polonsky, *Rise of the Sun God*, 531–638.

42 Frymer-Kensky, *Judicial Ordeal*, 493–94 and 527–28.

43 See Cardascia, "L'ordalie fluviale," 170–71 and 175; Cardascia, "L'ordalie par le fleuve," 25–32; Frymer-Kensky, *Judicial Ordeal*, 515–21; Heimpel, "River Ordeal," 12–13.

44 See Charpin, "Les champions," 29–38. In addition see discussion in Lafont, "The Ordeal," 205–6; Cardascia, "L'ordalie fluviale," 180; Heimpel, "River Ordeal," 10–13 and 16–18.

45 *CAD* Š/1, 273–74 s.v. *šalû* B. See discussion in Cardascia, "L'ordalie fluviale," 179–81; Frymer-Kensky, *Judicial Ordeal*, 528.

46 *CAD* Š/1, 214 s.v. *šalāmu* 2d; Frymer-Kensky, *Judicial Ordeal*, 491 and 529–30; Bottéro, "L'ordalie," 1022; Cardascia, "L'ordalie par le fleuve," 22.

47 *CAD* K, 104 s.v. *kalû* 11e (N-stem); *CAD* K, 278 s.v. *kašādu* 2e; see also the Sumerian term šu ri ri; Frymer-Kensky, *Judicial Ordeal*, 493; Bottéro, "L'ordalie," 1022; Cardascia, "L'ordalie par le fleuve," 22.

periods there is a contrast in legal terminology between a person who is cleared (*zâku*)[48] and a person who is found guilty (*târu*)[49] by the ordeal. In some instances, the use of the verb *mâtu* suggests that the river ordeal has resulted in death. According to the study of ordeals by Frymer-Kensky, however, after the Old Babylonian period, excepting the curious case described in the "King of Justice," the guilty do not drown.[50] Therefore, the intent of the river ordeal is to indict but not to punish, to determine truth and then allow the legal system to procure justice.

There have been various hypotheses about what may have occurred during the river ordeal: perhaps a contrast between floating and sinking; perhaps a form of trial by swimming.[51] Cardascia advocates for a sense of immersion in the water over plunging or diving.[52] Durand has suggested that at Mari the trial took place underwater "in the heart of the river god" (*ina libbi ilim*).[53] Certain texts from Mari describe holding objects during immersion or carrying objects across the river to prove the case.[54] Heimpel proposes that the river ordeal in the area of Mari and also in the case of the "King of Justice" was performed within a bitumen spring where both the temperature and the toxic fumes would provide a test for survival.[55]

Whatever transpires within the ordeal river, one individual is proven innocent and his or her claim is upheld, the other is proven guilty, and they are both returned to the courthouse to face punishment. The river ordeal, then, provides irrefutable proof (albeit through divine intervention) in situations where there is no prima facie evidence to determine a judgment. However, the river ordeal and the exact depic-

48 *CAD* Z, 26 s.v. *zakû* 1b; Frymer-Kensky, *Judicial Ordeal*, 491.

49 *CAD* T, 257–58 s.v. *târu* 3d, with the definition "to turn back from, refuse to take an oath." It should be noted that there are difficulties in understanding the verb *târu* with relation to the trial by ordeal, see Frymer-Kensky, *Judicial Ordeal*, 532–33; Cardascia, "L'ordalie fluviale," 178.

50 Frymer-Kensky, *Judicial Ordeal*, 531.

51 Bottéro, "L'ordalie," 1022; Cardascia, "L'ordalie fluviale," 179–80; Cardascia, "L'ordalie par le fleuve," 22; see also Heimpel's objections to the concept of an ordeal based on swimming, "River Ordeal," 7.

52 Cardascia, "L'ordalie fluviale," 179–81. Bottéro, however, consistently translates "plonger," see "L'ordalie," passim.

53 See Durand, "L'ordalie," 519, n. 62; Heimpel, "River Ordeal," 8.

54 Charpin, "Les champions," 29–38; Heimpel, "River Ordeal," 17–18; Sasson, "Thoughts of Zimri-Lim," 113–14.

55 Heimpel, "River Ordeal," 8. He places the bitumen spring on the west bank of the Euphrates close to Ḫit.

tion of its contents remain shrouded in mystery, as one would expect of a procedure involving faith, fear, and the workings of divine judgment.

The River Ordeal in BM 45690

The passage detailing the river ordeal in the "King of Justice" has been viewed against the backdrop of the ordeal texts. In the "King of Justice," the two participants, a man accused of committing murder and his accuser, are taken to the banks of the Euphrates River above the town of Sippar.[56] There they wait overnight surrounded by a heavy guard.[57] At sunrise the ordeal begins.[58] In attendance are the prince, governor, and troops at the command of the king.[59] Both parties go down to the river.[60] Under the auspices of the river-god, the first participant is submerged and is led safely to the bank.[61] The second participant sinks in the water.[62] From morning to noon no one sees him or hears anything of him.[63] A great hue and cry goes up when the body cannot be recovered. The guard troops that had watched by the river from evening to dawn are agitated as they set out to search, and question, "What shall we report? How can we answer the king?"[64] When the king hears of the situation he is furious at the troops. A courier goes back and forth. He asks, "Did you not watch over the man? Has he gotten across the river and lain down in open country?"[65] Since no one has seen him they are unable to answer, but the search continues along the river and both banks are watched.[66] Finally, at midday, the river gives up a bruised and battered corpse. It has been struck on the head and is bleeding from ears and nostrils, the top of the head is burned by fire, and the body is

---

56 Col. iii 21'–24'.

57 Col. iii 24'–26'.

58 Col. iii 26'.

59 Col. iii 27'–28'.

60 According to the reading and restoration by Schaudig, both parties submerge themselves in the river, col. iv 1: *ki-lal-la-an ú-ri-du* ÍD *i-š*[*a*]-*a*[*l-lu-u*].

61 Col. iv 4–5: *za-ku-*⸢*ú*⸣ [*šá* ᵈ]*i-ti ú-*⸢*šá*⸣*-áš-la-áš-šum-ma šal-mîš uṭ-ṭaḫ-ḫa-áš* ⸢*a*⸣-[*na kib-ri*]. It should be noted that the causative of the verb *šalû* is used, and this can be compared with the G-stem of the verb in col. iv 1, as well as with the use of the verb *ṭebû* in col. iv 6.

62 Col. iv 6.

63 Col. iv 6–7.

64 Col. iv 8–10.

65 Col. iv 11–13.

66 Col. iv 14–16.

covered with sores.[67] The people throughout the land see this and are terrified.[68] In a manner similar to the first case example, enemies and evildoers go into hiding.[69]

At this time the events in the above passage of the "King of Justice" have been interpreted as the river ordeal following its natural course. An accuser and accused are subjected to the ordeal, one is found innocent and the other guilty, and the guilty party drowns, punished by the divine river.[70] However, there are indications that this passage should be seen as just the opposite—an unnatural or subverted ritual and judicial procedure.

One indication is the overall nature, as well as the structure and style, of the "King of Justice" and the examples documented within it. Throughout the body of the text there are images of unbalance within the judicial system. The moral and economic misdeeds of the wealthy and powerful within the law courts are documented at the beginning of the preserved text. In addition, the judges themselves are accused of judicial misconduct, in particular actions that inhibit the normal course of justice and ignore the rights of the ordinary citizen. The reaction of the king to this situation is to cleanse the law courts and legal system of dishonorable procedures and reinstitute justice.

Examining the more detailed episodes of the "King of Justice," the first vignette describes an individual who seeks to retry his case using false means. The episode is documented in the following manner: (*a*) the attempt of the fraudulent litigant to manipulate the judicial procedure is detailed, (*b*) the reaction of the just king, the punishment for the crime is inflicted and recorded, (*c*) the criminal's severed head along with a permanent record in the form of a duplicate head inscribed with his offense are exhibited for all the land to see, and (*d*) as a result, criminals seek to conceal themselves. A similar structure is preserved in the example depicting the river ordeal: (*a*) the judicial procedure of the ordeal is described, (*b*) the reaction of the divine judge, an excessive punishment meted out to the ordalist is indicated, (*c*) his mutilated head and body are discovered and observed by all, causing fear and awe, and (*d*) criminals go into hiding. What is missing in the latter example as it has been interpreted is the element of manipulation of justice by the individual on trial. Therefore, taken in the context of the text as a whole,

67 Col. iv 17–20.

68 Col. iv 21–22.

69 Col. iv 23: *a-a-bi lem-nu u za-ma-nu pu-uz-rat i-ta-ḫaz*; see above col. iii 13'–14' and note 21.

70 This interpretation is represented throughout the secondary literature.

one might reasonably question whether the river ordeal presented in the "King of Justice" represents the correct procedure for the event and a fulfilled example of the river ordeal.

There are several signifiers of the true nature of the ordeal in the "King of Justice" within the narrative of the ordeal passage. A foreshadowing that things may be amiss occurs after the participants have arrived at the river. The scene is set and divine Ea, Lord of the Apsû, is present to ensure that justice is upheld.[71] At this moment, the action pauses and an observation that what follows "has not been seen or heard from far distant time" is interjected into the narrative.[72] Frymer-Kensky has suggested that this refers to the reinstitution of an ancient practice of trial by river ordeal that had fallen out of favor.[73] At the same time she contradicts this proposal, providing evidence for river ordeals in Babylonia from Sargonid times.[74] Beaulieu feels that this line signifies the miraculous character of the divine punishment of the ordalist.[75] It is very likely, however, that these lines just prior to the performance of the ordeal indicate that what is about to take place within the ritual itself is unnatural and unexpected.

Moving from the commencement to the outcome of the ordeal, it is apparent at this juncture that the judicial procedure has been resolved in an extraordinary manner. The second participant in the ordeal sinks in the river and is not seen from dawn until midday. When his body emerges, his head is bashed and bloody, his body is covered with sores, and it is as if he has been burned while submersed in the river.[76] It has always been difficult to explain the condition of the body of the second submerged individual upon its discovery. This clearly is not the body of a drowned man and as indicated above, in general, a determination of guilt at the river ordeal did not result in death. Both ancient observers[77]

---

71 Col. iv 2–3: ^{d}*é-a* LUGAL ABZU *na-ram* LUGAL-*ú-ti-šú a-n*[*a di-na-a*]*t* ⌜*kit-tu*⌝ *a-na nap-lu-su*.

72 Col. iv 3–4: *šá ul-tu ul-lu ina* I[GI^{II}] [*la in*]-⌜*nam-ru*⌝ *la iš-ši-ma-a ina* GEŠTUG^{II}.

73 Frymer-Kensky, *Judicial Ordeal*, 469. This is echoed by Foster, *Before the Muses*, 870; Foster, "Social Reform," 170.

74 Frymer-Kensky, *Judicial Ordeal*, 469.

75 Beaulieu, "Note on the River Ordeal," 60.

76 Col. iv 17–20: *ina* AN.BAR$_{7}$ *ina ka-šá-du šá-lam-tu-uš ul-tu* ÍD *i-lam-ma* SÌG-*iṣ* SAG.DU *iš-tu* KA GEŠTUG^{II} *u nap-pa-šú i-red-di* ÚŠ *u* UGU-*ḫi* GIN$_{7}$ *ši-kin* IZI-*im-ma ḫa-mi-iṭ* SU-*šú ma-li bu-bu-tu*.

77 The people react with fear, the world is overcome with awe, col. iv 21–22: *i-mu-ra-a* ÙG^{meš} *i-ta-ma-a pu-ul-ḫa-a-tú* KUR.KUR^{meš} *ka-li-ši-na ra-šub-bat za-a-na*.

and modern scholars have responded to the apparent punishment of the second ordalist by the divine river.

Frymer-Kensky questioned the death by drowning of the second participant in the ordeal, stating that the text does not treat this as a normal occurrence, but rather as an ordeal "gone awry."[78] Heimpel proposed a natural explanation for the condition of the body with relation to his theory of an ordeal trial by bitumen springs found in the Euphrates River. In this instance he feels that the body was inadvertently caught and trapped in the hot spring and that, by the time it was freed in the middle of the day, it had suffered battering and burning.[79] Beaulieu suggests a two-pronged outcome, with the guilty party first experiencing divine judgment by drowning in the river (therefore failing the ordeal) and then divine retribution through being burned by the divine splendor of the river-god because he was not rescued in a timely fashion.[80] Lafont agrees with this concept of proof of guilt and then punishment and, in addition, relates the act of divine retribution to the apologetic nature of the text.[81] Bottéro looks at the end result as a miracle and proof of the role of the "King of Justice" as an edifying tale.[82] All of these explanations view the treatment of the body of the second participant in the river ordeal by the river-god Ea as penalty for failure of the ordeal. A connection can be made, however, between the episode depicting the river ordeal and the earlier episode describing an attempt to falsely retry a case. In each instance the punishment was swift, severe, and corporeal, with emphasis placed on the head.[83] This suggests that the divine requital in the river ordeal passage might have been incurred for an attempt to sidestep justice.

The scene just after the second individual sinks in the river recounts an incredible flurry of activity suggesting that the witnesses themselves are aware that something is amiss.[84] The guards are anxious about what they have to report to the king. The king, in turn, is furious with them. The troops and boat crews are carefully watching over the banks of the river. In the midst of all the activity, a messenger is coming and going, questioning whether the missing participant has gotten across the river

---

78 Frymer-Kensky, *Judicial Ordeal*, 468, 531.

79 Heimpel, "River Ordeal," 8–9.

80 Beaulieu, "Note on the River Ordeal," 58–60.

81 Lafont, "The Ordeal," 204.

82 Bottéro, "L'ordalie," 1051–53.

83 I would like to thank M. Roth for bringing this connection to my attention, pers. comm., March 30, 2009.

84 Beaulieu, "Note on the River Ordeal," 58.

and lain down in the steppe.[85] No one can answer because no one has seen the ordalist. Why are the soldiers so anxious about a drowned body? What accounts for the king's fury at the troops for not being able to find the corpse? Why is there such a frantic and detailed search? And, most significantly, why does the messenger ask if the ordalist has crossed the river and reached open country?

An Alternate Explanation of the River Ordeal in BM 45690

It is proposed here that, just like the individual who unjustly submitted his case for retrial, one of the participants in the river ordeal is inclined to forego the normal route of justice. The crucial moment lies with the second individual in the river and the interpretation of the line that indicates his activity. Unfortunately, there has been little consensus about the reading or the interpretation of this line. Intense scrutiny has focused on the difficulties of the front part of the line.[86] The interpretation followed here is that of Schaudig and Foster, identifying the second participant as the accuser in the case.[87]

It is imperative, however, to understand the back part of the line, the moment when the ordalist enters the water.[88] The verb used to

---

85 Col. iv 13: *e-ber-tu*$_4$ ÍD *i-bir i-na-al* EDIN-*iš*. Heimpel, "River Ordeal," 9–10 and 16, translates this line with the sense that the missing ordalist crossed to the other bank of the river and escaped into the steppe. For the steppe as a traditional place for criminals to inhabit, see *CAD* Ṣ, 145 s.v. *ṣēru* A 3f.

86 Col. iv 6. When Lambert, "Nebuchadnezzar," 6, 9, first edited the text he read: ⸢*šá*⸣ UGU-*šú-nu tu-ru-ma*, and translated, "The one who returned to them." His reading was followed by Frymer-Kensky, *Judicial Ordeal*, 467, who translated, "The one who had 'turned' against him," and by Cardascia in "L'ordalie par le fleuve," 29, and "L'ordalie fluviale," 176, with n. 36, who suggested that the second participant at first refused the ordeal, but when the other ordalist was cleared, he returned to the judges and requested a second chance at the ordeal in which he subsequently drowned. See, however, von Soden, Review, 283, who emended the line: *šá* UGU-*sú ner*$^!$-*tu* ŠUB, and translated, "der ihn des Mordes bezichtigt hatte." Bottéro, "L'ordalie," 1049 and n. 34 read [*šá*] UGU-*šú là* TU.RU.MA, without translation. Heimpel, "River Ordeal," 16, n. 15, suggested *nu-tu-ru*, relating it to *nutturu* of uncertain meaning (see *CAD* N/2, 355–56), but did not offer a translation.

87 Schaudig, *Die Inschriften Nabonids*, 583, and n. 963, reads: ⸢*šá*⸣ UGU-*šú* NU-*tu* ŠUB-*ma*. He suggests that NU-*tu* should be understood as *nullâtu*, see *CAD* N/2, 334 s.v. meaning b: "malicious, treacherous talk." This reading is followed by Foster, *Before the Muses*, 872, who translates "the one who had frivolously charged him."

88 Col. iv 6: *ina* A^{meš} *ṭe-bi-ma*.

describe his action is *ṭebû*,[89] and it is important to note that the form of the verb is not causative as was the case with the first participant who was submerged in the river.[90] A translation of "drown" for the verb *ṭebû* in this passage does not allow for an ambiguity that the text seems to require. A more neutral translation of "submerge" or "sink" is appropriate.

Perhaps the best way to explain what is expressed in the text, the agitation of the troops, the anger of the king, and the intensive search and watchfulness is that this is an unexpected action, and the immersion of the second participant is a subversion of justice. The reader is kept in suspense in a manner similar to the troops of the guard, who are unsure what has happened. The accuser simply sinks beneath the water. The anxiety and investigation, however, is not for an ordalist known to have drowned, but for a participant who, as far as they know, has thwarted the divine decision of the river ordeal and who can no longer be accounted for among the living or dead.

When the corpse finally surfaces in the river it is apparent that he has suffered the anger of the deified river and divine retribution. Again, this punishment is not for a participant who failed the ordeal—and who then should have either been pulled out of the river and transported back to the courthouse for execution, or if the ordalist drowned in the course of the ritual, pulled dead from the water—but for a participant who tried to flee the ordeal, who attempted to escape and possibly hide in open country. His bid for freedom failed. Although, at the time, the troops, the onlookers, and the king were unaware, the divine river punished him for his violation of the sacred and secular system of justice embodied by the river ordeal.

When the section describing the river ordeal is understood in this manner, it conforms to the nature of the text as a whole. The interpretation of the action of the second ordalist in submersing himself in the river as an attempt to escape enables the river ordeal passage to be viewed as another illustration of a crime against the judicial system.

The just king battles social injustice, as is often portrayed in royal literature, but the "King of Justice" addresses the more insidious corruption both by officials and litigants within the court of law. This text considers the difficulty of enforcing a body of practices and beliefs that

---

89 Lambert, "Nebuchadnezzar," 9, translated the verb with the meaning "dive." See, however, *CAD* Ṭ, 68 s.v. *ṭebû* 1b with the meanings "to sink, to drown, to submerge." See also, the discussion in Cardascia, "L'ordalie fluviale," 176.

90 Described by the verb *šalû*, col. iv 5, and see supra note 61.

are intrinsically non-binding, bringing to the forefront the question of how to regulate and maintain beliefs in and respect for the moral, ethical, and religious underpinnings of the legal system.

The river ordeal is a primary example of faith-based, juridical procedures. At the same time, the passage depicting the river ordeal is a microcosm of the message of the "King of Justice." The ordeal itself seeks to establish truth, to uphold by divine decision what is just. The protagonists in the case narratives stand in opposition to truth, and perjure their judicial procedure: with false claims, false accusations, false participation, and false oaths. The Mesopotamian legal system, based on the talionic principle, ensures that false witnesses and false accusers suffer equal damages to that which would be inflicted upon the accused.[91] The response to the offenders in the "King of Justice"—the corporal punishment and mutilation, the vengeance of the king and the retribution of the god—reaches past the individual to address the masses and is designed to ensnare the nonbeliever, returning to the path of righteousness any who might circumvent the justice system.

The tablet of the "King of Justice," in a manner similar to the inscribed likeness of the individual attempting to receive a second judgment based on false claims and the scorched and battered visage of the guilty ordalist who tried to escape his trial, serves as a warning to the inhabitants of all the lands: Any attempt to compromise judicial procedure, to endanger the social fabric and the codes of belief that must be upheld for society to function, will evoke the wrath and retribution of the king and the gods. The ruler who commissioned the text defends his realm against a breakdown in the judicial system and the tenets that perpetuate social justice, moral responsibility, and juridical fairness. His edifying narratives are designed to disseminate both dread and respect throughout the land and to disrupt the activity of criminals, thereby allowing a return to societal norms, judicial stability, and ultimately prosperity.

WORKS CITED

Abusch, T. *Mesopotamian Witchcraft: Toward a History and Understanding of Babylonian Witchcraft Beliefs and Literature*. AMD 5. Leiden: Brill, 2002.

Alster, B. "Incantation to Utu." *ASJ* 13 (1991): 27–96.

91 See LU §28, LL §17, and LH §1–4, Roth, *Law Collections*, 20, 29, and 81–82; Frymer-Kensky, "Tit for Tat," 230–34; Westbrook, "Punishments and Crimes," 554–55.

Bartlett, R. *Trial by Fire and Water: The Medieval Judicial Ordeal*. Oxford: Clarendon Press, 1986.

Beaulieu, P.-A. *The Reign of Nabonidus, King of Babylon, 556–539 B.C.* YNER 10. New Haven: Yale University Press, 1989.

"A Note on the River Ordeal in the Literary Text 'Nebuchadnezzar King of Justice'." *NABU* (1992): 58–60 no. 77.

Bottéro, J. "L'Ordalie en Mésopotamie ancienne," *Annali della Scuola Normale Superiore de Pisa, Classe di Lettere e Filosofia*, Series III, 11 (1981): 1005–67.

Brichto, H. C. "The Case of the śōṭā and a Reconsideration of Biblical 'Law'." *HUCA* 46 (1975): 55–70.

Cardascia, G. "L'ordalie par le fleuve dans Lois assyriennes." *Festschrift für Wilhelm Eilers, Ein Dokument der internationalen Forschung zum 27. Sept. 1966*, edited by G. Wiessner, 19–36. Wiesbaden: Harrassowitz, 1967.

"L'ordalie fluviale dans la Mésopotamie ancienne." *Revue historique de droit français et étranger* 71 (1993): 169–84.

Castellino, G. R. "Incantation to Utu." *OrAnt* 8 (1969): 1–57.

Charpin, D. "Les champions, la meule et le fleuve." In *Florilegium marianum: recueil d'études en l'honneur de Michel Fleury*, edited by J.-M. Durand, 29–38. Mémoires de NABU 1. Paris: Société pour l'Étude du Proche-Orient Ancien, 1992.

Démare, S. "L'interprétation de Nb. 5, 31, à la lumiére des droits cuneiformes." In *La femme dans le Proche-Orient antique, Compte rendu de la XXXIIIe Rencontre assyriologique internationale, Paris, 7–10 Juillet 1986*, edited by J.-M. Durand, 49–52. Paris: Éditions Recherche sur les Civilisations, 1987.

Dossin, G. "Un cas d'ordalie par le dieu-fleuve." In *Symbolae ad iura orientis antiqui pertinentes Paulo Koschaker dedicatae*, edited by Th. Folkers et al., 112–18. Studia et documenta ad iura Orientis antiqui pertinentia 2. Leiden: Brill, 1939.

"L'ordalie à Mari." *Comptes-rendus des séances de l'année - Académie des inscriptions et belles-lettres* 102/4 (1958): 387–93.

Durand, J.-M. "L'ordalie." In *Archives épistolaires de Mari* I/1, 507–39. ARM 26. Paris: Éditions Recherche sur les Civilizations, 1988.

Fishbane, M. "Accusations of Adultery: A Study of Law and Scribal Practice in Numbers 5:11–31." *HUCA* 45 (1974): 25–45.

Foster, B. R. "Social Reform in Ancient Mesopotamia." In *Social Justice in the Ancient World*, edited by K. D. Irani and M. Silver, 165–77. Westport, Conn.: Greenwood Press, 1995.

Before the Muses: An Anthology of Akkadian Literature. Revised edition. Bethesda, Md.: CDL Press, 2005.

Akkadian Literature of the Late Period. Guides to the Mesopotamian Textual Record 2. Münster: Ugarit-Verlag, 2007.

Frymer-Kensky, T. *The Judicial Ordeal in the Ancient Near East*. PhD Dissertation, Yale University, 1977.

"Tit for Tat: The Principle of Equal Retribution in Near Eastern and Biblical Law." *BiAr* 43 (1980): 230–34.

Grayson, A. K. *Babylonian Historical-Literary Texts*. Toronto Semitic Texts and Studies 3. Toronto: University of Toronto Press, 1975.

Hallo, W. W., ed. *The Context of Scripture I: Canonical Compositions from the Biblical World*. Leiden: Brill, 1997.

Harper, Robert F. *Assyrian and Babylonian Letters Belonging to the Kouyunjik Collections of the British Museum*. Chicago, Ill.: Chicago University Press, 1892–1914.

Heimpel, W. "The River Ordeal in Hit." *RA* 90 (1996): 7–18.

Irani, K. D. "The Idea of Social Justice in the Ancient World." In *Social Justice in the Ancient World*, edited by K. D. Irani and M. Silver, 3–8. Westport, Conn.: Greenwood Press, 1995.

Irani, K. D., and M. Silver, eds. *Social Justice in the Ancient World*. Westport, Conn.: Greenwood Press, 1995.

Klíma, J. "L'ordalie par le fleuve en Elam." *RA* 66 (1972): 39–59.

Lafont, B. "The Ordeal." In *Everyday Life in Ancient Mesopotamia*, edited by J. Bottéro, 199–209. Baltimore: The Johns Hopkins University Press, 2001.

Lambert, W. G. "Nebuchadnezzar King of Justice." *Iraq* 27 (1965): 1–11.

Babylonian Wisdom Literature. Oxford: Clarendon Press, 1960; Winona Lake, Ind.: Eisenbrauns, 1996 reprint.

Lambert, W. G., and A. R. Millard. *Babylonian Literary Texts*. CT 46. London: Trustees of the British Museum, 1965.

Laroche, E. "Fleuve et ordalie en Asie mineure Hittite." In *Festschrift Heinrich Otten, 27. Dezember 1973*, edited by E. Neu and C. Rüster, 179–89. Wiesbaden: Harrassowitz, 1973.

Magnetti, D. L. "'Oath-Functions' and the 'Oath Process' in the Civil and Criminal Law of the Ancient Near East." *Brooklyn Journal of International Law* 5 (1979): 1–30.

McCarter, P. K. "The River Ordeal in Israelite Literature." *HTR* 66/4 (1973): 403–12.

Meier, G. "Beschwörung mittels eines Mehlkreises." *AfO* 11 (1936/37): 365–67.

Polonsky, J. *The Rise of the Sun God and the Determination of Destiny in Ancient Mesopotamia*. PhD Dissertation, University of Pennsylvania, 2002.

Reiner, E. *Šurpu: A Collection of Sumerian and Akkadian Incantations*. AfO Beiheft 11. Graz, 1958.

Roth, M. *Law Collections from Mesopotamia and Asia Minor*. 2nd ed. Writings from the Ancient World 6. Atlanta: Scholars Press, 1997.

San Nicolò, M. *Babylonische Rechtsurkunden des ausgehenden 8. und des 7. Jahrhunderts v. Chr. 1 Hälfte (Nr. 1–86)*. ABAW NF 34. München: Verlag der Bayerische Akademie der Wissenschaften, 1951.

Sasson, J. M. "Thoughts of Zimri-Lim." *BiAr* 47 (1984): 110–20.

Schaudig, H. *Die Inschriften Nabonids von Babylon und Kyros' des Großen samt den in ihrem Umfeld entstandenen Tendenzschriften: Textausgabe und Grammatik*. AOAT 256. Münster: Ugarit-Verlag, 2001.

Silver, M. "Prophets and Markets Revisited." In *Social Justice in the Ancient World*, edited by K. D. Irani and M. Silver, 179–198. Westport, Conn.: Greenwood Press, 1995.

von Soden, W. Review of *Babylonian Historical-Literary Texts* (Toronto Semitic Texts and Studies 3) by A. K. Grayson. *ZA* 65 (1975): 282–85.

"Kyros und Nabonid, Propaganda und Gegenpropoganda." In *Kunst, Kultur und Geschichte der Achämenidenzeit und ihr Fortleben*, edited by H. Koch and D. N. Mackenzie, 61–68. Archäologische Mitteilungen aus Iran, Ergänzungsheft 10. Berlin: D. Reimer, 1983.

von Weiher, E. "Bemerkungen zu §2 KH und zur Anwendung des Flußordals." *ZA* 71 (1981): 95–102.

Westbrook, R. "Punishments and Crimes." In *Anchor Bible Dictionary*, vol. 5, edited by D. N. Freedman, 546–56. New York: Doubleday, 1992.

"Social Justice in the Ancient Near East." In *Social Justice in the Ancient World*, edited by K. D. Irani and M. Silver, 149–63. Westport, Conn.: Greenwood Press, 1995.

THE PROPHET AS SUMMONER*

SHALOM E. HOLTZ
YESHIVA UNIVERSITY

Israelite prophets, in formulating their messages, employ terminology that originates in the realm of lawsuits and courts of law. Most famously, the identification of the so-called *rîb*, or "prophetic lawsuit," has drawn scholarly attention to the use of legal metaphors in biblical prophecies.[1] Even those who question the very existence of this genre of prophecy accept the fact that biblical prophecies incorporate legal imagery.[2]

---

* Abbreviations follow Alexander et al., *The SBL Handbook of Style*, §8.4, 89–152, and *CAD*. It is a privilege to contribute this study in honor of Professor Eichler, in gratitude for his continued mentorship. It was in his seminar on legal texts from Nuzi that I first encountered the *manzaduḫlu*. Over twenty years ago, he wrote of "a more sobering and responsible attitude toward the usefulness and importance of the Nuzi tablets for the study of the Bible," but nevertheless remained confident that "in conjunction with other cuneiform documents, the Nuzi texts will continue to illuminate biblical law, institutions, and practices" (Eichler, "Nuzi and the Bible," 119). This essay is humbly offered as an attempt to illustrate, and thus justify, the approach espoused in this latter assertion. Versions of this essay were read at "Tablet and Torah: Mesopotamia and the Biblical World: A Conference in Honor of Dr. Barry L. Eichler," and at the University of Chicago Divinity School. I am grateful to the audiences at both of these forums for their useful comments, as well as to my father, Professor Avraham Holtz, who read earlier drafts. This essay was revised for publication during a junior faculty leave supported by a visiting fellowship in Jewish law and interdisciplinary studies at the Center for Jewish Law and Contemporary Civilization of Yeshiva University's Benjamin N. Cardozo School of Law. Thanks for this fellowship are due to Suzanne Stone, director of the center, and to Yeshiva's provost, Morton Lowengrub, who provided a supplemental grant.

1 Gemser, "The *Rîb-* or Controversy-Pattern," 128–33. For the history of this area of inquiry, see the literature noted in Dijkstra, "Lawsuit," 251 n. 1.

2 For examples, see De Roche, "Yahweh's Rîb," 571–572; Daniels, "Is There a 'Prophetic Lawsuit' Genre?," 353–54; and Dijkstra, "Lawsuit," 254. Pietro Bovati suggests that the legal terminology comes from informal, bilateral resolution of disputes, rather than from formal mediation by judges. Yet,

Those who have studied legal language in prophetic texts, especially from the form-critical perspective, have assumed that the prophets' rhetoric is based on the procedures and terminology of actual courts of law in ancient Israel.[3] According to this assumption, the prophets' imagined courtrooms adopt procedures and use language that would have been used by actual courtrooms. But, as Meindert Dijkstra cautions:

> When looking for the origins of the lawsuit in Second Isaiah, certain elements of circular reasoning are not always apparent during debates. For instance, speaking of the original setting of the prophetic lawsuit, one has to be aware that the majority of texts on which reconstructions of the administration of justice and its distinctive speech forms are based, stem from prophecy and wisdom.[4]

Dijkstra's warning with regard to Second Isaiah applies to other prophets' lawsuits, as well. Because extra-biblical Israelite evidence is largely unavailable, most studies of Israelite courts of law have relied on information from within the Hebrew Bible itself.[5] Although the prophets use words with obviously juridical meanings, it is difficult to argue that the prophets' language imitates courtroom forms of speech without Israelite courtroom records, where one might find these purported legalisms in their original setting.

Recent comparative work, especially on the Neo-Babylonian legal corpus, has demonstrated the value of trial-related documents in Akkadian as a crucial supplement to the dearth of native Israelite material.[6] These documents attest to the workings of actual courts of law and to the legal formulations employed during trials. Thus, the Akkadian records open a window onto the procedures and language that stand behind the prophets' courtroom images, and courtroom imagery in the Hebrew Bible, in general.

---

regarding the informal procedure, even Bovati notes "le grand nombre d'éléments qu'il a en commun avec la structure de la procédure proprement judiciare." See Bovati, "Le langage juridique," 180.

3 Begrich, *Studien zu Deuterojesaja*, 27–28; Westermann, *Basic Forms of Prophetic Speech*, 131–35. The basic connection to human courts of law obtains even according to those who argue for a different *Sitz im Leben* for the prophetic lawsuit. See, for example, Huffmon, "The Covenant Lawsuit in the Prophets," 293; Harvey, "Le 'Rîb-Pattern'," 191; Limburg, *The Lawsuit of God*, 294–96.

4 Dijkstra, "Lawsuit," 254.

5 See, for example, Boecker, *Redeformen des Rechtslebens*, and Bovati, *Re-establishing Justice*.

6 Wells, *The Law of Testimony*; Magdalene, *Scales of Righteousness*; Holtz, "A Comparative Note"; Holtz, "Praying as a Plaintiff."

The purpose of this article is to examine one feature of the legal rhetoric of prophecy, the summoning to court, in light of the documentation available from functioning human legal systems in Mesopotamia. Working only with the Hebrew texts, scholars have observed that, at times, the prophets speak as agents of the divine court who summon the parties to the lawsuits.[7] For example, B. Gemser, in his well-known survey of "The *Rîb*- or Controversy-Pattern in Hebrew Mentality," writes that Micah "acts as summoner at divine command to the *rîb*."[8] Similarly, Claus Westermann identifies the "summons" (*Vorladung*) as one of the elements of Second Isaiah's "court speeches" (*Gerichtsrede*).[9] Parallels from Akkadian legal texts demonstrate that the image of the prophet as summoner is, in fact, anchored in a contemporary legal reality. The imaginary legal situations in which litigants are required to state their cases are known from actual legal texts. The prophets' language could well have been the language of ancient Israelite courts.

Summoning to Court in the Cuneiform Legal Tradition

Court records written in cuneiform indicate that in all periods, Mesopotamian courts of law, like their modern-day counterparts, faced the need to bring parties before them for trials. Texts from Nuzi, for example, use the verb *šasû* to indicate the "calling" of defendants to trial.[10] In Neo-Babylonian trial records, the verbs *abālu* and *abāku* indicate that judges "bring" defendants before them.[11] Officials responsible for this aspect of the proceedings are named in texts from various periods: the MAŠKIM in the Ur III period,[12] the *rābiṣum* in the Old Babylonian period,[13] and the *manzaduḫlu*-official from Nuzi[14] are among the titles found in court documents.

---

7 For an overview of the role of the prophet as a messenger of the heavenly council, see Jindo, *Biblical Metaphor Reconsidered*, 119 n. 128.

8 Gemser, "The *Rîb*- or Controversy Pattern," 130. Also see Gemser's similar remarks regarding Amos on 129 and "Trito-Isaiah" on 132.

9 Westermann, "Sprache und Struktur," 135–37.

10 See *CAD* Š/2 s.v. *šasû* 4a2', for examples. Compare the use of Hebrew *q-r-'* for summoning, studied in Magdalene, *Scales of Righteousness*, 141–42.

11 Holtz, *Neo-Babylonian Court Procedure*, 232–34; 275–78.

12 Falkenstein, *Gerichtsurkunden* 1, 53–54 and Falkenstein, *Gerichtsurkunden* 2, Nos. 121 and 138; Lafont and Westbrook, "Neo-Sumerian Period," 193–94.

13 As noted by Dombradi, *Die Darstellung des Rechtsaustrags*, 256, the Old Babylonian texts do not describe the summoning procedure itself in much detail.

14 Hayden, *Court Procedure at Nuzu*, 13–15. For texts, see Hayden, *Court Procedure at Nuzu*, 195 n. 45.

One text from Nuzi and several others from Neo-Babylonian Uruk afford a somewhat more detailed glimpse of the summoning process as it took place. The text from Nuzi describes an oral procedure by which the *manzaduḫlu*-officials confront the defendant in order to bring him to court. In this particular text, the *manzaduḫlu*-officials make the following statement upon their unsuccessful return to the court:[15]

16. *um-ma ma-za-du-uḫ-lu-ma a-na*
17. $^{m}PN_1$ *ni-ta-la-ak-mi*
18. *ù ni-iq-ta-a-bi*
19. *lišān-šu*$_4$ *ša* $^{m}PN_2$
20. *li-qa-am-mi ù al-ka*$_4$*-am-mi*
21. *um-ma* $^{m}PN_1$*-ma-mi*
22. *ù-la-a-mi i-na di-ni*
23. *la a-la-ak-mi*

16. Thus (said) the *manzaduḫlu*-officials:
16–20. "We came to PN_1 and said, 'Receive the declaration of PN_2, and come (to court)!'
21–22. "Thus (said) PN_1: 'No, I will not go to court!'"

According to their quoted report, the *manzaduḫlu*-officials give two orders to the summoned litigant. First, he must "receive the declaration" of the plaintiff (PN_2). Then, he must "come to court." In other words, the summoners are responsible not only for bringing the defendant to court, but also for conveying the complaint against him.

The only record of how the *manzaduḫlu*-officials presented the complaint to the defendant is the order, "Receive the declaration of PN_2." The actual procedure, however, must have included a fuller quotation of PN_2's charge. One imagines that the summoners fulfilled this part of their mission by reciting (from memory or, perhaps, from a written record) a formal version of the plaintiff's statement. The order actually quoted, then, is either the introduction or conclusion of this formal recitation of the charge.

A similar use of court messengers is attested much later, in the Neo-Babylonian period, in several texts from the Eanna at Uruk. One such text records proceedings, held in the presence of a royal judge and a scribe, concerning a cow stolen from the herd of the Lady-of-Uruk:[16]

---

15 HSS V 49:16–23, published in Speiser, *New Kirkuk Documents*, no. 34. Note that it is the extensive quotation, rather than the failure of the summoning procedure, that makes this text unique. Most of the Nuzi texts simply record the names of the men who were sent as *manzaduḫlu*-officials, the fact that they fulfilled their duty, and that the summoned individual refused to appear.

16 YOS 7 159. For complete discussion of this text, see von Bolla, "Drei

1. ^{m}*ba-zu-zu* A-*šú šá* ^{md}UTU-MU-DU ^{lú}NA.KAD *šá* ÁB.GU$_4$.ḪI.A
2. *šá* ^{d}GAŠAN *šá* UNUG^{ki} *šá ina ma-ḫar* ^{m}*ri-mut* ^{lú}DI.KU$_5$ LUGAL
3. *ù* ^{m}DA-^{d}AMAR.UTU ^{lú}UMBISAG *iq-bu-ú um-ma*
4. 1 ÁB.GAL *šá kak-kab-tu*$_4$ *še-en-de-e-ti ul-tu* ÁB.GU$_4$.ḪI.A-*ia*
5. *ina muḫ-ḫi* ÍD LUGAL *ki-i ta-am-mi-ir-ku-ú* ^{m}*la-a-ba-ši*
6. A-*šú šá* ^{m}*ku-na-a* A ^{lú}É.MAŠ ^{d}MAŠ *šá la-nu-ú-a i-ta-bak-šú*
7. ^{lú}DI.KU$_5$.ME ^{lú}DUMU! *šip-ri a-na muḫ-ḫi* ^{m}*la-a-ba-ši iš-pu-ru-ma*
8. *la in-na-mir iḫ-liq . . .*

1–3. Bazūzu son of Šamaš-šuma-ukīn, the herdsman of the cattle of the Lady-of-Uruk, who said thus before Rīmūt, the judge of the king, and Ile''i-Marduk, the scribe:

4-6. "When one cow branded with a star, from my herd of cows, lagged behind at the king's canal, Lâbāši, son of Kūnaya, descendant of Šangû-Ninurta, without my knowing, led it away."

7-8. The judges sent a messenger to Lâbāši, but he was not seen; he escaped.

In the wake of Bazūzu's accusation, the judges summon Lâbāši, the defendant, in what turns out to be a failed attempt to bring him to trial. According to the record, the summoning was carried out by a messenger sent for this purpose. Many Neo-Babylonian litigation records describe the successful "bringing" of the defendant before the judges, but do not say how this was accomplished. One may assume, based on this example of a failed attempt, that in other cases the judges also sent messengers who would confront the defendants directly and who succeeded in "bringing" them to court.

Apart from the narrative descriptions of the summoning procedure, additional evidence for summoning to court comes, at least in the Neo-Babylonian period, from a group of texts that require the summoned individuals to "argue their case" (*dīna* or *dibba dabābu*), that is, to defend themselves in the face of a claim that has already been made against them by an opposing party.[17] Failure to "argue the case" means that the sum-

Diebstahlsfälle von Tempeleigentum," 117–20. Two other texts that record the sending of messengers to summon accused parties are published in Jursa, "Auftragsmord," nos. 4 and 5.

17 These texts are described in Holtz, *Neo-Babylonian Court Procedure*, 117–27. According to Magdalene, *Scales of Righteousness*, 91, these texts are "writs of appeal that may have notified the appellant that his appeal to the higher court had been granted [and] summoned him to the court of review." Note that according to Magdalene, the Neo-Babylonian summonses are summonses to a court of appeal rather than the initial summons of a defendant.

moned individuals accept the charge and any obligations that it may carry. The following text, also from the Eanna at Uruk, is an example:[18]

1. U$_4$ 20-*kám šá* ITI GAN MU 4-*kám* ^{m}*ku-ra-áš*
2. LUGAL TIN.TIR^{ki} LUGAL KUR.KUR ^{m}PN$_1$
3. *a-na* TIN.TIR^{ki} *il-la-ka-ma*
4. *di-i-ni šá* 2 UDU.NITA.MEŠ *šá kak-kab-tu$_4$ še-en-du*
5. *šá* ^{m}*gi-mil-lu* A-*šú šá* ^{md}*in-nin*-MU-*ib-ni*
6. *ul-tu ṣe-e-ni šá* ^{m}PN$_1$ *i-bu-ku*
7. *it-ti* ^{m}PN$_2$ ^{lú}ŠÀ.TAM É.AN.NA
8. ^{m}PN$_3$ ^{lú}SAG-LUGAL ^{lú}EN *pi-qit-tu$_4$* É.AN.NA
9. *ù* ^{lú}UMBISAG.MEŠ *šá* É.AN.NA *ina* É *di-i-ni*
10. *šá* LUGAL *i-dab-ub-bu ki-i*
11. *la it-tal-ku* UDU.NITA-*a* 2
12. 1-*en* 30 *a-na* ^{d}GAŠAN *šá* UNUG^{ki} *i-nam-din*

1–3. On 20 Kislimu, year 4 of Cyrus, king of Babylon, king of the lands, PN$_1$ shall come to Babylon.

4–10. He shall argue the case regarding two sheep branded with a star—which Gimillu son of Innin-šuma-ibni led away from the flock of PN$_1$—against PN$_2$ the *šatammu* of the Eanna and PN$_3$, the king's administrative official in the Eanna, and the scribes of the Eanna, in the king's court of law.

10–12. If he does not come, he shall pay thirty-fold for these two sheep to the Lady of Uruk.

The summoned individual (PN$_1$) is responsible for two sheep that have been led away from his flock by the notoriously corrupt official named Gimillu.[19] Prior to the promulgation of this summons, PN$_1$ has been accused of mishandling the two sheep that were led away from his flock and has attempted to clear himself by challenging the accusation. PN$_1$ must now come to the king's court of law (*bīt dīni ša šarri*) in Babylon to "argue the case" against the officials from the Eanna (PN$_2$ and PN$_3$) who are probably those who made the accusation. If he does not, then he must pay the requisite thirty-fold penalty for the sheep.

Nevertheless, these texts remain relevant to the discussion of the terminology of summoning in general, and particularly to the biblical texts considered below.

18 YOS 7 31. For discussion of this text, see San Nicolò, "Parerga Babylonica VII," 337–39. Other examples of this type of summons include AnOr 8 37; AnOr 8 50; BE 8/1 48; *Nbn* 102; *VAS* 6 99; YOS 7 189. For Neo-Assyrian analogues, see Jas, *Neo-Assyrian Judicial Procedures*, nos. 4 and 54 (discussed in Holtz, *Neo-Babylonian Court Procedure*, 313–316).

19 For more on Gimillu, see Jursa, "Auftragsmord," 109–32, and the literature cited there.

Whereas the two earlier quotations provide direct, narrative descriptions of the summoning procedure, this last text and others like it seem to be one step removed from the process itself. They are probably not the actual legal instrument of summons.[20] Instead, they appear to be a record, formulated in the third person, that the oral summoning by a court-appointed messenger like the *manzaduḫlu* had taken place or had been authorized.[21] Even so, they offer a glimpse at terminology that might have been used as part of the procedure. By converting the documents' third-person formulations into direct address, one arrives at a plausible reconstruction of what a summoner might have actually said. One imagines the court messenger saying, "PN_1! Come and argue your case against PN_2 regarding such-and-such!"

In a number of ways, this reconstruction resembles the *manzaduḫlu*'s order recorded in the text from Nuzi. This, of course, is not surprising since the phrase fulfills the same court function. The reconstructed Neo-Babylonian version, however, is noteworthy for specifying that the purpose of "coming" to court is to "argue the case." Although it seems clear that the reason for summoning defendants to court is always for them to present their arguments, this purpose is only implied in the formulation from Nuzi, whereas the Neo-Babylonian formulation makes it explicit.

Second Isaiah as Summoner

With these Akkadian descriptions of the summoning procedure in mind, one can now turn to the biblical prophetic texts. Based on the Hebrew alone, the most obvious examples of summoning in prophecy occur in Second Isaiah. In three trial scenes, the prophet presents God's demand that his opponents present their case in court:

41:21–22:

קָרְבוּ רִיבְכֶם יֹאמַר ה' הַגִּישׁוּ עֲצֻמוֹתֵיכֶם יֹאמַר מֶלֶךְ יַעֲקֹב. יַגִּישׁוּ וְיַגִּידוּ לָנוּ אֵת אֲשֶׁר
תִּקְרֶינָה הָרִאשֹׁנוֹת מָה הֵנָּה הַגִּידוּ וְנָשִׂימָה לִבֵּנוּ וְנֵדְעָה אַחֲרִיתָן אוֹ הַבָּאוֹת הַשְׁמִיעֻנוּ.

> Present your case, says the Lord, put forward your arguments, says the King of Jacob. Let them put forward and declare to Us those (events) that will occur! First (events), what are they? Declare, so We may put our minds (to them) and know their outcomes! Or, those (events) that are yet to be – tell Us![22]

---

20 In this regard these texts resemble other cuneiform legal documents, such as contracts. See Westbrook, "Codification and Canonization," 124.

21 Holtz, *Neo-Babylonian Court Procedure*, 313.

22 On the use of first-person plural forms to denote God's speech in the divine council, see Cross, Jr., "The Council of Yahweh," 275 n. 4.

44:7:

וּמִי־כָמוֹנִי יִקְרָא וְיַגִּידֶהָ וְיַעְרְכֶהָ לִי מִשּׂוּמִי עַם־עוֹלָם וְאֹתִיּוֹת וַאֲשֶׁר תָּבֹאנָה יַגִּידוּ לָמוֹ.

Who can proclaim (the future) like Me,[23] since I established the eternal people?[24] Let him declare and set it before Me!
And future events, those that are yet to come,[25] let them declare for themselves![26]

45:20–21:

הִקָּבְצוּ וָבֹאוּ הִתְנַגְּשׁוּ יַחְדָּו פְּלִיטֵי הַגּוֹיִם לֹא יָדְעוּ הַנֹּשְׂאִים אֶת־עֵץ פִּסְלָם
וּמִתְפַּלְלִים אֶל־אֵל לֹא יוֹשִׁיעַ. הַגִּידוּ וְהַגִּישׁוּ אַף יִוָּעֲצוּ יַחְדָּו מִי הִשְׁמִיעַ זֹאת מִקֶּדֶם
מֵאָז הִגִּידָהּ הֲלוֹא אֲנִי ה' אֵין-עוֹד אֱלֹהִים מִבַּלְעָדַי אֵל־צַדִּיק וּמוֹשִׁיעַ אַיִן זוּלָתִי.

Assemble and come! Gather together, remnants among the nations. Those who carry their wooden images and pray to a god who cannot save, do not know!
Declare and put forward! Let them even consult one another! Who told of this from before, declared it since time past? Was it not I, the Lord?! There is no god besides Me, a victorious God, and there is no savior except Me!

---

23 For this translation, which follows the Masoretic cantillation, see NJPS. It is also possible to interpret the words *umî-kāmônî* as a self-standing nominal question about God. The word *yiqrā'* is then the first of three (rather than two) jussive verbs referring to actions in court that must be done by the opponents. For discussion, see Goldingay and Payne, *A Critical and Exegetical Commentary*, 338. Note, however, that typically the verb *'-m-r* (G-stem), rather than *q-r-'* (G-stem), introduces declarations in court, as in 1 Kgs 3:17, 22. Furthermore, as my colleague Moshe Bernstein has observed in personal conversation, if there is indeed a string of three verbs, one would prefer a 3fs suffix on the verb *yiqrā'*.

24 This translation retains MT as it stands, despite the many difficulties in doing so, since the interpretation of the words in question does not affect the argument. For this interpretation of the text, see Haran, *Between Ri'shonôt*, 51 (Hebrew); Blenkinsopp, *Isaiah 40–55*, 235; Goldingay and Payne, *A Critical and Exegetical Commentary*, 340; and Paul, *Isaiah 40–66*, 192 (Hebrew). For proposed emendations, see the literature cited in Goldingay and Payne, *A Critical and Exegetical Commentary*, 341.

25 The words *waᵃšer tābō'nâ* appear to be a gloss on *we'ōtîyyôt*. I am grateful to Moshe Bernstein for this suggestion. See also Qimḥi.

26 For this interpretation, see Goldingay and Payne, *A Critical and Exegetical Commentary*, 341. The suggested emendation of *lāmô* to read *lānû*, following the Targum, would furnish a fitting parallel to the 1cp pronouns in 41:22 and first-person plural language elsewhere in Isaiah's courtroom scenes, as noted in Cross, Jr., "The Council of Yahweh."

The lawsuit pertains to proof of prediction: the nations must prove that they (and their gods) can predict the future, like God himself. That this must be the nations' argument can best be seen from the use of the verb *n-g-š* (C-stem) in Isa 41:21–22. In 41:21, the prophet, speaking on God's behalf, orders the nations, "put forward your arguments" (*haggîšû ʿᵃṣumôtêkem*). In 41:22,[27] the same verb occurs, this time in the jussive, followed by a description of exactly what is to be "put forward," namely "those (events) that will occur" (*'ēt ʾᵃšer tiqrenā*). Based on this equivalence, it seems that the ability to predict is also what is to be "put forward" in 45:21, "set before" God (*ʿ-r-k*, G-stem)[28] in 44:7, or "declared" (*n-g-d*, C stem) in 44:7 and 45:21.[29]

It is the Neo-Babylonian formulation, with its explicit mention of "arguing the case" (*dibba dabābu*), that furnishes the clearest parallel to these verses in Isaiah. By using imperatives (41:21 and 45:21), the prophet speaks as the summoner might have, addressing the summoned individuals directly. In other verses (41:22, 44:7), the use of the jussive, marking indirect address, brings the prophet's words remarkably close to the third-person formulation of the Neo-Babylonian summonses themselves. However, the variations of vocabulary in the biblical formulations and their apparent variance from the Akkadian ones indicate beyond much doubt that the biblical phrases do not depend directly on the Neo-Babylonian texts. Rather, the parallel is functional: the Akkadian and the Hebrew formulations reflect, independently, the demands of the courts (one human, the other divine) that defendants present arguments to justify their cases. This similarity of function is sufficient to confirm the possibility that the prophet models the summonses to the foreign nations on a procedure and on language that originate in actual law courts.

The parallel between the biblical texts and the Neo-Babylonian summonses sheds light not only on the wording of the prophet's orders to the nations, but also, more generally, on the imagined legal situation, as well. The summoned individuals in the Neo-Babylonian texts face a

---

27 For the forensic meaning of this noun, noted already by Rashi and upheld by modern interpreters, see *HALOT*, 870 and Goldingay and Payne, *A Critical and Exegetical Commentary*, 193.

28 For the forensic use of this verb, compare Ps 50:21; Job 13:18 and 23:4. See Bovati, *Re-Establishing Justice*, 334 and Magdalene, *Scales of Righteousness*, 181, 242.

29 For the forensic use of this verb, compare Prov 12:17, where it might be translated "to testify." Although this usage is appropriate in these verses, note that in Second Isaiah, in general, the verb may simply refer to the ability to "declare" the future, without any forensic nuance. Compare the

claim against them and a concomitant penalty. The summonses afford them the opportunity to avoid paying the penalty by "arguing the case" in court. In Isaiah, no penalty is mentioned. Nevertheless, by ordering the nations to trial, God lets the nations have their day in court.[30] The summonses afford the nations an opportunity to make their case against God's claim that only he can foretell future events. If they cannot do so, they lose the case, and God is vindicated.

The Prophets and the manzaduḫlu-officials

Second Isaiah's extensive use of obvious courtroom metaphors eases the identification of parallels in actual litigation records. When the biblical text speaks of "presenting a case," the forensic context is clear and begs to be elucidated by examination of court procedure. Are there similar forensic parallels between the language used by other prophets and the language of actual courtroom procedure? In terms of the specific matter at hand, can one turn to Akkadian sources to shed light on these other prophets' role as summoners to court?

In literary prophecy, accusations are at times preceded by an order to "hear."[31] This order consists of the imperative *šimʿû* ("Hear!"),[32] addressed directly to the accused, often followed by the phrase *dᵉbar*-YHWH.[33] In this fuller form, the Hebrew introductory formula brings to mind the formulation of the *manzaduḫlu*-officials' order to the defendant: *lišān-šu*$_4$ *ša* ^{m}PN$_2$ *li-qa-am-mi ù al-ka*$_4$*-am-mi* ("Receive the declaration of PN$_2$, and come [to court]!"). Both the Akkadian and the Hebrew

use of the verb in Isa 45:21 above, as well as in Isa 41:26; 42:9; 43:9, 12; 46:10; 48:3, 5.

30 On the novelty of allowing the nations legal standing at trial, see Westermann, "Sprache und Struktur," 169.

31 For general discussion of the legal nuances of the verb *š-m-ʿ* (G-stem) and *ʾ-z-n* (C-stem) as introductions to forensic speech, see Magdalene, *Scales of Righteousness,* 120–21. Note that according to Westermann, *Basic Forms,* 142, "an investigation of these introductory phrases...does not...seem to be worthwhile."

32 Hos 5:1; Amos 4:1; 8:4; Mic 3:1, 9. Note the use of two additional, parallel verbs in Hos 5:1. On *š-m-ʿ* in the introduction to accusations, see Magdalene, *Scales of Righteousness,* 121; 206.

33 Isa 1:10; 28:14; Jer 2:4; 44:24; Ezek 13:2; Hos 4:1. See also Amos 7:16, where the phrase *šᵉmaʿ dᵉbar*-YHWH (in the singular) occurs. In Ezek 34:2, the *kō-ʾāmar* formula ("Thus said the Lord") serves a similar introductory function. The examples cited here and in the previous footnote are not meant to be an exhaustive list. And, of course, there are passages in which these formulas introduce speeches that are not accusatory.

phrases contain a verb in the imperative (Akkadian *leqû*, Hebrew *š-m-ʿ*) that calls the subject's attention to the "word of" (Akkadian *lišānšu ša*, Hebrew *d^ebar-*) the accuser.

This similarity of form and function between the prophets' orders and those of the *manzaduḫlu*-officials suggests that the role of the prophets corresponds to the role of the court messengers. Like the *manzaduḫlu*-officials, the prophets announce the accusation to the accused individuals. And, like their counterparts in the courts at Nuzi, the prophets specifically refer to the accuser by introducing the accusation as *d^ebar*-YHWH. In interpreting the biblical formula, one might argue that it mentions God because God is the judge who has commissioned the prophets as court messengers. The analogy to the Nuzi text suggests otherwise. Even though the *manzaduḫlu*-officials are court-appointed, their summoning speech does not refer to the judges or the court that appointed them. The "word" that the accused is supposed to "accept" (*leqû*) is explicitly the word of the accuser, rather than the "word" of the adjudicating authority. Similarly, even though the prophets play the role of summoners appointed by God, who will act as judge, they refer to the accusation as God's word because God is also the accuser.

One difference between the *šimʿû d^ebar*-YHWH formula and the orders of the *manzaduḫlu*-officials is that the Hebrew formula lacks an explicit summons to court. Analogues to the *manzaduḫlu*-officials' order to "come (to court)" (*alāku*), albeit with different semantic nuances, do, of course, appear in Second Isaiah's more explicit formulations. More typically, however, prophecies move from the accusation directly to God's judgment, without any explicit opportunity for a response in a trial. Nevertheless, the analogy between the first part of the *manzaduḫlu*-officials' speech and the prophetic formula remains apparent. In light of it, one may suggest that the order to "come to court" and respond to the accusation is implied. By conveying God's accusations, the prophets offer their audience, like the foreign nations in Second Isaiah, a chance to respond. With the accusation, the prophets summon the Israelites to their day in court, even if this summons is only implicit, and the weight of God's accusation is such that it goes unanswered.[34]

Conclusions

This article has considered the role of the prophets as summoners in light of the summoning procedure attested in Akkadian litigation

---

34 The work of Yochanan Muffs suggests that a response is expected and actually does come, from the prophets themselves, not as God's agents, but as representatives of the people. See Muffs, *Love and Joy*, 31–33.

records. It has pointed to Neo-Babylonian parallels to Second Isaiah's orders to the foreign nations to present evidence in court. Similarly, it has suggested the summoning terminology known from the Nuzi legal corpus as an analogue to the prophetic formula *šimʿu dᵉbar* YHWH. While the biblical texts alone allow the identification of the prophets' position as summoners, the Akkadian parallels anchor this depiction of the prophets in a position that is well attested in ancient court records. The prophets take on this role and "follow the script," as it were, by incorporating language analogous to the language used by their counterparts in actual courts of law.

The identification of these parallels adds a new dimension to the understanding of the prophetic office in general. Interpreters of prophecy's legal metaphor have focused on the prophets as those who deliver judgment.[35] That is to say, the prophet's role as messenger begins only once the case in the divine court is closed. The analogies between the prophets and the summoners known from the Akkadian texts suggest that the prophets begin their missions while the case is still open, when the outcome still remains unknown. As court messengers, the prophets are "on duty" throughout the legal proceedings and may be sent by the court to confront litigants well before the case is closed.

The implications of the prophets' role as summoners extend to the role played by God as well. Scholars have long recognized that prophetic courtroom imagery depicts God as both plaintiff and judge.[36] This ambiguity, of course, creates difficulties in interpretation of specific verses: is God speaking as a judicial authority or as a plaintiff?[37]

---

35 Baltzer, "Considerations Regarding the Office," 574; Cross, Jr., *Canaanite Myth and Hebrew Epic*, 188–89; Mullen, Jr., *Assembly of the Gods*, 209–26; Ross, "The Prophet as Yahweh's Messenger," 114–16; Gordon, "Standing in the Council," 190–96.

36 For literature, see De Roche, "Yahweh's Rîb," 563 n. 3.

37 A brief survey of modern commentaries on Isa 41:21–22; 44:7; and 45:20–21 illustrates the problem. Commentators who interpret these verses as spoken by a judge include, on Isa 41:21–22: Amos Ḥakham, *Sēper Yᵉšʿayāhû*, 439 (Hebrew); Baltzer, *Deutero-Isaiah*, 116 and Paul, *Isaiah 40–66*, 135 (Hebrew); and on Isa 44:7 and 45:20–21: Hanson, *Isaiah 40–66*, 87, 111. Commentators who see these verses as spoken by a plaintiff include, on Isa 41:21–22: Schoors, *I Am God*, 222 and Goldingay, *The Message of Isaiah 40–55*, 132; on Isa 44:7: Schoors, *I Am God*, 228 and Goldingay and Payne, *A Critical and Exegetical Commentary*, 328; on Isa 45:21: Berges, *Jesaja*, 432. In an interesting attempt to interpret this ambiguity in Isa 41:22, J. T. Walsh writes that "like a clever lawyer, Yahweh uses first person plural forms to imply an identification of his own point of view with that of the court" ("The Case for the Prosecution," 109).

Assigning the prophets to the role of court messenger, in light of the parallels considered above, offers some clarity on this question. It is God the plaintiff who makes the accusation, but it is God the judge who presides over the trial itself. Thus, it is God the judge, like the earthly analogues in the Akkadian legal sources, who commissions the prophets as summoners of the court.

In this capacity, the prophets are responsible both for presenting God's accusation to the accused and for summoning the parties to the trial. These two responsibilities are rarely manifest together in any given prophetic speech. Instead, the prophets as summoners may present the accusation by quoting the words of God, the plaintiff, but might not explicitly state God-the-judge's order to argue the case. Alternatively, as in the verses from Second Isaiah discussed above, they may issue clear orders to the litigants to appear in trial. These orders, with their overt procedural terminology, are best understood as the words of God the presiding judge, who has sent the prophet on court business.

WORKS CITED

Alexander, Patrick H., John F. Kutsko, James D. Ernest, Shirley Decker-Lucke, and David L. Petersen. *The SBL Handbook of Style for Ancient Near Eastern, Biblical, and Early Christian Studies*. Peabody, Mass: Hendrickson Publishers, Inc., 1999.

Baltzer, Klaus. "Considerations Regarding the Office and the Calling of the Prophet," *HTR* 61 (1968): 567–81.

Deutero-Isaiah. Hermeneia. Translated by Margaret Kohl. Minneapolis, Minn.: Fortress Press, 2001.

Begrich, Joachim. *Studien zu Deuterojesaja*. Theologische Bücherei 20. Munich: C. Kaiser, 1963.

Berges, Ulrich. *Jesaja 40-48*. Herders Theologischer Kommentar zum Alten Testament. Freiburg: Herder, 2008.

Blenkinsopp, Joseph. *Isaiah 40–55*. Anchor Bible. New York: Doubleday, 2002.

Boecker, Hans Jochen. *Redeformen des Rechtslebens im Alten Testament*. Neukirchen-Vluyn: Neukirchener Verlag, 1964.

Bovati, Pietro. "Le langage juridique du prophète Isaïe." In *The Book of Isaiah - Le livre d'Isaïe: Les oracles et leurs relectures unité et complexité de l'ouvrage*, edited by Jacques Vermeylen, 177–96. Bibliotheca Ephemeridum Theologicarum Lovaniensium 81. Leuven: Leuven University Press, 1989.

Re-establishing Justice: Legal Terms, Concepts and Procedures in the Hebrew Bible. JSOT Supplement 105. Translated by Michael J. Smith. Sheffield: Sheffield Academic Press, 1994.

Cross Jr., Frank Moore. "The Council of Yahweh in Second Isaiah." *JNES* 12 (1953): 274–77.

Canaanite Myth and Hebrew Epic. Cambridge, Mass.: Harvard University Press, 1973.

Daniels, Dwight R. "Is There a 'Prophetic Lawsuit' Genre?" *ZAW* 99 (1987): 339–60.

DeRoche, Michael. "Yahweh's Rîb against Israel: A Reassessment of the So-Called 'Prophetic Lawsuit' in the Preexilic Prophets." *JBL* 102 (1983): 563–74.

Dijkstra, Meindert. "Lawsuit, Debate and Wisdom Discourse in Second Isaiah." In *Studies in the Book of Isaiah: Festschrift Willem A. M. Beuken*, edited by J. Van Ruiten and M. Vervenne. Leuven: Leuven University Press, 1997.

Dombradi, Eva. *Die Darstellung des Rechtsaustrags in den Altbabylonischen Prozessurkunden*, Vol. 1. FAOS 20. Stuttgart: Franz Steiner, 1996.

Eichler, Barry L. "Nuzi and the Bible: A Retrospective." In *DUMU-É-DUB-BA-A: Studies in Honor of Åke W. Sjöberg*, Occasional Publications of the Samuel Noah Kramer Fund 11, edited by Hermann Behrens, Darlene Loding and Martha T. Roth, 107–20. Philadelphia, Pa.: The University Museum, 1989.

Falkenstein, Adam. *Die neusumerischen Gerichtsurkunden*, Vols. I, II. Bayerische Akademie der Wissenschaften, philosophisch-historisch Klasse 40. Munich: Bayerische Akademie der Wissenschaften, 1956–1957.

Gemser, B. "The *Rîb*- or Controversy-Pattern in Hebrew Mentality." In *Wisdom in Israel and in the Ancient Near East*, edited by M. Noth and D. Winton Thomas, 120–37. VT Supplement 3. Leiden: Brill, 1969.

Goldingay, John. *The Message of Isaiah 40–55*. London: T & T Clark, 2005.

Goldingay, John and David Payne. *A Critical and Exegetical Commentary on Isaiah 40–55*. ICC. London: T & T Clark, 2006.

Gordon, Robert P. "Standing in the Council: When Prophets Encounter God." In *The God of Israel*, edited by Robert P. Gordon, 190–204. Cambridge, U.K.: Cambridge University Press, 2007.

Ḥakham, Amos. *Isaiah*. Da'at Miqrā. Jerusalem: Mossad Harav Kook, 1984.

Hanson, Paul D. *Isaiah 40–66*. Interpretation. Louisville, Ky.: John Knox Press, 1995.

Haran, Menahem. *Between Ri'shonôt (Former Prophecies) and Ḥadashôt (New Prophecies): A Literary-Historical Study in the Group of Prophecies Isaiah XL–XLVIII*. Jerusalem: Magnes Press, 1963.

Harvey, Julien. "Le 'Rîb-Pattern,' réquisitoire prophétique sur la rupture de l'alliance." *Biblica* 43 (1962): 172–96.

Hayden, Roy Edmund. *Court Procedure at Nuzu*. Ph.D. Dissertation, Brandeis University, 1962.

Holtz, Shalom E. *Neo-Babylonian Court Procedure*. Cuneiform Monographs 38. Leiden: Brill, 2009.

"A Comparative Note on the Demand for Witnesses in Isa 43:9." *JBL* 129 (2010): 457–61.

"Praying as a Plaintiff." *VT* 61 (2011): 258–79.

Huffmon, Herbert B. "The Covenant Lawsuit in the Prophets." *JBL* 78 (1959): 285–95.

Jas, Remko. *Neo-Assyrian Judicial Procedures*. SAAS 5. Helsinki: The Neo-Assyrian Text Corpus Project, 1996.

Jindo, Job Y. *Biblical Metaphor Reconsidered: A Cognitive Approach to Poetic Prophecy in Jeremiah 1–24*. HSM 64. Winona Lake, Ind.: Eisenbrauns, 2010.

Jursa, Michael. "Auftragsmord, Veruntreuung und Falschaussagen: Neues von Gimillu," *WZKM* 94 (2004): 109–32.

Lafont, Bertrand and Raymond Westbrook. "Neo-Sumerian Period (Ur III)." In *A History of Ancient Near Eastern Law*, edited by Raymond Westbrook, 183–226. Leiden: Brill, 2003.

Limburg, James. *The Lawsuit of God in the Eighth-Century Prophets*. Th.D. Dissertation, Union Theological Seminary, 1969.

Magdalene, F. Rachel. *On the Scales of Righteousness: Neo-Babylonian Trial Law and the Book of Job*. Brown Judaic Studies 348. Providence, R.I.: Brown University Press, 2007.

Muffs, Yochanan. *Love and Joy: Law, Language and Religion in Ancient Israel*. New York: Jewish Theological Seminary of America, 1992.

Mullen Jr., E. Theodore. *The Assembly of the Gods: The Divine Council in Canaanite and Early Hebrew Literature.* HSM 24. Chico, Calif.: Scholars Press, 1980.

Paul, Shalom. *Isaiah 40–66*, Vol. 1. Mikra Leyisra'el. Tel Aviv: Am Oved, 2008.

Ross, James F. "The Prophet as Yahweh's Messenger." In *Prophecy in Israel: Search for an Identity*, edited by David L. Petersen, 112–21. Philadelphia, Pa.: Fortress Press, 1987.

San Nicolò, M. "Parerga Babylonica VII: Der §8 des Gesetzbuches Ḫammurapis in den neubabylonischen Urkunden." *ArOr* 4 (1932): 327–44.

Schoors, Anton. *I Am God Your Saviour: A Form-Critical Study of the Main Genres in Is. XL–LV*. VT Supplement 24. Leiden: Brill, 1973.

Speiser, E. A. *New Kirkuk Documents Relating to Family Laws*. AASOR 10. New Haven, Conn.: ASOR, 1928–29.

von Bolla, Sibylle. "Drei Diebstahlsfälle von Tempeleigentum in Uruk." *ArOr* 12 (1941): 113–20.

Walsh, J. T. "The Case for the Prosecution: Isaiah 41.21–42.17." In *Directions in Biblical Hebrew Poetry*, edited by Elaine R. Follis. JSOT Supplement 40. Sheffield: Sheffield Academic Press, 1987.

Wells, Bruce. *The Law of Testimony in the Pentateuchal Codes*. Beihefte zur Zeitschrift für Altorientalische und Biblische Rechtsgeschichte 4. Wiesbaden: Harrassowitz, 2004.

Westbrook, Raymond. "Codification and Canonization." In Raymond Westbrook, *Law from the Tigris to the Tiber: The Writings of Raymond Westbrook*, edited by Bruce Wells and F. Rachel Magdalene, 119–32. Winona Lake, Ind.: Eisenbrauns, 2009.

Westermann, Claus. "Sprache und Struktur der Prophetie Deuterojesajas." In *Forschung am Alten Testament*, 92–170. Theologische Bücherei 24. Munich: C. Kaiser, 1964.

Basic Forms of Prophetic Speech. Translated by Hugh Clayton White. Louisville, Ky.: Westminster John Knox, 1991.

DEATH-BED DEPOSITIONS IN THE HEBREW BIBLE*

MEIR MALUL
UNIVERSITY OF HAIFA

וְהָיָה כְּעֵץ שָׁתוּל עַל־פַּלְגֵי־מָיִם
אֲשֶׁר פִּרְיוֹ יִתֵּן בְּעִתּוֹ וְעָלֵהוּ לֹא־יִבּוֹל
וְכֹל אֲשֶׁר־יַעֲשֶׂה יַצְלִיחַ
(Ps 1:3)

In an article by Richard Hess titled "David and Abishag: The Purpose of 1 Kings 1:1–4," which has been published in the *Festschrift* of Prof. Bustenay Oded,[1] the author discusses the first four verses in 1 Kings 1, which describe David's advanced age and his bodily frailty. In his view, the main concern of these verses, rather than addressing David's sexual impotency, as is commonly understood by most interpreters, is the appointment of a successor and the continuity of the old king's dynasty, for which measures are taken by him and by his surroundings. His old age and imminent death are then in focus here, rather than his sexual weakness, for which, apparently, Abishag was hired to attend the king.[2] Hess looks closely into a few expressions in this pericope, firstly the idiom זָקֵן בָּא בַּיָּמִים "old (and well) advanced in years," and notes that in its occurrence in a few other contexts in the Bible, it always "precedes a final and important act." Thus, it pre-

* It is with great pleasure and a deep sense of honor that I humbly dedicate the following musings of mine to a great teacher, mentor, and man, Prof. Barry L. Eichler, whose legacy I try every day to pass on to my own students, I hope with as much success as his.

1 Galil, Geller, and Millard, eds., *Homeland and Exile*.

2 For a review of various views regarding the meaning and purpose of this pericope, see Section 1 of Hess's article, where he also cites a few scholars who hold impotence to be the main issue of the story and the main stimulus in Adonijah's behavior (see the scholars quoted in nn. 13–18). Noteworthy is M. Cogan's view, quoted by Hess, according to which David's impotence is significant in reflecting the king's old age rather than his sexual condition. As we shall presently see, demonstrating the king's old age and imminent death seem to be the main purposes of the passage, rather than his lack of sexual potency *per se*.

cedes the note regarding Isaac's birth in Gen 18:11ff.,[3] the procurement of a wife for Isaac in Genesis 24, the distribution of the land to the Israelite tribes according to Josh 13:1–2, and the renewal of the covenant between God and the people by Joshua in Joshua 23. More specifically, Hess notes that in all four cases, when this expression occurs, it applies to elderly people who, as death approaches, seek the fulfilment of the covenant with God and its application to the next generation.

Another expression in the pericope 1 Kgs 1:1–4 discussed by Hess is the verb *ḥmm* in vv. 1 and 2, describing David's inability to keep warm as a result of his advanced age:

> Now King David was old, advanced in age; and they covered him with clothes, but he could not keep warm (וְלֹא יִחַם לוֹ). Whereupon his servants say to him, "Let them seek a young virgin for my lord the king, and let her attend the king and become his nurse; and let her lie in your bosom, that my lord the king may keep warm (וְחַם לַאדֹנִי הַמֶּלֶךְ)."

This statement too has been understood by quite a few scholars cited by Hess as pointing to David's sexual impotence, and his lack of heat has been taken in a sexual sense. Hess, however—in my view correctly—relates this usage of the verb *ḥmm* to its usage in 2 Kgs 4:34, describing Elisha's efforts to restore life to the Shunammite's dead son:

> And he went up and lay on the child, and put his mouth on his mouth and his eyes on his eyes and his hands on his hands, and he stretched himself on him; and the flesh of the child became warm (וַיָּחָם בְּשַׂר הַיָּלֶד).

The parallelism between the two occurrences of the verb *ḥmm* shows that warmth and to be warm are signs of life; and the statement that David could not keep warm means then that he was on the brink of death, complementing thus the information supplied by the previous idiom discussed. The two idioms focus thus on the king's approaching an imminent death; this information was important and significant as a prelude to the "final and important act" of disposing one's last wish and had then to be duly underlined (see more below on this idea).

What Hess, in fact, is talking about here is a reflection, in all the cases he cites, of the phenomenon of death-bed dispositions, and the expressions he discusses seem to have been formal solemn formulae, either narrated by the author at the beginning of his description of such situations of death-bed dispositions[4] or placed in the mouth of the dying

---

3 For this episode, see more details below.

4 For Gen 18:11, which looks like an afterthought remark inserted by the author to underline Sarah's disbelief at the promise of a son in her advanced and post-menopausal age, rather than a clear case of a death-bed disposition, see further below. Below I shall also underline the "narra-

person, who is thus described as declaring his having become old and advanced in years, approaching his imminent death, and now discharging his last will. In other words, what we seem to have here are specimens of formal-legal declarations (*verba solemnia*), which carry what E. A. Speiser had called "definite socio-juridical implications."[5]

Hess thus seems to have definitely sensed the solemn nature of the expression זָקֵן בָּא בַּיָּמִים and he clearly notes its connection with the final wish of the testator and, in the case of David, with the disposal of his throne and house to his heir. However, he does not seem to be aware of the underlying legal-technical load of such idioms and expressions in the Bible nor of Speiser's 1955 article on the subject.[6] Having been much interested in this aspect of biblical and ancient Near Eastern research for quite some time, naturally Hess's article and argument have aroused my interest and curiosity to look afresh into the whole issue.

In the following, it is, therefore, my aim to review all the types of such death-bed declarations appearing in the Hebrew Bible in such—narratival!—contexts of final dispositions of dying patriarchs and leaders, trying to expose their formal, even legal-technical, load as defined by Speiser.

Let me start by first presenting Speiser's treatment of one famous death-bed declaration in the Hebrew Bible and its parallels in some cuneiform documents from the ancient Near East.

Isaac's Blessing (Genesis 27)

Speiser, in his 1955 study, called the attention of students of the Hebrew Bible to death-bed dispositions in cuneiform documents, mainly from Nuzi in the fifteenth century BCE, comparing them to similar dispositions in the Hebrew Bible.[7] Speiser duly underlined the dispositive nature of such declarations, claiming that they carried "socio-juridical implications."[8] Speiser discussed mainly the pregnant episode in Gen-

---

tival," rather than formal-technical, character of the biblical evidence, in which such reflections of assumed formal-solemn formulae sometime appear in the text as *en passant* remarks by the storyteller.

5 Speiser, "Day of My Death," 253.

6 See already C. H. Gordon's treatment of such death-bed dispositions and blessings back in 1940, Gordon, "Biblical Customs," 8.

7 See already Gordon, "Biblical Customs," 8.

8 Speiser, "Day of My Death," 253. Later, T. L. Thompson totally rejected Speiser's thesis, claiming that these declarations carry no such dispositive load, being merely summary in nature. See Thompson, *Historicity*, 285–92. Incidentally, Thompson (ibid., 286 n. 390) also dismisses the solemn nature of the biblical parallel statements to be reviewed below, which, in view of

esis 27, in which old Isaac, on what seems to have been his death-bed, decides to discharge his last will and blessing to his beloved son, Esaw. He points in particular to Isaac's declaration "Behold now, I have become old and I know not the day of my death" (v. 2), which he compares to a similar declaration occurring in the Nuzi document HSS 9 34:9: *u inanna anāku altīb* "now I have grown old," both statements carrying, in his view, a solemn dispositive power. Speiser cites a few more documents to bolster his thesis, the most significant, in my view, being AASOR 16 56,[9] in which a vivid and colorful picture of a death-bed situation is described. The significant lines read as follows (ll. 8–12):

> *abuya Ḫuya maruṣmi ina erši nāl u qātī abuya ṣabtu u kinanna ana iâši iqtabi*
>
> My father Ḫuya was ill and lying on (his) bed. And he took hold of my hand and thus he said to me.

Then follows the father's statement as regards a certain slave-girl who is to be given as a wife to the youngest son.[10] Speiser makes the observation, in my view a correct methodological observation, that such legal documents, as the ones harboring these colorful descriptions and statements, have no "room for casual observations," and recording such a statement as "now I have grown old," which on its face value seems to be a truism and, therefore, apparently superfluous, must needs reflect its "socio-juridical implications."[11] I would also add here the vivid description in AASOR 16 56:8–12 of the father holding his son's hand while lying sick and on his death-bed, as it, too, seems totally out of place in the context of a legal-technical document.[12]

---

the following analysis, is unwarranted. For Thompson's view, see more below.

9 Quoted also by Gordon, "Biblical Customs," and see also Pritchard, *ANET*, 220.

10 The document HSS 5 48, quoted by Speiser, "Day of My Death," 255, does not seem to reflect such a death-bed situation and, therefore, I do not include it in the following argumentation. Also, the document that seems to have originally triggered Speiser's interest in the topic of death-bed declarations, namely HSS 19 34, is hard to accommodate here and Thompson's criticisms in this regard do seem to be founded. See more below.

11 Speiser, "Day of My Death," 253.

12 For such descriptions and gestures in the context of death-bed dispositions in the Bible, see the discussion below. One of the main arguments against Thompson's critique of Speiser's thesis lies exactly here: Thompson ignores the above powerful methodological principle and thus he fails to explain the occurrence of such "narratival truisms" (my term) in such clear

Much later I devoted a detailed study to the whole colorful episode of Isaac's blessing, titled "Fabrication of Evidence in the Bible: Jacob's Imposture and Joseph's Blood-Stained Coat,"[13] in which I underlined the solemn-legal atmosphere of the whole situation and pointed to a few other legal-technical elements and expressions in the story. These include the meal requested by Isaac as a preparation for his act of blessing, which I interpreted as reflecting a ceremonial meal of the kind we find in the context of other solemn situations, particularly those of sealing treaties and other legal agreements;[14] his kissing of Jacob, which, as already explained above, may have been more than a mere sign of affection on the part of the loving father toward his son;[15] and especially the detailed procedure of closely examining of the evidence regarding the identity of the person claiming the blessing, by applying gradually the whole sensorial apparatus by old Isaac.[16] It is clear that Isaac made every effort to ascertain beyond any doubt that the person standing in front of him was actually the one he was claiming to be, whom he, Isaac, intended to bless, and not an impostor. I also pointed out, following Ian Ritchie,[17] the legal load of the sense of smell, serving as the most reliable instrument of judgment, perhaps occurring in this sense also in Isa 11:1ff. Finally, the reasons for such a careful and detailed examination of the evidence have also been examined, and these proved to have

---

legal-technical contexts. I myself have made much use of this methodological principle in a few of my publications, which has led to my discovering the legal-technical load of quite a few apparently "narratival" statements. See, e.g., my discussion of the kiss as a legal symbolic act in a Mesopotamian legal document (Malul, *Mesopotamian Legal Symbolism*, 181f.) and in a few contexts in the Bible (Malul, "Some Idioms," 202ff.; see also the kiss in Gen 27:26–27, for which, see more below). The most significant example of the working of this principle would seem to be in the identification of the legal-technical load of a few expressions and idioms in the colorful, and even poetic, passage in Ezek 16:3–7, which reflects the ancient Mesopotamian legal-social institution of adoption of foundlings (see Malul, "Adoption").

13 Malul, "Fabrication of Evidence."

14 Malul, *Mesopotamian Legal Symbolism*, 376ff.

15 Cf. in this context the gesture of the father holding his son's hand while making his disposition, reported in AASOR 16 56:8–12 quoted above. See more below.

16 Hearing, touch, taste, and finally smell. Sight is excluded due to Isaac's blindness because of his advanced age. For this bodily impediment and its possible significance in the context of the present discussion, see below.

17 Ritchie, "The Nose Knows."

their footing in the legal philosophy transpiring in biblical times, quite the opposite to what a modern person would expect. According to this philosophy, the person actually attending the solemn context and being granted the privilege intended by the testator, even if he is not the person actually intended by the testator but is, rather, an impostor, is considered to be the one who won the privilege; and being later discovered to have been an impostor, who had fraudulently appropriated what was meant for another person, did not abrogate what he had won.[18] Note Isaac's words pointing exactly to this situation: "Who was it, then, that hunted game and brought it to me…and I blessed him—and indeed he will be blessed!" (v. 33).[19] There are a few more episodes in the Hebrew Bible that also attest to the working of this philosophy, mainly the case of the Gibeonites who duped the Israelites into signing a treaty with them, pretending to be from a far away country (Josh 9, and see vv. 18–19); see also Esth 8:8; 7:8. The old and blind(!) patriarch, being aware of the way things worked in his time, was then forced to resort to a careful examination of the evidence presented to him regarding the person approaching him in order to make sure that what he was about to bequeath as his final wish would actually reach the person he had chosen.

To sum up, the above analysis of the whole episode of Isaac's blessing and the discovery of the various legal-technical building blocks strewn in it add support to Speiser's thesis and, at least in my view, more than strengthens his identification of the "socio-juridical implications" of Isaac's statement "I know not the day of my death," despite Thompson's critique.

However, as already hinted above (n. 10), Thompson's critique does seem to be valid at least with regard to Speiser's analysis and understanding of the Nuzi document that served as the main and first impetus for the whole thesis: HSS 9 34. As Thompson states, this is not a will and we do not seem to have here a clear death-bed statement. The document reports the transfer of responsibility from Ḫanaya, who has become old and probably unable anymore to take care of his holdings, to a group of apprentices who are expected to look out for the property. The supposedly pregnant expression *u inanna anāku altīb* "now I have grown old" is not, therefore, a declaration uttered by a dying person on his death-bed, as is clearly the case with Isaac in Gen 27:2, but rather a factual statement regarding the virtual incapacity of Ḫanaya to go on taking care of his holdings due to his advanced age. Having said that,

---

18 See Friedman, *To Kill and Inherit*, 60–84; and earlier Gordon, "Biblical Customs," 8.

19 Gordon, "Biblical Customs."

one still cannot ignore the fact that such a "narratival statement" is recorded in a clearly legal technical document and in that regard Speiser's methodological principle, mentioned above, is still valid.[20]

If we exclude this document too from the roster of "death-bed dispositions," we are left then with only AASOR 16 56, which, at least in my view, seems quite clear. Below, however, I shall call the reader's attention to a few (very few indeed) more documents in which such death-bed declarations seem to appear. Generally speaking, our trove of such declarations in the cuneiform evidence, compared to the finds in the Bible (see below), is quite poor, the reason probably being that these were oral statements, recorded only rarely in the written evidence. I shall address again this quality of rarity of such oral statements in the written evidence.

Let us now take a fresh and close look at the various death-bed dispositions occurring in various parts of the Hebrew Bible, which, on the force of the previously painted background, seem to betray their solemn and juridical nature, despite the fact that we are facing in all cases a narratival, rather than legal-technical, genre.

Prior to that, however, a few words regarding this narratival character of the biblical evidence, in contrast to the cuneiform legal sources, are in order. Let me start first with the latter: Cuneiform legal sources are formal, technical, and notoriously laconic. They focus on the subject matter at hand, use specific technical language, refrain from side remarks that have no specific and defined role in the legal issue at hand, and focus on the result rather than on the process leading to such a result.[21] Moreover, being basically evidentiary, rather than constitutive, instruments of law, the available cuneiform legal documents often fail to record the latter instruments, which, as already said above, seem to have been performed orally and performatively.[22] Those supposedly "narratival remarks" that one occasionally (and quite rarely indeed) encounters in such technical contexts could not then be coincidental, and they most probably allude to such constitutive instruments of law performed orally but rarely recorded.[23]

---

20 The next question would then be: "What could then be the 'socio-juridical implications' of this specific statement in this specific context? Was it specifically required of the aging person to formally state his deteriorating condition to be (legally?) allowed to relinquish his duties and bequeath them to other persons?"

21 See Malul, *Mesopotamian Legal Symbolism*, 13–17.

22 For the evidentiary, rather than constitutive, nature of the cuneiform legal documents, see also Malul, *Mesopotamian Legal Symbolism*, 449–52.

23 See again the above-discussed methodological principle (n. 12 above).

The biblical evidence, in contrast, is mostly of the narratival type, and even though there is a variegated assortment of genres in the biblical books, they are all different from the cuneiform technical documents, not only in language and phraseology, but also in goal and general outlook.[24] Now although the biblical narratives also abide by the law of economy in terms of conciseness of description, they do carry sometimes "narratival remarks" reflecting such orally-performed instruments of law, which appear at times to be strewn *en passant* in the text, but as part of the unfolding story. Applying again the above distinction between "result" and "process,"[25] in contrast to the cuneiform legal documents, which tersely report the result of some legal transaction, the biblical narratives by their very nature convey a sense of matters unfolding in front of one's eyes, as though a show is running, where various characters act, move, talk, and various activities take place. Those orally performed instruments of legal change are part of this unfolding process. It is the task of the modern scholar to glean and identify such formal elements in the text and expose their formal-legal load.[26] This is particularly true with regard to the subject under discussion here, for the various assumed death-bed statements identified and analyzed below are quite embedded in the story, and it is our task to identify their formulaic character and show that the narrator, when reciting a certain story, is making use, where needed, of formal-techni-

---

24 To follow W. W. Hallo's tripartite typological classification of cuneiform literature into "archival texts," "monumental texts," and "canonical texts" (in Hallo and Simpson, *The Ancient Near East*, 154–58), the biblical books definitely belong to the last group, whereas the cuneiform legal documents belong to the first. Incidentally, the argument of genre was one of the main arguments advanced by Thompson in rejecting previous scholars' attempts to find such legal-technical elements and reflections and other expressions of social customs in the Patriarchal Narratives. In his view (*Historicity*, 202, 294, 320f.), since these are stories, one should approach them with literary tools of analysis and understand them as stories rather than as documents reflecting legal and social reality. To these arguments I can only refer the reader to the approach of "Law in the Narrative" inaugurated by David Daube more than sixty years ago (*Studies in Biblical Law*, 1947), according to which the literary genre of our source material does not necessarily exclude the probability of gleaning from it social, even legal-technical, reflections and elements reflecting some socio-juridical reality behind the text. See Malul, "Adoption," 97f., and more below.

25 See Malul, *Mesopotamian Legal Symbolism*, 15.

26 See my treatment of the episode of Isaac's blessing in Genesis 27 in Malul, "Fabrication of Evidence," and the summary above.

cal language, and he is borrowing into his story legal idioms from the legal and social reality transpiring in his world.

Interestingly enough, it seems that exactly such narratival contexts, as we find in the Bible, "allowed" the preservation of such, definitely oral, formal declarations of the kind discussed here, which otherwise might have been lost to us. The cuneiform legal documents, laconic, technical, and basically evidentiary in outlook and purpose (see n. 22 above), failed in most cases to mention these unfolding instruments of legal change and this may explain the dearth of death-bed dispositions in the cuneiform evidence noted above.

Death-Bed Dispositions in the Hebrew Bible

Death-bed dispositions by old and dying persons in the context of solemnly disposing off their last will to their heirs have been known and are still known to have a dispositive and binding nature.[27] One may quote here the words of one of the Medieval Jewish commentators, Rabbi Obadiah ben Jacob Sforno (Sforno Italy, 1470–1550), who says in his commentary on Isaac's blessing in Gen 27:2 as follows:

> "I know not the day of my death." For indeed the blessing is more powerful when the blesser is approaching death, as in the cases of Jacob (Gen 49) and Moses (Deut 33), because at that time the soul is more distant from the flesh (lit. the matter).[28]

Interesting are also Aristotle's words as quoted by Gaster:

> A man's soul (*psyche*) is never more active than when he is at the point of death.[29]

Gaster underlines the widespread popular belief, reflections of which he finds in various places around the world, not least Classical and Late Antiquity, that the dying were considered to be prescient: "Gradually relinquishing the limitations of mortality, they become increasingly detached from the punctual and momentary and increasingly sensitive to that eternal continuum in which past, present, and future blend and blur."[30]

---

27 Cf. Westermann, *Genesis 12–36*, 437; Gordon, "Biblical Customs," 8; Gaster, *Myth, Legend, and Custom*, 214, Sec. 74.

28 My translation.

29 Gaster, *Myth, Legend, and Custom*, 214. See also the statement by Xenophon, "At the advent of death men become more divine, and hence they can foresee the future."

30 Gaster, *Myth, Legend, and Custom*, 214.

There are quite a few episodes in the Hebrew Bible describing the approaching death of some person. Famous, of course, are those concerning the patriarchs (Abraham in Genesis 24; Isaac in Genesis 27; and Jacob in Gen 47:29; 48:1, 10, 21), but see also David's last words in 1 Kgs 2:1–9; and a few others.[31] In most of these colorful episodes clear declarations occur, which—whether placed in the mouth of the testator or narrated by the author (see below)—formally and solemnly set out the testamentary nature of the situation and underline the status of the testator as a person on the brink of death.

Upon first impression, at least some of the death-bed statements occurring in various contexts in the biblical text, despite the narratival context, do seem to carry a solemn, even legal-formal, air and, in my view, they carry a legal-technical load, binding upon the persons involved in the death-bed situation described in the various passages.[32]

Another group of statements that we encounter in the Hebrew Bible seem to be summary in nature, merely stating the fact that the said person has reached old age and that his death is imminent, or that he has died in old age. This group includes such expressions as זָקֵן וּשְׂבַע יָמִים, "old and sated with days/years," said of Abraham (Gen 25:8), Isaac (35:29), and Job (Job 42:17); וְשָׂבַע יָמִים "sated with days/years," said of David (1 Chr 23:1) and Jehoiada (2 Chr 24:15); מלא ימים, "full of days," said of David in 2 Sam 7:12, 1 Chr 17:11; קרב קץ, "the end drew near," in Lam 4:18 (+ מלא ימים); זָקֵן בָּא בַאֲנָשִׁים, "old and advanced in years among men," said of Jesse in 1 Sam 17:12;[33] בא יומו, "his day has come,"

---

31 All the known episodes are listed in the following table, even those that do not clearly fall into the established pattern of death-bed dispositions. These, however, seem to share with the "real" death-bed dispositions some features worth noting and they add also to the clarification of the "real" ones. See the discussion below. Clear death-bed episodes are depicted also in some of the Apocrypha and Pseudepigrapha, such as the Book of Tobit (14:3ff.), the Assumption of Moses 1:15, the Testament of Job 1:1ff.; 51:2; 52:1ff., and particularly in all the Testaments of the Twelve Patriarchs. Significant details from these Pseudepigrapha will be adduced in appropriate places below.

32 See again my discussion of the episode of Isaac's blessing of Jacob (Malul, "Fabrication of Evidence"), which proved to be strewn with legal-technical terms and expressions, reflecting the solemnity and graveness of the situation in which a dying patriarch is disposing his last will to his descendant.

33 If we follow the Septuagint and the Peshita here, one should read בא בשנים and thus we would have the exact parallel to the expression בא בימים. In that case, this occurrence too should be placed in the first group and rightly

in 1 Sam 26:10, Jer 50:27, 31, Ezek 21:30, Ps 37:13 and more; and note also the description of the advanced age of Barzillai the Gilaadite in 2 Sam 19:32–38. In all these contexts it is clear that these statements are merely summary in nature.[34]

I am interested here in the former group of statements. All the relevant expressions and their occurrences in the text are listed in the following detailed table.

One should first note that beside the passages in which one of the expressions under discussion actually occurs, the table lists also a few others in which no expression is mentioned. These are noted by square brackets [ ]. Some of the latter passages occur in the text right after a passage that does contain a death-bed disposition and opens with one of the expressions. One then gets the impression that in these cases the latter passages just continue the previous ones and the death-bed dispositions in the former passages apply to the following as well. This seems to be the case in no. 4, in which Isaac blesses Jacob upon the latter's planned trip to Harran and admonishes him to take a wife from their family. It seems as though the death-bed situation at the start of Ch. 27 with Isaac's solemn declaration extends also to the next chapter.[35]

Similar are the cases of no. 7;[36] of no. 9, clearly alluding to a previous death-bed disposition; of no. 16, following the statement in no. 15 (Deut

---

so. Here, too, one faces a solemn and grave setting, the election of a new king who will replace Saul. See below.

34 For views regarding old age in ancient times, see Weinfeld, "Seventy Years"; Malamat, "Longevity." Interestingly enough, even the two age notifications listed in the Bible (Deut 31:2; 34:7, nos. 14 and 17, respectively, in the following table), stating the old age of Moses, which at first glance would seem to be clearly summary in nature, are included in the table and taken to reflect the same solemn load of the "real" death-bed statements. Age notifications are mentioned in most of the Testaments of the Twelve Patriarchs in the context of the death-bed episode and this may be taken as pointing to the formal load of such notifications. Note also Moses' reference to his death before entering the land in Deut 4:22, which continues the reference in Chap. 3:23–29 (no. 13 in the table) and thus may also carry the same formal air as the other references. See more below.

35 Note also Josh 24, relating the act of renewing the covenant between the people and God, which follows Ch. 23, vv. 1, 2 and 14 (no. 20), where the death-bed declaration of Joshua, preceding his farewell speech, is duly listed. Of course, this arrangement of the stories the way we have them in the MT must be the work of the editor, who may have thought along the lines postulated here. See Westermann's discussion of this editor and his guiding ideology (*Genesis 12–36*, 446f.).

36 Jacob's testament to his sons in Ch. 49 follows the death-bed declarations in Ch. 48 vv. 10 and 21.

No.	Expression	Reference	Said By	Said About	Context	Contextual Details	Other Expressions
1	זְקֵנִים בָּאִים בַּיָּמִים	Gen 18:11	Author	Abraham & Sarah	Promise of seed	(Ceremonial?) meal	צוה v. 19
2	זָקֵן בָּא בַּיָּמִים	Gen 24:1	Author	Abraham-testator	Choosing a wife for Isaac	Symbolic act; sworn pledge	שבע vv. 3, 9, 37; אלה v. 41
3	זָקֵן ... וַתִּכְהֶיןָ עֵינָיו מֵרְאֹת הִנֵּה-נָא זָקַנְתִּי, לֹא יָדַעְתִּי יוֹם מוֹתִי	Gen 27:1 Gen 27:2	Author Isaac-testator	Isaac-testator Isaac-testator	Blessing of heir	Ceremonial meal; kiss; smell evidence examination	ברך (x 16); ברכה (x 6); טרם/לפני מות vv. 4, 7
4	[ ]	Gen 28:1		Isaac-Testator	Blessing of heir to take a wife from family	Blessing of seed and land	צוה v. 1, 6; ברך vv. 1, 6
5	וַיִּקְרְבוּ יְמֵי-יִשְׂרָאֵל לָמוּת	Gen 47:29	Author	Jacob-testator	Final resting place	Death-bed; symbolic act; sworn pledge	חֶסֶד וֶאֱמֶת v. 29; שבע v. 31; רֹאשׁ הַמִּטָּה v. 31; וְשָׁכַבְתִּי עִם-אֲבֹתַי v. 30
6	וְעֵינֵי יִשְׂרָאֵל כָּבְדוּ מִזֹּקֶן הִנֵּה אָנֹכִי מֵת	Gen 48:10 Gen 48:21	Author Jacob-testator	Jacob-testator	Blessing, adoption, and appointing firstborn	Death-bed; symbolic act; kiss; blessing of seed and land	הִנֵּה אָבִיךָ חֹלֶה v. 1; עַל-הַמִּטָּה v. 2; ברך vv. 9, 15, 16, 20
7	[ ]	Gen 49	[Jacob-testator]	Jacob-testator	Blessing of posterity; final resting place	Death-bed (v. 29–33)	ברך v. 28; צוה vv. 29, 33; אֲנִי נֶאֱסָף אֶל-עַמִּי v. 29

No.	Expression	Reference	Said By	Said About	Context	Contextual Details	Other Expressions
8	הִנֵּה אָנֹכִי מֵת	Gen 50:5	Joseph/Jacob-testator	Jacob-testator	Final resting place	Sworn pledge	שבע vv. 5, 6; צוה v. 12
9	[ ]	Gen 50:16	[Brothers/ Jacob-testator]	Jacob-testator	Forgiving the brothers	Death-bed	צוה v. 16; לפני מות v. 16
10	אָנֹכִי מֵת	Gen 50:24	Joseph-testator	Joseph-testator	Final resting place	Death-bed; sworn pledge	שבע v. 25
11	[ ]	Num 20:22ff.	[ ]	Aaron	Death of Aaron; appointing Elazar successor	Dressing Elazar with Aaron's clothes	יֵאָסֵף אַהֲרֹן אֶל-עַמָּיו vv. 24, 26
12	[ ]	Num 27:12–14, 14ff.	[ ]	Moses	Death of Moses; appointing Joshua successor	In the presence of the priest and congregation; symbolic act; consulting the oracle	וְנֶאֱסַפְתָּ אֶל-עַמֶּיךָ v. 13; צוה vv. 19, 23
13	[ ]	Deut 3:23–29	[ ]	[Moses]	Death of Moses; appointing Joshua successor		צוה v. 28

No.	Expression	Reference	Said By	Said About	Context	Contextual Details	Other Expressions
14	Age notification	Deut 31:2	Moses-testator	Moses	Promise of land; appointing Joshua successor; laws	In the presence of all the people	צוה vv. 5, 10
15	הֵן קָרְבוּ יָמֶיךָ לָמוּת	Deut 31:14	God	Moses	Appointing Joshua successor; promise of land; admonitions & decreeing the future (+Ch. 32); covenant and laws	Standing in the Tent of Meeting; depositing the book of law; assembling the people	צוה vv. 14, 23, 25; שבע vv. 20, 21,23; העיד v. 28; היה לעד vv. 19, 21, 26; הִנְּךָ שֹׁכֵב עִם-אֲבֹתֶיךָ v. 16; אַחֲרֵי מוֹתִי vv. 27, 29
16	[ ]	Deut 32:48–52; 33	[ ]	Moses	Death of Moses	Preceding the blessing in Ch. 33	צוה v. 46; העיד v. 46; וְהֵאָסֵף אֶל-עַמֶּיךָ v. 50; ברך 33.1; ברכה 33:1; לפני מות 33:1

No.	Expression	Reference	Said By	Said About	Context	Contextual Details	Other Expressions
17	Age notification + לֹא-כָהֲתָה עֵינוֹ וְלֹא-נָס לֵחֹה	Deut 34:7	Author	Moses	Death of Moses; appointing Joshua successor	Symbolic act	צוה v. 9
18	[מֹשֶׁה עַבְדִּי מֵת]	Jos 1:2	God	Moses	Death of Moses; appointing Joshua successor; promise of land		צוה vv. 7, 9
19	וִיהוֹשֻׁעַ זָקֵן בָּא בַּיָּמִים אַתָּה זָקַנְתָּה בָּאתָ בַיָּמִים	Jos 13:1	Author God	Joshua	Inheritance of land	Joshua distributes the land to the tribes	צוה v. 6
20	וִיהוֹשֻׁעַ זָקֵן בָּא בַּיָּמִים אֲנִי זָקַנְתִּי בָּאתִי בַּיָּמִים וְהִנֵּה אָנֹכִי הוֹלֵךְ הַיּוֹם, בְּדֶרֶךְ כָּל-הָאָרֶץ	Jos 23:1 Jos 23:2 Jos 23:14	Author Joshua-testator Joshua-testator	Joshua-testator Joshua-testator Joshua-testator	Joshua's farewell speech: admonishing the people; renewing the covenant (Ch. 24)	Assembling the people and leaders; erecting a stone; Joshua dies	עדים/עדה 24:22, 27; כרת ברית v.25;

No.	Expression	Reference	Said By	Said About	Context	Contextual Details	Other Expressions
21	[וְעֵלִי זָקֵן מְאֹד] [וְעֵינָו הֵחֵלּוּ כֵהוֹת, לֹא יוּכַל לִרְאוֹת]	1 Sam. 2:22 1 Sam. 3:2	Author Author	Eli Eli	End of Eli's house (vv. 27–36; 3:11–14); Samuel the successor, v. 26; 3:1; 19–21		
22	[וַיְהִי כַּאֲשֶׁר זָקֵן שְׁמוּאֵל]	1 Sam. 8:1	Author	Samuel	Bequeathing authority to sons		
23	הִנֵּה אַתָּה זָקַנְתָּ	1 Sam. 8:5	People	Samuel	Request for a king	The law of the king vv. 11–17	העיד v. 9
24	וַאֲנִי זָקַנְתִּי וָשַׂבְתִּי	1 Sam. 12:2	Samuel	Samuel	Samuel's farewell speech; admonishing the people	A miracle: rain in summer vv. 17-18	עֵד v. 5
25	[וְאֵלֶּה דִּבְרֵי דָוִד הָאַחֲרֹנִים]	2 Sam. 23:1	Author	David	Farewell speech; spiritual testament		נְאֻם v. 1; ברית v. 5
26	וְהַמֶּלֶךְ דָּוִד זָקֵן בָּא בַּיָּמִים... וְלֹא יִחַם לוֹ וְהַמֶּלֶךְ זָקֵן מְאֹד	1 Kgs 1:1 1 Kgs 1:15	Author Author	David David	Appointing a successor	Sworn pledge; coronation ceremony	נשבע vv. 13, 17, 29, 30, 35; הודיע v. 27

No.	Expression	Reference	Said By	Said About	Context	Contextual Details	Other Expressions
27	וַיִּקְרְבוּ יְמֵי-דָוִד לָמוּת... אָנֹכִי הֹלֵךְ, בְּדֶרֶךְ כָּל-הָאָרֶץ	1 Kgs 2:1 1 Kgs 2:2	Author David-testator	David-testator David-testator	David's farewell speech ; admonishing Solomon		צוה v. 1; וַיִּשְׁכַּב דָּוִד עִם-אֲבֹתָיו v. 10
28	[וְאִישָׁהּ זָקֵן]	2 Kgs 4:14	Gehazi	Barren woman's husband	Promise of a son		
29	וֶאֱלִישָׁע חָלָה אֶת-חָלְיוֹ אֲשֶׁר יָמוּת בּוֹ	2 Kgs 13:14	Author	Elisha	Salvation prophecy		
30	חָלָה חִזְקִיָּהוּ לָמוּת צַו לְבֵיתֶךָ, כִּי מֵת אַתָּה וְלֹא תִחְיֶה	2 Kgs 20:1	Author Isaiah	Hezekiah	Death-bed		צוה לבית v. 1
31	וְדָוִיד זָקֵן וְשָׂבַע יָמִים	1 Chr 23:1	Author	David-testator	Appointing Solomon	Setting up temple administration	

31:14)[37] and, in its turn, preceding Ch. 33—Moses' blessing and testament.

In other cases (nos. 11, 12, 13, 18, 31) there is a clear connection between the death notification of the person and the appointment of his successor/heir, which betrays the deep significance of such death-bed situations (see further below).[38] A similar unfolding of events might be behind the descriptions in nos. 21 and 22, and perhaps also in nos. 23, 29, 30. The latter passages thus, though they do not reflect actual solemn death-bed situations as do those that actually harbor one of the expressions, still fall in the same pattern as the actual death-bed dispositions in one significant theme: the appointment of an heir/successor. Note especially nos. 21, 22, and 23, in which the statement about the old age of Eli/Samuel could, indeed, be interpreted as the reason for Eli's and Samuel's inability to control their unruly sons/successors; but it could also be understood as a preliminary remark leading to the appointment of a real successor (Samuel in the case of Eli, and a king in the case of Samuel). The latter seems to be the natural outcome of the first.

Thus, all the passages listed in the table allude somehow to the common death-bed situation of some person. Some actually let the audience/reader attend such situations as they occur, observing the procedure as it unfolds in a solemn and formal setting and witnessing/hearing the various solemn formulae declared by the persons involved.[39] Others just offer a summary of such situations.

Reviewing the various and variegated episodes of death-bed situations in the Hebrew Bible listed in the table, one may note that they basically fall into two sub-groups: (*a*) expressions coming from the pen of the author/writer and (*b*) expressions clearly placed in the mouth of the dying patriarch. A medium position is taken in a few occurrences in which the statement is placed in the mouth of God, addressing the dying person (nos. 15, 18, and 19), or in the mouth of some other pro-

---

37 Note that the appointment of Joshua in no. 15 is taken as a *fait accompli* in no. 16, when in Ch. 32:44 it is specified that "Moses came and recited all the words of this song in the hearing of the people, he and Joshua the son of Nun."

38 This is clear in no. 15, which starts with the statement by God to Moses הֵן קָרְבוּ יָמֶיךָ לָמוּת "Behold, the days approach when you must die," and right away moves to the appointment of Joshua as successor: קְרָא אֶת־יְהוֹשֻׁעַ ... וַאֲצַוֶּנּוּ "call Joshua…that I may command him."

39 See my remarks above regarding the "processual" character of the biblical evidence; and cf. the vivid picture described in AASOR 16 56:8–12 and the episodes depicted in the Pseudepigrapha consulted, in particular in the Testaments of the Twelve Patriarchs.

tagonist in the story (Joseph's brothers in no. 9 and the people in no. 23). The contexts in the latter episodes, however, would lead to placing these occurrences too in the second sub-group.

As regards the issues addressed in the various dispositions, these fall basically into two categories: (*a*) family affairs and (*b*) national affairs. In the first category we find such issues as the promise of a child/heir to a childless couple/woman (nos. 1, 28), the search for a suitable wife for the heir (nos. 2, 4), the blessing of the heir (nos. 3, 4, 6, 7), the appointment of the firstborn (nos. 3, 6), the worry for the right final resting place for the dying patriarch (nos. 5, 7, 8, 10), adoption (no. 6), and forgiveness for misbehavior inside the family (no. 9). In the second category the following issues occur: appointing a successor to the old leader (nos. 11, 12, 13–15, 17, 18, 21, [22], 26, 31), the promise of the land to the People (nos. 14, 15, 18), the inheritance of the land (no. 19), the fate of the People in the future (nos. 15, 16, 20, 24), sealing/renewing the covenant between the people and God (nos. 15, 20), appointing a king (no. 23), and giving detailed instructions to the successor to the throne, which carry clear significance not only for the royal house, but also for the nation as a whole (nos. 27, 30).

Those passages that colorfully describe actual death-bed situations share some features that appear to be patterned and fixed, and this, in turn, betrays their formality, solemnity, and even their "socio-juridical implications." Let us review briefly these common features.

(1) Both the declarations placed in the mouth of the old and dying person and the statements embedded in the stories, which seem to be details advanced by the author in his statement of the background data of the situation he is describing, focus on two basic and clearly important facts: the advanced age of the testator and his imminent death. The very fact that these observations appear to be, in terms of the information they convey, superfluous truisms, points, in my view, to their solemn-formal load: All knew that the dying person has reached old age and it is also obvious from the very situation of death-bed disposition. However, custom and formality required that this fact be solemnly and duly declared at the opening of such death-bed dispositions. Also, the statement of the approaching death, especially in the classic formulation placed in the mouth of Isaac "I know not the day of my death,"[40] which again, if taken literally, would appear to be a superfluous truism,

---

40 Other formulations include קרב ימים למות "the time to die drew near" (nos. 5, 15, 27), הִנֵּה אָנֹכִי מֵת "Behold, I am about to die" (nos. 6, 8, 10; and passim in the Testaments of the Twelve Patriarchs), מת "to die" (nos. 29, 30). And note also the expressions טרם/לפני מות "before (I) die" (nos. 3, 9, 16), as well

clearly appears to be of a solemn nature and it seems to have been one of the formalities required to be fulfilled in such situations to lend validity to the final disposition.[41]

Now, as regards the relationships between the above two subgroups of statements, one may safely conclude that so too the narratival statements by the author carry the same solemn and dispositive implications. That is to say, the storyteller, a figure outside the story, makes use of carefully chosen expressions and idioms to underline the solemn-dispositive nature of the whole situation he is describing.[42]

---

as the reference המטה (ראש)"upon the bed('s head)" in nos. 5, 6, clearly pointing at the death-bed. See also the interesting formulations in the Testament of Zebulun 10:4: ועתה הנני הולך למנוחתי כאשר עשו גם אבותי "And now I am going to my rest as also did my fathers"; in the Testament of Reuben 1:4: כי הנה אמותה הפעם "for I am now about to pass away"; and in the Book of Tobit 14:3 (short version): הנה זקנתי וקרוב אני לצאת מן החיים "Behold, I have become old and I am ready to depart out of this life." In the cuneiform texts we find only scattered and haphazard references to the approaching death of the testator, and usually wills start with the statement PN *šīmti bītišu išīm*, "PN has determined the disposition of his house (or children, or wife, or brothers, or estate, etc.)," and proceed to the details. In a few documents, some not actual wills, we find references to the coming death and in these cases too they seem to carry a solemn air. Note the statement *ina bāb muātišu*, "in the face of his death," which occurs in a few Old Assyrian documents (see *CAD* M/2, 422a b′; cf. Veenhof, "Old Assyrian and Ancient Anatolian," 139, n. 48). Veenhof cites also the expression *ina bāb mu-mì-tim*, "on her deathbed," in another Old Assyrian document. Note also the expression *ina pāni šīmtim*, "in the face of death," in two documents from Susa of the Old Babylonian period (MDP 22 137:5; 23, 285:4, 10; see Malul, *Mesopotamian Legal Symbolism*, 82f.). Finally, note the description in the above-quoted lines from the Nuzi document AASOR 16 56:8–12, in which the patriarch is said to be sick and on his (death?-)bed, Akkadian *eršu*.

41 These situations depict, in fact, what has been termed "donations in anticipation of death" (*donationes mortis causae*) (Stolper, "Testament of Mannu-Kâ-Attar," 467; cf. Westbrook, "Introduction," 58f.), and in Westbrook's words, "The core of the procedure appears to have been a *speech act* making the gift" (Westbrook, "Introduction," 58, italics mine). In the context of this "speech act," one also recalls statements addressing the volition of the testator and his free will in making his disposition, such as *ina ḫūd libbišu*, "voluntarily" (Stolper, "Testament of Mannu-Kâ-Attar," 469; and see also the statement *libbišu ūbilšu*, "he decided/made up his mind," ibid., 471 n. 10); *ina ṭūbātiša ina nar'amātiša*, "of her own free will" (MDP 22 137:1–2); *ina migrāt ramānišu šīmti bītišu išīm*, "in his full consent he determined the disposition of his house (or children, or wife, or brothers, or estate, etc.)" (*CAD* M/2, 49a b); etc.

42 Cf. my remarks above.

With these caveats in mind, one may see the reference in Gen 18:11 (no. 1 in the table) to the expressions זְקֵנִים בָּאִים בַּיָּמִים "old and well advanced in years" in a different light. It is more than a casual insertion by the author to underline Sarah's reaction of unbelief at the promise that she would shortly bear a son; it is a statement that seems to carry the same formal load of other such, supposedly casual, statements by the author, like those in nos. 2, 3, 5, etc. Note that the fulfillment of the promise in 21:1–7 clearly imparts the sense of a promise solemnly declared and this might add to the formal-solemn air of the episode related in Ch. 18.[43]

On the other hand, the statement in 2 Kgs 4:14, put in the mouth of Elisha's apprentice, Gehazi, which occurs in a similar context of a promise of a son to a(n old and?) barren woman,[44] is hard to place within the known pattern of death-bed dispositions.

(2) On the background of the foregoing remarks, the references to bodily frailties related to old age, such as, or mainly, weakness of eyesight or sheer blindness,[45] do not seem to be fortuitous, and in my view they too might have been a formality required by the solemn setting of the situation. If this is true, then the statement regarding David's inability to keep warm (no. 26) is also such a required formality, and it thus falls in line with the statement of blindness. This conclusion would then support Hess's suggestion, mentioned above, that this remark about David's lack of heat alludes not to David's sexual impotence, as believed

---

43 See also a few remarks below on the possible ceremonial character of the meal prepared by Abraham for the three men, his guests.

44 For the parallelism between this story and Gen 18:1–16a, see Westermann, *Genesis 12–36*, 279ff.

45 Nos. 3 - Isaac; 6 - Jacob; 21 - Eli. Note no. 17 where Moses' eyesight and vitality are said not to have faded away despite his extremely old age (and cf. in this context Caleb's words in Josh 14:10–11). Gen 48:1 states that Jacob חֹלֶה "is sick," and this too seems to be part of the necessary background details to the whole situation. In the testament discussed by Stolper a clear statement of the testator's illness is duly inserted into the text (Stolper, "Testament of Mannu-Kâ-Attar," 470f.). Note also the reference to the sickness of the testator in AASOR 16 56:8–12. Finally, in the testaments of Reuben (1:2, 5) and Simeon (1:2) a clear statement of the illness of the dying patriarch is listed. In other testaments (Levi [1:2], Issachar [7:9], Asher [1:2]), on the other hand, the patriarch is said to have expired while sound in health, recalling the statement regarding Moses. In Gen 27:19, Esaw, having returned from the field and having prepared a meal for his father, asks the latter to "please arise, sit and eat of my game," which shows that the aging father was lying (sick?) on his bed. For the effects of old age on the body, see the vivid description in Eccl 12:1–7.

by quite a few interpreters he cites, but is rather part of the formal-solemn statement זָקֵן בָּא בַּיָּמִים "old and well advanced in years."[46]

(3) Other contextual details, common to almost all the episodes listed in the table, also add to the solemnity and formality of the situations depicted therein: (*a*) Note first the root צוה "will, bequeath" (lit. "command"), from which the later Hebrew word צואה "will, testament," clearly setting forth the testamentary background of the whole situation;[47] (*b*) In a few episodes,[48] the verb שבע (השביע or נשבע "make someone take an oath" or "take an oath") occurs, referring to a pledge undertaken by some person on behalf of the testator.[49] In 1 Kgs 1:13, 17 the verb is attributed to David, the testator, who is said to have sworn a pledge to appoint Solomon as his successor, which he actually reinforces in vv. 29, 30.

(4) The episodes in which the verb שבע occurs are pregnant in other respects, such as the resort to accompanying solemn symbolic acts or gestures: (*a*) thus in the two pregnant episodes in the book of Genesis (Gen 24:2–9 [no. 2]; 47:29–31 [no. 5]) the person undertaking the pledge is asked to touch or grasp the thigh (= sexual organs) of the testator,

---

46 One recalls here the formula *ina bulṭišu*, "while he was of sound mind and body" (see *CAD* B, 311; and cf. the statements *pîša balṭu šaptāša balṭātā*, "her mouth sound, her lips sound" in MDP 22 137:3–4; 23, 285:2–3), frequently placed at the beginning of wills, stating the soundness of mind of the testator, thereby according validity to his testament. This, however, seems to fulfill a different function, while the reference to the body frailty of the testator was intended to underline the imminence of the testator's death, rendering his final disposition urgent.

47 López, "צוה *ṣwh*," 292. The verb and the noun occur *passim* in the Testaments of the Twelve Patriarchs. The reader's attention is called also to 2 Sam 17:23, where it is reported of Ahithophel, who, once his advice had been turned down, "saddled his donkey and went to his hometown. He left orders for his family and property (וַיְצַו אֶל-בֵּיתוֹ), and then he hanged himself." This remark may also reflect a death-bed disposition, of the kind listed in the table. However, because of its terse form I decided not to list it in the table. In the Testament of Job 1:2 we find the expression שים סדרים בבית "to give orders to the house," which means basically the same as the verb צוה and the word צואה.

48 Note, especially, nos. 2, 5, 8, 10; and see also nos. 15, 26.

49 E.g., the pledge undertaken by Abraham's servant, accompanied by a formal symbolic act (see anon), to bring a wife to Isaac from Abraham's family in Harran (Gen 24); or the pledge undertaken by Joseph to bury his father in the family sepulture in Canaan (Gen 47:30–31), etc. On the other hand, as we shall see anon, the testator himself could be depicted as making a promise to the heirs.

while taking the oath, a gesture shown to carry a clear legal load;[50] (*b*) other such pregnant symbolic acts having a clear solemn-formal load mentioned in the various episodes listed in the above table include the kiss reported in Gen 27:26–27 (no. 3), 48:10 (no. 6);[51] (*c*) the dressing of the successor with the dying man's clothes, signifying the transference of the authority and status of the former to the latter (no. 11);[52] (*d*) the

---

50 See Malul, "*PAḤAD YIṢḤĀQ*." Cf. the interesting and pregnant similar gesture mentioned in an Old Babylonian letter from Kisurra, brought to my attention by W. Mayer of the Pontifical Biblical Institute (see reference in Malul, "Touching the Sexual Organs"), in which the sender refers to some request he had previously asked from the addressee, which the latter is willing to grant on the condition the sender's envoy take an oath while grasping his (the addressee's) private parts: (11) *um-ma at-ta-a-ma* (12) *ma-ar ši-ip-ri-ka* (13) *iš-ki-ya* (14) *ù i-ša-ri* (15) *li-iṣ-ba-at-ma* (16) *lu-di-ku*[!]*-um*, "Thus you (have written to me): 'Let your envoy grasp my testicles and my penis, and then I will grant (it) to you'."

51 For the possible legal-technical load of the kiss in a few episodes in the Bible, see Malul, "Some Idioms," 202ff. These include, besides the above passages, also and mainly 1 Sam 10:1, where Samuel kisses Saul while anointing and solemnly declaring him king. See also 2 Sam 20:9–10; Exod 18:7; 2 Sam 14:33; and more. See also the Testament of Dan 7:1 and the Testament of Benjamin 1:2, where the old patriarchs are said to have kissed their sons while making their final disposition. See n. 12 above.

52 For the installation of a successor and the formulae used, particularly the verb צוה, see López, "צוה *ṣwh*," 291f. For the symbolism of clothes in such contexts, see Malul, *Mesopotamian Legal Symbolism*, 114ff. Compare the case of the treaty sealed between David and Jonathan, which involved the exchange of clothes (1 Sam 18:3–4); and see also the transfer of Elijah's coat to Elisha (2 Kgs 2:13–14, and see v. 16). Quite significant in this context, especially the clear requirement that the clothes put on the successor be those actually worn by the testator, are David's instructions in his last words (1 Kgs 1:33ff.) to mount Solomon, the appointed successor to the throne, on his *own* mule and lead him to the Gihon Creek to be solemnly anointed king. The fact that the intended successor mounts the old king's private mule (note the recurring formulation הַפִּרְדָּה אֲשֶׁר־לִי "my own mule," v. 33; עַל־פִּרְדַּת הַמֶּלֶךְ דָּוִד "on King David's mule," v. 38; עַל־פִּרְדַּת הַמֶּלֶךְ "on the king's mule," v. 44) definitely seems to carry deep significance in this context of disposing of the king's final wish. The reader may compare this story to the story of the investiture of Joseph in Gen 41:40–44, which also involved both the acts of dressing him with royal (the Pharaoh's own?) clothes and mounting him on the *king's* chariot (וַיַּרְכֵּב אֹתוֹ בְּמִרְכֶּבֶת הַמִּשְׁנֶה אֲשֶׁר־לוֹ "and he had him ride in the second chariot that he had," v. 43) and with the story of the elevation of Mordechai by the Persian king, again calling for dressing Mordechai with "a royal robe *which the king has worn*" and mounting him on "a horse on *which the king has ridden*," Est 6:8. In a lecture delivered at the University of Haifa on May 4th 2009 titled "The

laying of the hand on the appointed successor, again to signify the transference of authority from the testator to his successor;[53] (*e*) the placing of the heir between (or on) the testator's knees, which probably signified an act of adoption;[54] and (*f*) the ceremonial meal, attested mainly in Isaac's death-bed situation in Genesis 27 (no. 3), and perhaps also in Genesis 18 (no. 1), in the meal prepared by Abraham for his guests—the angels who promised the son and the continuity of his line (vv. 18–19)[55]—which may also be mentioned here as one of the formalities that accord these situations with their solemn and legally-binding force.[56]

Egyptian Background to the Investiture of Joseph," Susanne Binder focused in particular on the gold necklace said to be bestowed by the Pharaoh on Joseph (v. 42), seeing in it a reflection of the "Gold of Honor," a gold necklace formally and ceremonially bestowed in the presence of the pharaoh on selected deserving officials as a symbol of their special status vis-à-vis the king. See her book *The Gold of Honor in New Kingdom Egypt*.

53 Num 27:18, 23 (no. 12); Deut 34:9 (no. 17); and cf. also Gen 48:14ff. (no. 6), for which see more below. For the act of laying the hand as a gesture of investiture, see Fabry, "סָמַךְ *sāmak*," 281f. And see, of course, in this context the statement in the lines from the Nuzi document AASOR 16 56:8–12 quoted above about the dying father taking hold of his son's hand while making his disposition. Note that in no. 12, when Moses' successor is appointed, it is also specified that an act of divination by consulting the Urim and Thummim was to be performed to determine the legitimacy of the chosen future leader (Num 27:21). This also accords the situation with a clear formal-solemn air.

54 Gen 48:12 (no. 6). Cf. also the case of the adoption of little Obed by his grandmother, Naomi, in Ruth 4:16. For this symbolic act, see Sasson, *Ruth*, 170ff.; and already Köhler, "Die Adoptionsform."

55 According to Westermann's analysis of the complex of stories in Gen 18–19 (*Genesis 12–36*, 274ff.), he finds in Gen 18:1–16a the amalgam of two older stories: "(*a*) the promise of a child to a childless couple…, and (*b*) the visit of a divine messenger(s) or a god(s) who rewards the reception and hospitality with a gift, in this case the birth of a child" (ibid., 274). In his commentary to v. 11 (ibid., 280f.), Westermann points to its parenthetic nature, being inserted "subsequently as a parenthesis to explain what follows" (ibid., 280). Westermann's reconstruction of this story may be correct and he supports it with an impressive array of data, mainly comparative materials from other cultures. For our purpose here it would not appear far-fetched to surmise that the editor who put together the ancient separate stories and added the explanatory (parenthetic) statement in v. 11 may have thought along the lines of the known pattern of death-bed situations, in which a ceremonial meal might have held a central place in the ceremonial and solemn setting of the situation. And thus, the hospitality meal of one of the old stories making up Gen 18:1–16a, once the two stories were put together and the explanatory note in v. 11 was inserted,

(5) Parallel to the adjuration of some person, who then undertakes some pledge on behalf of the testator, the latter too may contribute to the death-bed disposition in terms of his blessing of his heir(s) and other promises and admonitions for the future: (*a*) for the testator's blessing of the heir(s) note first the episode in no. 3, which revolves mainly around the act of blessing, and the verb ברך occurs in it no less than 16 times, and the noun ברכה no less than 6 times; and the episodes in nos. 7 (Gen 49:28) and 16 (Deut 33:1);[57] (*b*) as regards admonitions and warnings for the future, note in particular the farewell speeches of some leaders, such as Jacob in Genesis 49,[58] Moses in Deut 31:14ff.,[59] 33; Joshua in Joshua 23; Samuel in 1 Samuel 12; and, of course, David's last words in 1 Kgs 2:1–10.[60] The promises declared by the testator revolve mainly around the seed and progeny and the inheritance of the land.

All the above elements, recurring in most of the episodes listed above—some of them clearly solemn and formal, and in at least the case of the symbolic acts can even be dubbed legal-technical—make it eminently reasonable that these stories of death-bed dispositions in the

---

turned into a ceremonial meal of the kind attested in the death-bed situation related in Genesis 27. Now, when one realizes that the hospitality meal itself carried almost the same formal-legal implications (Malul, "Biblical Hospitality," 241 with literature), this does not seem hard to accept. This ceremonial meal seems to be mentioned also in the Testament of Naphtali 1:2ff., and especially in 9:2: "And when he had eaten and drunken with them with a merry heart, he covered his face and died."

56 For the ceremonial meal, see already a few remarks above and literature.

57 For the significance of the blessing in the Bible, especially in such familial contexts as those reflected in Genesis 24, 27, 48, see Westermann, *Genesis 12–36*, 436f., where he also duly notes the solemn setting of the blessing and the vitality and irrevocability of the blessing; cf. already Gordon, "Biblical Customs," 8.

58 See v. 1: "And Jacob called unto his sons and said, 'Gather yourselves together, that I may tell you that which shall befall you in the last days. Gather yourselves together and hear, ye sons of Jacob, and hearken unto Israel your father'."

59 See also vv. 27 ("For I know how rebellious and stiff-necked you are. If you have been rebellious against the God while I am still alive and with you, how much more will you rebel *after I die*!") and 29 ("For I know that *after my death* you are sure to become utterly corrupt and to turn from the way I have commanded you").

60 In this context of admonitions, note the use in some of the episodes under discussion of the language העיד "testify against," and עד "witness," in Deut 31:26, 28; Josh 24:22, 27; 1 Sam 8:9, 12:5, all imparting the sense of some solemn warning for the future volunteered by the testator to his audience.

Hebrew Bible reflect formal and solemn situations in real life in which an old person approaching his death declares his final wish and will and bequeaths his legacy to his heirs and successors.[61] Moreover, these apparently expected statements regarding the old age and imminent death of the said person, which at first glance may appear to the reader as superfluous truisms, apparently adding no new information to the situation, must therefore, on the background of the foregoing listed formal elements, need be understood as formal and solemn statements, strictly required to be declared by the dying old man while making his final disposition, so as to accord the situation with legal and binding validity and "socio-juridical implications." Placed in the mouth of the old testator on his death-bed, these declarations are then simply specimens of formal *verba solemnia*, i.e., solemn declarations that are known to have carried clear legal dispositive force in various cultures around the world.[62]

One final question calls our attention. Above I divided all the passages listed in the table into two categories with regard to the nature of the issue dealt with in each episode: familial issues and national issues. If one would ask what then could have been the *Sitz im Leben* of these death-bed dispositions, the above exposition strongly suggests that it was in the family milieu, the narrow context of family life and affairs, and from within which this "socio-juridical" institution was borrowed unto the national level and applied to situations of significance to the larger group of the whole people. This would then be another reflection of the operation of the kinship principle on the national level, something evident in other aspects of life in biblical society.[63] If this is true, it would again underline the significance and solemn implications of these death-bed dispositions.

---

61 And see also the colorful situations of such death-bed episodes depicted in the various Pseudepigrapha cited above.

62 See Malul, *Mesopotamian Legal Symbolism*, 2ff.

63 In a large study under preparation (*The Kinship Basis of Israelite Society in Biblical Times*), I put to the test the hypothesis, commonly accepted in anthropological circles with regard to "primitive"/simplistic societies, that the kinship principle was the structural principle guiding the social perception in biblical society (this is in contrast to other structural principles guiding modern societies, such as the political and the economic). As has already been observed by anthropologists (see, e.g., Friedl, *The Human Portrait*, 220–221, 226, and passim), primitive or traditional societies are/were structured on the basis of the kinship principle, which means that various aspects and realms of life in society—

WORKS CITED

Binder, Susanne. *The Gold of Honor in New Kingdom Egypt*. The Australian Centre for Egyptology Studies 8. Oxford: Aris and Phillips, 2008.

Daube, D. *Studies in Biblical Law*. Cambridge: University Press, 1947, republished in New York: KTAV Publishing House, 1969.

Fabry, H.-J. "סָמַךְ *sāmak̲*; שְׁמִיכָה *ś*ᵉ*mîk̲â*." In *TDOT* 10: 278–86. Grand Rapids, Mich.: Eerdmans Publishing Company, 1986.

Friedl, J. *The Human Portrait. Introduction to Cultural Anthropology*. Englewood Cliffs, N.J.: Prentice-Hall Inc., 1981.

Friedman, D. *To Kill and Inherit*. Tel Aviv: Dvir Publishing House, 2000 (Hebrew).

Gaster, T. H. *Myth, Legend, and Custom in the Old Testament*. New York and Evanston: Harper & Row, Publishers, 1969.

Gordon, C. H. "Biblical Customs and the Nuzu Tablets." *BA* 3 (1940): 1–12.

Hallo, W. W., and W. K. Simpson, *The Ancient Near East. A History*, New York: Harcourt Brace Jovanovich, 1971.

Hess, R. "David and Abishag: The Purpose of 1 Kings 1: 1–4." In *Homeland and Exile: Biblical and Ancient Near Eastern Studies in Honour of Bustenay Oded*, edited by G. Galil, M. Geller, and A. Millard, 427-38. Vetus Testamentum Supplement 130. Leiden: Brill, 2009.

Köhler, L. "Die Adoptionsform von Rt 4^{16}." *ZAW* 29 (1909): 312–14.

López, F. García. "צוה *ṣwh*." *TDOT* 12: 276–96, Grand Rapids, Mich.: Eerdmans Publishing Company, 2003.

Malamat, A. "Longevity: Biblical Concepts and Some Ancient Near Eastern Parallels." In *Vorträge gehalten auf der 28. Rencontre Assyriologique Internationale in Wien 6.–10. Juli 1981*, edited by H. Hirsch and H. Hunger, 215–18. Archiv für Orientforschung

---

such as political and economic relationships, distribution of power, distribution of food resources, assignment of roles and tasks among the members, education, the relationships between the individual and/or the group and the property (in particular the land), the way property (again, mainly the land) changes hands, marriage relationships and the related incest laws—all these and other aspects are not only expressed by terminology taken from the kinship nomenclature, but their very operation is dictated by the kinship-familial principle.

Beiheft 19. Horn: Verlag Ferdinand Berger & Söhne Gesellschaft, 1982.

Malul, M. "More on *PAḤAD YIṢḤĀQ* (Genesis xxxi 42, 53) and the Oath by the Thigh." *VT* 35 (1985): 192–200.

"Touching the Sexual Organs as an Oath Ceremony in an Akkadian Letter." *VT* 37 (1987): 491–92.

Studies in Mesopotamian Legal Symbolism. AOAT 221. Kevelaer: Butzon & Bercker, 1988.

"Adoption of Foundlings in the Bible and Mesopotamian Document—A Study of Some Legal Metaphors in Ez. 16, 1–7." *JSOT* 46 (1990): 97–126

"Fabrication of Evidence in the Bible: Jacob's Imposture and Joseph's Blood-Stained Coat." *Diné Israel* 22 (2003): 203–20 (Hebrew).

"Some Aspects of Biblical Hospitality and Their Significance." In *Tesûrôt LeAvishur. Studies in the Bible and the Ancient Near East, in Hebrew and Semitic Languages Presented to Professor Yitzhak Avishur at Sixty*, edited by M. Heltzer and M. Malul, 233–52 (Hebrew). Tel Aviv: Archaeological Center Publication, 2004.

"Some Idioms and Expressions in Biblical Hebrew Originating in Symbolic Acts in the Realm of Treaty-Making." *HaIvrit WeAhyoteha. Studies in Hebrew Language and its Contacts with Semitic Languages and Jewish Languages* 4–5 (2004–2005): 189–208 (Hebrew).

Ritchie, I. "The Nose Knows: Bodily Knowing in Isaiah 11.3." *JSOT* 87 (2000): 59–73.

Sasson, J. M. *Ruth*. Baltimore, Md.: Johns Hopkins University Press, 1976.

Speiser, E. A. "I Know Not the Day of My Death." *JBL* 74 (1955): 252–56.

Stolper, M. "The Testament of Mannu-Kâ-Attar." In *Veenhof Anniversary Volume. Studies Presented to Klaas R. Veenhof on the Occasion of His Sixty-Fifth Birthday*, edited by W. H. van Soldt, J. G. Dercksen, N. J. C. Kouwenberg, and Th. J. H. Krispijn, 467–473. Leiden: Nederlands Instituut voor het Nabije Oosten, 2001.

Thompson, T. L. *The Historicity of the Patriarchal Narratives. The Quest for the Historical Abraham*. BZAW 133. Berlin: Walter de Gruyter, 1974.

Veenhof, K. R. "Old Assyrian and Ancient Anatolian Evidence for the Care of the Elderly." In *The Care of the Elderly in the Ancient Near East*, edited by M. Stol & S. P. Vleeming, 119–60. Leiden: Brill, 1998.

Weinfeld, M. "Seventy Years—Old Age, Eighty Years—Extreme Old Age: A Mesopotamian Parallel." In *Dr. Baruch ben Yehudah's Book. Studies in the Bible and Jewish Thought*, edited by B. Z. Luria, 312–317. Tel Aviv: The Society of Biblical Research in Israel, 1981 (Hebrew).

Westbrook, R. "Introduction: The Character of Ancient Near Eastern Law." In *A History of Ancient Near Eastern Law*, edited by R. Westbrook, 1–90. Leiden: Brill, 2003.

Westermann, C. *Genesis 12–36. A Commentary*. Translated by J. J. Scullion. Minneapolis, Minn.: Augsburg Publishing House, 1985.

UGARITIC COMMERCIAL PRACTICES AND BIBLICAL LAW*

KEVIN M. McGEOUGH
UNIVERSITY OF LETHBRIDGE

This paper seeks to demonstrate how the study of commercial practices at the Late Bronze Age site of Ugarit can help us to better understand biblical law and social institutions. By first examining the nature of credit and debt practices at the Late Bronze Age city of Ugarit, this paper shall explore how these practices inform laws relating to debt within the Hebrew Bible. At Ugarit, royal and non-royal elites used credit and debt as means of storing wealth, as well as gaining access to the goods and labor of debtors. Credit acted as a means of facilitating exchange in a non-monetary economy and allowed these elites to develop and store wealth. Given this, biblical laws regarding debt, especially in Deuteronomy, appear not just to be humanitarian but also to be attempts to undermine the economic power of royal institutions and elite economic actors.

Using Ugaritic materials to better understand the Bible is not a unique approach; the earliest textual work on Ugaritic documents was in many ways devoted to this kind of comparison. Similarities between Ugaritic literature and the Psalms were readily apparent and liturgical texts helped make sense of the sacrificial terminology of the Hebrew Bible. Initial efforts at this enterprise were varied in their methodology and methodological appropriateness.[1] In terms of commercial practices, scholars have already noted a number of areas worth comparing between Ugaritic practices toward merchants and biblical law dealing with merchant activity. For example, a number of Ugaritic letters and possibly treaties (although the designation of treaty for some of these documents has recently come into question) between the city and the

* I would like to dedicate this paper to Barry Eichler—a wonderful teacher with whom I feel quite lucky to have had the opportunity to study at the University of Pennsylvania—in thanks for all his mentorship in and out of the classroom. His careful attention to his students and his thoughtfulness in designing his classes have modeled excellent teaching for me.

1 For a discussion of the history of how the field of Ugaritic studies has contributed to the field of biblical studies, see Smith, *The Bible and Ugaritic Studies*.

Hittite king Hattushilis deal with the compensation for the murder of foreign merchants.[2] To some, this is reminiscent of pentateuchal legal traditions, which demanded that foreigners be treated well while in the land (as in Deut 24:17), albeit the actual legal rights of foreigners differed from those of residents.

Comparative approaches are often fraught with difficulty since arguments are built based on analogy. The Iron Age context of the biblical law corpora is very different from the Late Bronze Age internationalism of Ugarit. Yet, two shared aspects of these cultures make this kind of comparison valid, (*a*) participation in the larger cuneiform legal tradition, and (*b*) the absence of money or currency in either society. In regards to the first issue, the shared cuneiform legal tradition, it is debatable how static this tradition was and how "shared" it should be considered. Regardless of how similar or different one takes the Ugaritic legal tradition to be from the biblical tradition, there are enough shared traits to warrant a comparative approach as an heuristic device, if nothing else. It is the second issue—the absence of money or currency within the economy—that is more germane to this argument. The absence of currency in a complex economy necessitates certain behaviors and institutions in order to enable goods and services to be exchanged and wealth to be stored.

Rather than comparing Ugaritic laws or legal practices regarding merchants with biblical law, this paper studies how Ugaritic commercial practices can inform our understanding of biblical law. This is an attempt to broaden the comparative framework of these two very different types of data sets and rather than comparing isolated lexemes or lines, I shall demonstrate that analysis of larger cultural institutions and contexts can be useful. Thus, rather than list Ugaritic commercial terms that may appear as cognates in biblical legal materials, what follows is a reconstruction of commercial practices at Ugarit that can shed light on institutions and legal formulae in the Hebrew Bible, with the acknowledgment that these are cultures that are separated by both time and space.

My recent research on the site of Ugarit has concentrated on the analysis of economic behavior at the site and economic relationships with other sites in the eastern Mediterranean. This study focused on

---

2 The letters include RS 17.42, 17.145, 17.158, and 17.234. The possible treaties include RS 17.146, 17.230, and 18.115. For discussion of these documents, see Greengus, "Comparability of Laws," 65–71; Klengel, "Mord und Bussleistung," 189–97; and Westbrook, *Studies in Biblical and Cuneiform Law*, 51–52.

exchange relationships and encounters since those types of economic activities are visible in both the archaeological and textual record. This tangible type of economic behavior was used as the basis for the analysis as a means of avoiding problems that appear in some other studies of the Ugaritic economy. Previous work on the Ugaritic economy had been limited by the application of social scientific models that were "too strong" for the evidence. That is to say, these models, at times, overpowered the data and in many ways were tautological, smoothing over differences, obscuring the complexities of ancient economic life, and embedding modern political ideologies into the analysis.[3]

One issue in the reconstruction of the Ugaritic economy is the widespread acceptance of Michael Heltzer's interpretation of the term *bnš mlk*. Heltzer understood this term as referring to anyone who is under the authority of the king and he equates this to *arde šarri*.[4] However, the polyglots from Ugarit are very clear—*bnš* is described as equivalent to Akkadian *awīlum*, which refers to either a particular class of individual, explicitly distinguished from a *wardum* in the Code of Hammurabi, or refers explicitly to a "man" in the generic sense. It does not mean servant. Heltzer furthers this mistake by taking *bnš* as a short form of *bnš mlk* whenever it appears and uses this to postulate that there are two distinct spheres of people at Ugarit, *bnš*, who are under the authority of the king, and non-*bnš*, who would be anybody else, part of what he understands as the primitive or village sector of the community over which the palace has no control. There is no evidence at Ugarit to indicate that there were any groups of people who resided there that were not under the authority of the king. Marquez Rowe has convincingly argued that the expression *bnš mlk* refers to a type of antichretic debt relationship in which the debtor pledges labor or the use of land in exchange for credit.[5] The expression appears only in eight tablets (which is surprising given the prominent role it has played in reconstructions of Ugaritic society) and each instance reflects a situation in which the *bnš mlk* perform some kind of service for the king.[6]

There is limited evidence to suggest that royal and primitive sectors were strictly distinguished within Ugaritic society. There were, however, numerous situations in which debt and credit facilitated the ex-

---

3 For more on these models, as well as extended criticism, see McGeough, *Exchange Relationships*, 39–88.

4 For example, see Heltzer, *Internal Organization*, 3.

5 Marquez Rowe, "The King's Men in Ugarit," 1–19.

6 For extended discussion of this term, see McGeough, *Exchange Relationships*, 90–94 and Rowe, "The King's Men in Ugarit," 1–19.

change relationships. Three broad categories of economic actors are identifiable at Ugarit: royal elites, non-royal elites, and non-elites.[7] Although the reality of the situation was much more complex than this, categorizing the economic agents as such is a useful heuristic device and well reflects the different types of exchange activities that are in evidence for each group.

The dominant economic actor at Ugarit was the royal palace, which sat at the center of a variety of different types of exchange relationships. The scholars who first worked on the economic texts from Ugarit made the logical assumption that much of the palace's revenue came from taxation, from skimming off the top of local producers.[8] There is minimal direct evidence for this kind of taxation. Taxation records found at the palace indicate that taxes were paid far more frequently in the form of military service and perhaps labor (although the labor records are inconclusive). The tribute records indicate that when goods were collected, these goods were collected as part of tribute owed to the Hittites, whose suzerainty Ugarit was under. The palace itself directly organized production and this is how the palace gained access to a variety of products. Craft-specialists produced bronze, textiles, and other classes of commodities under the palace's supervision. The palace organized significant agricultural production at estates called *gittu* (*dimtu* in Akkadian according to the polyglots) and sometimes called *gintu* in Amarna Akkadian.[9] Cereal and vine crops were grown on these estates and agricultural products (such as wine and olive oil) were manufactured on these estates. These products were distributed by the palace—sometimes they were sold. These situations are obvious when the expression "x item *ntn b ksp*" (x item given for silver), an expression that is clearly derived from the Akkadian expression *ana kaspim nadānum*, is used. Often though, the motivation for the distribution of commodities is ambiguous.

The palace also engaged in international exchanges through the commercial activities of non-royal elites who traveled to other cities and engaged both in their own trade and in trade and diplomatic missions on behalf of the palace. These non-royal elites seem to have made the bulk of their living through these large-scale commercial enterprises. There is minimal evidence (archaeologically or textually) to indicate

---

7 For a complete discussion of the activities of these groups, see McGeough, *Exchange Relationships*.

8 See, for example, Rainey, *The Social Stratification of* Ugarit, 79–81.

9 The Ugaritic *gt* and scholarship on it are discussed in McGeough, *Exchange Relationships*, 130 and 376–78.

that these elites engaged in any kind of direct production. Their income came from profits from exchange and from selling international goods locally. Numerous debt records found in non-royal elite homes attest to this means of wealth accumulation.[10] Wealth hoarding and status accumulation seem to have been two of the primary activities of these elites.

Non-elites at Ugarit engaged in some form of small-scale primary production for their households, including agriculture, textile manufacture, and the production of secondary food products. They were also able to act as laborers but, given the nature of the evidence, it is impossible to determine how much their work as laborers would have contributed to their incomes.

The palace engaged in the most exchange activities at Ugarit and stored a considerable proportion of its wealth in terms of debt—important since much of the production activities in which the palace engaged revolved around perishable foodstuffs or products that had a very rapid diminishing marginal utility. The palace's position at the center of many nodes of production allowed it to gain considerable economic power, by being able to easily transfer resources between various nodes. Likewise, the juridical and military authority of the palace gave added gravitas and authority to the exchange relations. However, the palace was only one economic agent and clearly was not "in control" of the economy; as such, it is unlikely that the palace "set up" the economy.

At Ugarit, credit and debt were among the primary structuring mechanisms for facilitating exchanges and for the storage of wealth. In a non-monetary economy, the storage of wealth can be particularly difficult, especially when much of the real forms of wealth would have been perishable foodstuffs. The importance of debt and credit as means of storing wealth are well recognized for Mesopotamia proper and it certainly was the case at Ugarit as well.[11] Extending credit to non-elites allowed non-elites access to goods necessary for their subsistence work (such as seed and tools for agriculture before the harvest), as well as to luxury goods for the maintenance and creation of social capital. Likewise, by having payment take the form of debt as opposed to real goods, the palace and non-royal elites were able to store their wealth in a form that would not go bad. Thus, rather than stockpiling grain or

---

10 See, for example, *KTU* 4.258, 4.262, 4.283, 4.313, 4.634, 4.690, and 4.699, all found in private contexts. This list is not exhaustive, merely illustrative.

11 Numerous recent studies on debt and credit in Mesopotamia have helped shed light on this issue. See, for example: Dercksen, ed., *Trade and Finance in Ancient Mesopotamia*; Hudson and van de Mieroop, eds., *Debt and Renewal in the Ancient Near East*; and Westbrook and Jasnow, eds., *Security for Debt in Ancient Near Eastern Law*.

olives, which would eventually spoil or perhaps were unneeded, the creditors could stockpile wealth in terms of individual obligations. Thus, much of the economic clout of these institutions was kept in these "non-real" terms. It is my contention that the primacy of debt as a means of storing wealth furthered the collapse of Ugarit after its destruction by the Sea People's at the end of the Bronze Age since wealth-stored-as-debt does not survive calamities well.[12] The importance of debt and credit in a non-monetary complex economy should not be underestimated. Debt and credit allows complexity, in an economic sense, to develop. Simple barter does not work on a large scale and the trade of precious metals does not work well at a small scale unless those precious metals reflect an abstract form of state-sanctioned wealth, as coins would eventually do.

Steinkeller has made a number of observations about understanding debt and credit in Ur III Mesopotamia that are important to consider, despite the fact that the situation seems to have been substantially more complex in Mesopotamia than in Bronze Age Syria or Iron Age Israel. Steinkeller notes that despite formal similarities between ancient and modern loans, the two situations are quite different, and in many ways not comparable.[13] Steinkeller's analysis suggests that the primary goals of debts were not "interest-operated profit" but rather to gain access to the borrower's labor or land, in his words, "interest was a tool and not an economic end in itself."[14] In these Ur III debt situations, the rate of interest was immaterial so long as it was sufficient to prevent the debtor from ever being able to pay off the principal of the loan. What modern observers might take to be evidence for security in these loans is, to Steinkeller's mind, not equivalent to modern forms of security. He states:

> Although land and labor pledged in this way superficially resemble modern security, the fact that their primary objective was other than protecting lenders, argues, in my view, against lending them this classification. In fact, this phenomenon escapes all modern legal definition, which underscores once again the conceptual autonomy of ancient and "primitive" legal systems, and the difficulty of conforming their facts to our own understanding of normative legal and economic behavior.[15]

---

12 McGeough, "The Unwinding of the Late Bronze Age" (paper presented at the annual meeting of the American Schools of Oriental Research, Boston, Mass., November 19–22, 2008).

13 Steinkeller, "The Ur III Period," 48.

14 Ibid., 48.

15 Ibid., 55.

In other words, "security" on loans is not actually "security" but the point of extending credit is to gain access to land and labor. This reading well reflects the situation at Ugarit. It is worth emphasizing, more than Steinkeller does, the practical aspect of these antichretic debt relationships as means of storing wealth in an economic context that lacks a stable form of currency or abstract wealth.

The laws regarding debt that are preserved in the Pentateuch (and elsewhere in the Hebrew Bible) can be understood within the context of these observations of how elites, non-elites, and palatial institutions utilized debt and credit at Ugarit and Mesopotamia. Modern readers have considered these laws in the context of humanitarianism, emphasizing their roles in reducing poverty within the Iron Age kingdoms.[16] These laws allowed the very poor a means of escaping the cycles of debt that kept them impoverished. This kind of reading is valid and certainly there is substantial textual evidence to suggest this. For example, amongst the debt laws in Deuteronomy, Deut 15:4 (NRSV) reads: "There will, however, be no one in need among you, because the Lord is sure to bless you in the land that the Lord your God is giving you as a possession to occupy, if only you will obey the Lord your God by diligently observing this entire commandment that I command you today." More explicitly, Deut 15:11 (NRSV) reads: "Since there will never cease to be some in need on the earth, I therefore command you, 'Open your hand to the poor and needy neighbor in your land.'" Statements such as these, throughout the legal corpora, frame the discussion of these laws, to the modern reader, in terms of humanitarian ideals. Frymer-Kensky is right to note that the biblical credit laws reflect an economic situation in which money is not borrowed as means of engaging in entrepreneurial speculation but rather is borrowed as "a device by which the poor stave off disaster."[17] However, the situation may be more complex than this and that, despite the humanitarian benefits of extending credit, there were real benefits to the creditor, that, while different from benefits derived from earning interest, were benefits nonetheless.

It is not uncommon for economic activities and principles to be framed in one manner that disguises other intentions. An obvious example from the ancient world is the description of tribute as "gifts" in

---

16 Craigie, for example, describes these laws as humanitarian and also emphasizes that Deuteronomy is arguing that the prosperity of the land will be associated with divine grace. Craigie, *Book of Deuteronomy*, 236–37.

17 Frymer-Kensky, "Israel," 251.

Late Bronze Age international correspondence.[18] This may also occur in the legal material relating to debts preserved in the Hebrew Bible, where motivations for these laws are described in terms that any reader will be "on-side" with but in fact other motivations may lie beneath the laws.

The laws in Deuteronomy 15 relating to the remission of debts are worth considering within the context of Near Eastern credit practices. According to Deut 15:1–4, every seventh year debts were to have been remitted amongst the Israelites. Deut 15:9–10 further forbids creditors from withholding credit when the seventh year is approaching and thus within the context of the verses previously cited, the remission of these debts can be understood as a type of charity. Deut 15:3 indicates that debts could still be exacted from foreigners, however; thus limits to the charity are established.

Tigay has compared these laws with *mīšarum* edicts from Mesopotamia, which Mesopotamian monarchs would sometimes announce at the beginning of their reigns (and at other times), that would remit debts and release servants. As Tigay describes, "[t]hese practices rectified extreme and dangerous disparities between social classes and ingratiated the new ruler with certain elements of the public."[19] The comparison is apt but there is a major difference between these laws and the *mīšarum* edicts.[20] Whereas the *mīšarum* edicts were enacted by monarchical authority as a means of currying favor and supporting the monarch, the laws in Deuteronomy bear no such monarchical authority. In fact, if debt was as significant a means of storing wealth for the monarchs of Judah and Israel as it was for the monarchs of Ugarit, then these regulations, enacted from an outside institution, would mark a significant attack on the economic clout of the palace.

This observation is in keeping with observations about anti-monarchical tendencies (or at least understandings that the power of the monarchy should be limited) contained within Deuteronomy. As Tigay describes:

---

18 In these instances, the mandatory nature of the provision of tribute (and the power relations that are implied) go unacknowledged in the letters, despite the fact that gifts are never free. For more on this, see Liverani, *International Relations in the Ancient Near East*.

19 Tigay, *Deuteronomy*, 145.

20 Westbrook has a slightly different reading of *mīšarum* edicts in his comparison of them with the biblical material. He states that they "were acts involving an element of desperation, which, like price-fixing regulations, attempted to curb the worst effects of an economic condition without approaching the underlying causes thereof." Westbrook, *Property and the Family*, 47.

> Deuteronomy is hardly designed to advance royal interests: it portrays the monarchy as a grudging concession to human initiative, pejoratively describing it as a desire to be like other nations...It assigns no significant role to the king (such as appointing judges or commanding the army), but severely restricts the king's freedom to accumulate capital and describes him as a figurehead whose main role is studying God's Teaching so that he will not become arrogant.[21]

Tigay's observations about Deuteronomy's attempts to limit the power of the king are borne out by other sections within the legal material. As Tigay has observed in his commentary, these laws seek to prevent monarchical excesses. This is clear in Deut 17:16, which forbids the king from acquiring many horses (or selling his subjects into slavery in order to gain more horses) and in Deut 17:17 (NRSV), which states: "he must not acquire many wives for himself, or else his heart will turn away; also silver and gold he must not acquire in great quantity for himself."

Since it is apparent that there is an emphasis within the laws in Deuteronomy on limiting the economic power of the monarchy, reading the debt remission laws of Deuteronomy 15 as a further attempt to limit the accumulation of wealth by the palace is not a stretch. This does not mean that these laws are *solely* designed to limit kingly wealth; no doubt they were also intended to act as a check on non-royal elite attempts to accumulate wealth.

When the laws regarding the remittance of debt in Deuteronomy are compared to other law collections preserved in the Hebrew Bible, the attempts on the part of Deuteronomy to limit the economic power of the palace appear to be unique. Exod 21:1–6 provides similar laws about the manumission of slaves every seven years but lacks the broader mandate regarding credit.[22] Given the similarities between other aspects of the legal literature in Deuteronomy and Exodus, the absence of these laws in Exodus is significant. Thus, debt accumulated by elites, in the form of human labor, is limited by Exodus. However, debt in the form of credit obligations is not limited by Exodus. This is a very explicit attack on the wealth accumulation capabilities of elites but would not

---

21 Tigay, *Deuteronomy*, 461.

22 Recognition of the similarities between the manumission of slaves laws in Deuteronomy and the Covenant Code leads to divergent possible source-critical interpretations of the two legal codes. For example, Westbrook ("What is the Covenant Code?," 35) sees the appearance of the same law in both an earlier and later legal text as insufficient evidence that there were attempts to edit the legal texts. Matthews ("Anthropology of Slavery," 120–21) takes the opposite stance and sees this as proof of the evolution of social and legal life in Israel through the Iron Age.

serve the same purpose in regards to a larger institution such as a palace.

Leviticus 25 provides similar but not identical instructions. In proclaiming that every fifty years should be a Jubilee Year, Leviticus aims to institute a system that, in a sense, "resets" changes that occur to landholdings through buying and selling, limiting, in a sense, the alienability of land from those to whom God had initially granted the land. Whereas the King of Ugarit appears to have been the *de facto* owner of all land, in Leviticus it is clearly God, not the monarchy, who owns the land. So while this is an ideological limit on the authority of the crown, in practical terms, Leviticus does not provide mandates to limit the accumulation of debt relationships by the palace in the same way that Deuteronomy does.

The appearance of regulations ensuring the remittance of debt every seven years reflects a very innovative approach on the part of Deuteronomy to limit the economic growth of the palace and elites. In a non-monetary economy, debt and credit are absolutely vital mechanisms for facilitating the circulation of goods and allowing an individual or institution to store and maintain wealth over extended periods of time. As is apparent at Ugarit, debt was a primary economic basis of palatial authority, outside of military, legal, and juridical authority. When the laws in Deuteronomy are considered within the context of a pre-monetary economy, these laws should not be understood as merely humanitarian. They are direct attempts to check the wealth of various groups and were direct attacks on wealthy elites.

WORKS CITED

Craigie, P. C. *The Book of Deuteronomy*. New International Commentary of the Old Testament. Grand Rapids, Mich.: Eerdmans, 1976.

Dercksen, J. G., ed. *Trade and Finance in Ancient Mesopotamia: Proceedings of the First MOS Symposium*. MOS Studies 1. Istanbul: Nederlands Historisch-Archaeologisch Instituut; Leiden: Nederlands Instituut voor het Nabije Oosten, 1999.

Frymer-Kensky, T. "Israel." In *Security for Debt in Ancient Near Eastern Law*, edited by R. Westbrook and R. Jasnow, 251–64. Culture and History of the Ancient Near East 9. Leiden: Brill, 2001.

Greengus, S. "Some Issues Relating to the Comparability of Laws and the Coherence of the Legal Tradition." In *Theory and Method in Biblical and Cuneiform Law: Revision, Interpretation, and Development*, edited by B. Levinson, 60–87. Journal for the Study of the

Old Testament Supplement Series 181. Sheffield: Sheffield Academic Press, 1994.

Heltzer, M. *The Internal Organization of the Kingdom of Ugarit*. Wiesbaden: Ludwig Reichert, 1982.

Hudson, M., and M. van de Mieroop, eds. *Debt and Renewal in the Ancient Near East*. Bethesda, Md.: CDL Press, 2001.

Klengel, H. "Mord und Bussleistung im Spätbronzezeitlichen Syrien." In *Death in Mesopotamia*, edited by B. Alster, 189–97. Mesopotamia 8. Copenhagen: Akademisk Forlag, 1990.

Liverani, M. *International Relations in the Ancient Near East, 1600–1100 BC*. New York: Palgrave, 2001.

Marquez Rowe, I. "The King's Men in Ugarit and Society in Late Bronze Age Syria." *Journal of the Economic and Social History of the Orient* 45.1 (2002): 1–19.

Matthews, V. "The Anthropology of Slavery in the Covenant Code." In *Theory and Method in Biblical and Cuneiform Law: Revision, Interpretation, and Development*, edited by B. Levinson, 119–35. Journal for the Study of the Old Testament Supplement Series 181. Sheffield: Sheffield Academic Press, 1994.

McGeough, K. *Exchange Relationships at Ugarit*. Ancient Near Eastern Studies Supplement 26. Leuven: Peeters Press, 2007.

Rainey, A. *The Social Stratification of Ugarit*. Ph.D. Dissertation, Brandeis University, 1962.

Smith, M. S. *The Bible and Ugaritic Studies in the Twentieth Century*. Peabody, Mass.: Hendrickson, 2001.

Steinkeller, P. "The Ur III Period." In *Security for Debt in Ancient Near Eastern Law*, edited by R. Westbrook, and R. Jasnow, 47–62. Culture and History of the Ancient Near East 9. Leiden: Brill, 2001.

Tigay, J. *Deuteronomy*. JPS Torah Commentary 5. Philadelphia, Pa.: Jewish Publication Society, 1996.

Westbrook, R. *Studies in Biblical and Cuneiform Law*. Cahiers de la Revue Biblique 26. Paris: Gabalda, 1988.

Property and the Family in Biblical Law. Journal for the Study of the Old Testament Supplement Series 113. Sheffield: Sheffield Academic Press, 1991.

"What Is the Covenant Code?" In *Theory and Method in Biblical and Cuneiform Law: Revision, Interpretation, and Development*, edited by B. Levinson, 15–36. Journal for the Study of the Old

Testament Supplement Series 181. Sheffield: Sheffield Academic Press, 1994.

Westbrook, R, and R. Jasnow, eds. *Security for Debt in Ancient Near Eastern Law*. Culture and History of the Ancient Near East 9. Leiden: Brill, 2001.

A SCANDAL IN LARSA*

MARTHA T. ROTH
UNIVERSITY OF CHICAGO

TCL 18 153[1] (AO 6768) is a Late Old Babylonian tablet in the collections of Le Musée du Louvre. My interest in the text derives from its references to a posthumous birth and legitimation, topics to which a larger work-in-progress is concerned. The tablet was acquired by the museum from the antiquarian dealer Élias Géjou in 1914 and most likely comes from illegal excavations at Larsa.[2] Erich Ebeling did not include it in his 1942 edition of the Larsa letters.[3] The first edition and commentary was by Martin David in 1973.[4] A second edition was published by Klaas Veenhof in 2005, in AbB 14.[5]

In his AbB edition, Veenhof labeled the text a *ze'pum* tablet, a communication type that does not appear before the time of King Ammiditana (r. 1683–1647). The characteristics of a *ze'pum* tablet include: (1) the absence of the names of the addressee and sender and the blessings per the usual opening formulae of a letter; (2) a shape typically more square than rectangle and with tapered edges; and (3) the absence of horizontal guide lines.[6] Finkelstein noted that *ze'pum* tablets "may be characterized as 'business directives' and are to be distinguished from

---

* It is a privilege to dedicate this paper to Prof. Barry Eichler, teacher, scholar, and exemplar of all the best of professional and personal integrity.

1 Dossin, *Lettres de la première dynastie babylonienne.*

2 See Veenhof, AbB 14, xi with n. 7.

3 Ebeling, *Altbabylonische Briefe der Louvre-Sammlung aus Larsa*, 124: "153.154. nicht behandelt, weil keine Briefe."

4 David, "Kritik," 90–94; see 90 n. 3, where David acknowledges the help of B. Landsberger and F. R. Kraus. David, whose restorations of broken sections of the text differ markedly from Veenhof's and from mine, has an overall interpretation that cannot be sustained; only some details of his interpretation will be addressed here.

5 Veenhof, AbB 14, 188–89 no. 207.

6 See Sallaberger "Wenn Du mein Bruder bist," 26, with prior literature, to which add Walker, *Cuneiform Texts from Babylonian Tablets* 52 (unpaginated, Preface p. 2).

the mainstream of Old Babylonian letters, which cover a larger range of subjects, including political and social matters."[7] Our text, however, although indeed lacking the opening epistolary formulae and the horizontal guide lines, and although its edges are tapered or pinched, differs in other characteristics: it is not square but rectangular (the catalogue in TCL gives its dimensions as 95×47 mm) and it is certainly not a "business directive." It gives the impression more than anything of being a "second page," a continuation of a letter, the first "page" (or tablet) of which probably contained the relevant personal information. Personal examination of the tablet,[8] furthermore, reveals it to be unbaked and with the contents distributed unequally on the two surfaces: the obverse is filled with the first seventeen lines, many of which extend across the right edge and onto the reverse surface; there are only five lines written on the reverse, leaving about two-thirds of that surface blank.

Below I present an edition of the text with some suggestions for new readings and translations, followed by some remarks on its content and import.

1. [*aš*]-*šum di-ni-im ša* ^{d}UTU-TAB.BA.E
2. *ša ta-aš-pu-ra-aš-ši-im*
3. NITA.GABA *iš-tu um-ma-šu*
4. *ez-bé-et ša-nu-um*
5. *i-ḫu-zu-ši-ma*
6. *i-na bi-it a-ḫi-zi-i-ša*
7. *wa-ar-ki-im*
8. *ú-li-is-sú*
9. *a-na mu-ti-i-ša wa-ar-ki-im*
10. *ki-a-am iz-ku-ur um-ma ši-i-ma*
11. *a-na ka-ši-im-ma*
12. [*lu*] *wa-li-da-ku*
13. [*aš-š*]*um ki-a-am iz-ku-ru*
14. [*di-na-am*(?)] *i-ta-pí-iš* ^{d}UTU-TAB.BA.E
15. [x x x] ⌜*i*⌝-*za-a-uz*
16. [*ù* x x x SA]G.ARAD-*sú ú-x*
17. [*e-pe-šum a*]*n-nu-um*

REV.

18. *i-na* LARSAM^{ki} *ma-ti-i-ma*

---

[7] Finkelstein, *Late Old Babylonian Documents*, 6. See also Saggs, "An Unaddressed Old Babylonian Letter," 56–58.

[8] July 2009. I thank Béatrice André-Salvini, conservateur général, Musée du Louvre, for her courtesy in allowing me to examine the tablet.

19. *ú-ul ib-ba-ši*
20. *a-bi ma-ri* SAG.ARAD-*sú*
21. *a-na ma-ru-ti-im*
22. *ú-ul i-*⌜*ša*⌝*-ka-an*

(1–2) As for the legal decision involving Šamaš-tappê about which you sent a message to her ([f]PN, unkn.):

(3–8) (Concerning) the suckling child—after his mother was left (pregnant and abandoned or widowed), another took her in marriage, and she gave birth to him in the house of her second spouse. (9–10) She swore an oath to her second husband, as follows: (11–12) "Indeed I am the progenitrix for you."

(13–16) Because she swore thus, he made [a decision(?)], he …-ed Šamaš-tappê […], and he …-ed … his slave.

(17–22) Such [a thing] has never before occurred in Larsa: a father with sons simply does not establish his slave into sonship!

NOTES

1. *di-ni-im* with copy (typo in AbB 14 207).

3. There is no vertical wedge at the beginning of the line, per collation by J. Nougayrol, reported in David, "Kritik," 94; see also the collation in Veenhof, AbB 14, 232, and confirmed by personal collation. David, "Kritik," 92 n. 6, reports the suggestion of F. R. Kraus to read 1 DUMU GABA "1 Brustkind." David and Veenhof read RA.GABA and RÁ.GABA, *rakbûm* "messenger, envoy," which makes no sense in the context. The copy clearly supports reading the first sign NITA; NITA.GABA is thus the preposed topic, with the resumptive accusative pronominal suffixes in *ummašu* and *ulissu*.

12. David, "Kritik," 92: "[nicht] geboren" (restoring [*la*] rather than [*lu*]). *CAD* A/1, 341 s.v. *ālidu* adj. (although more accurately a participle) cites our passage at usage b-1': *umma šîma ana kâšimma lu* [sic] *wa-li-da-ku*, she declared (under oath) "I have borne (the child) for you (the second husband)," understanding *ālittum* (fem.) as a predicate adjective with the enclitic subject pronoun (and omitting the markings of restoration around *lu*). So too Veenhof, AbB 14 207: "It is truly to you that I have borne (him)!" with p. 189 n. b: "*wālidāku* must be a stative of the partic[i]ple."

14. *i-ta-pí-iš* is confirmed by personal collation. David, "Kritik," 91 reads […] *i-na bi-it*. Veenhof, AbB 14 207 reads [x x] *i-ta(-)-bi-it*; see Veenhof, AbB 14, 189 n. c: the final sign "… id is damaged, … the second sign [is] not na..." The restoration of *dīnam* at the beginning is tentative.

15. Neither David nor Veenhof restores the break at the beginning of the line, but David translates ("Kritik," 92 and comments, ibid., 93) "wird er [eine Tochter] ... [nicht] heiraten."

    In the second half of the line, ⸢*i*⸣-*za-a-uz* presents considerable difficulties. The first sign (rendered here in half brackets) is damaged and not complete although there can be little doubt about the reading. David, after proposing and rejecting *i-za*$^{(!)?}$-*a*-UZ (with restoring ḪA.LA at the beginning of line 14, for *zittam zâzum*), accepted *iḫḫaz*, G present from *aḫāzum*. Veenhof, while transliterating *i-ḫa-a-UZ*, left the verb untranslated and concluded that "a reference to a marriage does not make sen[s]e. L. 14–16 must mention the adoption." My own collation concludes that the Winkelhacken that distinguish the graphemes /ḪA/ and /ZA/ are not visible, and thus I read /ZA/. The broken writing (CV_1-V_1-V_2C) suggests a middle weak verb (*zâzum*), but it is not out of the question to read a corrupt form of *uzuzzum*. Of course, in the Old Babylonian period we most frequently find writings that preserve the doubling of the first consonant of finite forms of *uzuzzu* (G present *izzaz*, G preterite *izziz*); see Huehnergard, "*izuzzum* and *itūlum*," 165; but note *i-za-az-ku-um* BIN 7 29:13, *i-za-zu* UET 5 127:8 (both cited *CAD* U/W, s.v. *uzuzzu* mng. 12b).

16. See the collation in Veenhof, AbB 14, 232, confirmed by my own examination, although there is a more distinct separation of the grapheme /Ú/ from the following constellation of wedges than Veenhof represents. David, "Kritik," 93 suggests SAG.ARAD-*su-ú-ma*(!), "vielmehr er ist sein Sklave."[9]

17. David restored [*dīnum*] at the beginning of the line, in accordance with his understanding that the text of lines 20–22 records the official pronouncement of a judicial body: an articulated principle for Larsa if not a "law" for all of Babylonia ("Kritik," 91). There is certainly enough room in the break for three signs (David: [*di-nu-um a*]*n-nu-um*; Veenhof: [*e-pe-šum*] *an-nu-um*); the restoration of only one sign, /*di*/ (that is, [*di*]-*nu-um*), in *CAD* A/2, 244 s.v. *ardu* mng. 1c, is not likely.

22. Note the use of *šakānum* here. The formation of an adoption is most commonly expressed in Old Babylonian with the complementary *ana mārūtim leqûm*, "to take in adoption" and *ana mārūtim nadānum*,

---

9 Veenhof, AbB 14, 189 n. d, proposes and rejects *ú-pil* (*uppil*, **uppulu*, denominative verb from *aplu* "heir"), citing Kouwenberg, *Gemination in the Akkadian Verb*, 312, where reference is made to LH § 178:17; rather, that reference is certainly from *apālu* A, although not in either *CAD* or *AHw*.

"to give in adoption." To my knowledge the only other use of *šakānum* in OB adoption is in BE 6/1 96:1–8:[10] ^{f}PN *qadu mārat irtim mārat* ${}^{f}PN_2$ *nadīt Šamaš ša* ${}^{f}PN_2$ *nadīt Šamaš ummaša udammiqušima ana mārūtiša iškunuši* [*u*] ${}^{f}PN_2$ *nadīt Šamaš mārat* PN_3 *ullilši* [*panī*]*ša ana ṣīt šamšim iškun*, "(Concerning) ^{f}PN together with an infant daughter, the daughter of ${}^{f}PN_2$, the *nadītum* of Šamaš—whom ${}^{f}PN_2$, the *nadītum* of Šamaš, her mother, treated her well (*udammiqušima*) and established her (*iškunuši*) as her heir/into sonship—${}^{f}PN_2$, the *nadītum* of Šamaš, daughter of PN_3, manumitted her, she placed (*iškun*) her face toward sunrise."

DISCUSSION

1. *The Dramatis Personae*

There are at least seven and possibly eight persons in this story. The first three are observers. They may have a stake in the matter, but their relationships to one another and to the actors in the mini-drama related in the body of the letter are unknown:

(1) The letter writer, unnamed.
(2) The person (male or female) who sent the original inquiry or complaint (*dīnum*) (*tašpuraššim* "you sent a message ...," line 2).
(3) The woman to whom that inquiry was sent (*tašpuraššim* "... to her," line 2).

Then there are the actors in the drama:

(4) Šamaš-tappê is the only individual referred to by name in this letter. The legal matter involves him (line 1) and he reappears in the crucial and broken clause in line 14. He is likely a plaintiff or defendant in the case (*aššum dīnim ša Šamaš-tappê*, "as for the case concerning/involving/brought by/brought against Šamaš-tappê," line 1).
(5) The woman who was left pregnant by her first husband, remarried, gave birth, and swore an oath.
(6) The infant.
(7) The second husband.

---

10 See *CAD* M/1, 319 s.v. *mārūtu* mng. 1b–2' (incorrect in *CAD* D, 63 s.v. *damāqu* mng. 2c–1' and in Harris, *Sippar*, 347): the bound form *ummasa* (which of course could be either nominative or accusative) must be nominative and in opposition to ${}^{f}PN_2$ *nadīt Šamaš*, and the two subjunctive verbs in hendiadys *udammiqušima* and *iškunuši* have the same subject and object.

(8) The slave (line 16), who might be identical with either Šamaš-tappê or (less likely) the infant.

2. The Opening (lines 1–2)

Whether or not TCL 18 153 is formally a *ze'pum*, it certainly continues or refers to a story the beginning of which we are ignorant. We know only that there is a matter in which one Šamaš-tappê is involved and about which a message was sent to a certain woman.

3. The Drama, Part One (lines 3–12)

The first part of the drama relates the events that culminated in the wife's oath. We learn first that she was pregnant when her second husband married her and that she gave birth to her baby in the latter's house. The location of the birth is important; it establishes the appearance if not the biological certitude that the child belongs to the second husband's household.

The use of *ezēbum* to signify a husband "leaving" behind a pregnant woman after his death is seen also in PBS 5 100 ii 13ff.: *inūma ... īzibuma imūtu ariātma īzibši.*[11] David and Veenhof both understand *ezēbum* here in the sense of "divorce." The principal difficulty in understanding formal divorce is contextual: it is implausible that her first husband would divorce her if she were pregnant, barrenness generally being the only valid reason for divorce. And if she had been divorced because of apparent barrenness (if, perhaps, she did not yet know she was pregnant) it is even more implausible that another man would have married her.

The important point is that she is somehow free to create, to reify, a new parentage for her child. This must mean that there is no first husband and, equally important, no family of her first husband to claim the child, whether that first husband is dead, missing in battle, or otherwise absent. That there was a first husband is clearly implied by the language of the text, which refers to a second husband: *āḫizum warkûm, mutum warkûm*. Thus it is certain that she was not, for example, a prostitute or otherwise a "single mother."

The oath then is quoted: "Indeed I am the progenitrix for you." Note the force of the asseverative marker *lu*, which can express the positive injunction "let it be so" in an assertory oath with a verbless clause. Thus the force of the assertory oath is to construct a legal relationship: whether or not her second husband is the biological father of the child is not relevant; she affirms under oath the relationship between the newborn and her second husband: she bears the child to him.

---

11 See Roth, "Reading Mesopotamian Law Cases," 243ff.

4. The Drama, Part Two (lines 13–16)

What follows as a consequence of her oath is then expressed in three verbal clauses, each of which is problematic: *i-ta-pí-iš ... i-za-a-uz ... ú-x*. The *aššum* clause ("Because she swore thus") is the key element for understanding the force of this missive: the legal decision (*dīnum*, line 1) and the ensuing actions enumerated are the consequence of her oath.[12] Syntactically, the subject of each of the three verbs must be the same person;[13] logically that person must be the second husband. In my provisional understanding of these lines, the second husband takes certain actions that settle the inheritance rights of this new-born child and takes some action relative to a slave whom he had previously designated as his heir; whether or not Šamaš-tappê is that slave is unclear to me.

5. The Closing (lines 17–22)

The closing appears to have two parts. The first part (lines 17–19) expresses outrage and the singularity of this event: "Such a thing has never before occurred in Larsa!" The second part could very well be quoting a popular expression or otherwise expressing conventional wisdom: a man with legitimate sons simply does not make the effort to make a slave his heir.[14]

IMPLICATIONS

There are two related concerns about inheritance that arise from our document. The first has to do with establishing filiation in the absence of a living father in order for a posthumous child to have inheritance rights. The second has to do with the inheritance rights of biological children versus those of adopted children; the latter could be slaves sired by the master upon his slave woman.

---

12 For the *aššum* clause providing the legal rationale for what follows, see Roth, "The Because Clause," 407ff.

13 Grammatically and in isolation, Šamaš-tappê could be the subject of the verb in lines 14–15 ("Šamaš-tappê …-ed …").

14 Note that the expression of common practice echoes the statement made by Laban to Jacob recorded in Genesis 29:26. After working for seven years, Jacob had demanded that Laban fulfill his commitment to give Rachel as wife. Laban deceived him, however, and substituted his older daughter Leah, with whom Jacob consummated the marriage. When confronted with the deception, Laban justified his action and agreed to give Rachel for an additional service term of another seven years. The opening of Laban's remarks is: "One does not do thus in our place, to marry off the younger before the older."

1. Establishing Filiation

PBS 5 100 is a prominent example documenting the elaborate lengths to which a family would go to be certain of the biological relationship of a posthumous child.[15] In that text as in ours, a pregnant woman was left widowed or divorced. In PBS 5 100, however, the detailed process is intended to establish that the first, now deceased husband was indeed the father. (This is not to be confused with establishing the inheritance rights of children raised, after their biological father's death, in the household of another—a circumstance in which filiation is not in question. Such a situation is addressed, for example, in LH § 177.)

There is one provision from the law collections that deals with the inheritance rights of a posthumous child, MAL A § 28:[16]

> *šumma almattu ana bēt a'īle tētarab u mārаša ḫurda ilteša naṣṣat ina bēt āḫizānіša irtibi u ṭuppu ša mārūtišu la šaṭrat zitta ina bēt murabbiānišu la ilaqqe ḫubullē la inašši ina bēt ālidānišu zitta kî qātišu ilaqqe*

> If a widow should enter a man's house and she is carrying (in her arms?, in her womb?) her son, the posthumous-child-of-her-dead-husband (*ḫurdu*), with her, and he grows up in the house of the-man-who-took-her (*bēt āḫizānіša*), but a tablet of his adoption (or: sonship) is never written—he will not take an inheritance share from the house of the-one-who-raised-him (*bēt murabbiānišu*) and he will not be responsible for (the estate's) debts. (Rather) he will take a proportionate inheritance share from the house of his begetter (*bēt ālidānišu*).

The rare word *ḫurdu* appears, in addition to the Middle Assyrian reference just cited, also in Old Assyrian, in the letter TCL 20 91, where one of a number of debtors is identified by name as: *Nūr-Ištar ḫurdim ša Ennamaja*, "Nūr-Ištar, the posthumous son of Ennamaja."[17] It is found also in a Neo-Assyrian letter, CT 53 149[18]:

> The LÚ.GAR.U.U, whom your royal father consecrated (*ugallibuni*), used to enter the ablution chamber, and moreover your royal father put him in charge of the statues—now he died in Elul (month VI). But he has a posthumous son (DUMU-*šú ḫurdu ibašši*); he is a novice and is unconsecrated (TA *pirte izzaz*, lit., remains/stands with hair). If it is acceptable to the king, my lord, let them consecrate him.

15 See Roth, "Reading Mesopotamian Law Cases," 243ff.

16 Roth, *Law Collections*, 163.

17 Edited by Larsen, *The Aššur-nādā Archive*, 49ff.

18 See Parpola, *LAS* 310 and Parpola, SAA 10 97.

These references, albeit few in number and from other periods, support the reasonable assumption that posthumous births pose a problem for the legal systems. In our text, TCL 18 153, the biological fact that the child was not sired by the second husband is assumed and subverted by the force of the mother's oath. She *alters* that biological fact in order to create a new legal parentage.

2. (Reconciling) Inheritance Rights of Biological and Adopted Heirs

Adoption in Mesopotamia typically occurred in two circumstances: when a childless couple or a parentless child creates a new familial structure, or when a person of property was facing a future without a legitimate heir and without support in her dotage—what Elizabeth Stone calls "familial adoptions" and "economic adoptions."[19] In the latter situation, economic adoptions, which concern us here, the adopter has a number of options: adoption of an unrelated child or adult; adoption of a child born to a current spouse's previous marriage; adoption of one's own biological child born to (or sired by) a slave (or prostitute).

The Old Babylonian law collections, which always maintain a focus on the economic implications of any circumstance, include provisions that address potential conflicts between heirs that arise when more than one avenue to inheritance is open. Thus there are law provisions concerned with competing inheritance rights of children born to first and second wives (LL § 24, LH § 167), of children born to a prostitute (LL § 27), and of children born to a wife and a slave woman (LL §§ 25, 26, LH §§ 170, 171).[20]

Our text deals with a wrinkle not anticipated in the law provisions: a man without biological sons who had adopted his slave as heir, then accepted a child born in his household as his biological son and heir. This is not completely unforeseen in adoption documents of the period, however, in which we find clauses such as: 10 *mārē* PN *liršīma* PN_2 *apilšu*, "should PN (adopter) have even ten children, PN_2 (adoptee) is still his (primary) heir."[21] The difference between these adoption contract clauses and our situation in TCL 18 153, of course, is that our adopter did not himself sire children. In TCL 18 153, the adopter made a slave from his household his heir, then later took in marriage a woman who was at the time pregnant by her previous husband, publicly

19 Stone, "Adoption in Old Babylonian Nippur," 1–2. For adoption, see Westbrook, ed., *A History of Ancient Near Eastern Law*, passim; for the Old Babylonian period, see 391ff.

20 Roth, *Law Collections*, 31 and 113–14.

21 VAS 8 73:7 and 127:9; Szlechter, *Tablettes*, 3 MAH 15.951:14–15; *BAP* 95:8; ARM 8 1:22; etc.

accepted and acknowledged the child she then bore as his own, and finally reconfirmed the slave as his heir.

CONCLUSION

The letter TCL 18 153 provides a partial and tantalizing glimpse into a family drama. Someone wrote to an unnamed and unknown woman complaining about a situation in which one man's biological child was accepted into another man's household and assumed a place as heir. That situation upset the existing inheritance structures, affecting Šamaš-tappê (whose precise relationship to the birthing woman or her second husband is not clear) and perhaps another person. Details are elusive, but from the final lines it appears logical to me to assume that the second husband both accepted the newborn as a son and affirmed the inheritance rights of a previously adopted slave.

In my understanding of this letter, there is a situation that, as the letter writer declares in his final statement, never before occurred in Larsa or, to be less dramatic, a situation that should not normally occur in Larsa (or anywhere else): a father with heirs adopts his slave into sonship and heirship. But, as this letter demonstrates, this aberrant situation did happen, and I conclude with some final speculations.

A play by John Webster and William Rowley, first performed in London in 1625, titled "A Cure for a Cuckold" is a typically tangled web of jealousies, misunderstandings, and confused identities.[22] The play has a subplot in which a sailor returns after four years at sea to find his wife with a one-year-old baby. Instead of outrage, the sailor, in fact, embraces the child, upholds his wife's honor, and accepts the child as his own offspring. The title's "cure" for cuckoldry is, in other words, simply ignoring it and publicly declaring the bastard to be legitimate. In a final scene, the cuckold husband and the man who actually sired the infant both claim the child; in a trial in a tavern, the judge declares the child belongs to neither man—but to its mother.

I don't suggest that the second husband in our Old Babylonian letter was a cuckold. But I do suggest that one possible key to understanding the letter is the person of the mother and the force of her public declaration. Unlike the men involved, our Larsa woman's biological relationship to the child is not a matter of speculation or contestation. Her statement, therefore, carries legal and social force. What she says about the father—biological or fictive—is what matters.

---

22 I thank my colleague Bradin Cormack for bringing this play to my attention.

WORKS CITED

David, M. "Kritik an einem Rechtsspruch aus Larsa (TCL 18, 153)." In *Symbolae Biblicae et Mesopotamicae Francisco Mario Theodoro de Liagre Böhl Dedicatae*, edited by M.A. Beek et al., 90–94. Leiden: Brill, 1973.

Dossin, G. *Lettres de la première dynastie babylonienne* 2. TCL 18. Paris: Geuthner, 1934.

Ebeling, E. *Altbabylonische Briefe der Louvre-Sammlung aus Larsa*. Mitteilungen der Altorientalischen Gesellschaft 15. Leipzig: Harrassowitz, 1942.

Finkelstein, J. J. *Late Old Babylonian Documents and Letters*. YOS 13. New Haven and London: Yale University Press, 1972.

Harris, R. *Ancient Sippar: A Demographic Study of an Old-Babylonian City (1894–1595 B.C.)*. PIHANS 36. Leiden: Nederlands Historisch-Archaeologisch Instituut te Istanbul, 1975.

Huehnergard, J. "*izuzzum* and *itūlum*." In *Riches Hidden in Secret Places: Ancient Near Eastern Studies in Memory of Thorkild Jacobsen*, edited by Tzvi Abusch, 161–85. Winona Lake, Ind.: Eisenbrauns, 2002.

Kouwenberg, N. J. C. *Gemination in the Akkadian Verb*. PhD Dissertation, University of Leiden, 1997.

Larsen, M. T. *The Aššur-nādā Archive*. Old Assyrian Archives 1. PIHANS 96. Leiden: Nederlands Instituut voor het Nabije Oosten, 2002.

Parpola, S. *Letters from Assyrian Scholars to the Kings Esarhaddon and Assurbanipal*. 2 vols. AOAT 5/1-2. Kevelaer: Butzon & Bercker; Neukirchen-Vluyn: Neukirchener Verlag, 1970–1983.

Letters from Assyrian and Babylonian Scholars. SAA 10. Helsinki: Helsinki University Press, 1993.

Roth, M. *Law Collections from Mesopotamia and Asia Minor*. 2nd ed. Writings from the Ancient World 6. Atlanta: Scholars Press, 1997.

"Reading Mesopotamian Law Cases, PBS 5 100: A Question of Filiation." *JESHO* 44 (2001): 243–92.

"The Because Clause: Punishment Rationalization in Mesopotamian Laws." In *Veenhof Anniversary Volume*, edited by W. H. van Soldt et al., 407–12. PIHANS 89. Leiden: Nederlands Instituut voor het Nabije Oosten, 2001.

Saggs, H. W. F. "An Unaddressed Old Babylonian Letter." *JCS* 14 (1960): 56–58.

Stone, E. "Adoption in Old Babylonian Nippur." In *Adoption in Old Babylonian Nippur and the Archive of Mannum-mešu-liṣṣur*, by E. C. Stone and D. I. Owen, with a contribution by J. R. Mitchell, 1–33. Mesopotamian Civilizations 3. Winona Lake, Ind.: Eisenbrauns, 1991.

Szlechter, É. *Tablettes juridiques de la 1re dynastie de Babylone, conservées au Musée d'Art et d'Histoire de Genève*. 2 vols. Paris: Recueil Sirey, 1958.

Veenhof, K. R. *Letters in the Louvre.* AbB 14. Leiden and Boston: Brill, 2005.

Walker, C. B. F. *Old Babylonian Letters*. CT 52. London: British Museum Publications, 1976.

Westbrook, R., ed. *A History of Ancient Near Eastern Law*. Handbook of Oriental Studies 1/72/2. Leiden: Brill, 2003.

THE ROLE OF THE ELDERS IN THE LAWS OF DEUTERONOMY

JEFFREY H. TIGAY
UNIVERSITY OF PENNSYLVANIA

It is a great pleasure for me to take part in this volume honoring Barry Eichler. For more than forty years, most of them when we were colleagues at Penn, I have found in him a dear friend, a wise counselor and teacher, and a model of rigorous and penetrating scholarship. Among the many subjects of his interest, at the core lies the study of biblical law in its ancient Near Eastern context, and I offer the following study as a token of my affection and admiration.

In addition to cases that the laws of Deuteronomy assign to professional, appointed judges for adjudication,[1] several others are assigned for some purpose to the elders. These are the cases of accidental homicide (Deut 19:12), the insubordinate son (21:19–20), the accused bride (22:13–21), and refusal to perform levirate marriage (25:5–10). It is commonly assumed that in these cases the elders serve as judges,[2] and this division of labor between the elders and professional judges has prompted many attempts at explanation revolving around the question of whether the two groups functioned simultaneously in the same judicial system, handling different categories of cases, or whether these cases reflect different strata in the development of biblical law, with the elders judging in the traditional tribal society whereas professional judges are a later development from the period of the monarchy.[3]

---

1 Deut 17:9, 12; 19:17–18; and 25:1–2. By "professional" judges I mean simply those called *šōpĕṭîm*, whose appointment is commanded in Deut 16:18, without implying that they were paid or were full-time judges.

2 See already m. Yebamot 12:1; Sanhedrin 8:4; Makkot 2:6; b. Ketubbot 46a; Maimonides, Hilkhot Roṣeaḥ 5:7; Mamrim 7:7; Naarah Betulah 3:6; Yibbum 4:1. For moderns see, e.g., Driver, *A Critical and Exegetical Commentary on Deuteronomy*, 233; Hoffmann, *Sefer Devarim*, 374; Weinfeld, *Deuteronomy and the Deuteronomic School*, 234; Phillips, *Deuteronomy*, 115; Mayes, *Deuteronomy*, 304 and 310; Craigie, *The Book of Deuteronomy*, 268. For more recent scholarship see the sources cited in the works listed in the next note.

3 The bibliography on this subject is extensive. See Rofé, "The Organization of the Judiciary in Deuteronomy," 92–112; Levinson, *Deuteronomy and the*

It seems to me that the premise of this debate—that the elders serve as judges in Deuteronomic law—is dubious. In no case are they explicitly said to judge, and in 21:2 elders and judges are referred to as separate groups (as they are Josh 8:33; 23:2; 24:1; Ezra 10:14). The elders are never said to engage in the activities typical of judges, such as investigate, inquire, or interrogate (19:18; cf. 13:15; 17:4), convict, acquit, or announce a verdict (17:19–21; 25:1), nor are they ever mentioned in contexts that refer to such activities. Looking beyond Deuteronomy, it is notable that when Moses and Joshua go up to Mount Sinai, Moses says to the elders: "Wait here for us until we return to you. You have Aaron and Hur with you; let anyone who has a legal matter approach them" (Exod 24:14).[4] Aaron and Hur, not the elders, serve as judges.

What, then, is the role of Deuteronomy's elders in the legal passages that mention them?

The common denominator in the cases of the insubordinate son, the accused bride, and refusal to perform levirate marriage, is that the outcome in each case is entirely determined not by the elders but by a declaration or action made or performed before them. Their role is to serve as a public forum for procedures that require publicity. The case regarding levirate marriage requires publicity in order to bring public pressure to bear on the reluctant brother-in-law and, if he continues to refuse, to make it publicly known that his brother's widow is free to remarry.[5] In the case of the slandered bride, presenting the evidence of virginity requires publicity in order to restore her reputation and that of her parents, which was publicly defamed by her husband who "put out [*hôṣîʾ*] a bad name for her" and so as to show the public the justice of her husband's punishment, and perhaps also to deter other husbands from making such charges public. In these cases, the ceremony of removing the brother-in-law's sandal and the bride's parents' presentation of the signs of virginity suffice to determine the outcome. The judges' role in

---

Hermeneutics of Legal Innovation, 98–143, esp. 124–27, and briefly in Berlin and Brettler, eds., *The Jewish Study Bible*, 403; Wells, "Competing or Complementary? Judges and Elders in Biblical and Neo-Babylonian Law" (my thanks to Prof. Wells for kindly allowing me to read and cite his paper in advance of its publication).

4 Translation from *Tanakh: The Holy Scriptures*.

5 In b. *Yebamot* 101b certain rabbis required a quorum of five elders (instead of the standard three) for the sandal-removal ceremony, "in order that the matter be given due publicity" (*lĕparsûmê millĕtāʾ*) "so no priest would marry her; while prospective husbands, on hearing that she had been freed by halizah from her levirate bond, might begin to woo her" (n. 61 *ad loc.* in *The Babylonian Talmud, Seder Nashim, Translated into English*).

such cases is similar to their role as "witnesses" (as a "notarial forum") to the agreement that Boaz and the redeemer make at the city gate in Ruth 4:1–11a[6] and to the role of "all who entered the gate" of Hebron in whose sight Ephron the Hethite sold the field and cave of Machpelah to Abraham (Genesis 23). As Sarna put it: "the negotiations…are carried out at the city gate….The transaction is given the widest possible publicity in order to avoid the likelihood of future litigation."[7] Since the gate was the most public place in the city, conducting such procedures in the presence of those gathered there served in the same way as the required publication of information important to the public, such as real estate transactions, in newspapers today.

The elders' role as a public notarial forum is comparable to the role of the assembly (*'ēdâ*) in the Elephantine documents, as described by R. Yaron: The *'ēdâ* served as

> the forum before which declarations of divorce might be made. We have no ground for attributing a judicial nature to the function of the *'edah* [at Elephantine, unlike the *'ēdâ* in Numbers 35:12 and 24–25]; it merely provides for the necessary publicity. This would prevent subsequent uncertainty and possible allegations of adultery against the divorced wife."[8]

Such a role is known from Mesopotamia as well. A letter from the Old Babylonian period refers to a man who assembled twenty of the city's elders in order to tell them about his adoptive brother who had run away and to remove him from his status as brother.[9] This is reminiscent of publishing in newspapers that one is no longer responsible for somebody's debts. A number of Neo-Babylonian documents mention declarations to the Assembly (the *puḫrum*). In one, a widow appears before the assembly in a time of famine and dedicates her two sons as slaves to the temple of Ishtar of Uruk so that the temple would feed them and officials of the temple accept them.[10] In another, a woman declares that the true father of her son is not the man her son had named but another man, and the son agrees to change the name of his father in all his documents.[11] (Since the assembly also functioned regularly as a court, it is clear from such cases that the notarial forum did

---

6 Reviv, *The Elders in Ancient Israel: a Study of a Biblical Institution*, 66. The term "notarial forum" is Reviv's.

7 Sarna, *The JPS Torah Commentary: Genesis*, 159.

8 Yaron, *Introduction to the Law of the Aramaic Papyri*, 28.

9 Stol, *Letters from Yale*, 36–37.

10 Dougherty, *Shirkûtu*, 33–34.

11 TCL 13 138, in Pohl, *Neubabylonische Rechtsurkunden*, no. 47.

not necessarily have to be a non-judicial body; the two functions could be performed by the same body. In other words, notwithstanding what seems to be the case in Deuteronomy and at Elephantine, a court could also play this role.)

The elders play a non-judicial role also in the case of the insubordinate son (Deut 21:19). The parents' declaration that their son is insubordinate requires a public forum so as to place his execution under communal supervision and prevent a hasty or arbitrary decision by the frustrated, insulted parents, and so that the public will know that his execution is justified. In the light of 25:8, where the elders summon the resistant brother-in-law and talk to him, it is conceivable that bringing the case of the insubordinate son to the elders would give them the opportunity to mediate between parents and son. But in this case the law does not say that the elders should speak to the parents and the context indicates that the parents' declaration is all that is required to seal the fate of their son.

The law concerning asylum cities is different from the others in which the elders play a role. Here, too, no judicial process is mentioned, but in addition, the law does not describe a procedure of any kind that takes place in their presence. Their role is simply to extradite the intentional killer from the city of asylum and hand him over to the blood avenger. The parallel passages in Num 35:12, 24–25 and Josh 20:6, 9 do describe a trial, conducted by the assembly (*ʿēdâ*), but these passages are from P[12] and are not decisive as far as Deuteronomic law is concerned. Of course, from a legal point of view it would be reasonable to assume that in a case such as this there would be a trial. It is generally assumed that Deut 19:12 presupposes that a trial has already taken place in which the killer was convicted of intentional homicide.[13] If so, we would have to assume that the text is extremely elliptical. If we do assume that, we might further assume that it was the elders, "the only officials explicitly mentioned in the text,"[14] who conduct the trial. But this would be the

---

12 Rofé, "The History of the Cities of Refuge in Biblical Law," 228–30.

13 See the halakhic exegesis summed up in Maimonides, Hilkhot Roṣeaḥ 5:7; Luzzatto, *Il Pentateuco*, at Deut 19:12 (he assumes a two-part trial: a preliminary hearing preceding v. 12 and a final trial between vv. 12a and 12b); Wells, "Competing or Complementary? Judges and Elders in Biblical and Neo-Babylonian Law," p. 7 of draft, following n. 23: "testimonial and other types of evidence are already available and further investigation of the matters at hand is unnecessary." Cf. Rofé, "History of the Cities of Refuge," 228 (repr., 138–39).

14 Wells, "Competing or Complementary? Judges and Elders in Biblical and Neo-Babylonian Law," p. 20 of draft, just after n. 77.

only case, not only in Deuteronomy but in the entire Torah, in which the elders serve as judges, and it seems just as likely, if not more so, that if the law does presuppose a trial, it would be conducted by professional judges and that following the conviction the elders would merely be exercising the administrative function of extraditing the killer under their executive authority as leaders of the city (cf. Josh 20:4 in which they admit the killer to the city merely on the basis of his own statement).

On the other hand, since the text does not mention a trial, perhaps there is none. It may be that the role of the elders is to act on the basis of their knowledge, as the family heads in the city, about the past relations between the killer and the victim. Apparently this is the only basis for a decision in Deuteronomy, since the killing took place in the woods where there would have been no witnesses.[15] In the absence of witnesses, that the killer "lay in wait" may simply be an inference from the past enmity (cf. 22:23–27, in which an execution is likewise carried out based on circumstantial evidence). Another possibility is that their role is to ensure that the killer is not executed on the basis of a private agreement between his family and that of his victim: "Where the families of the victim and the perpetrator both agree on the details and the circumstances of the tragedy, there is no need to turn to the judgment of the elders, that is, to the judgment of the heads of the city's families. The elders are needed only if there is an accusation of premeditated murder; then, even if all are agreed on the details of the deed, some sort of higher authority is needed to make the decision and take the initiative in carrying out the sentence of death."[16]

We do not have enough cases to be sure that in Israel it was generally the elders who served as the public/notarial forum or if it played this role only in certain types of cases. Most of the cases we have reviewed deal with matters concerning families: the insubordinate son, accusations of premarital unchastity, and refusal to perform levirate marriage. In the case of murder, blood vengeance is also a family matter, between the killer and the victim's family.

---

15 The proximity to this law of Deut 19:15–21, about witnesses at trials, might suggest that our law does involve witnesses, and hence a trial, as does the parallel law in Numbers 35, where v. 30 requires two witnesses for execution. However, unlike the case in Numbers 35, Deuteronomy separates the law of witnesses from the law about accidental homicide with v. 14, which deals with an unrelated topic (landmarks), indicating that to Deuteronomy these are separate laws.

16 Rofé, "History of the Cities of Refuge," 229 (repr., 139).

In the rest of the Bible, too, there is hardly a case in which the elders function as judges. As noted above, Exod 24:14 indicates clearly that the elders do not judge, and elders and judges are mentioned as different groups in several other passages. The one exceptional case in which elders serve among the judges in a criminal case is in the trial of Naboth in 1 Kings 21. They are involved (along with the "nobles" [*ḥōrîm*]) apparently because Naboth's conviction for *lèse majesté* would lead to the confiscation of his ancestral land by the king (cf. the document from Alalakh that refers to the confiscation of the estate of a man convicted of *lèse majesté*[17]).[18]

None of this excludes the possibility that individual elders, on the strength of their prestige and experience, were among the appointed professional judges. Indeed, from an anthropological perspective it is certainly plausible that the authority of the elders as a group once included adjudication. But as far as the biblical evidence reflects actual practice in Israel during the biblical period, that must have been in the distant past.

To sum up: Deuteronomy assigns several legal cases to the elders. It is generally assumed that in these cases the elders, rather than appointed professional judges, serve as the judges, and this has prompted attempts to clarify whether the elders and professional judges functioned simultaneously in the same judicial system, handling different categories of cases, or whether these cases reflect different strata in the development of biblical law. But the premise of the discussion—that the elders serve as judges—is dubious since Deuteronomy never actually says that they are to engage in judicial activities. Nor is this picture contradicted in the rest of the Torah. In Exod 24:14, Moses tells the elders that in his absence Aaron and Hur, not they, will serve as judges (Exod 24:14). It seems, then, that the elders' role is different. In the cases of the insubordinate son, the accused bride, and a brother's refusal to perform levirate marriage, they serve as a public forum for procedures that require publicity, like the elders in the book of Ruth (chapter 4) and "all who entered the gate" of Hebron who witness Ephron's sale of his field and cave to Abraham (Genesis 23), and like the assemblies at Elephantine and in certain Mesopotamian documents. In the case of accidental murder, the elders' role is less clear, but there, too, they are not explicitly assigned a judicial role and it is not likely that they play one.

---

17 Pritchard, *ANET*, 546, no. 15.

18 Cf. Loewenstamm, "Notes on the Alalakh Tablets," 225 (repr., 25–26).

WORKS CITED

Berlin, A., and M. Z. Brettler, eds. *The Jewish Study Bible*. Oxford and New York: Oxford University Press, 2004.

Craigie, P. C. *The Book of Deuteronomy*. New International Commentary on the Old Testament. Grand Rapids, MI: Eerdmans, 1976.

Dougherty, R. P. *The Shirkûtu of Babylonian Deities*. YOR 5/2. New Haven, CT: Yale University Press, 1923.

Driver, S. R. *A Critical and Exegetical Commentary on Deuteronomy*. ICC. New York: Charles Scribner's Sons, 1916.

Hoffmann, D. Z. *Sefer Devarim*, vol. 2. Tel Aviv: Netsaḥ, 1961 [in Hebrew].

Levinson, B. M. *Deuteronomy and the Hermeneutics of Legal Innovation*. New York, Oxford: Oxford University Press, 1997.

Loewenstamm, S. E. "Notes on the Alalakh Tablets." *IEJ* 6 (1956): 217–25. Reprinted in his *Comparative Studies in Biblical and Ancient Oriental Literatures*, 25–26. AOAT 204. Kevelaer: Butzon & Bercker; Neukirchen-Vluyn: Neukirchener Verlag, 1980.

Luzzatto, S. D. *Il Pentateuco*, vol. 5: *Deuteronomio*. Padua: Sacchetto, 1876.

Mayes, A. D. H. *Deuteronomy*. New Century Bible Commentary. Grand Rapids, Mich.: Eerdmans; London: Marshall, Morgan & Scott, 1979.

Phillips, A. *Deuteronomy*. Cambridge Bible Commentary. Cambridge: Cambridge University Press, 1973.

Pohl, A. *Neubabylonische Rechtsurkunden aus der Berliner Staatlichen Museen*. AnOr 8. Rome: Pontifical Biblical Institute, 1933–34.

Pritchard, J. B., ed. *Ancient Near Eastern Texts Relating to the Old Testament*. Third edition with Supplement. Princeton: Princeton University Press. 1969.

Reviv, H. *The Elders in Ancient Israel: A Study of a Biblical Institution*. Jerusalem: Magnes, 1989.

Rofé, A. "The History of the Cities of Refuge in Biblical Law." In *Studies in Bible*, edited by S. Japhet, 228–30. Scripta Hierosolymitana 31. Jerusalem: Magnes Press, 1986. Reprinted in his *Deuteronomy: Issues and Interpretation*, 138–40. London: T&T Clark, 2002.

"Joshua 20: Historico-Literary Criticism Illustrated." In *Empirical Models for Biblical Criticism*, edited by J. H. Tigay, 131–47. Philadelphia: University of Pennsylvania Press, 1985.

"The Organization of the Judiciary in Deuteronomy." In *The World of the Aramaeans*, vol. 1, edited by P. M. M. Daviau, J. W. Wevers, and M. Weigl, 92–112. Sheffield: Sheffield Academic Press, 2001. Reprinted in his *Deuteronomy: Issues and Interpretation*. London and New York: T & T Clark, 2002.

Sarna, N. M. *The JPS Torah Commentary: Genesis*. Philadelphia: Jewish Publication Society, 1989.

Stol, M. *Letters from Yale*. AbB 9. Leiden: Brill, 1981.

Tanakh: The Holy Scriptures: A New Translation of the Holy Scriptures According to the Traditional Hebrew Text. Philadelphia: The Jewish Publication Society, 1985.

The Babylonian Talmud, Seder Nashim, translated into English, vols. 1–2: *Yebamoth*. Translated by I. W. Slotki. London: Soncino Press, 1936.

Weinfeld, M. *Deuteronomy and the Deuteronomic School*. Oxford: Clarendon Press, 1972.

Wells, Bruce. "Competing or Complementary? Judges and Elders in Biblical and Neo-Babylonian Law." In *Reichsrecht und Lokalrecht: Zu Konkurrenz und wechselseitigem Einfluss divergenter Rechtsordnungen im Alten Orient*, edited by H. Neumann. Beihefte zur Zeitschrift für Altorientalische und biblische Rechtsgeschichte 12. Wiesbaden: Harrassowitz, forthcoming.

Yaron, R. *Introduction to the Law of the Aramaic Papyri*. Oxford: Clarendon Press, 1961.

THE EXODUS NARRATIVE AS AN EXPRESSION OF THE COSMIC COMBAT MOTIF

SHAWN ZELIG ASTER
YESHIVA UNIVERSITY

I am very grateful for the opportunity to participate in this volume in honor of my teacher Professor Eichler. This study compares the narrative structure of Exodus 3–15 to that of the Baal Cycle and *Enūma eliš*. It is particularly appropriate that Professor Eichler, who devoted so much of his career to teaching and mentoring students with untold patience and diligence, is honored with a study that itself began as a course lecture.[1] This essay will apply some of the methodologies for which Professor Eichler is known to an issue that has been considered by comparative scholars for more than half a century.

Introduction

Any cursory reading of the Hebrew Bible will demonstrate that the event of the Exodus is narrated multiple times. The familiar story in the first fifteen chapters of the book of Exodus stands alongside such shorter narrations as Num 20:13–16, Num 33:3–5, Deut 26:5–10, Josh 24:4–7, and I Sam 12:8. We also find poetic recitations that mention many of the salient events of Exodus 1–15 in Ps 78:43–53, Ps 105:23–38, and Ps 136:10–15.[2] All this is besides the later historiography, appearing in such books as Ezra and Chronicles.

This is by no means an exhaustive catalog of all the Exodus narratives in the Hebrew Bible. But this selection of some developed narratives from the Pentateuch and Historical Prophets, along with Psalms, is broad enough to allow for a comparative literary study. The implications of the repeated mentions of the Exodus for reconstructing the

---

1 In a course entitled "Religion in Biblical Israel and the Ancient Near East" that I co-taught with Prof. Wayne Horowitz at a Summer Institute of the Rothberg International School of the Hebrew University in 2006. The present article has benefited substantially from my having had the opportunity to consider the issues together with Prof. Horowitz.

2 Besides these, a number of passages in Psalms mention only the splitting of the sea and the rescue of the Israelites. These include 66:5–8, 74:13–15, 77:15–21, and Ps 114.

history of ancient Israel have been discussed widely and provide a basis for the argument that this narrative was fundamental to ancient Israel's perception of its own origins.[3] But prior consideration of these narratives using a comparative literary approach is a desideratum.

Such an approach can clarify the features that distinguish Exodus 1–15 from the many narrative presentations of the exodus within the Hebrew Bible. The sequence of events in all these presentations includes an Israelite presence in Egypt, divine intervention in favor of Israel and/or against Egypt, and the resulting Israelite exodus from Egypt. But other events, familiar to us from Exodus 1–15, appear only in some of these narratives.

Narratological Tools for Analyzing the Transition from Event to Story

The tools used by scholars of comparative literature for comparing narratives from different cultures or media can be productively applied to comparing these narratives. These comparisons often focus on the complex transition from event to story. Two or more levels of narrative structure are frequently posited. Seymour Chatman refers to structuralist theory in arguing that:

> Each narrative has two parts: a story (histoire), the content or chain of events (actions, happenings), plus what may be called the existents (characters, items of setting); and a discourse (discours), that is the expression, the means by which the content is communicated.[4]

While this division is useful in analyzing a story and in separating between *what* is depicted and *how* it is depicted, it omits a critical intermediate stage. In order for events to become narrative discourse, some means must be found to tie together the events in a logical and directional sequence. Most narratologists follow Vladimir Propp in recognizing this intermediate stage. Propp argued that an immanent story

---

3 Because of this, many archeologists have devoted significant attention to the historicity of the whole Exodus-Conquest cycle of stories: precisely because the narrative is so pervasive in early Israelite historiography, the lack of archeological corroboration is of concern. It is in this sense that William Dever calls the Exodus stories both mythical and true: "True in that they convey forcefully later Israel's self-awareness as a liberated people" (*What Did the Biblical Writers Know*, 121). Dever raises the possibility that among the groups who coalesced into Israel was a group who indeed stemmed originally from Egypt and that "when they told the story of Israel's origins, they assumed naturally that they spoke for all Israel." His comments are important to us because they convey how central this story is in biblical thought, and how often it is repeated.

4 Chatman, *Story and Discourse*, 19.

structure can be isolated from the narrative discourse. Three stages thus emerge: the events, the story structure, and the narrative discourse that results.

Considerable effort has been devoted to developing a narrative grammar to define these stages. But since my goal here is to harness these discussions for comparative purposes, I confine myself to two highly accessible and lucid presentations of these stages.

The first such presentation is that of Barbara Herrnstein Smith.[5] In her presentation, she defines the first stage as the selection of events to be narrated.[6] The second is the "basic story," or "deep structure," terms she uses to describe a level underlying the narrative. I will use the term "basic story" to describe the way the events narrated are tied together into a logical trajectory so that they can be presented to the reader. This logical trajectory is made manifest in the narrative discourse by means of emphasis (the choice of which events to emphasize) and sequence (the order in which events are presented). Third is the narrative discourse, the stage in which "the basic story is actualized, realized, expressed, or manifested."[7] The text we have before us is the narrative discourse.

Another highly accessible discussion of the stages of narrative is that of Shlomith Rimmon-Kenan. She uses the term "story" for the intermediate stage, which I have called "basic story." Although made of separable components (the events), the "story" has a structured character, made of networks of internal relations among the events. Furthermore:

> (s)tory is an abstraction from: (1) the specific style of the text in question…, (2) the language in which the text is written (English, French, Hebrew) and (3) the medium or sign-system (words, cinematic shots, gestures). Starting with story, rather than with the text from which it is abstracted, the former may be grasped as transferable from medium to medium, from language to language, and within the same language.[8]

5 Smith, "Narrative Versions," 209–30.

6 No text can include all events, as the most patient historian will be forced to realize. A particularly lucid discussion on the importance of "choosing one's facts" can be found in Carr, "The Historian and His Facts," 3–32.

7 Smith, "Narrative Versions," 210. I have omitted her quotation marks.

8 Rimmon-Kennan, *Narrative Fiction*, 21. The discussion above summarizes some key points from ibid., 19–24.

The idea that story is transferable from medium to medium (that is, from text to text) expresses the view that story is a sort of "common structural trunk"[9] and that structure is a fundamental part of the concept of story.

Exodus 1–15 and Other Biblical Narratives of the Exodus

In my discussion, I will show how the story found in the Exodus 1–15 narrative differs from the story found in other biblical Exodus narratives. I will then compare this story to other ancient Near Eastern narratives that use it. The ways in which Exodus 1–15 differs from other biblical Exodus narratives, and the ways in which it is similar to ancient Near Eastern narratives, enable us to perceive important aspects of the message of the Exodus 1–15 narrative that are often overlooked.

Before analyzing the different basic stories found in the various Exodus narratives, it is relevant to group the narratives into two groups, based on the choice of events narrated. The first group consists of those narratives that emphasize both the mistreatment of the Israelites in Egypt and the role of a divine emissary in achieving their liberation. These include Num 20:13–16 and I Sam 12:8. Neither the plagues nor the defeat of the Egyptians is mentioned in either. The basic story that emerges from this particular sequence of events does not focus on miracles, but on divine justice, realized by means of a human savior, who carries out the basic imperative of justice, viz. to save the mistreated from their oppressor.

The second group, in contrast, contains narratives that emphasize the miraculous nature of the liberation and include the plagues among the events narrated. These speak about the defeat of the Egyptians but do not necessarily mention their mistreatment of the Israelites, focusing on the miraculous defeat of the Egyptians, not on the savior rescuing the oppressed. These include Num 33:3–5, Josh 24:4–7, as well as three passages from Psalms: 78:43–53, 105:23–38, and 136:10–15. The basic story is not one of justice through rescue from oppression, but of a miraculous victory against the Egyptians achieved through divine plagues. In most of the narratives in this group (all except Num 33:3–5), the Exodus is presented as part of a larger historical pattern of events for which Israel should be grateful.

Two of the passages, however, cross this boundary and narrate a sequence of events that includes elements found in both groups. Deut 26:5–10 includes many of the events narrated in both groups and Exod

---

9 The formulation is that of Greimas, "Elements of a Narrative Grammar," 23, as cited in Rimmon-Kenan, *Narrative Fiction*, 20.

1–15 includes all of them. Both Deut 26:5–10 and Exod 1–15 include the Egyptian mistreatment of the Israelites, divine intervention, and the miraculous nature of the plagues.[10] Since the events narrated in these passages show the strongest similarities to each other, a literary comparison between them is likely to be the most fruitful. Such a comparison shows that despite the similarity in events narrated, the basic story of each narrative differs markedly.

Above, I noted the importance of structure and logical trajectory in any discussion of "basic story." In Deut 26:5–10 that trajectory is that of the rags-to-riches motif, which is known from many civilizations, in which an individual moves from extreme privation to great wealth.[11]

> (5) My ancestor was a wandering Aramean, he went down to Egypt and with a small number of people, he dwelled there. There he became a great nation, powerful and numerous. (6) The Egyptians mistreated us and humbled us, and placed upon us difficult labor. (7) We called out to the Lord, God of our fathers. The Lord heard our voices and saw that we had been humbled, our trouble, and our oppression. (8) The Lord took us out of Egypt with a strong hand and an outstretched arm, with great terror, with signs and wonders. (9) He brought us to this place, he gave us this land, a land flowing with milk and honey.

The events narrated are intentionally ordered and formulated so as to allow this basic story to emerge. Deut 26:5 emphasizes the privation of the ancestor, v. 6 highlights the mistreatment by the Egyptians, vv. 7–8 describe the turning point in which divine intervention is engaged. The narrative concludes with the giving of the land in v. 9, emphasizing the land's great abundance. The narrative discourse, especially the details in vv. 6 and 9, thus exposes the logical trajectory that ties together the different events. It moves from the single displaced homeless

---

10 Deut 26:5–10 is somewhat more similar to the second group described above, since it narrates the Exodus as part of a larger historical sequence, beginning with the ancestors of the Israelites of the Exodus and ending with the settlement in the land of Israel, and since it omits any mention of a divine emissary. However, it narrates the mistreatment of the Israelites at the hands of the Egyptians and thus it does not properly belong in either group.

11 See the discussion by Smith, "Narrative Versions," 212–17, in which she demonstrates that the studies of the Cinderella story by Cox (*Cinderella; Three Hundred and Forty-Five Variants*) and by Rooth (*The Cinderella Cycle*) incorrectly assume that all such stories have a common origin. Smith also notes the difficulties in defining which stories share a common "basic story" or "deep structure," and suggests that rags-to-riches stories develop in many cultures and that the stories defined as "Cinderella" stories are all developments of this motif.

ancestor, with "a small number of people," to the "us/here," a nation living in a land flowing with milk and honey. By identifying the homeless ancestor with the us/here, a rags-to-riches trajectory is created.

The rags-to-riches motif, however, is only part of the message of the narrative. The details in vv. 7 and 8 emphasize the attentive and miraculous nature of the divine intervention. Along with the rags-to-riches motif, these aspects of the divine intervention teach the lesson of the landed Israelite's indebtedness to God, the munificent benefactor who transmuted the homeless ancestor into a nation with a rich land.

Exodus 1–15

The narrative of Exodus 1–15, despite its far greater length, narrates events similar to those found in Deut 26:6–8. But a very different basic story is used to order these events and create a logical trajectory.

In these chapters, the basic story is the battle for supremacy between God and Pharaoh. The question of Israel's redemption from Egypt takes an almost secondary position in some portions of this narrative. In the initial exposition in Exod 3:7–11, Moses' mission is described as "to Pharaoh," and the mission "to the children of Israel" is mentioned only in 3:13, in Moses' response. Verses 15–22 in chapter 3 are the most detailed exposition of the dual nature of Moses' mission: to the Israelites and to Pharaoh. Even in these verses, the goal of speaking to the Israelites is clearly to gather the Israelite elders for a meeting with Pharaoh. In 3:18, Moses and the elders are to come to Pharaoh and demand that the Israelites be allowed to acknowledge God's sovereignty through worship, not that they be liberated from servitude. This demand highlights the pith of the conflict between God and Pharaoh, because acknowledging God's sovereignty is exactly what Pharaoh refuses to do. At this point in the narrative (3:19–20), the future conflict over sovereignty between God and Pharaoh is predicted:

> (19) But I know that Egypt's king will not allow you to go, unless by a strong arm. (20) So I will send my arm and strike Egypt with all my wonders that I will work in his midst, and afterwards he will release you.

Thus, the opening of the narrative sets up a conflict whose topic is sovereignty over Israel. It explicitly refers to the role of "wonders" (נפלאות) in resolving this conflict. These wonders are narrated as a demonstration of God's sovereignty over Pharaoh.[12]

---

12 Source critics have noted that different sources in Exodus use different terms to refer to these wonders. The passage discussed here is usually attributed to E. But the wonders, by whatever name they are designated, appear in passages attributed to each source.

Two points bear noting. First, narrating the plagues in this way is a deliberate choice. The narrative of the plagues in Ps 78:43–53 presents the plagues as a series of attacks on the Egyptians and as an integral part of the process of liberating the Israelites. It does this by focusing on the harm they caused to the Egyptians (omitting Exodus' dialogues and confrontations between Moses and Pharaoh) and by embedding this narrative between two mentions of God's liberating the Israelites, in vv. 42 and 52–53. Similarly, the brief narrative in Deut 26:8 presents the "signs and wonders" as part of the process of liberation, omitting any mention of the confrontations between Moses and Pharaoh.

In contrast, Exodus 7–12 uses the dialogues between Moses and Pharaoh to tie together the events of the plagues and to create a very different basic story. Nahum Sarna has shown that elements recorded in the Moses-Pharaoh encounters in these chapters serve to organize the plagues in a rigidly ordered pattern.[13] The dialogues also expose the purpose of the plagues: in 8:7, "that you may know that none is like the Lord our God"; in 8:18, "that you may know that I am the Lord in the midst of the land"; in 9:16 "in order to show you my strength and to tell my Name throughout the world"; and in 9:29, "that you may know that the earth is the Lord's." In these passages, the purpose of the plagues is clearly to demonstrate the sovereignty of God over Pharaoh. The basic story of the plagues in Exodus 7–12 is not that the plagues arrived in order to facilitate the liberation of the Israelites, but to demonstrate divine sovereignty over Pharaoh.

The second point is that this emphasis is not restricted to texts associated with one particular strand among those identified by source critics in Exodus 1–15. A full discussion of the source critical work on these chapters (or even on Exodus 7–11, which are most relevant to our discussion) is well beyond the scope of the present essay, but most scholars detect three sources in these chapters (besides the redactional strata).[14] The material attributed to the E source demonstrates this most blatantly, and the verses cited above from chapters 8 and 9 are usually attributed to E. But material attributed to other sources makes a similar point, as in 11:9, "Pharaoh will not heed you, that my wonders be multiplied in the land of Egypt"[15] and 7:5, "And Egypt will know that I am YHWH, in my extending my arm over Egypt" is attributed to P.

---

13 For the elements of this pattern, see Sarna, *Exploring Exodus*, 76–78. Sarna notes that "(t)he meaning and function of the structural symmetry are always to emphasize that what has occurred is the vindication of God's active presence in the life of the world" (ibid., 78).

14 See the bibliographical notes in Propp, *Exodus 1–18*, 310.

15 This verse is seen by Eissfeldt as the beginning of a P passage. Even Propp,

The similar vocabulary used in verses attributed to different sources also highlights this emphasis: 7:5 uses the phrase "to know the Lord," to indicate acceptance of Divine Sovereignty, and very similar phrases are used in 8:7 and 18 and in 9:16 and 29 (cited above), attributed to E. These formulations cast the issue of recognizing Divine Sovereignty, rather than release of the Israelites, as the pith of the conflict driving the narrative. Thus, in a summary of the argument at the very beginning of the encounter between Moses and Pharaoh, in Exod 5:2 (variously attributed to J and E), Pharaoh brazenly states "I have not known the Lord. Moreover I will not release Israel."[16]

Since the basic story joining together the events of the plagues is the conflict over sovereignty, it is necessary for the narrative to explain how the plagues relate to the Israelites (such an explanation is unnecessary in the other narratives of the exodus, in which the events of the plagues are tied together by the basic story of the liberation of Israel). Such an explanation is provided first in 10:2 (variously assigned to J or E), in which Moses is told that the plagues are accomplished for the benefit of future generations of Israelites "that you may tell into your son's ears and your son's son how I toyed with Egypt and my signs that I set among them, that *you* may know that I am the Lord."

This statement echoes the emphasis on re-telling the events of the Exodus, found in chapters 12 and 13. In those chapters, the re-telling is explicitly linked to the Passover festival. According to 12:25–26, re-telling the events of the final plague is the purpose and goal of the festival. In 13:9, and again in 13:14, a more general formulation for the re-telling is given, which includes all the events of the plagues: "With a strong arm the Lord took us out from Egypt." The re-telling is specifically associated with the Paschal lamb ceremony, but other elements of the festival are also connected to the commemoration of the plagues. The abstention from leaven is included as part of this commemoration in

---

who assigns the overwhelming majority of the plagues material to E, sees this as a redactional intrusion (Eissfeldt, *The Old Testament*, 189; Propp, *Exodus 1–18*, 292).

16 Childs has argued that in the material assigned to P, it is only the events at the Sea that demonstrate YHWH's sovereignty to the Egyptians and that it is in 14:4 and 8 that the program of 7:5 is accomplished (see the very clear discussion in Childs, *The Book of Exodus*, 140). But Propp has noted in several places that P's narrative of the plagues assumes knowledge of JE prototypes (Propp, *Exodus 1–18*, 286–317). Thus, while the demonstration of YHWH's sovereignty reaches its culmination at the sea in the material assigned to P, one cannot argue that the plagues in P are entirely disconnected from this goal.

13:6–7 (the "sign" on the arm and the "memorial" or "frontlets" between the eyes are also said to commemorate this "strong arm" in 13:9 and 13:16).[17]

The narrative trajectory here is fascinating. In the other biblical passages discussed above, the events of the exodus from Egypt are narrated using the trajectory Enslavement-Liberation-Exodus. But here, that trajectory is interrupted by the laws ordaining the festival commemorating aspects of the Exodus. As the culmination of the conflict over sovereignty is about to be reached, the festival celebrating this sovereignty is ordained. As 10:2 indicates, the plague narrative, with its conflict between Pharaoh and God, leads up not to the liberation of the Israelites but to the festival, with its recital of Divine Sovereignty.

The basic story underlying the presentation of events leads up to a present and future festival that celebrates the Exodus as an expression of divine power, at least as much as it leads up to the actual liberation of the Israelites. The inclusion of this element as part of the events narrated is unique to this narrative and deserves careful consideration.

So too does the inclusion of the Red Sea events, narrated in chapter 14. This narrative in this chapter seems designed to provide a climax to the narrative in chapters 3–13. Themes found in the earlier chapters are resumed, including the demand that Pharaoh "know that I am the Lord" (14:8 and 18, echoing 7:5 and 17) and the portrayal of the divine arm plaguing Pharaoh (14:31, echoing 3:20, 6:1, 7:5, 9:3). Moses' arm, stretched out over the sea, represents the arm of God, which is seen as the motivator of the plagues in the previous chapters, and Egypt recognizes that it is ranged against God in a battle: "for it is the Lord who fights for them against Egypt." (14:25). Most important is the double-entendre found in Exod 14:17–18:

> And I will achieve glory over Pharaoh and over all his force, over his chariotry and his horsemen. And Egypt will know that I am the Lord, through my achieving glory over Pharaoh, over his chariotry and his horsemen.

The verb אכבדה, here translated "I will achieve glory," also means "I will deal harshly." The harsh dealing of YHWH against Egypt is what has allowed God to be recognized as sovereign. The conflict for supremacy, which forms the basic story of the plagues narrative and

17 The source attribution of this material is debated. Although clearly similar to much of the material attributed to E, the emphasis on re-telling history has led some to argue that these passages were inserted by a Deuteronomic or Deuteronomistic redactor. See the summary of the discussion in Propp, *Exodus 1–18*, 376.

which is encapsulated in the challenge to "know the Lord," is now decisively won by God. The verb "to battle" in 14:14 and 14:23 describes the conflict that has been ongoing since chapter 3.[18]

The "Basic Story" of Exodus 1–15

Thus, the overall structure, or "basic story," of the Exodus 1–15 narrative can be described as:

(1) An initial exposition of the conflict between God and Pharaoh for sovereignty over the earth, which will be determined by the question of Israel's release from Egypt;

(2) An ongoing conflict in which the plagues are vehicles for achieving Pharaoh's recognition of Divine Sovereignty;

(3) A festival celebrating the achieving of Divine Sovereignty, which led to the release of the Israelites;

(4) The final climactic victory at the sea.

In considering the various narratives of the Exodus in the biblical corpus, and especially when compared to Deut 26:5–10, this is indeed a unique "basic story." No other narrative places the fate of the Israelites in a comparative secondary position and narrates the Enslavement-Liberation-Exodus cycle with such attention to the conflict over Sovereignty.

Although the Conflict over Sovereignty occupies a prominent place throughout Exodus 1–15, Cross focused on its presence in Exodus 15, and excluded the preceding 14 narrative chapters from his discussion. He saw in this "epic" a reflection of the Ugaritic motif of the battle of a god against the sea, which biblical writers identified with a historical battle in which YHWH defeated the Egyptians at the Sea of Reeds.

> In choosing the event of the sea, Israel drew upon available symbols and language which retained power and meaning even when the old mythic patters which gave them birth had been attenuated or broken by Israel's austere historical consciousness.[19]

---

[18] The passages cited are all usually attributed to P, and it is generally held that the events at the Sea of Reeds are the culmination of the demonstration of Divine Sovereignty in P, and serve a function similar to that of the plagues in material attributed to E (see above note 16). But the battle of YHWH against Egypt at the Sea of Reeds is represented in all sources, and the specific language of "YHWH fighting Egypt" is found in 14:25 (attributed to E), and again in 15:3–4, the antiquity of which is generally acknowledged, along with that of the rest of the Song.

[19] Cross, *Canaanite Myth*, 138.

But it is important to recognize that the literary context of Exodus 15 must play a prominent part in this discussion. Exodus 15 is part of a larger literary whole and its focus on Divine Sovereignty mirrors and complements a literary emphasis found in the preceding narrative. The signal contribution of Exodus 15 to this motif is the explicit mention of the establishment of a sanctuary, established by God, in which his sovereignty is celebrated: "An establishment for you to dwell You have fashioned O Lord, a Temple, O God, have Your hands established. The Lord shall reign forever and ever" (Exod 15:17–18).

Thus, the trajectory of the narrative in Exodus 1–15 can be expanded, and it includes:

(1) An initial exposition of the conflict between God and Pharaoh for sovereignty over the earth;
(2) Pharaoh's recognition of Divine Sovereignty, achieved by means of the plagues;
(3) A festival celebrating the achieving of Divine Sovereignty;
(4) The final climactic victory at the sea, which resumes the themes exposed in the plagues;
(5) The establishment of the Temple, connected to the Sovereignty of God.

Ancient Near Eastern Sources to the "Basic Story" in Exodus 1–15

This list will prove extremely important to understanding the origins and rhetorical thrust of the "basic story" in Exodus 1–15.

Cassuto was among the first to probe Exodus 15 for similarities to the expressions and motifs appearing in the Ugaritic material.[20] Cross also noted similarities between the events described in Exodus 15, on the one hand, and those of the Baal cycle from Ugarit and *Enūma eliš*, on the other.[21] Although Cross accepted the argument of Jacobsen, suggesting a connection between *Enūma eliš* and the Ugaritic myth of Baal's battle with Yamm, no incontrovertible connection between these two epics could be established at the time.[22] Hanson also addressed the similarities between these conflict myths and argued for much broader

20 Cassuto, "The Israelite Epic," 121–42 (translated in Cassuto, *Biblical and Oriental Studies*, 69–109).

21 Cross, *Canaanite Myth*, 93. Cross notes the following structure to the Baal cycle: Threat; Combat-Victory; Building of a Temple; Banquet Celebration; Manifestation of Baal's Universal Reign; Theophany of the Divine Warrior; Fertility of Restored Order.

22 Jacobsen, "Battle between Marduk and Tiamat," 104–8.

connections to apocalyptic literature.[23] The scholarship on the structural connections between the Baal cycle and *Enūma eliš*, and between the Baal cycle and several biblical passages, has been surveyed by Rummel.[24]

More recent research has shown that there is a specific connection between the Mesopotamian *Enūma eliš* and the Ugaritic Baal narrative, which were seen as related in antiquity. Jean-Marie Durand demonstrated that in Aleppo in the eighteenth century BCE, Adad was considered to have defeated Tiamat in battle, and the arms that he is said to have used were enshrined in a temple.[25] Furthermore, Durand has shown that several characteristics link Adad and Marduk:

(1) Both are considered gods of justice, above personal desires;
(2) Both provide the basis for human rulership and royalty;
(3) The sovereignty of both derives from the victory each won over the original chaos and, as such, both Marduk and Adad are considered to be the source of order in society.

The perception that the narratives were related in antiquity derives from the fact that the events described in them are similar, and they share a "basic story." Any analysis of the two epics connected with these gods shows that the similarity in "basic story" goes beyond the cosmic combat. In both narratives, the victorious god replaces an older god. At the conclusion of both narratives, the victorious god becomes sovereign and his sovereignty is recited and celebrated in a cultic ritual. Particular temples were connected to this recital, and this is a key element of the epic, as Durand has shown from the mention of the enshrining of the weapons of Adad. The shared features of *Enūma eliš* and the Baal Cycle are precisely those that are unique to the Exodus 1–15 narrative.

These features include a divinity battling to achieve sovereignty and winning a decisive victory over the forces of disorder; this sovereignty serving as the basis for order in the society that venerates this deity; the dedication of a festival celebrating this achievement of sovereignty; and finally, the recital at this festival of the acts by which the deity achieved sovereignty.

Since these features were well known in the ancient Near East and were part of a known and defined literary "trajectory," "basic story," or central motif as early as the thirteenth century BCE, it would appear that

---

23 P. Hanson in "Zechariah 9," 37–59, and later in *The Dawn of Apocalyptic*.

24 Rummel, "Narrative Structures," 221–332.

25 Durand, "Le combat entre le dieu," 41–61.

their appearance in Exodus 1–15 is not accidental. Rather, the narrative of Exodus 1–15 uses these specific elements as the "basic story" that structures its unique narrative of the Enslavement-Liberation-Exodus cycle. Only by recognizing the uniqueness of the "basic story" in the Exodus 1–15 narrative, which differs from those of the many Enslavement-Liberation-Exodus narratives in the Bible, can one recognize the similarity between this "basic story" and that of two other ancient Near Eastern narratives that treat Divine Sovereignty, the Baal Cycle and *Enūma eliš*.

Conclusion

Exodus 1–15 uses the events of the Enslavement-Liberation-Exodus cycle and structures these around the "basic story" used in Divine Sovereignty narratives known in the ancient Near East. By referencing and using this basic story, Exodus 1–15 deliberately argues for a different perspective on Divine Sovereignty. *Inter alia*, it argues that:

(1) Creation is disconnected from the battle for Divine Sovereignty;

(2) YHWH has no predecessor, and his sovereignty did not begin with a battle;

(3) YHWH does not battle other gods, but only powerful humans.

The combination of event and basic story that we find in the Exodus 1–15 narrative then exercises a decisive influence on later biblical writers. One example of this, which merits further discussion, can be found in Isa 10:5–12:6. Throughout this unit (much of which I attribute to the late eighth-century prophet) references to Divine Sovereignty are tied to the Exodus motif. Thus, the defeat of the Assyrian challengers is compared to God's battle in Egypt (10:26), the return of Israelites from Assyrian exile in 11:15–16 uses phrases that evoke the splitting of the sea in Exodus 14, and Isaiah 12 is modeled on Exodus 15. All these are part of a process leading to universal recognition of Divine Sovereignty, as is clear from Isa 10:9: "The earth will be as full of knowledge of YHWH as the water covers the sea."

In this passage and in many others, Exodus 1–15 plays a key role in connecting the concept of Divine Sovereignty to the event of the Exodus.

WORKS CITED

Carr, E. H. "The Historian and His Facts." In *What Is History?* New York: Knopf, 1962.

Cassuto, U. "The Israelite Epic" (in Hebrew). *Kenesset* 8 (1943): 121–42. *Biblical and Oriental Studies*, vol. 2. Translated by I. Abrahams. Jerusalem: Magnes, 1973.

Chatman, S. *Story and Discourse: Narrative Structure in Fiction and Film.* Ithaca, N.Y.: Cornell University Press, 1978.

Childs, B. *The Book of Exodus.* OTL. Philadelphia: Westminster, 1974.

Cox, M. R. *Cinderella; Three Hundred and Forty-Five Variants.* London: The Folk-Lore Society, 1893.

Cross, F. M. *Canaanite Myth and Hebrew Epic: Essays in the History of the Religion of Israel.* Cambridge, Mass.: Harvard University Press, 1973.

Dever, W. *What Did the Biblical Writers Know, and When Did They Know It? What Archaeology Can Tell Us about the Reality of Ancient Israel.*" Grand Rapids, Mich.: Eerdman's Pub. Co., 2001.

Durand, J. M. "Le combat entre le dieu de l'orage et la mer." *MARI* 7 (1993): 41–61.

Eissfeldt, O. *The Old Testament: An Introduction.* Translated by P. Ackroyd. New York: Harper, 1965.

Greimas, A. J. "Elements of a Narrative Grammar." *Diacritics* 7.1 (1977): 23–40.

Hanson, P. "Zechariah 9 and the Recapitulation of an Ancient Ritual Pattern." *JBL 92.1* (1973): 37–59.

The Dawn of Apocalyptic: The Historical and Sociological Roots of Jewish Apocalyptic Eschatology. Philadelphia: Fortress, 1975; rev. ed., 1979.

Jacobsen, T. "The Battle between Marduk and Tiamat." *JAOS* 88.1 (1968): 104–8.

Propp, W. H. C. *Exodus 1–18.* Anchor Bible 2. New Haven, Conn.: Yale University Press, 1998.

Rimmon-Kennan, S. *Narrative Fiction: Contemporary Poetics.* Florence: Routledge, 1983.

Rooth, A. B. *The Cinderella Cycle.* Lund: C. W. K. Gleerup, 1951.

Rummel, S. "Narrative Structures in the Ugaritic Texts." In *Ras Shamra Parallels: The Texts from Ugarit and the Bible*, vol. 3, edited by L. R. Fisher, 221–332. AnOr 51. Rome: Pontifical Biblical Institute, 1981.

Sarna, N. M. *Exploring Exodus: The Heritage of Biblical Israel*. New York: Schocken, 1986.

Smith, B. H. "Narrative Versions, Narrative Theories." In *On Narrative*, edited by W. J. T. Mitchell, 209–32. Chicago, Ill.: University of Chicago Press, 1980.

WHAT IS THE BOOK OF JOB ABOUT?*

ADELE BERLIN
UNIVERSITY OF MARYLAND

What is the Book of Job about? The standard response is: The book is about why the righteous suffer. But if this is the book's main question, it leaves us without an answer. Because we were privy to what transpired in heaven between the *Satan* and God, we know that Job's suffering resulted from a wager to see if he would abandon his piety when it brought him no reward. But that explanation cannot satisfy Job. Job, confined as he is to an earthly perspective, spends most of the book searching for a reason for his suffering, but the reasons put forth by his friends—that suffering results from sin or that it is a form of divine discipline—are rejected by Job and, indeed, the author wants us, the readers, to reject them, too. Job never does find a reason for his suffering. What Job *does* find in the end, I suggest, is an acceptance of his human condition.

While the question of suffering forms the hinge around which the book revolves, I view it more as a pretext, a point of entrée, to a larger set of questions with which biblical wisdom literature concerns itself. Wisdom literature as found in Job and in Ecclesiastes poses questions to which there are no ready-made answers. It pushes ideas to their furthest limit, examining in the most abstract way the nature of humanity, the nature of God, and the nature of the universe. In the case of Job, as in Ecclesiastes, the underlying problem is how to understand the human condition, of which suffering is a definitive part. Both Job and Ecclesiastes use the word *'amal*, "toil, trouble," to signify world-weariness, the burdensomeness of life. Ecclesiastes inquires into the purpose of life, asking what in human life is of lasting value. The book of Job poses a related question. While many people see in Job an inquiry into the nature of God and his justice, I want to read Job as putting the emphasis more on the nature of humans and less on God, although in the end Job

---

* An earlier version of this essay was presented at the Awards Ceremony for the John Templeton Awards for Theological Promise, Heidelberg, May 23, 2008. I am pleased to dedicate it to my dear friend and colleague Barry Eichler, a man who is תם וישר וירא אלהים וסר מרע.

will admittedly learn about himself by learning more about God. I would say that the book of Job is an inquiry into the human condition and what it means to be a human being.

Job initially resists the idea that suffering is part of his humanity, for to accept suffering is to admit an imperfection in the human condition; and Job is not only perfect, he is a perfectionist. Job, of course, is more advanced than his friends in regard to life and suffering, for his friends assume that a life free of suffering is at least theoretically possible if one does not sin. Job knows, from his own bitter experience, that to be sinless does not necessarily mean to be free of suffering. But he fights long and hard against the conclusion that sinlessness and suffering may not be mutually exclusive. Carol Newsom, who has written brilliantly about the book of Job, puts it more elegantly: "The human passion for moral order...is a passion to deny the tragic in existence."[1] This tension between a moral universe and human tragedy and suffering is at the heart of the book and it is never resolved, except to conclude, as we shall see, that suffering is a natural part of the world order. In a way, albeit a somewhat simplistic way, Job told us that in the prologue (2:10): "Shall we accept the good from God and not accept the bad?" The Job of the prologue may have known this all along, but the Job of the dialogues needed to probe the tension in depth.

So if we do not learn the reason for human suffering, what is it that we learn from the book of Job? Like all wisdom writing, the book of Job is a search for Wisdom. The famous poem on wisdom in chapter 28 expresses this most explicitly. "Where can wisdom be found? Where does wisdom come from?" It is not an object to be found by humans anywhere in the cosmos, even in its deepest recesses or at its farthest reaches. Only God knows its source, for wisdom belongs to God; it is the principle by which he created the universe. A similar idea is found in Prov 8:22–31, where Wisdom says: "The Lord created me at the beginning of his course, as the first of his works of old. In the distant past I was fashioned, at the beginning, at the origin of earth." Proverbs wants to demonstrate the antiquity of wisdom, which existed prior to the cosmos, and thereby to prove its value and authority. Proverbs takes the position that wisdom is easily accessible to everyone who seeks it. Wisdom is a woman calling out at the crossroads, at the city gate, at every public place, encouraging everyone to learn her ways (Prov 8:1–11). Wisdom in Proverbs is the commonly accepted traditional wisdom, the sum of generations of human teachings, of the type that Job's friends advocate.

---

1 Newsom, *The Book of Job*, 253.

In Job, however, the commonly accepted wisdom has been shown to have its limitations. One might say that the book of Job problematizes the wisdom of Proverbs. Job requires a level of wisdom beyond what the tradition has to offer. Human beings cannot acquire this higher level of wisdom on their own, for it is in the domain of God and it must be "revealed" to them by God. As Job 28:23 says, answering its question about where wisdom can be found: "God understands the way to it; He knows its source." The implication is that any wisdom that humans acquire is a gift from God. We see clearly here that the ancients, unlike post-enlightenment moderns, did not make an impenetrable barrier between religion and science. Rather, they saw religion as the path leading to knowledge. Chapter 28 says that the way humans acquire wisdom is by fearing God: "To fear the Lord is wisdom, to shun evil is understanding" (28:28). The same message is found in Proverbs and in Ecclesiastes, so all the biblical wisdom books agree that piety is a prerequisite for wisdom. Michael Fox is, therefore, correct when he says of the book of Job that "the teaching of the book is essentially pietistic, which is to say, it makes faith the prime virtue."[2] And he is also correct to insist that Job is pious and that he remains so throughout the book. Job is not the skeptic or religious rebel that some have made him out to be. In fact, the first thing we are told about Job is that he was God-fearing and shunned evil. These words of the narrator are confirmed by God (1:8) and later by Eliphaz (4:6), so there is no doubt about Job's piety. And we can deduce from this that Job is also wise, at least in the traditional sense, although his friends may not always think so and Job himself may be entertaining serious doubts. The problem is that Job's traditional wisdom has proved to be insufficient in his present circumstance; it cannot explain his suffering. Human wisdom has reached its limits.

Towards the end of the book, in what readers rightly take to be its climax, Job is given a glimpse of what I will call divine wisdom, by which I mean wisdom in its most perfect and complete form, the kind of wisdom by which God created the world.[3] It is the wisdom to which humans aspire but can never fully reach. This wisdom is revealed to Job during the theophanic encounter with God, who speaks to him out of

---

2 Fox, "Job the Pious," 351.

3 Mayer Gruber also speaks of human and divine wisdom, but he then equates human wisdom with the wisdom of non-Israelites, as opposed to the wisdom of Israel. I do not think this opposition is present in the book. The wisdom of Job's non-Israelite friends is similar to the wisdom of Proverbs. Indeed, there are no Israelite characters in the book (with the exception of God). See Gruber, "Human and Divine Wisdom," 88–102.

the windstorm (chapters 38–41). Several scholars have described these God-speeches in terms of the sublime: the description of something that is indescribable, that exceeds the imagination, that evokes the feeling of being overwhelmed by something too vast or too powerful to be grasped by the mind. The sublime is an experience rather than an object. It evokes a sense of elation and awe, a sense of being transported to a different level of existence. This has led some scholars to conclude that the sublime replaces the rational with the emotional. Yet I doubt that the book of Job would move away from the root of wisdom thought, which is based on reason, and surely not on emotion. And besides, the dichotomy between reason and emotion is very unbiblical. So Tod Linafelt and Carol Newsom, who have each independently invoked the idea of the sublime in their discussions of these God-speeches, are correct that reason is involved, albeit a different type or level of reason. Newsom refers to the "aesthetic dimensions of understanding," a phrase that clearly makes a place for cognition, as well as for emotion.[4] Linafelt notes that the sublime "is the feeling evoked by that which exceeds the imagination. It is literally *unpresentable,* that is, it cannot be comprehended by the imagination and therefore cannot be *presented* in a way that allows one to understand. The object of the sublime...can only be *apprehended* not comprehended."[5] But later he speaks of "a second movement of thought, in which reason triumphs in its ability to *conceive* that which the imagination is unable to *represent.*"[6] In other words, the mind can conceive of the unimaginable. Job is able to conceive of a world more terrifyingly beautiful than can be imagined or adequately described, even by the magnificent rhetoric of the divine speeches.

The divine speeches present verbal pictures of the edge of the cosmos where chaos and creation meet—the mysterious place far from human habitation where darkness turns to dawn, where snow and hail are stored, where wild animals go about their lives unaided by man. In that place are, to put it in more modern terms, the denizens of outer space (the constellations), and the dinosaur and the Loch Ness Monster, which is how I like to think of the Behemot and the Leviathan. If science fiction had been invented in ancient Israel, this would have been the place to use it. But, of course, the purpose of these images was not to stretch the imagination or to entertain. Nor was it to frighten Job into submission, as some people might think. It was to lift Job to a new level of reality, a God's-eye view of the universe, where all things, even suf-

---

4 Newsom, *The Book of Job*, 236.

5 Linafelt, "The Wizard of Uz," 101.

6 Ibid., 103.

fering and death, have their place and God does not have to explain why. Human concepts of morality do not pertain here.[7] From a human perspective, this is not a perfect place, for it includes elements of chaos that, though under God's control, continue to be present in the universe; moreover, they are cared for by God, on whom they depend for their existence. For all that God's speeches may appear terrifying, I also find them comforting, for they reassure us and Job that the world was indeed created through divine wisdom and that it continues to operate that way.

This higher dimension of wisdom enables Job to accept his humanity, along with its suffering. This acceptance is not resignation, but a celebration of existence, the result of the experience of the sublime.[8] Job's death-wish, which hung so heavy in the first part of the book, has vanished. Job has been granted something even more precious than an explanation for his suffering. He has experienced for a brief moment something of divine wisdom, a kind of wisdom that surpasses human wisdom although it is the source of human wisdom. Job has seen more of divine wisdom than any other person, and it has changed him forever.

It may be instructive to compare Job with Utnapishtim, the survivor of the flood in the *Gilgamesh Epic*. That epic is concerned with the quest for immortality, which is a different facet of the inquiry into the human condition. Utnapishtim is the only person (along with his wife) ever to have transcended his human-ness, his mortality, by having been granted eternal life. The Hebrew Bible has no counterpart; no one in the Hebrew Bible lives forever. But I have come to view Job as a parallel to Utnapishtim in that both men were granted a divine gift given to no other person: immortality for Utnapishtim and a first-hand encounter with divine wisdom for Job.[9] It is interesting that the Garden of Eden story, the Bible's etiology of human mortality, equates the loss of immortality with the gaining of wisdom, the knowledge of good and

---

7 The idea that the natural world is amoral, having no principle of natural justice, is found in Matitiahu Tsevat and accepted by Norman Habel, *The Book of Job*, 65.

8 See Newsom, *The Book of Job*, 256.

9 It seems that the Mesopotamian idea of what distinguishes the gods from humans is that the gods are immortal and humans are not. While this idea is also present in Gen 3:22 and 6:3, for the most part, the Hebrew Bible identifies God's divinity not by his immortality but by the fact that he created the world and rules over it as sovereign. Thus it is fitting that God demonstrates to Job his sovereignty by recounting the wisdom whereby he created the universe.

evil. Both qualities are God-like. "Indeed, the man has become like one of us, knowing good and evil; so now, what if he were to put out his hand and take also from the tree of life and eat, and live forever." (Gen 3:22). If, says Genesis, human beings have God-like wisdom, they may not also have God-like immortality. So, too, Gilgamesh, "who saw the wellspring" and "was wise in all things" (*Gilg* I 1, 5), was denied immortality.[10] Wisdom is, then, both a blessing and a curse. Wisdom is what makes humans God-like and also what makes them mortal. This, I think, is what Job learned from his encounter with God.

It is in this context that I want to understand Job's last words (42:5–6):

לְשֵׁמַע־אֹזֶן שְׁמַעְתִּיךָ וְעַתָּה עֵינִי רָאָתְךָ.
עַל־כֵּן אֶמְאַס וְנִחַמְתִּי עַל־עָפָר וָאֵפֶר.

I translate: "I heard you through hearing and now my eyes have seen you. Therefore I reject and change my mind about dust and ashes."[11] In v. 5, hearing, which represents traditional teaching as told by one generation to another, is joined by seeing, Job's own first-hand encounter with God.[12] These are the two modes of knowing that are placed in opposition throughout most of the book, with the friends advocating the first—wisdom of the ages—and Job relying on the second—his own experience, which includes the divine theophany.[13] At the end of the book these two opposing modes come together and Job reaches a unified understanding of God. Verse 6 is enigmatic and numerous interpretations have been proposed. I prefer to interpret it in the context of my argument about Job's acceptance of his human condition. Having achieved a more complete understanding of divine wisdom, Job regrets having spoken as he did before, when he set up the opposition between the divine and the human, played out as a contest between himself and

---

10 Translation from Foster, *Epic of Gilgamesh*, 3.

11 My translation of v. 6 is close to that of Edwin Good (*In Turns of Tempest*, 26, 375–78) but my interpretation is slightly different. This verse was recently discussed by Daniel Timmer, "God's Speeches, Job's Responses," 298–300. Timmer's translation (ibid., 300) is close to mine: "Therefore I reject and repent concerning my human frailty."

12 On this interpretation of שמע אזן see Tsevat, "The Meaning of the Book of Job," 206.

13 Habel, *The Book of Job*, 68, writes that "The message of Job...is bound up with the interplay of tradition and experience." Edward Greenstein develops the opposition between tradition and experience at length in "'On My Skin and in My Flesh,'" 333–62. I would note that Qohelet, too, bases his conclusion on experience, even experiments.

God. Job now rejects that opposition, and aligns himself with God rather than against him. He no longer wants to take God to court; he no longer wishes to die in order to escape from God. He accepts, and I like to think he takes comfort in, being dust and ashes, in being a mortal human being, which means being subject to suffering.[14] For, after all, humans were fashioned by the same wisdom through which God created the world and they, like all the exotic phenomena and strange creatures in the divine speeches, continue to be cared for by God. One senses that Job is now more at ease with himself and his place in the world.

If Job was wise at the beginning of the story, he is even wiser at its end, especially about God's ways. His wisdom far surpasses that of his friends, who "did not speak correctly" about God as Job did (42:7). And we the readers, who saw in the prologue a God that Job did not see and thought that we knew more about the workings of God than Job knew, must now admit that our knowledge of God was also severely limited. By learning first-hand about God's wisdom, Job learned about what it means to be human. Our human-ness is most evident in our drive to acquire wisdom at any price, as we see from the Garden of Eden story, a story which, by the way, not only says that the acquisition of wisdom eliminated the possibility of immortality, but also tells us that the result of this acquisition is that the human condition is one of pain and toil. At the same time, despite God's concern that wisdom renders humans God-like, human wisdom will never reach the level of God's wisdom. It can only approximate divine wisdom when it is accompanied by the fear of the Lord, the Bible's *sine qua non* for wisdom. This, of course, is the teaching of all the biblical wisdom books. Job, however, needed to learn it for himself, for throughout the book Job based his knowledge on personal experience rather than on traditional teachings. Does the book of Job, then, add nothing to the traditional teachings? Does it take us on that tortuous journey of the mind only to return us empty to our starting-place? Yes and no. Like Gilgamesh, whose quest for immortality is the flip side of Job's quest for understanding, we return home without the answer we set out to find, but we are much wiser for the journey. So what does the book add to traditional teachings? Let me suggest that if traditional teaching says that the fear of the Lord leads to wisdom, the book of Job shows that wisdom leads to the fear of the Lord.

---

14 עפר ואפר. For the meaning "mortal," as opposed to God, see Gen 18:27; Job 30:19; and also (in part) Ps 103:14. That humans are dust evokes Gen 2:7, the Garden of Eden story, whose undercurrents I have noted at several points in this paper.

WORKS CITED*

Clines, David J. A. *Job 1–20*. Word Biblical Commentary 17. Waco, Tex.: Word Books, 1989.

Job 21–37. Word Biblical Commentary 18. Dallas, Tex.: Word Books, 2006.

Cooper, Alan. "The Sense of the Book of Job." *Prooftexts* 17 (1997): 227–44.

Fox, Michael V. "Job the Pious." *ZAW* 117.3 (2005): 351–66.

Geller, Stephen A. "Nature's Answer: The Meaning of the Book of Job in Its Intellectual Context." In *Judaism and Ecology; Created World and Revealed Word*, edited by Hava Tirosh-Samuelson, 109–32. Cambridge, Mass: Center for the Study of World Religions, Harvard Divinity School, 2002.

Good, Edwin M. *In Turns of Tempest: A Reading of Job, with a Translation*. Stanford, Calif.: Stanford University Press, 1990.

Greenstein, Edward L. "'On My Skin and in My Flesh': Personal Experience as a Source of Knowledge in the Book of Job." In *Bringing the Hidden to Light: The Process of Interpretation. Studies in Honor of Stephen A. Geller*, edited by K. F. Kravitz and D. M. Sharon, 63–77. Winona Lake, Ind.: Eisenbrauns, 2007.

"The Problem of Evil in the Book of Job." In *Mishneh Todah. Studies in Deuteronomy and Its Cultural Environment in Honor of Jeffrey H. Tigay*, edited by Nili Sacher Fox, David A. Glatt-Gilad, and Michael J. Williams, 333–62. Winona Lake, Ind.: Eisenbrauns, 2009.

Gruber, Mayer. "Human and Divine Wisdom in the Book of Job." In *Boundaries of the Ancient Near Eastern World: A Tribute to Cyrus H.* Gordon, edited by Meir Lubetski, Claire Gottlieb, and Sharon Keller, 88–102. Sheffield: Sheffield Academic Press, 1998.

"The Book of Job as Anthropodicy." *Biblische Notizen* 136 (2008): 59–71.

Habel, Norman. *The Book of Job. A Commentary*. OTL. Philadelphia: Westminster, 1985.

"Wisdom in the Book of Job." In *Sitting with Job. Selected Studies on the Book of Job*, edited by Roy B. Zuck, 303–315. Grand Rapids, Mich.: Baker Book House, 1992.

---

* This essay has been informed by the works listed above. Especially relevant to my argument are the writings of N. Habel, C. Newsom, and M. Tsevat.

Linafelt, Tod. "The Wizard of Uz: Job, Dorothy, and the Limits of the Sublime." *Biblical Interpretation* 14.1–2 (2006): 94–109.

Newsom, Carol A. *The Book of Job: A Contest of Moral Imaginations*. Oxford and New York: Oxford University Press, 2003.

"The Book of Job." In *The New Interpreter's Bible*, Vol. IV, 317–637. Nashville, Tenn.: Abingdon, 1996.

Pope, Marvin. *Job. Introduction, Translation, and Notes*. Anchor Bible. Garden City, N.Y.: Doubleday, 1973.

Timmer, Daniel, "God's Speeches, Job's Responses, and the Problem of Coherence in the Book of Job: Sapiential Pedagogy Revisited." *CBQ* 71/2 (2009): 286–305.

Tsevat, Matitiahu. "The Meaning of the Book of Job." In *Sitting with Job. Selected Studies on the Book of Job*, edited by Roy B. Zuck, 189–218. Grand Rapids, Mich.: Baker Book House, 1992.

"INANA AND EBIḪ" AND THE SCRIBAL TRADITION

PAUL DELNERO
THE JOHNS HOPKINS UNIVERSITY

The study of Sumerian literature is no longer what it used to be. As few as fifty years ago very little of the rich corpus of Sumerian literary compositions was known beyond a handful of duplicates published as hand copies during the first decades of the twentieth century. When Adam Falkenstein, one of the pioneers of Sumerology, put together the first editions of these texts in the 1940s and 50s, he was rarely able to base his translations on more than five or six sources. This situation changed dramatically when the renowned Sumerologist, Samuel Noah Kramer, began publishing hand copies of hundreds of new Sumerian literary sources he had identified in large cuneiform tablet collections in Istanbul, Jena, and London. With the publication of *SLTN* (1944),[1] *ISET* I and II (1969 and 1976), TMH 3 and 4 (1961 and 1967), and UET 6/1–2 (1963 and 1966), as well as the identification of over one thousand new sources in the University Museum of the University of Pennsylvania,[2] it became possible, for the first time, to reconstruct the content of nearly all the Sumerian literary compositions that have been discovered to date.

---

1 Unless otherwise indicated, all abbreviations are those used in the Cuneiform Digital Library Initiative (CDLI) abbreviation list, which contains more detailed bibliographic references to these publications.

2 A complete list of all these sources, along with numerous others, was compiled by Miguel Civil in an unpublished manuscript, which has circulated for years under the title "Index to the Corpus of Sumerian Literature," and has undergone several revisions, most recently by Steve Tinney in 1999. Although its publication is still forthcoming, many of the sources listed in this catalogue can now be found in the lists of sources following the transliterations of each of the Sumerian literary compositions edited by *ETCSL*. Without this invaluable resource, which has formed the basis for nearly every text edition of a Sumerian literary work that has been published since its appearance, the substantial advances that have been made in the reconstruction and understanding of these compositions would not have been possible.

One of the many compositions identified by Kramer was a text he called *Inana and Ebiḫ*. The discovery of this composition was announced in his book *Sumerian Mythology*, along with a brief summary of its content.[3] Unlike many of the major literary works he identified, Kramer never published a full edition of this text.[4] He chose to leave this task instead to Barry Eichler, who had just completed his dissertation at the University of Pennsylvania. Since Barry generously permitted me to include a complete score of *Inana and Ebiḫ* in my dissertation,[5] it is a pleasure to dedicate to him a few observations about this fascinating composition, and in particular its place in the Old Babylonian scribal curriculum.

I. The Textual Reconstruction of Inana and Ebiḫ

Although Bottéro and Kramer published a translation of *Inana and Ebiḫ*,[6] and the composition is frequently cited in discussions of Sumerian literary and mythological works, a full edition has yet to be published. Until the complete transliteration in Pascal Attinger's 1998 article,[7] based on the published sources and an earlier version of Eichler's unpublished score, only the last third of this text, which Limet had transliterated in his publication of PUL 551—a tablet containing lines 122 to 181—had appeared in transliteration.[8] Attinger's transliteration, which includes a translation and a brief philological commentary, was followed by another transliteration and translation of the entire composition, without commentary, by *ETCSL*,[9] as well as the publication of five new sources by Margaret Jaques.[10]

When Kramer first summarized *Inana and Ebiḫ* only eight sources were known.[11] The number of preserved duplicates has since grown to eighty sources. All but six of these sources are listed and included in a

---

3 Kramer, *Sumerian Mythology*, 82–83.

4 See, for example, Kramer's editions of *Lamentation over the Destruction of Ur* (1940), *Enki and Ninḫursag* (1945), *Gilgameš and the Land of the Living* (*Gilgameš and Ḫuwawa, Version A*) (1947), *Schooldays* (1949), and *Enmerkar and the Lord of Aratta* (1952).

5 Delnero, *Variation in Sumerian Literary Compositions*, 2290–2358.

6 Bottéro and Kramer, *Lorsque les dieux*, 219–29.

7 Attinger, "Inana et Ebiḫ," 164–95.

8 Limet, "Le poème épique."

9 *ETCSL* 1.3.2.

10 Jaques, "Inanna et Ebiḫ," 202–25. This article includes a transliteration and translation of the first nine lines (from Sb 12367), and a transliteration of lines 29–52 and 83–130 (from the other four sources).

11 See Kramer, *Sumerian Mythology*, 82 with notes 78–79.

score of *Inana and Ebiḫ* compiled for the author's dissertation, a study of orthographic and grammatical variation in a group of ten Sumerian literary compositions known as the Decad.[12] With the new list, which includes additional sources and numerous joins and employs sigla that identify both the provenience and tablet type of each source (e.g. "N" for sources from Nippur, "Ur" for sources from Ur, "Si" for sources from Sippar; as well as the subscripts "$_{I}$" for multi-column or Type I sources, "$_{III}$" for single column extracts or Type III sources, and "$_{P}$" for prisms), instead of the common practice of arbitrarily assigning letters of the alphabet, the following additions and revisions can be made to Attinger's list:

JOINS[13]

- Attinger's source A joins source DD (physical join confirmed by author), the new siglum for this source, which includes this join, is N_{I7} (i 1–42[, ii] 52–88, iii 89–128[, iv 136–81[14])
- Source D joins N 1333, N 6149, N 1328, N 6433, N 6128 (identification and join of this fragment by J. Peterson), and N 7265 (identified and joined by J. Peterson), the new siglum for this source, with joins, is N_{I1} (i 1–18[, ii]46–62[, iii]114–41[, iv]154–81)
- Source H joins source L, as well as N 3001 and N 7417 (identification and join of these two fragments, as well as another unnumbered fragment by J. Peterson) = N_{III2} with joins (obv.]2–19[, rev.]26–42)
- Source K joins source WW as well as 3 N-T 916, 354 = N_{III24} (obv. 1–9[, rev.]12–18[)

12 Delnero, *Variation in Sumerian Literary Compositions*; see 2290–2297 for the list of sources and 2298–2358 for the score. Before this list, a similar list of sources was included in Attinger, "Inana et Ebiḫ," 167. Unless otherwise indicated all further references to the sources of this compositions and their content are from the list and score in Delnero, *Variation in Sumerian Literary Compositions*.

13 This section has benefited substantially from Jeremiah Peterson's work identifying and joining previously unknown fragments to existing sources, and the countless hours of concentrated labor this task involved. Special thanks are owed to him for sharing some of the joins and new fragments listed in this section with me before their publication.

14 The line numbers cited here and, unless otherwise indicated, throughout this article, follow the score in Delnero, *Variation in Sumerian Literary Compositions*. The line numbers in this score are identical to the line numbers in Attinger's composite text from 1–112. However, Attinger's l. 113—a line that appears only in two sources—is numbered l. 112a, so that Attinger's ll. 114–82 = ll. 113–81.

- Source N joins source X as well as N 3257 = N_{I2} (i]3–48, ii 49–97, iii 98–142, iv 143–76[)
- Source O joins CBS 7206 = N_{P1} (i]18–34, ii 35–37 and 53–67[, iii 69–104, iv 105–41[, v]165–81)
- Source P (CBS 4586) joins JJ = N_{I4} (i]20–36, iii]100–8[, iv]138–56[)
- Source EE joins CBS 13977, CBS 15146, N 5131, and N 7233 = N_{I6} (i]39–46[, ii]69–89, iii 90–114[, iv 135–41[)
- Source PP joins RR (Ni 4042) = N_{III16} (obv.]122–30[, rev.]142–59[)
- Source DDD probably joins Ni 9790 (*ISET* 3 150) = N_{III21} (obv. 158–75, rev. 176–81)

NEW SOURCES

- 3 N-T 554 (UM 55–21–346) = N_{I9} (ii]84–87, iii 88–94[)
- N 6535 = N_{III3} (obv.]30–34[, rev.]51–54[)
- N 4199 + N 4142 + N 5783 (fragment identified and joined by J. Peterson) = N_{III8} (obv.]61–67[, rev.]75–86[)
- N 1357 = N_{III10} (obv.]66–77, rev.]79–83[)
- N 5769 + N 4219 + N 4242 + N 4231 + N 6546 + N 6936 + N 6768 (fragment identified and joined by J. Peterson) = N_{III13} (obv. 113–36[, rev.]143–62[)
- N 3262 = N_{III22} (obv.]165–70[, rev. 173–81)
- N 7685 + N 3651 = N_{U5} (obv.?]83–89, rev.? 90–98[)
- CBS 10338 = N_{U6} (obv.?]158–60[)
- 2 N-T 55 (UM 55-21-14) = N_{U7} (obv.? 1–2[)
- UET 6/3 744 = Ur_4 (obv.?]65–68[)
- VAT 6795 = X_3 (obv. 118–27, rev. 128–34)
- Sb 12367 = Su_1 (Jaques, "Inanna et Ebiḫ")
- Sb 12368 = Su_2 (Jaques, "Inanna et Ebiḫ")
- H 174 = M_1 (Jaques, "Inanna et Ebiḫ")
- MAH 16123 (+) MAH 16127 = X_2 (Jaques, "Inanna et Ebiḫ")
- CBS 12670 (identified by J. Peterson) (obv.]27–31[, rev.]35–41[)
- N 3210 (identified by J. Peterson) (obv.?]37–49)
- N 3211 (identified by J. Peterson) (obv.?]88–101[)
- N 6335 (identified by J. Peterson) (obv.?]111–17[)
- CBS 3967 (identified by J. Peterson) (obv. 124–27[, rev.]151)

- YRL SC 1813-BxX-X (obv. 54-72; rev. uninscribed)[15]

ADDITIONS AND CORRECTIONS

- Attinger's source G (= N_{III32}) has lines 137–41[, not lines 1–4
- U (= N_{III5}), the last line on the reverse is l. 54
- Join between MM (N_{III12}) and RR (N_{III16}) is not possible because the obverse of RR ends with l. 131 and the reverse of MM begins with l. 131; also RR joins PP (see above)

---

15 This source, which was kindly brought to my attention by S. Brumfield and L. Allred, is in the Special Collections of UCLA in Los Angeles, and is published in photograph and transliteration by CDLI under the number P387610 (http://cdli.ucla.edu/P387610). The tablet, the provenience of which is unknown, is written in a cursive ductus characteristic of many late Old Babylonian tablets. The format and layout of the source are unusual because the tablet is ruled into two columns on the obverse, but only the first of the two columns is inscribed. Since the tablet begins with an extract from the middle of the composition, rather than from the beginning of the text, it is unclear why these lines were written on what looks like a Type I tablet instead of a Type III tablet, or why the second column on the obverse was left uninscribed. The source also contains a number of idiosyncratic variants, including DU for **du$_{11}$** for the verbal form in l. 54, **saĝ imin-am$_3$** for **saĝ imin-e** in l. 56, **ki-ni-a** for **ki-na** in l. 62, **an-na** for **an(-ne$_2$)** in l. 65, **inim-ĝu$_{10}$** UN (or **du$_{11}$-mu-un**?) for **inim-ĝu$_{10}$** in l. 66, the addition of an extra phrase after **suḫuš gi-na** (possibly **saĝ an-še$_3$? il$_2$?**) at the end of l. 69 not attested in any of the other preserved sources with this line, and **šita$_4$-a-ka** for **šita$_4$(-a)-ke$_4$** in l. 70. In addition there are at least three variants that are more evidently erroneous: **mi-in-be$_2$-e** for **mi-ni-ib-e$_3$** in l. 58, **nesaĝ-ra** for **ne-saĝ-ĝa$_2$** in l. 60 (in which **ne-saĝ** is written phonetically and the dative affix **-ra** was erroneously carried over from the form **an-ra** at the beginning of the line), and **mu-bu-bu?-um?-x** for **mu-bu-um-gin$_7$** in l. 70. One of the errors in the source—the variant **ma-ra-ab(-)**KA**(-)ĝu$_{10}$-še$_3$** for **ma-ra-ab-be$_2$-en inim-ĝu$_{10}$-še$_3$**—is particularly interesting, because it would seem that before writing the verb **e** (the *marû* form of the verb **du$_{11}$**, "to speak"), the scribe, associating **e** with **du$_{11}$**, which is written with the KA sign, mentally jumped ahead to **inim** (which like **du$_{11}$** is written also with the KA sign) and omitted all the signs before **inim**. Errors such as this, in which a scribe omits everything between two occurrences of the same letter (or sign), are a common type of copying error known in some studies of textual criticism as paralepsis. Since the association between **e** and **inim** involves a mental process that has both a visual/graphic and a cognitive/grammatical component, and is more complex than other errors of this type that typically occur when a scribe is copying directly from another exemplar and his or her eye merely skips from one occurrence of the same letter to the next, this variant, along with the phonetic variant **nesaĝ** for **ne-saĝ** and some of the other idiosyncratic writings in the source, suggests that the scribe who produced the tablet was copying from memory.

- Join between 3 N-T 916, 356 and 3 N-T 905, 189 (joined as Attinger's source WW) is unlikely, since it seems more probable that 3 N-T 916, 356 joins source K (N_{III24}) (see above)
- Attinger's source ZZ (N_{III33}) has lines]144–54, 155–63[, not lines 144–62; 177–81

The transliterations published by Attinger and *ETCSL* are composite texts in which each line has been selected from all the known sources, as opposed to a single duplicate thought to represent the best version. Since there are frequently variants or differing writings and forms among the sources for a given line, the transliteration for the composite text was chosen on the basis of which source or sources were considered to have the most accurate or "correct" version of the line. Attinger's transliterations generally reflect the version of the line that is present in the majority of preserved sources, and is also the most consistent with his interpretation of the orthography and grammar of the text.

The criteria applied in compiling the composite text for *ETCSL*, which is also generally accurate, are less clear. In the first section of the text, for example, the composite text seems to follow the version found in source Ur_1 (UET 6/1 12), which is the only preserved source that contains the forms **mud-bi** for **mud** and **u_3-tu-ud-da-za** for **u_3-tu-za** selected for the *ETCSL* composite text in lines 2 and 17. At the same time, however, *ETCSL* adds a line between lines 17 and 18 that is not attested in Ur_1 or any of the other sources used to compile the score.[16] Furthermore, for lines 32–51 and 91–110, which contain identical passages that are repeated in the text, there are a number of inconsistencies in the transliterations of some of these lines: the verbal form is transliterated **na-ma-ra-ab-te-a-gin_7** in *ETCSL* l. 34 (=l. 33) but without the infix **-ra-** in *ETCSL* l. 93 (=l. 92), which should be identical to l. 34; the first verb is **ḫub_2 šu_2** in *ETCSL* l. 39 (=l. 38) but **UŠ šub** in *ETCSL* l. 98 (=l. 97); in *ETCSL* l. 40 (=l. 39) the verbal form is rendered **si ga-ba-ab-sa_2**, but **ga-ba-ab-sar-sar** in *ETCSL* l. 99 (=l. 98), etc.

Since many of the inconsistencies in *ETCSL*'s transliteration, and a few of the forms in Attinger's transliteration, can be improved in light of the new sources for the composition, the following modifications to both composite texts are suggested:

---

16 The addition of this line, as well as the rendering of l. 127 as two separate lines, leads to the following discrepancies between the line numbering in the score of *Inana and Ebiḫ* in Delnero, *Variation in Sumerian Literary Compositions*, and the composite text in *ETCSL*: *ETCSL* ll. 19–127 = ll. 18–126, *ETCSL* ll. 128–29 = l. 127, and *ETCSL* 130–83 = ll. 128–81.

ll. 6–7 As noted by Attinger in his commentary to these lines,[17] a significant number of sources for these lines write the verbal forms with the pre-verbal element /n/. For the first verbal form in l. 6 three sources (two of which are from Nippur) have **i-ni-in-BAD** instead of the expected form for second person, *ḫamṭu* **i-ni-BAD**, in which the pre-verbal slot contains the element **-i/e-**, which appears in three Nippur sources. Similarly, in l. 7 four sources (three of which are from Nippur) have **i-ni-in-gi$_4$** against only two sources (both from Nippur) with **i-ni-gi$_4$** and again for the second form four sources have **i-ni-in-sig$_3$** against two with **i-ni-sig$_3$**. Moreover, only one of the sources (N_{I1}) that omits pre-verbal /n/ consistently omits it in all three forms, whereas three other sources (N_{I7}, N_{III24}, and Ur_1) omit it inconsistently (cf. N_{I7} **i-ni-BAD** in l. 6 but **i-ni-in-gi$_4$** in l. 7; N_{III24} with **i-ni-BAD** and **i-ni-gi$_4$** in ll. 6–7 but **i-ni-in-sig$_3$** in l. 7; and Ur_1 with **i-ni-in-BAD** and **i-ni-in-gi$_4$** in ll. 6–7 but **i-ni-sig$_3$** in l. 7). The frequency with which the pre-verbal element /n/ is written in these forms in contrast to the frequency and inconsistency with which it is omitted therefore suggests that the presence of /n/ was intended in the OB/Nippur recension of these lines, and that its occasional omission was either accidental or the result of intentional shorthand. Since it is unlikely that the tense of the verbal forms switched from third to second person between lines 6–7 and 8 (as evidenced by the unambiguously second-person verbal form **ba-gub-be$_2$-en** in l. 8) the grammatical function of /n/ in these verbal forms is difficult to interpret. However, the comparable distribution of sources with and without /n/ in the first-person verbal forms in lines 171–77 (in l. 171 three of the six sources for the line have **mi-ni-in-gi-en** instead of **mi-ni-gi-en**, in l. 173 six of the eight sources have **mu-na-an-šum$_2$** instead of **mu-na-šum$_2$**, in l. 174 five of the seven sources have **mu-ni-in-AK** instead of **mu-ni-AK**, in l. 175 four of the six sources have **ba-an-šum$_2$** instead of **ba(-a)-šum$_2$**, and in l. 177 four of the six sources have **ba-an-sur** instead of **ba(-a)-sur**) suggests that the morphological distinction between first, second, and third-person verbal forms was in the process of being lost at the time that the written transmission of this composition was becoming fixed.[18]

---

17 Attinger, "Inana et Ebiḫ," 182.

18 For a more extensive discussion of textual variation involving pre-verbal /n/ in *Inana and Ebiḫ* and the other compositions in the Decad see Delnero, "Pre-verbal /n/."

l. 17 The majority of preserved sources have **u$_3$-tu-za**.

ll. 18–19 The signs used to write the verbal forms in these lines (Attinger **kur$_4$-kur$_4$** and **gur$_4$-gur$_4$**, *ETCSL* **gur$_4$-gur$_4$** and **gur$_4$-gur$_4$**) are graphically distinct in nearly all the preserved sources for each line: in l. 18 most sources write the verb as LAGAB with two horizontal wedges inside the sign (**TUG$_2$** = **mu$_4$**) and in l. 19 as LAGAB without horizontal wedges inside the sign (**LAGAB** = **gur$_4$**).

ll. 29–31 The majority of preserved sources have **na-ma-ra-ab-AK** instead of **na-ma-ra-AK**.

ll. 35/94 Nearly all the preserved sources render the verbal chain for both verbal forms as **ga-am$_3$-mi-ib$_{(2)}$-** (and none of the sources for these lines has **ga-mi-ib-zu** as the second verbal form).

ll. 36–37/95–96 The correct verbal form is probably **ga-ba-ši-ib-gub**. The sources from Ur (Ur$_2$ for ll. 36–37 and Ur$_5$ for ll. 95–96) are the only sources that consistently have **-in-** instead of **-ib-**, whereas only one Nippur source (N$_{I3}$) has **-in-** in ll. 36–37 against three in l. 36 (N$_{I2}$, N$_{I7}$, and N$_{III27}$) and three in l. 37 (N$_{I2}$, N$_{I7}$, and N$_{III4}$) with **-ib-**, and none of the Nippur sources has **-in-** in ll. 95–96, whereas two Nippur sources for l. 95 (N$_{I6}$ and N$_{U5}$) and one for l. 96 (N$_{U5}$) have **-ib-**. Since the verb **gub** in these lines is transitive and has an inanimate object, the form with /b/ is also the grammatically expected form with the cohortative element **ga-**.

ll. 38/97 Most (and possibly all) of the sources have **ḫub$_2$** instead of **UŠ**. Also most of the preserved sources render the second verbal form as **ga-mu-ni-ib-sar**.

ll. 39/98 The form **ga-ba-ab-sa$_2$-sa$_2$** occurs the most consistently as the second verbal form in the preserved sources for these lines.

ll. 40/99 Although all the preserved sources for l. 99 have the verb **si sa$_2$** ("to set straight," "put in order"), four sources (N$_{I7}$, N$_{III4}$, N$_{III5}$, and N$_{III27}$) for l. 40 have **sa sa$_2$** (referring to placing the arrow straight on the thread of the bow?) against two sources (N$_{IIII1}$ and Ur$_2$) with **si sa$_2$**. As the less typical (or more difficult) form the reading **sa sa$_2$** is probably to be preferred.

ll. 42–43/101–2 When the total number of sources for both lines 42 and 101 are counted, there are more sources with the form **ga-am$_3$-ma-ab-AK** than with **ga-ba-ab-AK** or **ga-na-ab-AK**. The same distribution can be observed for the verbal chain in lines 43 and 102 (where the verb **si sa$_2$-sa$_2$** is certain, and occurs in all the preserved sources).

ll. 45/102 The variant **-du$_{11}$** for **-DU** in source Ur$_2$ for l. 45, which contains other phonetic writings for forms in this composition (cf. **ebiḫ** for

ebiḫ$_2$ in l. 41, **-su** for **-su$_3$** in l. 47, and **gu$_3$-bi** for **gu$_2$-bi** in l. 49) speaks against the reading **-gub** in *ETCSL*. Note also the variant form **ga-ba-ši-in-ti** in source N$_{III4}$ for l. 45.

ll. 46/103 As in ll. 42–43/101–2 the verbal chain **ga-am$_3$-ma(-an)-** occurs the most consistently in the preserved sources.

ll. 51/110 When the total number of sources for both lines is counted, only one source has **ebiḫ^{ki}-e** (N$_{I1}$ for l. 51) against four sources with **ebiḫ^{ki}-a** and eight sources with **ebiḫ^{ki}**.

l. 58 All the Nippur sources and one source from Ur (Ur$_3$) have **u$_2$-sa$_{11}$-an-na** instead of **usan$_x$(AN.USAN)^{an}-na**.

l. 59 Three of the seven sources have **u$_6$ di-de$_3$** instead of **u$_6$ di**.

l. 62 The verbal form **ba-an-tuš** is to be preferred to *ETCSL*'s **ba-e-tuš**. The three sources with **ba-e-**, two of which are from Ur, were probably influenced by the verbal form **ba-e-si** in all the sources for the next line.

l. 63 The majority of sources have **an-na-ke$_4$** instead of **an-na-ka**.

l. 64 Note the Emesal writing **e-ne-em$_3$-ĝu$_{10}$-še$_3$ MU.UŠ.TUG$_2$.PI-zu** for **inim-ĝu$_{10}$-še$_3$ GIŠ.TUG$_2$.PI-zu** in source N$_{III4}$.

l. 65 Four sources (N$_{I2}$, N$_{I7}$, N$_{III4}$, and N$_{III8}$), all which are from Nippur, have **an**, against four sources (N$_{I3}$, Ur$_2$, Ur$_3$, and W$_1$), only one of which is from Nippur, which have **an-ne$_2$**. The forms without the ergative element may be intended as vocatives and, if this is the case, it is possible that the verb is intended to be in the second person. In support of this position, note the similar distribution of forms with and without pre-verbal /n/ (three sources—N$_{I7}$, N$_{I8}$, and YRL SC 1813—have **mi-ni-ri** vs. three sources—N$_{III4}$, N$_{III9}$, and Ur$_3$—with **mi-ni-in-ri**), which is similar to the distribution of forms discussed in the note to lines 6–7, suggesting that the morphological distinction between first and third-person verbal forms was in the process of becoming lost.

l. 66 Both Nippur sources (N$_{I8}$ and N$_{III4}$) have **la-ba-ni-in-tuku** instead of **la-ba-e-ni-tuku**, which is only unambiguously preserved in source Ur$_3$. Note also the form **li-bi$_2$-ni-in-tuku** in YRL SC 1813.

l. 70 One source (N$_{P1}$) preserves the entire form **^{ĝiš}mu-bu-um-gin$_7$**, and at least three additional sources (N$_{III4}$, Ur$_3$, and W$_1$) have **mu-bu-um-gin$_7$** suggesting that this reading is to be preferred to Attinger's **mu/ĝiš-BU dub-gin$_7$**.[19]

---

[19] Attinger, "Inana et Ebiḫ," 172 with n. 70.

l. 71 Only one source (Ur_3) has **ḫa-ḫa-ze$_2$** instead of **ḫa-ḫa(-a)-za**, which is preserved in five sources.

l. 80 The majority of preserved sources have the verbal form **ḫu-mu-da(-an)-dub$_2$-be$_2$**.

l. 82 All the preserved sources have **kur-kur-re** instead of **kur-kur-ra**. Note also that none of the preserved sources has **šu** instead of **TUG$_2$**.

l. 83 At least four sources (N_{I7}, N_{I8}, N_{III10}, and N_{III29}) have **e$_{11}$**—the expected form for indicating vertical movement—instead of **e$_3$**.

l. 85 Nearly all the preserved sources have **an-na-ka-še$_3$** instead of **an-na-ka**.

ll. 86–87 In l. 86 five sources (N_{I7}, N_{I8}, N_{I9}, N_{III29}, and N_{P1}) have **ga-ne-diri** against one (N_{I3}) with **ga-en-ne-diri**, one (X_2) with **ga-e-ne-diri**, and one (N_{I6}) with **ga-an-ni/ne$_2$-diri**. Note also that each source in which the verbal form in l. 87 is preserved seems to have the same verbal chain with -**ĝen** that it has with -**diri** in l. 86, with the exception of source N_{I6}, which has **ba-ĝen**.

ll. 88–90 All the preserved sources have different verbal forms for these lines, but only one source (N_{I3}) writes the verbal base as **ta** instead of **te**. The sources with **-te-a(-ta)** may therefore contain the best form (cf. also **-te-te** in sources N_{P1} and N_{U5}).

ll. 112–14 Note once again the distribution of forms with and without pre-verbal /n/ (discussed in the notes to ll. 6–7 and 65): in l. 112 four sources have **bi$_2$-in-du$_{11}$** against three sources with **bi$_2$-du$_{11}$**, and in l. 113 and l. 114 five sources have **bi$_2$-in-du$_{11}$** against three sources with **bi$_2$-du$_{11}$**.

l. 115 All the preserved sources have -**ri** instead of -**ri-ri** (in *ETCSL*).

l. 118 All the preserved source have pre-verbal /n/ in the form **(sa-) mu-un-ri** and only two (N_{III12} and M_1) of eight sources have **kur-kur** instead of **kur-kur-ra**.

l. 123 All but one source (X_5) has **ni$_2$-bi-a** instead of **ni$_2$-ba** and the verb in all the preserved sources is unambiguously -**lu**.

l. 125 Three sources (N_{I2}, N_{III15}, and X_4) have **ḫur-saĝ-ĝa$_2$-ke$_4$** against two sources (N_{P2} and X_5) with **ḫur-saĝ-ĝa$_2$-ka** and one source (X_3) with **ḫur-saĝ**.

l. 127 All but one source (N_{P2}) have -**un-de$_3$**- instead of -**e-de$_3$**- in the verbal chain and only one source (X_5) has **ḫuš-am$_3$** instead of **ḫuš-a**.

l. 128 Only one source (N_{I2}) has a form similar to the verbal form in *ETCSL*'s transliteration; the remaining sources have a form that ends with -**ab-(b)e$_{(2)}$** followed by either -**ak(-ka)** or -**a-ka**.

l. 132 All but one of the Nippur sources (N_{I2}, N_{III12}, N_{III13}, and N_{III15}) have **ba-ra-an-e$_3$-a(m$_3$)** instead of **ba-ra(-an)-e$_3$** in four other sources (N_{P2}, Ur_6, X_3, and X_5).

l. 133 *ETCSL* omits this line entirely, although it is not omitted in any of the ten preserved sources.

l. 136 None of the preserved sources has **ḫul**, but instead a sign that looks similar either to **u$_3$** or to **u$_6$** or **u$_8$**.

l. 140 Three sources (N_{III17}, N_{III18}, and X_5) have **ebiḫ^{ki}-e**, two sources (N_{I1} and N_{I4}) have **ebiḫ^{ki}-a**, and one source (N_{I7}) has **ebiḫ^{ki}**.

l. 141 Only one source (N_{I4}) has **ĝir$_2$**, against six sources with **mir**.

l. 144 Although the form **dub-dab$_5$** is clearly expected (and is commonly attested in constructions with the verb **-za**), it is not unambiguously present in any of the preserved sources: two sources (N_{I2} and N_{I4}) have **dub-dub**, one source (X_5) has **dub**, and at least three (N_{I7}, N_{III18}, and N_{III19}) and possibly five have **dub-ba** (the traces of the sign after the first **dub** in N_{III12} and N_{III15} are consistent with **ba** but not enough of the sign is preserved to determine this with certainty). Along with the incorrect use of pre-verbal /n/, this may be another indication that the version(s) of the composition on which these sources was based was compiled at a relatively late date (Isin-Larsa/early OB?).

l. 145 Three sources (N_{I2}, N_{I5}, and N_{I8}) have **gal-gal-(l)e**, three sources (N_{III18}, N_{III33}, and X_5) have **gal-gal-la**, and one source (N_{I7}) has **gal-gal**.

l. 147 Only one source (N_{I4}) has **su-ba**, whereas the remaining six sources have either **KA** or **KA** inscribed with another sign (cf. N_{III33} with **KA×SA**). Note also that seven of the preserved sources have **mi-ni-in-ug$_5$** against only two (N_{III33} and X_5) with **mi-ni-ug$_5$**.

l. 150 The presence of the form **-gi$_4$** for the verb in three sources (N_{I7}, N_{I8}, and N_{III33}) may suggest that the form in four other sources (N_{I4}, N_{I5}, N_{III13}, and N_{III15}) should be read **-gi$_{18}$** instead of **-dim$_2$**; on the other hand, the form **-du$_3$** in Ur_7 may support the latter reading.

ll. 154–55 Only three (N_{III13}, Si_1, and Ur_7) of the fourteen preserved sources write these lines in the sequence in which they appear in *ETCSL* and Attinger's composite texts; the other eleven reverse their order.

l. 154 Only one source (Ur_7) has **an-ne$_2$** instead of **an-na**, which occurs in six sources.

l. 155 Only N_{III20} and Ur_7 have **ku$_3$-ga** vs. six sources with **ku$_3$-ge**.

l. 158 All the preserved sources have **šа$_3$** instead of **ki**. Also, read **mu-un-ug$_5$-ge(-en)**, since four sources (N_{III16}, N_{III20}, Is_3, and X_5) include **-en** and four sources (N_{I1}, N_{I2}, N_{III13}, and N_{U6}) omit it.

l. 161 Four of the preserved sources have the verb **šub** and render the verbal form as either **mu(-un)-šub-be$_2$** (N_{I2}, N_{I7}, and N_{III33}) or **mu-šub-be$_2$-en** (N_{III20}); Ur_7 is the only source with **mu-ri-ib$_2$-us$_2$**.

l. 164 Two of the three sources (N_{I2} and N_{I7}) have **im-ma-an(-u$_2$)-us$_2$**.

l. 167 Only one source (X_5) has **zi-da-ĝa$_2$** instead of **zi-da-ĝu$_{10}$** (in seven sources).

l. 169 All the preserved sources begin the verbal form with **i$_3$-** instead of **in-**. For the writing and omission of pre-verbal /n/ in lines 171–77 see the note to ll. 6–7.

l. 179 Only one source (X_5) has **ebiḫ^{ki}-e** against three sources (N_{III19}, N_{III31}, and M_1) with **ebiḫ^{ki}-a** and two sources (Ur_7 and X_2) with **ebiḫ^{ki}**.

II. The Content and Structure of Inana and Ebiḫ

Inana and Ebiḫ is one of several Sumerian literary works that showcase the bellicose attributes of Inana, a goddess associated also with erotic love. The content of the composition can be summarized succinctly. After a short hymnic prologue in which Inana is extolled for her prowess as a warrior, replete with images of her rushing into battle like a storm, carrying an axe bathed in blood, the narration switches to a first person speech delivered by the goddess herself, in which Inana promises to destroy the mountain Ebiḫ for failing to bow down and show her respect. She petitions her father An, the god of the heavens, for permission, but he warns her that the mountain is both too verdant to merit destruction and too fearsome to oppose. Insulted, Inana sets off in anger to wage war against Ebiḫ before An has even finished speaking. After driving her dagger into its side, setting fire to its trees, causing rocks to tumble down its sides with a shattering roar, and leaving the mountain, which she has lain to waste, smoldering in smoke, she delivers a final speech, boasting of her victory and praising her own might.

The literary structure of the text is relatively uncomplicated. The first nineteen lines of the composition contain a hymn in praise of Inana narrated in the first person (cf. **nin-ĝu$_{10}$** "my queen" in l. 10), and addressed to Inana in the second person (cf. the second person verbal forms in ll. 6–9 and the non-finite, pronominal conjugations with **-za** in ll. 10–19). Many of the descriptions of Inana in her capacity as a warrior and destroyer in these lines are similar to epithets of the goddess in other literary compositions, such as *The Exaltation of Inana* and *Inana C* (in-nin ša$_3$ gur$_4$-ra), that also contain hymnic passages that celebrate the aggressive side of Inana. In l. 2 she is described as "clothed in the blood of battle" (**mud me$_3$ gu$_2$ e$_3$**), which can be compared to "clothed in terrifying radiance" (**su-lim ḫuš gu$_2$ e$_3$**) in l. 19 of *Inana Hymn C*; in l. 7 she "fills the heaven and earth with a roar like a lion" (**pirig̑-gin$_7$ an ki-a šeg̑$_{11}$ i-ni-gi$_4$**), just as in *The Exaltation of Inana* l. 10 she "roars like Iškur" (**^{d}iškur-gin$_7$ ki šeg̑$_{11}$ gi$_4$-a-za**; cf. also *Inana Hymn C* l. 52). Similarly, in both l. 6 of *Inana and Ebiḫ* and l. 17 of *The Exaltation of Inana* she is identified as the "destroyer of lands" (**kur gul-gul**). The first nine lines of this prologue are followed by a passage with another ten lines that end with non-finite verbal forms ending in **-za**, which is analogous to a section of *The Exaltation of Inana* (ll. 123–33) with the same type of second-person pronominal verbal constructions, and several similar expressions (cf. ll. 10–11 **... an-gin$_7$ bulug̑$_3$-g̑a$_2$-za ... ki-gin$_7$ maḫ-a-za** "...that you are high like heaven .. that you are majestic like the earth" with *The Exaltation of Inana* ll. 123–24 **an-gin$_7$ maḫ-a-za ... ki-gin$_7$ dag̑al-la-za ...** "that you are majestic like heaven...that you are broad like the earth..."). This section concludes with the people of Sumer bursting into an *ilulama* song in praise of Inana (ll. 20–21), and the narrator expressing his or her desire to praise the goddess (ll. 22–23). The composition continues with a passage (ll. 24–51) in which Inana, in the first person, describes her trajectory through the heavens and her anger, when after approaching the mountain Ebiḫ, it refuses to bow down to her. Her journey to Ebiḫ, which requires passing the lands of Elam, Subir, and Lullubi, from the southeast to the northeast of southern Mesopotamia, is depicted in similar terms in ll. 113–14 of the composition *Inana and Šu-kale-tuda* (**^{d}inana an mu-un-nig̑in$_2$-na-ta ki mu-un-nig̑in$_2$-na-ta / elam^{ki} su-bir$_4$^{ki} mu-un-nig̑in$_2$-na-ta**: "Inana, after going around the heavens, after going around the earth / after she went around Elam and Subir").

The occurrence of the same description in two very different narrative contexts has led some to suggest that the path described alludes to Inana's regular movement, as the planet Venus, through the heavens in distinct phases, as opposed to a specific military campaign.[20] The description of Inana's arrival culminates in a detailed account of her plans to decimate Ebiḫ (ll. 32–51) by besieging it (ll. 36–37: **a$_2$ maḫ-bi-še$_3$ gu$_4$ maḫ ga-ba-ši-gub / a$_2$ tur-bi-še$_3$ gu$_4$ tur ga-ba-ši-gub** "At its large flanks I will place large siege engines, at its small flanks I will place small siege engines) and burning down its forests"; (l. 44: **$^{g̑iš}$tir us$_2$-sa-bi-še$_3$ izi ga-am$_3$-sig$_3$** "I will set fire to its immense forests"). This passage is repeated verbatim in ll. 91–110 of the next section of the text when Inana, after adorning herself (ll. 52–58), presenting herself before her

20 Volk, *Inanna und Šukaletuda*, 31; Cooper, "Literature and History," 143.

father An (ll. 59–63), and reminding him that he has given her power over all heaven and earth to rule and put down revolts (ll. 64–83), tells him of her intentions (ll. 84–110). In a speech intended to soothe Inana's anger (ll. 111–27), An warns the goddess against attacking Ebiḫ but is interrupted when she, in a fit of rage, rushes away to carry out her plans (ll. 128–64). The last sixteen lines of the composition (ll. 165–80), before the doxology (l. 181), conclude with Inana praising herself for her victory over Ebiḫ, which she has just successfully destroyed.

The interpretations of this ostensibly simple composition have been varied. In an article about politicizing tendencies in Sumerian literary compositions, Claus Wilcke argued that *Inana and Ebiḫ* contains a subtext pertaining to the expansionist politics of the Akkadian dynasty and, in particular, of the rulers Sargon and Naram-Suen, who established a vast territorial state through aggressive military expansion in the late third millennium BCE.[21] Assuming that Inana, in certain mythological narratives, symbolically represents Akkad and its interests in the guise of its patron deity Ištar/Inana, Wilcke proposed that myths in which Inana is depicted in a positive light are pro-Akkad, whereas those in which Inana is criticized are anti-Akkad.[22] Wilcke initially interpreted *Inana and Ebiḫ* as a pro-Akkad myth, which, by extolling Inana for conquering Ebiḫ, implicitly endorses the military campaigns undertaken by the Akkadian rulers to extend their territorial holdings to the north and northeast of Akkad. But later, as more of the text could be reconstructed, he modified this view, interpreting *Inana and Ebiḫ* instead as an anti-Akkad myth, on the grounds that Inana's father An does not support her decision to destroy Ebiḫ.[23] A similar approach to understanding *Inana and Ebiḫ* was adopted by Annette Zgoll, a student of Wilcke's, who also identified an anti-Akkad subtext in the composition, but argued more specifically that An's refusal to support Inana is grounded in his concern for the cultic cities of Sumer, which would have to pay a heavy price in human life (due to military conscription) for a successful campaign.[24]

Central to both of these interpretations is the assumption that *Inana and Ebiḫ* alludes to actual historical events and circumstances. The strongest point in favor of this notion is the likelihood that mount Ebiḫ is a real place and not a mythological location. On the basis of descriptions in second and first-millennium Assyrian annals in which the top-

---

[21] Wilcke, "Politische Opposition," 54–55.

[22] Wilcke, "Politische Opposition," 56–57.

[23] Wilcke, "Politik im Spiegel," 48–49.

[24] Zgoll, *Rechtsfall der En-ḫedu-Ana*, 91–92; Zgoll, "Ebeḫ und andere Gebirge."

onym occurs, Ebiḫ can be situated between the Lower Zab and Diyala rivers in the vicinity of Assur, where the Jebel Ḥamrīn, the mountain range with which Ebiḫ has most plausibly been identified, is located.[25] Since Ebiḫ is situated geographically in an area that the powerful Old Akkadian rulers, Sargon and Naram-Suen, claim to have conquered in their royal inscriptions, this composition could conceivably allude to the military activities of these rulers.

Less plausible, however, is the theory that An and Inana are simply literary devices for critiquing the imperial ambitions of earlier rulers. In a critique of Wilcke's interpretation, Jerrold Cooper calls attention to the numerous overtly political literary works, such as the *Curse of Agade* and the *Lamentation over the Destruction of Sumer and Ur*, that mention actual rulers by name, and sees no compelling reason why it would have been necessary to conceal political figures and policies allegorically in mythological narratives.[26] In support of this position, he noted that the depiction of Inana in *Inana and Ebiḫ* is entirely consistent with the way she is described in other mythological texts from the same period, and therefore concluded that it is not necessary to interpret these compositions politically.[27] In *Inana's Descent to the Netherworld*, for example, Inana also sets out impulsively to conquer the region below the earth where the dead reside, and to dethrone its queen Ereškigal. Similarly, in *Inana Hymn C*, lines such as "to destroy, to build up, to tear out, and to settle are yours, Inana" (l. 119: **gul-lu dim$_2$-me zi-zi ĝa$_2$-ĝa$_2$ ^{d}inana za-a-kam**) and "wherever she (turns)? cities become ruin mounds and haunted places, and shrines become waste land" (l. 16: **ki ib$_2$-[...]-ni-še$_3$ uru^{ki} du$_6$-du$_6$-da e$_2$ lil$_2$-la$_2$-še$_3$ uzug e$_2$-ri-a-še$_3$ i$_3$-ĝal$_2$**) describe her as a willful destroyer. This text is also the only other composition that refers directly to Inana's conquest of Ebiḫ (in ll. 110–12), strengthening the connection between *Inana and Ebiḫ* and another "non-political" mythological literary work. Furthermore, one of the critical passages in the interpretation of *Inana and Ebiḫ* as an anti-Akkad polemic is An's refusal to grant Inana's request to attack Ebiḫ. However, an analogous interaction between An and Inana, in which An uses similar language and an almost identical line of argumentation to dissuade Inana from carrying out an equally destructive act is recounted in the Sumerian composition *Gilgameš and Bull Heaven*. In his sixteen-line

---

25 See, for example, Thureau-Dangin, "Notes assyriologiques," 84–86; Gelb, "Topography of Western Asia," 67–68; and Edzard and Farber, *Die Orts- und Gewässernamen*, 38 for additional references.

26 Cooper, "Literature and History," 135–36 with n. 20.

27 Cooper, "Literature and History," 134–35.

speech to Inana in *Inana and Ebiḫ* (ll. 112–27), An begins his refusal with an appeal to reason:

112. lu$_2$-tur-ĝu$_{10}$ kur-re al bi$_2$-du$_{11}$ ša$_3$-bi a-na ab-AK
113. ^{d}inana me-en kur-re al bi$_2$-du$_{11}$ ša$_3$-bi a-na ab-AK
114. ḫur-saĝ ebiḫ^{ki}-ke$_4$ al bi$_2$-du$_{11}$ ša$_3$-bi a-na ab-AK

My young one, you have requested the mountain—what is the reason?
You, Inana, you have requested the mountain—what is the reason?
You have requested the mountain Ebiḫ—what is the reason?

His speech continues by calling attention to Ebiḫ's fear-inspiring aura (ll. 115–18) and describing the mountain as a place of abundance, with fruit-bearing gardens (l. 120), immense trees (l. 121), and coupling lions and stags (ll. 122–23), before concluding by stating that Inana will not be capable of successfully overcoming Ebiḫ:

126. ni$_2$-bi ḫuš-a nu-mu-da-an-ku$_4$-ku$_4$
127. ḫur-saĝ-ĝa$_2$ me-lim$_x$-bi ḫuš-a ki-sikil ^{d}inana saĝ nu-mu-un-de$_3$-ĝa$_2$-ĝa$_2$

Its radiance is terrifying—you will not be able to enter there.
The aura of the mountain is terrifying—young maiden Inana, you will not be able to oppose it.

The same narrative structure of a reasoned appeal, followed by concern for the consequences, and concluding with a statement about the impossibility of the task can be found in An's equally unsuccessful argument to talk his impulsive daughter out of using the bull of heaven to punish Gilgameš:

Appeal to reason followed by concern for the consequences:

(Segment B) 38: lu$_2$-tur-ĝu$_{10}$ a-ba-kam a ši-im-lu$_3$-lu$_3$-e šurum [gur$_4$-gur$_4$-re]

My young one, what (use) is it? It will muddy the water and leave thick cow pats.

Concluding with a statement of impossibility:

(Segment B) 47–48: lu$_2$-tur-ĝu$_{10}$ gu$_4$ an-na u$_2$-ku$_2$-bi in-nu an-ur$_2$-ra u$_2$-ku$_2$-bi-im /
ki-sikil ^{d}inana gu$_4$ an-na ki ^{d}utu e$_3$-a-še$_3$ u$_2$ im-da-ku$_2$-e

My child, the bull of heaven could not pasture—its pasture is on the horizon /
Young maiden Inana, the bull of heaven is only able to pasture where the sun rises.

Inana's response to An's speech is more or less the same in both compositions. In *Inana and Ebiḫ* she sets out in a rage to destroy Ebiḫ anyway, and in *Gilgameš and the Bull of Heaven* she gets so angry that she threatens to scream so that An gives in, permitting her to use his bull against Gilgameš's city Uruk. The similarity in the portrayal of Inana and An in separate contexts therefore strongly suggests that the interaction between An and Inana in *Inana and Ebiḫ*, as well as in *Gilgameš and the Bull of Heaven*, is intended to underscore an essential aspect of the relationship between Inana and her father—the impulsive, easily angered daughter Inana, and the father, who always give her what she wants, even when he knows it is unreasonable or destructive—and not as a subtle political critique.

III. Place and Function of Inana and Ebiḫ *in the Scribal Curriculum*

More recently another interpretative approach to understanding *Inana and Ebiḫ* has been proposed. Taking into account that all or nearly all the preserved copies of Sumerian literary works were copied by apprentice scribes learning to read and write Sumerian, the meaning of these texts is derived primarily from their function as scribal exercises. By examining various aspects of the tablets containing these compositions, including their physical format and archaeological context, the scholars Niek Veldhuis, Steve Tinney, and Eleanor Robson have been able to reconstruct the approximate sequence of texts copied by apprentice scribes at different stages in their training.[28] They argue that texts copied on tablets with both a model extract and a pupil's copy were learned during the elementary phase of scribal education, and that texts copied without a model were learned at a later stage.[29] According to this argument, literary compositions, which occur almost exclusively on tablets without a model, were copied in the second or advanced phase of the

---

28 For the reconstruction of the first or elementary phase of the curriculum, and the evidence for it, see Veldhuis, *Elementary Education*; for the intermediate or transitional phase between the elementary and advanced curriculum see Tinney, "On the Curricular Setting"; and for the advanced phase when most Sumerian literary compositions were learned see Robson, "The Tablet House." For a summary of these theories and a detailed discussion of the evidence for the reconstruction of all three phases of the scribal curriculum see Delnero, *Variation in Sumerian Literary Compositions*, 64–147.

29 For the role of tablet typology in determining the sequence of the curriculum see, in particular, Veldhuis, *Elementary Education*, 35–36 and Tinney, "Texts, Tablets, and Teaching." For the function of the tablet types used during the advanced phase of the curriculum see Delnero, "Sumerian Extract Tablets and Scribal Education."

scribal curriculum. *Inana and Ebiḫ* can be placed even more precisely within the sequence of texts that were learned in this phase. Observing that the first ten entries in two Old Babylonian lists of literary texts, known as the Nippur and Louvre catalogues, are identical, Tinney has argued that these entries refer to a group of compositions, which he calls the Decad, that were learned at the beginning of the second phase of the curriculum.[30] Collective tablets and catch-lines that connect the individual texts in the Decad in the same sequence in which they are listed in the catalogues provide further evidence for this.[31] Including *Inana and Ebiḫ*, the Decad comprises the following compositions:[32]

1. *ŠA*: *A praise poem of Šulgi* (*Šulgi A*)[33]
2. *LiA*: *A praise poem of Lipit-Eštar* (*Lipit-Eštar A*)[34]
3. *Al*: *The Song of the Hoe*[35]
4. *InB*: *The Exaltation of Inana* (*Inana B*)[36]
5. *EnA*: *Enlil in the E-kur* (*Enlil A*)[37]
6. *KH*: *The Keš Temple Hymn*[38]
7. *ErH*: *Enki's Journey to Nibru*[39]
8. *IEb*: *Inana and Ebiḫ*[40]
9. *Nu*: *A hymn to Nungal* (*Nungal A*)[41]
10. *GH*: *Gilgameš and Ḫuwawa* (*Version A*)[42]

---

30 Tinney, "On the Curricular Setting," 168–70.

31 For a list of these sources see Tinney, "On the Curricular Setting," 169 and Delnero, *Variation in Sumerian Literary Compositions*, 31–33 (with additional sources).

32 For an extensive discussion of the Decad as a curricular grouping, which includes references to previous studies and a detailed bibliography of editions and discussions of each of the ten compositions in this group, see Delnero, *Variation in Sumerian Literary Compositions*, 22–147.

33 *ETCSL* 2.4.2.01.

34 *ETCSL* 2.5.5.1.

35 *ETCSL* 5.5.4.

36 *ETCSL* 4.07.2.

37 *ETCSL* 4.05.1.

38 *ETCSL* 4.80.2.

39 *ETCSL* 1.1.4.

40 *ETCSL* 1.3.2.

41 *ETCSL* 4.28.1.

42 *ETCSL* 1.8.1.5.

The observation that literary compositions were learned as advanced exercises has had a significant influence on how *Inana and Ebiḫ* and other works of Sumerian literature are interpreted. Instead of studying these texts in isolation, their content is now understood from both a functional-pedagogical and an ideological perspective. The didactic function of these compositions is especially clear in the elementary stages of the curriculum, in which the sequence of exercises that were copied was graded according to difficulty to teach pupils fundamental aspects of the Sumerian language and the cuneiform writing system. Scribal training began with *Syllable Alphabet B* and *Tu-ta-ti*, lists that taught basic cuneiform signs and their phonetic values, and continued with thematic lexical lists, model contracts, and short Sumerian proverbs, which would have been useful for learning vocabulary, syntax, and simple grammatical sentences. Extending this logic to the second phase of the curriculum, it can be argued that the literary compositions at the beginning of this stage, including *Inana and Ebiḫ* and the other texts in the Decad, were intended to introduce apprentice scribes to more complex grammar and longer, continuous texts.

Since by this stage in their training scribes would presumably have been able to understand the content of the compositions they were copying, the ideological function of these texts has also been considered. In his recent edition of the literary composition *Nanše and the Birds*, Veldhuis put forward the theory that the works of literature in the scribal curriculum were intended to convey the notion of a unified Sumerian heritage.[43] This knowledge would have served to indoctrinate a small circle of elites who were being trained as bureaucrats to believe that they shared a common history and culture, inspiring loyalty to the state that employed them. From this perspective, *Inana and Ebiḫ* would have been one of many compositions in which apprentice scribes encountered a central deity in the national pantheon. In addition to Inana, they learned about Enki in *Enki's Journey to Nippur*, Enlil in *Enlil in the Ekur*, Nungal in the *Nungal Hymn*, Nintu in the *Kesh Temple Hymn*, and Šamaš in *Gilgameš and Ḫuwawa A*. Learning about these deities would have created the sense of a single, coherent religious tradition. Since these gods and goddesses were also the patron deities of important urban centers in Sumer, learning compositions about them and their cities would have also reinforced the more overtly political message of the first two texts in the Decad, the royal hymns *Šulgi A* and *Lipit-Eštar A*, which glorified powerful rulers of the not-so-distant past.

---

43 Veldhuis, *Religion, Literature, and Scholarship*, 66–80.

While the curricular approach has certainly revealed a dimension that had previously been overlooked, it also has limitations. One of its most substantial weaknesses is that the proposed reconstruction of the sequence of the scribal curriculum is less certain than it may have first appeared. For one, it now seems very unlikely that the Nippur and Louvre catalogues, the two lists that serve as the primary basis for reconstructing the advanced curriculum, give the sequence of literary compositions that were learned at this stage. The number of similarities between these two sources and other lists from the same period that can be identified with certainty as tablet inventories strongly suggests that these catalogues are also inventories, and not curricular lists.[44] The most apparent similarity is the manner in which the entries in these lists are grouped. The Nippur and Louvre catalogues and the other composition lists contain groups of entries that are arranged either thematically, by their first sign or signs, in sections that end with dividing lines, generic rubrics or subtotals, or some combination of these methods. Since all these grouping devices have a clear archival function, it is probable that all the lists that employ them, including the Nippur and Louvre catalogues, are inventories, and therefore cannot be used reliably to determine the sequence of the scribal curriculum.

Another shortcoming of the curricular approach is that most of what is known about scribal education is based entirely on evidence from only one city, without considering how scribes were trained in other locations in southern Mesopotamia. At present, approximately 400 compositions that were copied during the Old Babylonian Period have been identified that can be classified as literary works. Nearly ninety percent of the preserved sources for these texts come from Nippur, the religious center of Sumer in the third and second millennia. Nippur was undoubtedly a major center for scribal education, and the thousands of tablets it has yielded provide the most data for reconstructing the scribal curriculum. But it is not the only place where scribal training was conducted. School tablets containing exercises from both the elementary and advanced stages of the curriculum, including the compositions in the Decad, have been found at Ur, Babylon, Sippar, Isin, Uruk, Kish, Larsa, and other Mesopotamian cities. If there was a standard scribal curriculum it remains to be shown that similar sequences of exercises were learned outside Nippur. In the absence of

---

44 For this theory and a more detailed discussion and argument of the evidence for it see Delnero, "Sumerian Literary Catalogues and the Scribal Curriculum," and Delnero, *Variation in Sumerian Literary Compositions*, 107–41.

indications for this, it is equally possible that the texts that were copied differed from place to place and there was no set curricular sequence at all.

One way of addressing this issue is by comparing what is known about scribal education at Nippur to evidence from another site that provides sufficient comparative data, the city of Ur. At both Nippur and Ur groups of tablets from each stage of the curriculum were found in private houses that have been identified as schools. One of these groups, consisting of approximately one thousand tablets, was excavated at Nippur in a house known as "House F" and another group of about half that size was found in a house at Ur known as "#1 Broad Street." Dated administrative texts from the two houses indicate that these groups of tablets were copied in the nineteenth and eighteenth centuries BCE. House F was abandoned in the tenth year of Samsuiluna, around 1740, and the school tablets, which had not yet been recycled, were presumably produced shortly before the abandonment of the house.[45] Similarly, the administrative texts from #1 Broad Street span the period from 2020 to 1790.[46] If the tablets in this house were found *in situ* on the floor along the wall where they had fallen from shelves, as Woolley supposed,[47] and not brought in as fill from different places,[48] then they would have been produced within fifty years of the tablets from House F. Dating to the same period, and spanning the entire sequence of the curriculum, the tablets from House F and #1 Broad Street therefore provide a reliable basis for comparing how scribal training was conducted in different cities.

In a recent article, Eleanor Robson analyzed the sequence of the curriculum at House F in detail,[49] while the archaeological context of the tablets from #1 Broad Street has been examined by both Dominique Charpin and Paolo Brusasco.[50] Robson's analysis is based on the distribution of tablets from House F, which were excavated by McCown and Haines during the third season of post-war excavations at Nippur conducted in 1951 and 52. The tablets from House F, which were inventoried with 3 N-T numbers, were studied from fragments and casts of the original tablets, housed in the University Museum of the University of

45 Robson, "The Tablet House," 42.

46 Brusasco, "Family Archives," 125–26.

47 Woolley and Mallowan, UE 7, 137.

48 Cf. Charpin, *Le clergé d'Ur*, 484–85.

49 Robson, "The Tablet House."

50 Charpin, *Le clergé d'Ur*, 434–86; Brusasco, "Family Archives," 124–26 and 159–61.

Pennsylvania and the Oriental Institute of the University of Chicago. Detailed archaeological data about the tablets from House F could be obtained from the original site report published by McCown and Haines,[51] the catalogue of tablets from House F in Elizabeth Stone's book *Nippur Neighborhoods*,[52] and field notebooks with find spot information recorded at the site. To investigate scribal education at Ur, Charpin and Brusasco provide valuable descriptions of the archaeological context for the tablets from #1 Broad Street. Charpin's discussion is based on Woolley's excavation report of the Old Babylonian period at Ur,[53] while Brusasco reassessed this data taking into account discrepancies between the final report and earlier versions of the field catalogue to correct identifiable inaccuracies. These descriptions can be supplemented with the three parts of *Ur Excavations: Texts*, Volume Six, which contain catalogues and hand copies of the school texts from Ur. With the appearance of the third and final volume in the series in 2006,[54] it is now possible to study the distribution of all the scribal exercise tablets from #1 Broad Street as a group.

Many of the compositions that are well represented at House F are attested in multiple duplicates also from #1 Broad Street. There are a total of forty texts that were copied at both houses. In addition to all ten compositions in the Decad, these texts comprise:

> *Išbi-Erra E* (1 source from House F; 1 source from #1 Broad Street), *Ewe and Wheat* (20; 5), *Curse of Agade* (17; 3), *Dumuzi's Dream* (20; 8), *The Instructions of Šuruppak* (21; 6), *Gilgameš, Enkidu, and the Netherworld* (17; 13), *Hoe and Plough* (27; 3), *Šulgi B* (17; 4), *Tree and Reed* (1; 1); *Summer and Winter* (4; 3); *The Ur Lament* (17; 7); *The Nippur Lament* (8; 1); *Lamentation over the Destruction of Sumer and Ur* (3; 14); *Lugalbanda in the Mountain Cave* (8; 2); *Lugalbanda and the Anzu Bird* (8; 1); *Inana's Descent to the Netherworld* (3; 6); *Inana and Šukaletuda* (1; 2); *Dialogue between Two Scribes* (*Dialogue 1*) (21; 5); *Father and Son* (*Eduba B*) (12; 5); *Two Women* (*Dialogue 5*) (9; 8); *Enkiḫegal and Enkitalu* (*Dialogue 2*) (4; 6); *Enkimansum and Girniisag* (*Dialogue 3*) (3; 2); *The Deeds and Exploits of Ninurta* (5; 9); *Inana Hymn C* (in-nin ša$_3$-gur$_4$-ra) (9; 2); *Ninurta's Return to Nibru* (10; 1); *Išme-Dagan A* (2; 5); *Bird and Fish* (2; 5); *The Tummal Inscription* (2; 3); *Enlil-Bani A* (2; 1); *Lisin's Song* (1; 1)

51 McCown and Haines, *Nippur I*.

52 Stone, *Nippur Neighborhoods*, 161–212.

53 Woolley and Mallowan, UE 7.

54 Shaffer, UET 6/3.

However, there are also numerous differences in the distribution of texts at both houses. At House F there are copies of twenty-one compositions that are not attested at #1 Broad Street:

> *Gilgameš and the Bull of Heaven* (4 copies); *Gilgameš and Agga* (1); *Enlil and Ninlil* (4); *Nanše A* (5); *Heron and the Turtle* (2); *Enmerkar and Ensuḫkešdana* (2); *Enki and the World Order* (3); *Inana Hymn D* (1); *Schooldays (Eduba A)* (19); *Supervisor to the Scribe* (13); *The Farmer's Instructions* (21); *Lipit-Eštar B* (3); *Iddin-Dagan A* (1); *The Death of Urnamma* (1); *Enlil and Namzitara* (1); *Nintinugga's Dog* (1); *The Axe of Nergal* (3); *The Fowler and his Wife* (1); *Nignam* (1); *Minor Composition 1* (1); *Minor Composition 4* (1)

There is also a much larger group of thirty-three texts found at #1 Broad Street, but not at House F:

> *Nisaba A* (7 copies); *The Sumerian King List* (2); *Nanna's Journey to Nibru* (1); *Home of the Fish* (3); *Eridu Lament* (1); *Uruk Lament* (4); *Enmerkar and the Lord of Aratta* (2); *The Collection of Temple Hymns* (8); *Scribal Activities (Eduba D)* (1); *The Eduba Regulations* (2); *Man and His God* (3); *Ninurta and the Turtle* (2); *Ningišzida and Ninazimua* (1); *Ningišzida and Damu* (1); *Ur-Namma D* (2); *Šulgi S* (3); *Amar-Suen and Enki's Temple* (2); *Iddin-Dagan B* (1); *Lipit-Eštar E* (2); *Sin-iddinam A* (1); *Sin-iddinam B* (1); *Crane and Raven* (1); *The Old Woman from Girsu* (1); *Minor Composition 2* (1); *Bau Hymn A* (1); *Dumuzi-Inana E* (1); *Dumuzi-Inana G* (2); *Nanna Hymn E* (1); *Nanna Hymn F* (1); *Ningišzida B* (1); *Ningišzida E* (1); *Ninisina D* (1); *Eduba E* (2)

Moreover, one of the compositions in the Decad, the *Nungal Hymn*, is preserved in nineteen duplicates from House F, but in only two fragmentary copies from Ur that may belong to the same source.[55] A school lentil from Ur that was previously thought to be a duplicate of this text contains only five lines, three of which are similar but not identical to lines found in other sources for the *Nungal Hymn*, and two of which are otherwise unattested.[56] Although some of the same compositions were used for training scribes at both House F and #1 Broad Street, the differences in distribution suggest that the sequence of exercises at the two houses was not fixed in the same way, even perhaps within the Decad.

Further evidence that compositions were not copied in the same order is suggested by a group of extract tablets from Ur. Over half the

---

55 UET 6/3 593 and 594.

56 UET 6/1 75.

tablets from #1 Broad Street contain twenty to seventy lines extracted from a longer text. In many instances these extract tablets are part of a series containing a full composition divided into connected sections. For example, the entire text of *Ewe and Wheat* is written on a group of three sources with lines 1 through 62, 63 to 123, and 124 to 190 of this composition.[57] Similar groups of extract tablets are preserved for *Inana and Ebiḫ; Lamentation over the Destruction of Sumer and Ur; Gilgameš, Enkidu and the Netherworld; The Kesh Temple Hymn; The Instructions of Šuruppak*; and *Bird and Fish*. In a few instances the extract tablets from #1 Broad Street end with colophons that give the name of the scribe who wrote the tablet and the day and month on which the work was completed. On the basis of this information, five of these tablets can be identified as extracts written by a scribe named Damqi-ilišu: UET 6/1 33 and 34 (*Ewe and Wheat*), UET 6/2 131 (*Lamentation over the Destruction of Sumer and Ur*), UET 6/2 163 (*Father and Son*), and UET 6/2 169 (*The Instruction of Šuruppak*). Three of his tablets are of particular interest because they were written within a two-week period. Two extracts with lines 1–62 and 63–123 of *Ewe and Wheat* were written on the 14th and 24th day of the month "eš$_3$-e$_3$,"[58] and a third, with an extract of *Lamentation over the Destruction of Sumer and Ur*, was written on the 21st day of the same month.[59] Since there are numerous extracts from #1 Broad Street written during this month, and very few that were written in other months, it is very likely that the tablets dating to this month were all copied during the same year. If this is the case, then Damqi-ilišu began learning another composition before he had finished copying *Ewe and Wheat*. These sources show that pupils did not always learn one composition completely before proceeding to another composition, but rather may have learned two or more compositions at the same time. Therefore, even if it were possible that identical compositions were copied at both Ur and Nippur, it is very unlikely that there was a sequence of texts that were taught in the same prescribed order, another indication that the texts copied at Ur were not learned in the same linear sequence.

In conclusion, one of the primary limitations of recent reconstructions of the scribal curriculum is that they are based almost entirely on cuneiform sources from Nippur. In order to demonstrate that there was, in fact, a standard or even similar sequence of exercises, as opposed to an unstructured assemblage of texts from which specific exercises could be selected more or less arbitrarily it is necessary to identify

---

[57] UET 6/1 33, 34, and 35.

[58] UET 6/1 33 and 34.

[59] UET 6/2 131.

groups of exercises that were copied in the same order at different sites. In the absence of evidence for this, questions about the nature of the Old Babylonian curriculum, if indeed there even was one, must remain open.

WORKS CITED

Attinger, P. "Inana et Ebiḫ." *ZA* 88 (1998): 164–95.

Bottéro, J., and S. N. Kramer. *Lorsque les dieux faisaient l'homme: mythologie mésopotamienne*. Paris: Gallimard, 1989.

Brusasco, P. "Family Archives and the Social Use of Space in Old Babylonian Houses at Ur." *Mesopotamia* 34–35 (1999–2000): 3–173.

Charpin, D. *Le clergé d'Ur au siècle d'Hammurabi (XIXe-XVIIIe siècles av. J.-C.)*. Hautes Études Orientales 22. Paris: Libraire Droz, 1986.

Cooper, J. S. "Literature and History: The Historical and Political Referents of Sumerian Literary Texts." In *Historiography in the Cuneiform World*, edited by T. Abusch, et al., 131–47. CRRAI 45. Bethesda, Md.: CDL Press, 2001.

Delnero, P. *Variation in Sumerian Literary Compositions: A Case Study Based on the Decad*. PhD Dissertation, University of Pennsylvania, 2006.

"Pre-verbal /n/: Function, Distribution, and Stability." In *Analysing Literary Sumerian: Corpus-based Approaches*, edited by J. Ebeling and G. Cunningham, 105–43. London: Equinox Publishing, 2007.

"Sumerian Literary Catalogues and the Scribal Curriculum." *ZA* 100 (2010): 32-55.

"Sumerian Extract Tablets and Scribal Education." *JCS* 62 (2010): 53-69.

Edzard, D. O., and G. Farber. *Die Orts- und Gewässernamen der Zeit der 3. Dynastie von Ur*. Répertoire géographique des textes cunéiforms 2. Beihefte zum Tübingen Atlas der Vorderen Orients, Reihe B (Geisteswissenschaften), 7/2. Wiesbaden: Ludwig Reichert, 1974.

Gadd, C. J., and S. N. Kramer. *Literary and Religious Texts. First Part*. UET 6/1. London: Trustees of the Two Museums, 1963.

Literary and Religious Texts. Second Part. UET 6/2. London: Trustees of the Two Museums, 1966.

Gelb, I. J. "Studies in the Topography of Western Asia." *The American Journal of Semitic Languages and Literature* 55 (1938): 67–68.

Jaques, M. "Inanna et Ebiḫ: Nouveaux textes et remarques sur le vocabulaire du combat et de la victoire." *ZA* 94 (2004): 202–225.

Kramer, S. N. *Lamentation over the Destruction of Ur*. AS 12. Chicago: The University of Chicago Press, 1940.

Sumerian Mythology: A Study of the Spiritual and Literary Achievement in the 3rd Millennium B.C. Memoirs of the American Philosophical Society 21. Philadelphia: The American Philosophical Society, 1944.

Enki and Ninhursag: A Sumerian 'Paradise' Myth. Bulletin of the American Schools of Oriental Research, Supplemental Series 1. New Haven: American Schools of Oriental Research, 1945.

"Gilgamesh and the Land of the Living." *JCS* 1 (1947): 3–46.

"Schooldays: A Sumerian Composition Relating to the Education of a Scribe." *JAOS* 69 (1949): 199–215.

Enmerkar and the Lord of Aratta: A Sumerian Epic Tale of Iraq and Iran. Museum Monographs. Philadelphia: The University Museum of the University of Pennsylvania, 1952.

Limet, H. "Le poème épique 'Innina et Ebiḫ': une version des lignes 123 à 182." *Or*NS 40 (1971): 11–28.

McCown, D. E., and R. C. Haines. *Nippur I: Temple of Enlil, Scribal Quarter, and Soundings*. OIP 78. Chicago: The University of Chicago Press, 1967.

Robson, E. "The Tablet House: A Scribal School in Old Babylonian Nippur." *RA* 95 (2001): 39–66.

Shaffer, A. *Literary and Religious Texts, Third Part*. UET 6/3. London: British Museum Press, 2006.

Stone, E. *Nippur Neighborhoods*. Studies in Ancient Oriental Civilization 44. Chicago: The Oriental Institute of the University of Chicago, 1987.

Thureau-Dangin, F. "Notes assyriologiques." *RA* 31 (1934): 84–86.

Tinney, S. "Texts, Tablets, and Teaching: Scribal Education in Nippur and Ur." *Expedition* 40 (1998): 40–50.

"On the Curricular Setting of Sumerian Literature." *Iraq* 41 (1999): 159–72.

Veldhuis, N. *Elementary Education at Nippur: The Lists of Trees and Wooden Objects*. PhD Dissertation, Rijksuniversiteit Groningen, 1997.

Religion, Literature, and Scholarship: the Sumerian Composition 'Nanše and the Birds'. Cuneiform Monographs 22. Leiden: Brill, 2004.

Volk, K. *Inanna und Šukaletuda. Zur historisch-politischen Deutung eines sumerischen Literaturwerkes*. SANTAG 3. Wiesbaden: Harrassowitz, 1995.

Wilcke, C. "Politische Opposition nach sumerischen Quellen: Der Konflikt zwischen Königtum und Ratsversammlung. Literaturwerke als politische Tendenzschriften." In *La Voix de l'Opposition en Mésopotamie*, edited by A. Finet, 37–65. Bruxelles: Institut des Hautes Études, 1974.

"Politik im Spiegel der Literatur, Literatur als Mittel der Politik im älteren Babylonien." In *Anfänge politischen Denkens in der Antike*, edited by K. Raaflaub, 29–75. Schriften des Historischen Kollegs 24. München: Oldenbourg, 1993.

Woolley, L., and M. Mallowan. *The Old Babylonian Period*. Ur Excavations 7. London: British Museum Publications, 1976.

Zgoll, A. *Der Rechtsfall der En-ḫedu-Ana im Lied nin-me-šara*. AOAT 246. Münster: Ugarit-Verlag, 1997.

"Ebeḫ und andere Gebirge in der politischen Landschaft der Akkadzeit." In *Landscapes: Territories, Frontiers and Horizons in the Ancient Near East (Pt. II: Geography and Cultural Landscapes)*, edited by L. Milano, S. de Martino, F. M. Fales, and G. B. Lanfranchi, 83–90. CRRAI 44. History of the Ancient Near East Monographs 3/2. Padova: Sargon, 2000.

A NEW LOOK AT THE THEOLOGICAL BACKGROUND OF THE MESOPOTAMIAN AND BIBLICAL FLOOD STORIES

JACOB KLEIN
BAR-ILAN UNIVERSITY

For Barry, *šeš ku-li-ĝu*$_{10}$
May you enjoy *zi-u*$_4$*-sud-rá*!

According to modern biblical criticism, the story of the flood in Genesis 6:5–9:17 consists of two documentary sources: J and P.[1] Since the differences between these two hypothetical sources are marginal, we can regard the biblical story as belonging to one single, more or less uniform, tradition that can be compared to the parallel Mesopotamian traditions.

The Mesopotamian Flood Story is known from three different but complementary sources. The major and most important source is the Old Babylonian *Atra-ḫasīs* myth.[2] It begins with man's creation, a cos-

---

1 For a generally accepted layout and analysis of the two alleged sources of the biblical Flood Story, see Westermann, *Genesis 1–11*, 395–98. According to Westermann, the basic stock of the story is that of P, with J worked into it. An examination of the composite text, according to him, reveals that both sources contained "the same event with the same division, and only the slightest variations." From this he concludes that "the narrative was already well fixed in form before it came to J and P" (ibid., 394). Among those few modern exegetes who question the above documentary hypothesis or reject it is Cassuto. Cassuto assumes an underlying poetic tradition, which may have originated from several oral traditions, and was recorded in the Pentateuch in an elevated prose style; in his commentary on Genesis he tries to explain the stylistic differences and the seeming thematic contradictions in the text in a harmonizing way (Cassuto, *From Noah to Abraham*, 22–29). For another, highly speculative, reconstruction of the development of the biblical Flood Story, see Shaviv, "Polytheistic Origins," 527–48.

2 *Editio princeps:* Lambert and Millard, *Atra-ḫasīs: The Babylonian Story of the Flood*. For recent translations of the myth based on the above edition, see Bottéro and Kramer, *Lorsque les dieux*, 526–601; Dalley, *Myths from Mesopotamia*, 1–38; von Soden, apud Keiser (ed.), *Texte aus der Umwelt des Alten Testaments III/4*, 612–45; Shifra and Klein, *In Those Distant Days*, 88–130 (in Hebrew); Foster, *Before the Muses*, 227–80 (cf. ibid., 278 for an updated bibliography).

mic event, which was the ultimate cause for the flood. The second source is the eleventh tablet of the Standard *Epic of Gilgameš*, wherein Ūt-napištim, the Mesopotamian Noah, tells the main part of the story to Gilgameš as his personal experience.[3] The third source is a relatively late Sumerian composition, of which only one third is preserved.[4] In its original complete form it probably contained a report of the creation of man, the institution of kingship, the founding of the first cities, and the Flood Story.[5] Although the three Mesopotamian sources come from two different periods, almost a millennium apart, they are close enough to each other to be compared to the biblical tradition.

The subject of this study, as its title indicates, is the theological background of the flood in the biblical and the Mesopotamian traditions. In more concrete terms, the discussion will focus on the reason for the divine decision to bring the flood upon humanity in both traditions. Before we compare the two traditions from this point of view, it is important to note that both of them see in the flood a turning point in history. In the Bible, as well as in the Mesopotamian sources, this event separates "pre-history" from "history." Just as the Bible counts ten generations before the flood (Gen 5:1–32) and ten generations after the flood (Gen 10:1–32), so the Sumerian King List[6] counts the royal dynasties that ruled in five ancient cities before the flood and the royal dynasties that ruled Mesopotamia after the flood, until the end of the Isin dynasty.

The biblical Flood Story is the concluding episode in the broader framework of the early history of mankind. This history began with the creation of man, continued with man's repeated sins and rebellions against God, reaching its climax with the harsh statement (Gen 6:11): "The earth became corrupt before God; the earth was filled with injustice (*ḥāmās*, חמס)," and ended in the destruction of humanity and the creation of a new human world.[7] The meaning of the poetic-legal term *ḥāmās*, which is used to ex-

---

3 George, *Babylonian Gilgamesh Epic* I-II, 509–30; 700–25. See recently Greenstein, "Retelling of the Flood Story," 97–204.

4 Civil, "The Sumerian Flood Story," 138–45; Jacobsen, "The Eridu Genesis," 513–29; Kramer, "The Sumerian Deluge Myth," 115–21.

5 Cf. Jacobsen, "The Eridu Genesis," 513–14.

6 *Editio princeps*: Jacobsen, *The Sumerian King List*. For a full list of sources and studies published subsequently until 2004, see Glassner, *Mesopotamian Chronicles*, 117–18. See further Steinkeller, "An Ur III Manuscript," 267–92; Klein, "The Brockmon Collection Duplicate," 77–91.

7 According to Müller, just as the Creation Story is a myth, the Flood Story is an anti-myth, because it destroys all that was created (cf. idem, "Das Motiv für die Sintflut," 295–316). For a comprehensive survey of the

press the ultimate cause of the flood (see also Gen 6:13), is rather elusive, as indicated by its widely divergent renderings.[8] Its basic meaning seems to be: robbery,[9] which is interpreted in certain contexts also as oppression, extortion, violence, injustice, and the like.[10] It is especially Ezekiel who uses the idiom "filled with injustice" (*malᵉʾāh/malᵉʾū ḥāmās*) borrowed from Genesis, in his prophecies of doom against Judah and its Canaanite neigh-

---

various hypotheses as to the literary and thematic structure of the primeval history (Gen 1–11) and the place of the Flood Story within this literary framework, see Tsumura, "Genesis and Ancient Near Eastern Stories," 45–51.

8 Note the following representative sample of renderings of the noun *ḥāmās*: "injustice" (NJPS; *HALOT*); "lawlessness" (Speiser, *Genesis*, 1964; Gesenius-Donner); "wrong" (BDB; *DCH*; *HALOT* 1994); "violence" (BDB; *DCH*; JPS; ESV; Westermann, *Genesis 1–11*; Gesenius-Donner[18]; *HALOT* 1994); "robbery, oppression, extortion" (Kaddari, *DBH*, 318). According to von Soden, this word is attested in Middle/Neo-Assyrian in the forms *ḫamsu*, "false," and *ḫimsātu*, "unlawful property/plunder" (*AHw*, 318a; 346b). However, according to *CAD*, these nouns derive from Akk. *ḫamāṣu* "to strip, rob" (*CAD* Ḫ, 60f.; 191f. s.v. *ḫimṣātu*). As to the verb derived from the same root, *ḥāmas*, its meaning is somewhat clearer; it is agreed upon that it means "to rob, treat violently, oppress" and the like. Hebrew *ḥāmas* and Akk. *ḫamāṣu*, seem to be etymologically and semantically related, the Akk. form appearing in the Bible twice, in the words *ḥōmēṣ* (Ps 71:4) and *ḥāmōṣ* (Isa 1:17).

9 Cf., e.g., Jer 6:7; Am 3:10. This was already observed in Jewish rabbinical interpretation; cf. Bab. Talmud, Sanhedrin 108a: "R. Johanan said: Come and see how great is the power of robbery, for lo, though the generation of the flood transgressed all laws, their decree of punishment was sealed only because they stretched out their hands to rob, as it is written (Gen 6:13), for the earth is filled with violence through them, and, behold, I will destroy them with the earth."

10 Cf., e.g., Ex 23:1; Deut 19:16; Ps 27:12. For a recent comprehensive and systematic survey of Hebrew *ḥāmas/ḥāmās*, see Gemeren (ed.), *New International*, 177–80. According to this study, the verb denotes "do violence, treat violently, harm, oppress," and the noun denotes accordingly "violence, wrong, bloodshed, unrighteousness, wickedness." These socio-ethical crimes are committed always by man against his fellow man. Usually, they take the form of physical and psychological violence, such as murder and destruction (Gen 49:5; Jud 9:24; Ps 7:16; Hab 1a; Joel 4:19); occasionally they constitute injustice in juridical or social contexts (Gen 16:5; Ex 23:1; Isa 59:6; Jer 6:7). It is important to note that *ḥāmās* may also corrupt the earth, which involves the destruction of plant and animal life (cf. Hab 2:17a), a phenomenon that has a close relevance to the flood episode (Gen 6:11, 13).

bors.[11] The ultimate reason for bringing the flood upon mankind, according to the Bible, was thus moral corruption in society, which manifested itself in all the evil acts covered by the general term *ḥāmās*.

The Babylonian myth *Atra-ḫasīs* likewise introduces the Flood Story with an account of the creation of man, and ascribes to humanity a series of "misdeeds" that aroused the displeasure of Enlil, motivating him to bring upon them the flood. However, it is unclear whether we can see in these "misdeeds" actual sin. The unique and surprising element in the Mesopotamian tradition is the fact that, prior to the flood, the gods made three attempts to diminish mankind by reducing their number. According to this myth, twelve hundred years after the creation of man, humanity multiplied and their tumult made the supreme god Enlil restless. Consequently, he decided to reduce their number by means of a plague. However, Enki-Ea, the god of wisdom, the creator of man, thwarted Enlil's plan: he advised King Atra-ḫasīs, his protégé, to instruct the people to worship only Namtar, the god of pestilence, bribing him with copious food offerings. The people followed the advice, and the plague was lifted.[12] This story repeats itself two more times: The people multiply again and again, making Enlil restless with their noise; and Enlil makes two more attempts to diminish their number, this time by the means of droughts and severe famine. Enki, with his cunning frustrates these attempts too.[13]

Ever since the *Atra-ḫasīs* myth was coherently reconstructed, scholars have been divided over the question: Why did the gods order the annihilation of mankind by the flood according to Mesopotamian tra-

---

11 Cf. Ez 7:23; 8:17; 28:16. Frymer-Kensky, in a very stimulating article ("The Atrahasis Epic," 150–54), suggests that *ḥāmās* in the present context refers particularly to "bloodshed," which polluted (Heb. *hišḥīt*) the earth, having prompted God to erase everything from the earth and start anew. This she concludes, among others, from the phrase "the land is full of *dāmim*" in Ez 9:9, which parallels the phrase "the earth was filled with *ḥāmās*," in the flood episode, as well as from the fact that immediately after the flood God issues the commandment that neither beast nor man can kill a human being, "for man is created in God's image" (Gen 9:5–6). Although this hypothesis provides a more rational explanation to the harshness of the divine punishment meted out to humanity, it cannot be proven on the basis of the term *ḥāmās*, whose wide range of meanings in the Bible, as admitted by the author herself, "encompasses almost the entire spectrum of evil" (ibid., 153a).

12 *Atra-ḫasīs* I 352–414.

13 *Atra-ḫasīs* II i 1–iv 20 (cf. Foster, *Before the Muses*, 241–45); due to the fragmentary state of the sources these two episodes could be only partly reconstructed.

dition? Several answers have been offered, of which two merit consideration. According to one opinion, mankind committed some kind of offence against the gods, thereby bringing upon itself the flood as punishment; according to another opinion, the problem that the gods wanted to solve with the flood was humanity's overpopulation.

The key passages that may provide a clue to the solution of this problem are found at the beginning and the end of the Flood Story. According to the beginning of the myth, the trouble with mankind began with its proliferation, which is described as follows:

> Twelve hundred years had not yet been passed
> When the land extended and the people multiplied.
> The land was bellowing like a bull,
> The god was disturbed with their uproar (= *ina ḫubūrišina*)
> Enlil heard their clamor (=*rigimšin*)
> And addressed the great gods:
> "The clamor of mankind has become burdensome to me,
> With their uproar I am deprived of sleep.
> Command that there be a plague,
> Let Namtar diminish their clamor!"[14]

As early as 1950, Speiser, in his translation of *Atra-ḫasīs*, expressed the opinion that this epic cycle deals "with man's sins and his consequent punishment through plagues and the deluge."[15] Speiser did not disclose his reasoning behind the above interpretation of the myth, but Finkelstein, in his essay on the religious and ethical differences between Babylonian mythology and the Bible, published eight years later, was more explicit and assertive in following Speiser's hypothesis. Finkelstein was convinced that "there can be little doubt that the noise of mankind that disturbs Enlil's repose is only the metaphoric or mythological guise for what is clearly meant to be the wicked behavior of man." However, Finkelstein could not pinpoint the exact nature of man's wickedness according to the myth, claiming that Babylonian myth does not go beyond generalization in describing his alleged wickedness.[16]

The first Assyriologist who undertook a thorough study to demonstrate the nature of man's alleged wickedness according to the *Atra-ḫasīs* myth was Pettinato. In an article published in 1968, a year before the appearance of the masterful edition of the myth by Lambert-Mill-

---

14 *Atra-ḫasīs* I 352–60. The text of this passage has been restored on the basis of the following parallels: II i 1–8; S rev. iv 1–8; 37–42 (Lambert-Millard, *Atra-ḫasīs*, 106f.); x rev. I 1–3 (ibid., 116).

15 Speiser, "Atrahasis," 104.

16 Finkelstein, "Bible and Babel," 437.

ard, Pettinato investigated in detail the problem under discussion, reaching the conclusion that the sin of mankind in the Babylonian myth was even graver than the sin of mankind according to the biblical tradition.[17]

The starting point of Pettinato's interpretation of the above passage, which provides Enlil's motives for attempting to diminish the number of mankind, is the history of religion. In his opinion it is inconceivable that the Babylonian mythographer would not provide a theologically reasonable motive for such a grave cosmic disaster as the flood. Therefore, Pettinato excludes à priori the assumption that Enlil's action against mankind was arbitrarily motivated, assuming that it must have been a punishment for a crime.[18]

Pettinato affirms the interpretation that the words *ḫubūru* and *rigmu* are not neutral expressions, referring simply to the "uproar" and "clamor" (respectively) raised by multitudes of human beings, but rather connote evil conduct. These expressions, in his opinion, allude to man's rebellious protest against his lot of having to toil for the gods, which amounted to outright rebellion. Pettinato supports his interpretation by referring to Landsberger's contention that *ḫubūru* in Akkadian literature generally denotes a rebellious uproar[19] and by the observation that in the first episode of the same myth the expression *rigmum* refers to the rebellious uproar of the Igigi gods.[20] From this he infers that mankind

---

17 Pettinato, "Die Bestrafung," 165–200. Although Pettinato's above article was published one year before the appearance of the edition of *Atra-ḫasīs* by Lambert-Millard, he was able to reconstruct Tablet I of this myth, containing the events that led to the flood, from the copies of the cuneiform sources (CT 46, pls. 1–15). For a subsequent analysis of the *Atra-ḫasīs* myth, following and supplementing that of Pettinato, see especially Oden, "Divine Aspirations," 197–216.

18 Pettinato, "Die Bestrafung," 174f.

19 Cf. Landsberger, "Ḫabiru and Lulaḫḫu," 328. For a full documentation of this poetic word see *CAD* Ḫ, 221 s.v. *ḫubūru* B. See below for another, recent interpretation of this term.

20 Cf. I 77: *rigma išemmû š*[*a Igigi*]. Note that elsewhere, *rigmu* is used only in the meaning of "legal claim" or "complaint" (cf. *CAD* R, 334 s.v. *rigmu* 6), never referring to rebellious uproar. Oden in his defense of Pettinato's interpretation (cf. Oden, "Divine Aspirations," 210) compares the expressions "uproar" and "clamor" in *Atra-ḫasīs* to the biblical expressions זעקה, "uproar" and צעקה, "outcry" in Gen 18:20 (for this false comparison, see already Finkelstein, "Bible and Babel," 437). In that episode, God says to Abraham: "Because the uproar of Sodom and Gomorrah is great, and their sin is very grave, I will descend and see whether they have acted altogether according to the outcry that has reached Me." In his opinion, just

after its creation followed the example of the Igigi gods by imitating and repeating their rebellion. He concludes, therefore, that according to Mesopotamian tradition the flood was brought upon mankind as punishment for grave sins, not unlike in the biblical tradition.[21]

The other key passage with which Pettinato supports his hypothesis is the apologetic address of Enki to Enlil toward the end of the composition. After Enlil had realized that some human beings survived the flood and became enraged at the Igigi, one of the major gods[22] accused Enki of having thwarted Enlil's plan to exterminate the people. Enki reacts with a counter accusation.[23] He blames Enlil's rashness in sending the deluge, thereby inflicting punishment indiscriminately without regard for guilt. Instead he should have used less drastic measures, such as decimating the people by the means of wild animals, famine, or plague.[24] In Enki's own words (*Epic of Gilgameš* XI 183–95):

> You, the sage of the gods, the hero,
> How could you lack counsel and cause the deluge?
> On him who commits a sin, inflict his crime!
> On him who does wrong, inflict his wrong-doing!...
> Instead of the deluge you caused,
> A lion could arise to diminish the people!
> Instead of the deluge you caused,
> A wolf could arise to diminish the people!
> Instead of the deluge you caused,

---

as the expressions "uproar" and "outcry" in the biblical passage refer to crimes committed by the citizens of Sodom and Gomorrah, so also the "uproar" and "clamor" of mankind in the Babylonian Flood Story refer to rebellious acts by the people against the gods. However, Moran is right in pointing out that in the biblical story זעקה and צעקה do not refer to the sinful clamor of the two evil cities, but to the "outcry" of the oppressed people against their oppressors in the two cities; consequently, these two biblical expressions cannot be adduced in support of Pettinato's interpretation of the *Atra-ḫasīs* episode.

21 Pettinato, "Die Bestrafung," 184–90.

22 Anu (according to *Atra-ḫasīs*) or Ninurta (according to the *Epic of Gilgameš* XI).

23 *Atra-ḫasīs* III vi 16–40; *Epic of Gilgameš* XI 177–98.

24 To similar lists of natural disasters as divine punishment, cf. Lev 26:21–26; Ez 14:12–20. It is needless to stress that according to both the Mesopotamian authors and Ezekiel, such divinely ordained disasters affected only the sinners, whereas all those who escaped them were considered righteous people.

A famine could happen to slaughter the land!
Instead of the deluge you caused,
Erra could arise to slaughter the land![25]

According to Pettinato, Enki's above words affirm that the repeated attempts to diminish humanity and the subsequent attempt to annihilate them by the means of the flood were punishment for their rebellious complaint over the hard labor imposed upon them, which could not be suppressed by any other measures.[26] Consequently, Pettinato reaches the provocative conclusion that the reason given in the Mesopotamian

---

25 Although Enki's corresponding address in *Atra-ḫasīs* III vi 16–26 is extremely damaged, the surviving traces indicate that it was more or less identical to the address in the *Epic of Gilgameš*. The following is a conjectural reconstruction of this passage:

[^{d}*en-ki*] *pí-a-šu i-*⸢*pu*⸣*-ša-am-*[*ma*]
[*is-sà-qar*] *a-na i-li ra-bu-ti*
[*lu-ú e*]*-pu-uš i-na pa-ni-*⸢*ku*⸣*-u*[*n*]
[*ú-uš-t*]*a-ṣi-ra na-pí-i*[*š-tam* x x x [x x]
[*at*]-⸢*ta*⸣$^{?}$ [*apkal*] *i-l*[*i* x x x] x bi$^{?}$
[*ki-i la tam-ta-li-ik-ma*$^{?}$ *taš-kun a-b*]*u-ba*
[*a-wi-lu-ti ana ka-ra-ši-im ta*]*-aš*$^{?!}$*-ku-un*
[*li-nu-uḫ*$^{?}$ *a-i-is-bu-us*$^{?}$ *l*]*i-ib-ba-ka*
[x x x *šu-du-ud*] *ù ru-um-mi*
[*be-el ar-n*]*im šu-ku-un še-re-et-ka*
[*ù*] ⸢*a*⸣*-iu ša ú-ša-a*[*s*]*-sà-ku a-wa-at-ka*

Enki opened his mouth
[And addressed] the great gods:
"[I] did it [indeed] *for your sake*!
[I caused] to save life, ...!
[Yo]u [*the sage*] of the god[s] ....,
[*How could you lack counsel and cause*] the deluge?
[You ex]posed [*humanity to annihilation*!]
[*May*] your heart [*calm down, may it not rage*!]
[.......... *pull taut*] and slacken!
Impose your punishment [on the criminal]
[And] whoever disregards your command."

26 Pettinato, "Die Bestrafung," 193. Compare Finkelstein's earlier remarks on Ea's above apologetic speech: "Numerous Babylonian religious texts such as hymns and prayers had been already published which reflected a high moral and ethical consciousness and a deep awareness of sin and retribution" (432), and therefore "The speech of Ea...is an indication that, to the mind of the Babylonian the decision [to bring the Flood] was in the

tradition to the flood is more reasonable and justified than the reason given to the same in the biblical tradition. Whereas the biblical author gives to this event a general, vague, and somewhat forced moral reason: lawlessness and violence,[27] the Babylonian author provides to the same event a well-defined, specific, and plausible reason: man's rebellion against the very purpose for which he was created.

Soon after the appearance of Pettinato's article, William Moran and Ann Kilmer responded to it in two independent studies in which they expressed a radically different interpretation as to the motive of Enlil in inflicting the flood upon mankind.[28] Contrary to Pettinato, Moran and Kilmer argued that "uproar" and "clamor" in the Babylonian Flood Story cannot refer to rebellious outcry; these expressions rather refer to the tumult raised by innocent people, who naturally multiplied without any evil intentions. In their opinion, the problem with mankind was their ever-increasing population, which resulted in such a din and racket that it disturbed the peace (literally "sleep") of Enlil.[29]

---

first place prompted by man's evil behavior" ("Bible and Babel," 436). Heidel, on the other hand, points out that, according to Ea's speech, in Mesopotamian tradition "the destruction is intended for all alike, for the just and for the unjust," indicating a defective law of retribution (Heidel, *The Gilgamesh Epic and Old Testament Parallels*, 226).

27 Pettinato, "Die Bestrafung," 199f. The feeling that the motive provided for the Flood in the Bible is general and vague has been expressed already by Finkelstein ("Bible and Babel," 437) and by other biblical exegetes; cf. e.g. Müller, "Das Motive," 296–98; Shaviv, "Polytheistic Origins," 545–46. For the hypothesis of T. Frymer-Kensky, that *ḥāmās* in this context refers to "bloodshed," cf. n. 11 above.

28 Moran, "Atrahasis," 51–61; Kilmer, "Mesopotamian Concept of Overpopulation," 160–77. Moran reaffirmed his hypothesis in two subsequent articles; cf. Moran, "Some Considerations," 251–55; Moran, "The Gilgamesh Epic," 2327–36.

29 Cf. Moran, "Atrahasis," 55ff.; Moran, "Some Considerations," 253f.; Kilmer, "Mesopotamian Concept of Overpopulation," 167ff. Most scholars who subsequently dealt with this issue tended to agree with Moran and Kilmer's hypothesis; cf., e.g., Müller, "Das Motive," 300–1; Kvanvig, "Gen 6,1–4," 95–98. According to Müller ("Das Motiv," 298), just as the flood is not motivated by a clearly visible sin by man, so the saving of Atra-ḫasis by Enki cannot be based on his righteousness or piety. He is saved because Enki favors him. Millard, on the contrary, claims that the true meaning of the name Atra-ḫasīs is "the exceedingly devout" (rather than "the exceedingly wise") and, therefore, he was saved by his piety, not by his wisdom (Millard, "A New Babylonian 'Genesis' Story," 124). The most recent study dealing with the problem under discussion is Y. Chen's doctoral thesis on the emergence and development of the Mesopotamian

Moran further asserted that, notwithstanding Enki's above speech, the *Atra-ḫasīs* myth ignores altogether the ideas of sin and punishment. In his opinion, man's innocent clamor became so intense that it caused a sort of chaos and imbalance in the antediluvian world. One is reminded of other Mesopotamian myths such as the Epic of Creation, *Enūma Eliš*, where the so called "sleep" of the otiose elder gods was disturbed by the clamor raised by the dynamic younger gods, a development that resulted in a total war between the two groups.[30]

That Moran and Kilmer pointed in the right direction in solving the problem under discussion is indicated by the concluding episode of *Atra-ḫasīs*. It consists of a passage of about 80 lines, which, in spite of its fragmentary state, can be reconstructed and reasonably understood. In this passage, Enlil orders Enki and the birth-goddess Nintu to find a solution to man's uncontrolled multiplying by devising measures for putting it under control. The first measure that Enki proposes to Nintu is the most effective one: limiting the lifespan of man (III vi 45–50):

> [*Enki pī*]*šu īpušamma*
> [*issaqar*] *ana Nintu sassūri*
> [*attī sa*]*ssūru bāniat šīmāti*
> [*mūta šuknī*] *ana nišī*[31]
>
> Enki opened his mouth
> And [addressed] Nintu, the birth-goddess:
> "[You], birth goddess, creatress of destinies,
> [Impose death] on the people…!"

The other measures for controlling birth, as proposed by Enki, are the barrenness of women, the death of infants by the hand of a female demon, and the creation of certain categories of priestesses who were forbidden to conceive and give birth.[32]

---

flood traditions. According to Chen, while the Sumerian Flood Story did not offer any rational reason for the catastrophe, the author of the Babylonian epic resorted to the motif of human noise to explain the annihilation of humanity in the flood, alluding to it as some kind of sinful behavior. This author, however, did not clarify the sinful nature of the noise, rather emphasizing the disproportional and indiscriminate nature of the punishment, through the admonishing address of Enki to Enlil after the flood. Nevertheless, both flood traditions developed from earlier Sumerian lament literature, which generally fails to provide logical and moral reasons for natural or political disasters (Chen, *The Emergence*, vol. I, pp. 391-402).

30 Moran, "Atrahasis," 57–59.

31 For the restoration of this line see Lambert, "The Theology of Death," 58.

32 *Atra-ḫasīs* III vi 50–51; vii 1–9.

In view of the above measures taken by the gods to limit and control man's proliferation, it turns out that, according to Mesopotamian belief, the gods made a fatal mistake when they created man: they created him male and female, granting him the potential to procreate and multiply, but forgot to limit his lifespan, most probably having destined him for immortality.[33] As a result, humanity multiplied without control, and this overpopulation brought upon them the flood. Only after the flood did it occur to the gods to correct their mistake: they limited man's lifespan and took other measures to check their proliferation. As correctly pointed out by Lambert,[34] this is confirmed also by Ūt-napištim's admonitory address to Gilgameš, before telling him the story of the flood. After relating to Gilgameš the cruel facts of life and death in the grimmest terms, Ūt-napištim concludes his words saying (*Epic of Gilgameš* X 318–22):

Mortal-man, young-man, after [Enlil] blessed me,[35]
The Anunnaki, the great gods, assembled,
Mammītum, the creatress of destiny, made a decree with them:
Death and life they did establish,
The day of death they did not reveal![36]

Whether the authors of the Sumerian King List shared the above belief as to the origin of death or not cannot be determined with certainty. Nevertheless, the fact that they ascribed to antediluvian kings much longer reigns than to postdiluvian kings[37] seems to indicate that

---

33 Man's original immortality could have resulted from the divine "flesh and blood" with which his clay was mixed; cf. *Atra-ḫasīs* I 211–12: *ina šīrišu u damišu Nintu liballil ṭiṭṭa ilumma u awīlum libtallilū puḫur ina ṭiṭṭa*, "From his (=the slaughtered god) flesh and blood let Nintu mix clay, so that god and man may be thoroughly mixed in the clay." See also *Enūma eliš* VI 31–34 (Talon, *The Standard Babylonian Creation Myth*, 63); Lambert, "The Relationship of Sumerian and Babylonian Myth," 133–34.

34 Lambert, "The Theology of Death," 54–57.

35 Restoring *lullû amēlu eṭel ultu ikrubu*[*ni Enlil*?] (for a similar restoration of this line see Schott, *Das Gilgamesch-Epos*, 85 vi 35). For a different restoration and reading of this line, see George, *Babylonian Gilgamesh Epic*, 696. On the basis of his above restoration George concludes that there was another tradition in Mesopotamia, according to which death was the doom of mankind from its creation. This tradition, as he points out (George ibid., 507–8), is clearly reflected in the address of the ale-wife to Gilgameš in the OB version of the epic (OB VA + BM iii 2-5), as well as in the address of Enlil to Ūt-napištim in the Standard Babylonian epic (XI 202–3).

36 Akk. *ša mūti ul uddû ūmīšu*; cf. George, *Babylonian Gilgamesh Epic*, 696–99.

37 Whereas the regnal years of the antediluvian kings range between 108,000

they, too, saw in the flood a turning point, at which the human lifespan was drastically reduced. Accordingly, even if we assume that according to the authors of the King List man was not destined at the time of his creation to immortality, they still granted him an extremely long lifespan, and he still had the potential to multiply disproportionately, disturbing Enlil's peace.

The belief that man's lifespan was not limited at all at the time of his creation seems to be reflected also in the Bible. In the second, more popular, creation story we are told that after the creation of man, God planted in the Garden of Eden all manner of fruit trees, with the tree of life and the tree of knowledge of good and bad in its center (Gen 2:8–9). A few verses further the author tells us that "God commanded man saying: 'Of Every tree of the garden you are free to eat; but as for the tree of knowledge of good and bad, you must not eat of it; for as soon as you eat of it, you shall be doomed to die'"[38] (Gen 2:16–17). According to the plain sense of the text, God initially forbade man only to eat from the tree of knowledge, allowing him tacitly to eat from the tree of life, and thus live forever.[39] Only when man trespassed the prohibition against eating from the "tree of knowledge" did God prevent him from eating from the "tree of life" by expelling him from the Garden of Eden (Gen 3:22–24). God explains this act of his against man as follows:

> Now that the man has become like one of us, knowing good and bad, what if he should stretch out his hand and take also from the tree of life
> and eat, and live forever![40]

to 18,600 years, those of the postdiluvian kings do not exceed a maximum of 1500 years (Etana), gradually diminishing, and becoming reduced to realistic numbers after Dumuzi and Gilgameš of the Uruk I dynasty (cf. Glassner, *Mesopotamian Chronicles,* 119–27).

38 Literally: "for when you eat from it you will surely die."

39 Whether becoming immortal by eating from it once or by eating from it periodically and thus always renewing his youth. For the former possibility, cf. the "food of life" (*akal balāṭi*) and "water of life" (*mê balāṭi*), which were offered to Adapa in heaven but refused by him, whereby he lost the opportunity to become immortal (cf. Izre'el, *Adapa and the South Wind,* 20:60′–63′); for the latter possibility cf. the "plant of heartbeat" (*šammu nikitti*), which makes the old man grow young, in the *Epic of Gilgameš* XI 295–300 (George, *Babylonian Gilgamesh Epic,* 722). The fact that man could still become immortal by eating from the tree of life, after he was sentenced to death (Gen 3:22; see below), may support the latter interpretation.

40 Gen 3:22. Many Bible critics consider the verses relating to the "tree of life"

It follows from the above episode that biblical tradition agrees with Babylonian tradition as to the original divine plan concerning man's longevity. According to both traditions, when man was created, he was destined for immortality. However, contrary to the Babylonian flood tradition, death according to the Bible was imposed on man not after the flood as a result of his uncontrolled proliferation, but very soon after his creation, even before he began to multiply; and the reason for imposing death on him was his first attempt to transgress his boundaries and become like God by eating from the "tree of knowledge."[41]

However, according to the Bible, although death was meted out to man not long after his creation, the death sentence did not take effect immediately; and Adam and his descendents were allowed unusually long life spans. This is reflected in the first two genealogical lists in Genesis (5:1–31 and 11:10–27), wherein all personages live hundreds of years. In this respect, biblical tradition agrees with that of the Mesopotamian King List in three points: (1) the generations close to creation enjoyed extraordinary longevity, which gradually diminished in the course of time, proportionately to their remoteness from the time of creation;[42] (2) the antediluvian patriarchs were assigned much longer life-spans than the postdiluvian patriarchs;[43] and (3) this privilege of lon-

---

in Gen 2–3 as secondary interpolations (cf., e.g., Skinner, *Genesis* [ICC], 52f.). The conspicuous parallels to the Babylonian tradition, however, seem to demonstrate that they are integral parts of the text.

41 In a recent comparative study of the above episode and the myth of Adapa, Hallo claims that both Adapa and Adam were given the choice between eating from the tree/food of life, thereby acquiring immortality, or eating from the tree of knowledge, which meant for both of them death; and both of them deliberately chose death, rejecting eternal life (cf. Hallo, "Adapa Reconstructed," 267–77; see especially ibid., 276f.). In fact, however, neither Adapa nor Adam was aware of the consequences of his decision. Mislead by the ill-advice of cunning Ea, Adapa believed that the food and water offered him meant death, and he rejected them (Izre'el, *Adapa and the South Wind*, 18:28′–31′); similarly, misled by the ruse of the serpent (Gen 3:4–5), Adam did not believe that upon eating from the tree of knowledge he would die and, therefore, he ate from it.

42 The longevity of the earlier generations was most probably due to man's divine origin, either by having been infused with the blood of a god (according to Mesopotamian tradition; see already n. 33 above) or by having been infused with divine spirit, "the breath of life," directly by God (according to the Bible; cf. Gen 2:7); see Cassuto, *A Commentary on the Book of Genesis*, 262–64; 297–98.

43 Whereas the life-spans of the antediluvian patriarchs range from 777 to 969 years, those of the postdiluvian patriarchs range from 464 to 205 years (except of Noah's son, Shem, who is assigned 610 years).

gevity brought trouble upon antediluvian man, for we read in the passage preceding the Flood Story (Gen 6:1): "When men began to increase on earth and daughters were born to them, the divine beings[44] saw how beautiful the daughters of man were, and they took as wives any they liked." This intermarriage between divine and human beings resulted in man transgressing the limits set for him, thereby incurring God's displeasure.[45] Consequently, God decided to limit the lifespan of humanity, saying (Gen 6:3):

> My spirit shall not last in man forever, since he is flesh;
> let the days allowed him be one hundred and twenty years.

The relationship of this episode to the subsequent Flood Story, and the exact meaning of the sentence "let the days allowed him (lit. "his days") be one hundred and twenty years" (Hebrew: *w^e^hayū yāmâw meāh w^e^esrîm šānāh*) had long been a matter of controversy among Bible commentators. According to one opinion, our episode is a prelude to the Flood Story, and hence "his days" refers here to the generation of the flood, whose punishment was postponed for a period of 120 years, to allow them to repent;[46] according to another opinion, our episode is not

---

44 Literally "the sons of God" (Hebrew *b^e^nê ha-elōhīm*). In the history of biblical exegesis many different interpretations have been put forward as to the identification of these super-human beings. Both early Jewish and Christian exegetes tended to identify them as human beings possessed of outstanding power, especially identifying them with the Sethites or Cainites, an apologetic interpretation that is still maintained by some very recent interpreters (cf. Hartley, *Genesis*, 96–97; Clines, "The Significance of the 'Sons of God' Episode," 33–38); others saw in them angels. Modern exegetes emphasize the origin of the term in ancient Ugaritic and Canaanite mythology, upon which the present translation "divine beings" is based (cf. especially Gunkel's pertinent discussion in his *Genesis*, 59). For surveys of former interpretations cf. Westermann, *Genesis 1–11*, 371–73; Kvanvig, "Gen 6,1–4," 86–87. No question that we have here a vestige of a mythological episode, which excludes the probability that the reference is to human beings.

45 It had been observed by many commentators that these illicit intermarriages cannot be considered as a sinful transgression on the part of man, because they were initiated by the "divine beings" and not by human beings. However, the ultimate cause for this incident was still man's unlimited proliferation, which had to be checked less it get out of control. Therefore, the reaction of God is not a punishment, but a measure taken to correct an inherent defect in mankind from its creation.

46 This position was held by most ancient and medieval Jewish interpreters, and it is still adhered today by a minority of modern exegetes. See

connected to the Flood Story, but belongs to the preceding primeval history, and therefore these words refer to the maximum lifespan, which a human being was allowed to attain hereafter.[47]

In an article that I published twenty years ago,[48] I demonstrated that the figure 120 in the present context must refer to the maximum lifespan of any individual in future days.[49] In that article I pointed out that the figure of 120 years as the upper limit of human lifespan already appears in a wisdom composition from Emar, which is a bilingual version of the Sumerian folktale *Enlil and Namzitara*.[50] In this tale, Namzitara reminds Enlil of the transience of human life, saying to him as follows (ll. 19′–26′):

> The days of the human-being are approaching,
> Day to day they verily decrease,
> Month after month they verily decrease,
> Year after year they verily decrease!

---

bibliography by Westermann, *Genesis 1–11*. 368f.; Heidel, *The Gilgamesh Epic*, 226. Davidson (in *Genesis 1–11*), who considers Gen 6:1–4 "a fragment of pagan mythology" and sees in Gen 6:1–8 J's introduction to the Flood Story. As to the sentence "let the days allowed him be one hundred and twenty years," he cannot decide whether it refers to man's lifespan or to the limited period that was left for humanity to repent before the flood.

47 This interpretation is now generally acknowledged in modern biblical scholarship. However, many modern commentators still consider this episode to be an introduction to the Flood Story, furnishing the main reason for God's decision to punish mankind, and illustrating the statement that "all flesh corrupted its ways on earth" (Gen 6:12).

Since the intermarriages between the divine beings and the daughters of man serves here (originally or secondarily) as an etiology for the origin of the "fallen heroes" (Gen 6:4), it had been generally assumed that the latter, by virtue of descending from divine fathers, were expected to attain immortality and, therefore, the divine decree concerning the limiting of the lifespan to 120 years, relates especially to them. According to Westermann, the sons of the gods "aspired to raise the status of the human race and so forced the creator to intervene" (*Genesis 1–11*, 374; cf. Kvanvig, "Gen 6,1–4," 86).

48 Klein, "The 'Bane' of Humanity," 57–70.

49 I further draw attention to the fact that after the forefathers, who enjoyed the prestige of the primeval generations, no one was allowed by the biblical authors a lifespan of 120 years except for Moses (Deut 31:2; 34:7); cf. Klein, "The 'Bane' of Humanity," 60–62.

50 For the latest edition of this bilingual MB version see Alster, *Wisdom of Ancient Sumer*, 336–37.

One hundred twenty years (are) the years of mankind—verily it is their bane;
(This is so) from the time that humanity exists until today![51]

We have seen that in both the Mesopotamian and the biblical traditions man before the flood had a very high potential for multiplying, which was bound to get out of control. In both traditions man's proliferation caused him to displease the supreme god; and in both traditions measures were taken to put man's propagation under control, especially by limiting his lifespan to the maximum of 120 years. The major difference between the two traditions is that according to the Bible, man's lifespan was limited before the flood, whereas in Mesopotamian mythology, his lifespan was limited after the flood. The reason for this difference is obvious. The incident of the intermarriage between divine and human beings (Gen 6:1–4) belongs to an older layer of tradition, of a semi-mythological nature, being very close to the Ancient Near Eastern traditions. In this tradition the concern is still the rivalry between god and man, and the fear that man may transgress his boundaries and upset the cosmic equilibrium. The Flood Story, on the other hand, is a purely monotheistic source, based on an absolute separation between man and the transcendent God. The sole concern in this story is therefore man's morality vis-à-vis his fellow man. Therefore, in the biblical Flood Story the deity is not concerned with the disturbance of cosmic equilibrium, but rather with the social and moral state of humanity. Accordingly, when he reaches the conclusion that humanity has become hopelessly corrupt, he decides to wipe it out and build a new

51 Contrary to all former interpretations of this folktale (including mine), the "vanity theme" speech is delivered by Namzitara and not by Enlil (this was pointed out to me by Yoram Cohen, who will demonstrate this in a future publication). In my above study I suggested that the figure of 120 years as the maximum lifespan may derive from a West-Semitic tradition. However, I will not be surprised if this figure will turn up in one of the now missing versions of the Babylonian Flood Story. It should be noted that although most biblical commentaries and studies relating to Gen 6:1–4 that subsequently appeared either ignored or overlooked my above article, the over-whelming majority of them reached the same conclusion, namely that the figure of 120 years refers here to the limitation of the lifespan of any individual in future days. One of these scholars is H. Kvanvig, who in her sophisticated study of Gen 6:1–4 observed the close relationship between this episode and *Atra-ḫasīs*, and reached similar conclusions to those of the present author. However, ignoring the Emar parallel and overlooking the lifespan attributed to Moses, she speculates that the figure 120 is perhaps based on the number 1200 (=2 *nēru* or 1/3 *šāru*), given for the intervals between the three attempts to reduce the number of humanity in the *Atra-ḫasīs* myth, reducing the number by one zero (Kvanvig, "Gen 6,1–4," 99).

and better human society from the stock of a righteous family.[52] Therefore, the biblical author (or redactor) draws a clear line between the problem of overpopulation and the problem of morality and social equilibrium.

In Mesopotamian mythological thought the concern of the gods is fundamentally different. Man's uncontrolled proliferation generated an unbearable "din," which disturbed Enlil's "sleep." As has been correctly pointed out by Peter Machinist, *ḫubūru*, "uproar," and *rigmu*, "clamor," in this and similar contexts, refer to excessive, energetic activity, in contrast to *ṣalālu*, "sleeping," which refers to rest and inactivity.[53] In his opinion, "activity is necessary for the universe to function. But too much activity brings on violence and potential chaos."[54] Accordingly, Enlil was concerned here primarily with the overpopulation of mankind, which generated excessive activity on its part and caused chronic disorders and crises, as a result of which the world was bound to return into a chaotic state.

Another possible motive for the bringing of the flood upon mankind could have been Enlil's fear that if man's procreative powers went unchecked, he would fill up the surface of the earth, evicting from it the gods, his creators. An analogous situation is depicted in Inana's threatening words to Anu, when she demands from him the Bull of Heaven to punish the defiant Gilgameš (*Epic of Gilgameš* VI 94–100):

> O my father, give me, please, the Bull of Heaven,
> That I may slay Gilgameš in his dwelling.
> If you will not give me the Bull of Heaven,
> I shall smash the netherworld together with its dwelling place,
> I shall raze the nether regions to the ground.
> I shall bring up the dead to consume the living,
> I shall make the dead outnumber the living.[55]

Thus it is not impossible that Enlil feared that mankind, created to serve the gods, would become so numerous that no living space would be left upon the earth for the gods, its creators.

---

52 Cf. Frymer-Kensky's pertinent remarks in her article "The Atrahasis Epic," 150.

53 Machinist, "Rest and Violence in the Poem of Erra," 221–35; see also Michalowski, "Presence at the Creation," 385–89.

54 Machinist, "Rest and Violence in the Poem of Erra," 225.

55 For a similar threatening address of Inana-Ištar, cf. *Descent of Ištar* 13–20 (Borger, *Babylonisch-Assyrische Lesestücke* II, 499); Lapinkivi, *The Neo-Assyrian Myth*, 25, 29, 46–49.

But perhaps we attribute to Enlil a greater measure of rationality than he deserves. The possibility cannot be excluded that his displeasure with the din and intense activity of mankind evolved from his otiose character.[56]

Whatever the reason for Enlil's vexation may have been, his solution to the crisis was violent and ill considered. His intended total annihilation of mankind would have deprived the gods of their sustenance and the world would have returned to chaos. In Mesopotamian thought, man and god were interdependent. Man provided the god with all his basic needs and, in return, the god offered him protection. This was understood only by the wise Enki-Ea. Hence, when the gods decided upon the flood, he immediately took preventive measures against the foreseen disaster. Actually, Enki saved the righteous king Atra-ḫasīs not so much for his piety and righteousness, as for seeing in him an indispensable instrument for his and his fellow gods' survival.[57]

Interestingly, the problem created by the uproar (*ḫubūru*) of the people, i.e., their excessive and energetic activity, reappears in the *Poem of Erra*[58] in a context quite similar to that of *Atra-ḫasīs*.[59] Introducing the *Sibittu*, the seven destructive divine weapons of Erra and Išum, the poet tells us that they were given to Erra by Anu, to help him massacre the people of the land "when the clamor of human habitations (*ša nišī dadmē ḫuburšina*)" becomes noisome to him.[60] Subsequently, the *Sibittu* deliver a long address to Erra[61] in which they urge him to rise from his "sleep" (i.e. inactivity) in the city and go out to the battlefield to arouse war. The principal reason behind their call-to-arms is that they are bored and out of training. But they camouflage it with various pretexts, especially

56 Cf. n. 30 above. See further in this connection Müller's pertinent remarks ("Das Motiv," 300–1): "The 'uproar' 'clamor' of humanity in *Atra-ḫasīs* can mean neither rebellion nor tumult raised by extra...work...The people seem to humbly accept their duty as the servants of the gods. The reason that Enlil is disturbed about the 'noise' of humanity is his otiose character (which he shares with Anu): these gods are antagonistic to the individuation of the cosmos, and strive for pre-creational unity, chaos (i.e. to the situation when the gods were still like men)."

57 Cf. pertinent remarks in Michalowski, "Presence at the Creation," 388f.

58 Latest, updated edition: Cagni, *L'epopea di Erra*; cf. Edzard, "Irra (Erra) Epos." For recent translations, see Cagni, *The Poem of Erra*; Foster, *Before the Muses*, 880–911.

59 This has been pointed out already by Machinist (cf. his "Rest and Violence in the Poem of Erra," referred to in n. 53 above).

60 *Erra* I 40–44.

61 *Erra* I 46–91.

extolling the heroic excitement of the campaign and the honor, prestige, and gratification it brings. A long passage in which they depict the terrifying impact of Erra's warfare on everyone, including the gods, nature, man, and beast, concludes with the words (*Erra* I 73–75):

> Let men be frightened and their clamor subside,[62]
> Let beasts tremble and return to clay,
> Let the gods, your ancestors, see and praise your valor!

Toward the end of their inciting address, the *Sibittu* bring up the old charge that human clamor disturbs the sleep of the Anunnakū, the chthonic gods (*Erra* I 79–86):

> Ere the whole land outgrows us,[63]
> Do a kindly deed for the Anunnakū, who delight in deathly stillness,
> The Anunnakū cannot fall asleep for the clamor of humankind[64]

The motif of human clamor is mentioned once more in the poem, in the longest address of Išum to Erra, in which he describes the terrible devastation and havoc that was created in the cities of Babylon, by the civil war that was generated by Erra.[65] Išum, among others, quotes the lament of Ištaran, the patron deity of Dēr, over his city (*Erra* IV 66–69):

> You (=Erra) turned the city of Dēr into a wasteland,
> You fractured the people therein like reeds,
> You extinguished their clamor like foam on the water's face![66]
> And as for me, you did not spare me but gave me over to the Sutean nomads!

Cagni follows Pettinato in assuming that "clamor" (*ḫubūru*), both in *Atra-ḫasīs* and the *Poem of Erra*, refers to "the rebellion of humanity against the destiny to work in the service of the gods."[67] One could sup-

---

62 Akk.: *nišī liplaḫāma litquna ḫubursi*[*n*].

63 So Foster; Cagni translates: "Before the whole country overwhelms us." Akkadian: *adi mātu napḫarša irbû elīni.*

64 Akk.: *Anunnakī ina ḫubūr nišī ul ireḫḫû šittum.*

65 *Erra* III 57–IV 127.

66 Akk: *kî ḫubuš pān mê ḫubūršina tuballi.*

67 Cagni, *The Poem of Erra*, 29, n. 12; see also his discussion of lines 79–86 in his edition (*L'epopea di Erra*, 172–74). Just as a curiosity it is interesting to note that already A. L. Oppenheim suspected the term *ḫubūru* in *Enūma eliš* and the *Poem of Erra* to be a euphemism ("substitution") for sinful doings (such as incest), which the poet allegedly intended to conceal from the sensitive reader (cf. his "Mesopotamian Mythology I," 210 with n. 3). For

port this hypothesis by a nine-line passage in the concluding part of Išum's address to Erra (IV 104–12), in which he accuses Erra that in the terrible civil war that he created in Babylonia the righteous and unrighteous were being killed alike (*Erra* IV 104–7):

> O warrior Erra, you have put the righteous person to death,
> You have put the unrighteous person to death,
> He who sinned against you, you put him to death,
> He who did not sin against you, you put him to death

These reproachful words of Išum recall Enki-Ea's apologetic address in the story of the flood in which he accused Enlil of bringing on humanity collective punishment.[68] However, just as in *Atra-ḫasīs*, one cannot find in the beginning of the *Poem of Erra* any allusion to a rebellion against the gods on the part of the people of Babylon that could have prompted Erra to mete out a devastating punishment to them.[69] On the contrary, Erra's warlike activity seems to have been dictated by his capricious and vainglorious character, and bolstered by the instigation of his seven divine weapons. Accordingly, I cannot see in the sporadic and selective use of the expression "clamor" (*ḫubūru*) in the *Poem of Erra* reference to man's rebellion against the gods.[70] On the other hand, one can infer from the warlike speech of the *Sibittu* that their main concern was, not unlike that of Enlil in *Atra-ḫasīs*, the overpopulation of the citizens of the land, which threatened the cosmic equilibrium established after the flood.[71]

The last point that should be discussed here is Enki's address to Enlil at the end of the flood episode and its relation to the rest of the myth. In this address,[72] Enki seems to admonish Enlil for his rashness in

---

this bibliographical reference, as well as for other useful comments to the final draft of this article, I am indebted to Yitschak Sefati.

68 See above notes 23–25; and further discussion below.

69 It is true that Ištaran, in his lament, complains that "Man forsook truth and took up violence, / They abandoned justice and were plotting wickedness" (*Erra* IV 73–74). However, the complaint is against Erra himself, whose violent acts brought about these social misdeeds.

70 For a similar interpretation of the *Poem of Erra*, see Black and Green, *Gods, Demons and Symbols*, 36: "In the Babylonian poem...the god acquires temporary control of the world and (apparently because destruction is simply in his nature, rather than to punish any sin) ravages and lays waste Babylonia."

71 Cf. *Erra* I 79 quoted above (n. 62).

72 *Atra-ḫasīs* III vi 16–40; *Epic of Gilgamesh* XI 181–95 quoted above (cf. notes 23–25).

sending the deluge, thereby inflicting punishment indiscriminately without regard for guilt. If I was correct in my contention that the flood was not brought upon mankind as a punishment for any kind of intentional sin, then Enki's address to Enlil contradicts the beginning of the myth. Moran does not attach much importance to Enki's speech, asserting that its purpose was to reveal Enlil's character as brute force.[73] Von Soden, who takes Enki's speech at face value, suggests that it is a later addition in the Old Babylonian myth.[74]

In my opinion, one can agree with von Soden that Enki's speech is an attempt to provide the flood with an ethical basis, and still assume that the entire myth came from the hands of one and the same author. It stands to reason that the Akkadian *Atra-ḫasīs* myth is based on a Sumerian prototype, very similar to the extant Sumerian version of the flood.[75] Although the section that contained the motive for bringing the flood is not preserved in the Sumerian version, we may assume that it was very similar to the corresponding section in the Babylonian composition. In other words, in all probability, the basic theology behind the Babylonian myth was borrowed from Sumerian tradition without

---

73 Moran, "Atrahasis," 57, n. 1.

74 von Soden, "Religion und Sittlichkeit," 153, n. 4.

75 See n. 4 above. To be sure, it is generally agreed that the only extant copy of the Sumerian Flood Story (CBS 10673) was made in the late Old Babylonian period, exhibiting the grammatical features of late, inferior Sumerian dialect, and therefore it could not have been composed before the end of the Isin-Larsa period (cf. Poebel, PBS 4/1, 66–69; Jacobsen, *The Harps that Once*, 145; Civil, "The Sumerian Flood Story," 138–39). Accordingly, it has been generally assumed that the primeval flood was not an ancient Sumerian mythological motif and that it is based on late traditions, from the end of the Isin-Larsa period, such as reflected in the myth of *Atra-ḫasīs* (cf. Civil, "The Sumerian Flood Story"; Glassner, *Mesopotamian Chronicles*, 56–68; 109). The above hypothesis as to the relatively late Old Babylonian origin of the flood tradition has been reinforced and effectively defended in a recent doctoral dissertation by Y. Chen (cf. Chen, *The Emergence*, vol. I, 232ff.; 241ff.). Nevertheless, Chen is well aware of the fact that the Babylonian tradition of the flood itself is heavily dependent in its literary motifs and theological ideas on previous third and second-millennia Sumerian lament literature (ibid., 347ff.). Contrary to the above widespread hypothesis, it is assumed here that the Sumerian tradition of the flood, together with the history of urban civilization and the five cities that ruled Mesopotamia before it, was a genuine old Sumerian tradition that surfaced later and was secondarily appended to the standard version of the King List (see the following note; Jacobsen, *The Sumerian King List*, 55–68; Hallo and Simpson, *The Ancient Near East: A History*, 28–29; 35–37).

any substantial alteration.[76] However, this tradition apparently did not satisfy the Old Babylonian author of the composition, whose theological beliefs were more advanced and who adhered to the doctrine of retribution. Consequently, he added to Enki's apologetic speech a theological element that implies that the flood, after all, was a deserved punishment for some misdeeds on the part of mankind, without clarifying the nature of these misdeeds and overlooking the contradiction, which this addition created with the beginning of the myth. Such tensions and inner contradictions are quite common in Mesopotamian and biblical compositions and their existence does not indicate multiple authorship or editorial insertions.

In conclusion, we may sum up the differences between the Mesopotamian and biblical motivation for the flood as follows: Original Mesopotamian mythology saw in overpopulation, which became a threat to the cosmic equilibrium, the ultimate reason for the flood, and its attempt to provide for this cosmic catastrophe an ethical reason, justifying the divine decree, was only secondary and vague. Biblical theology, on the other hand, carefully and explicitly separated the flood from the problem of overpopulation, and provided it with a clear ethical motive. Moral corruption in society, for which man himself was responsible. Thus, while the polytheistic Babylonians were able to develop only a limited and inconsistent ethical system, biblical monotheism provided man with an ultimate and consistent moral-ethical doctrine, thus giving him the feeling that he was master over his own fate.[77]

WORKS CITED

Alster, B. *Wisdom of Ancient Sumer*. Bethesda, Md.: CDL Press, 2005.

Black, J., and A. Green. *Gods, Demons and Symbols of Ancient Mesopotamia*. London: British Museum Press, 1992.

Borger, R. *Babylonisch-Assyrische Lesestücke*, Vol. II. Rome: Pontificium Institutum Biblicum, 1969.

---

[76] As a matter of fact, the bilingual Neo-Babylonian Royal Chronicle (cf. Glassner, *Mesopotamian Chronicles*, 126–35) contains an allusion to Enlil's disturbance by the din of humanity, which caused him to bring upon it the flood (ll. 30–34). It is reasonable to assume with Jacobsen (*The Sumerian King List*, 60, n. 113; cf. Glassner, *Mesopotamian Chronicles*, 126) that the first part of this chronicle is a late and abbreviated version of the Sumerian Flood Story incorporated into the King List.

[77] Cf. Finkelstein, "Bible and Babel," 438–41.

Bottéro, J., and S. N. Kramer, *Lorsque les dieux faisaient l'homme*, Paris: Gallimard, 1989.

Cagni, L. *L'epopea di Erra*. Studi Semitici 34. Rome: Istituto di Studi del Vicino Oriente, 1969.

The Poem of Erra. Sources and Monographs from the Ancient Near East 1/3. Malibu, Calif.: Undena Publications, 1977.

Cassuto, U. *From Noah to Abraham* (in Hebrew). Jerusalem: Magness Press: 1959.

A Commentary on the Book of Genesis. Jerusalem: Magness Press, 1961.

Chen, Yi Samuel. *The Emergence and Development of Sumerian and Babylonian Traditions Related to the Primeval Flood Catastrophe from the Old Babylonian Period*. PhD Dissertation, University of Oxford, 2009.

Civil, M. "The Sumerian Flood Story." In *Atra-ḫasīs: The Babylonian Story of the Flood*, edited by W. G. Lambert and A. R. Millard. Oxford: The Clarendon Press, 1969.

Clines, J. A. "The Significance of the 'Sons of God' Episode (Genesis 6:1–4) in the Context of the 'Primeval History' (Genesis 1:1–11)." *JSOT* 13 (1979), 33–38.

Dalley, S. *Myths from Mesopotamia*. Oxford: Oxford University Press, 1989.

Davidson, Robert. *Genesis 1–11*. Cambridge Bible Commentary. Cambridge: University Press, 1973.

Edzard, D. O. "Irra (Erra) Epos." *RlA* 5 (1976–80): 166–70.

Finkelstein, J. J. "Bible and Babel." *Commentary* 26 (1958): 431–34.

Foster, B. R. *Before the Muses*. Bethesda, Md.: CDL Press, 2005.

Frymer-Kensky, Tikva. "The Atrahasis Epic and Its Significance for Our Understanding of Genesis 1–9." *Biblical Archeologist* 40 (1977): 150–54.

Gemeren, W. A., ed. *New International Dictionary of Old Testament Theology and Exegesis*, Vol. 2. Grand Rapids, Mich.: Zondervan Pub. House, 1997.

George, A. R. *The Babylonian Gilgamesh Epic* I-II. Oxford: Oxford University Press, 2003.

Glassner, J.-J. *Mesopotamian Chronicles*. SBL Writings from the Ancient World 19. Atlanta, Ga.: SBL, 2004.

Greenstein, E. L. "The Retelling of the Flood Story in the Gilgamesh Epic." In *Hesed ve-Emet: Studies in Honor of Ernest S. Frerichs*, edited by J. Magness and S. Gitin, 197–204. Brown Judaic Studies 320. Atlanta, Ga.: Scholars Press, 1998.

Hallo, W. W. "Adapa Reconsidered: Life and Death in Contextual Perspective." *Scriptura* 87 (2004): 267–77.

Hallo, W. W., and W. K. Simpson. *The Ancient Near East: A History*. New York: Harcourt Brace Jovanovich, 1971.

Hartley, J. E. *Genesis*. New International Biblical Commentary. Peabody, Mass.: Hendrickson Publishers, Inc., 2000.

Heidel, A. *The Gilgamesh Epic and Old Testament Parallels*. Chicago: The University of Chicago Press, 1949.

Izre'el, Sh. *Adapa and the South Wind*. Winona Lake, Ind.: Eisenbrauns, 2001.

Jacobsen, Th. *The Sumerian King List*. Assyriological Studies 11. Chicago: The University of Chicago Press, 1939.

"The Eridu Genesis." *JBL* 100 (1981): 513–29.

The Harps that Once…: Sumerian Poetry in Translation. New Haven: Yale University Press, 1987.

Kilmer, A. Draffkorn. "The Mesopotamian Concept of Overpopulation and Its Solution as Reflected in Mythology." *Or*NS 41 (1972): 160–77.

Klein, J. "The 'Bane' of Humanity: A Lifespan of One Hundred Twenty Years." *Acta Sumerologica* 12 (1990): 57–70.

"The Brockmon Collection Duplicate of the Sumerian Kinglist (BT 14)." In *On the Third Dynasty of Ur: Studies in Honor of Marcel Sigrist*, edited by P. Michalowski, 77–91. Journal of Cuneiform Studies Supplementary Series 1. Boston, Mass.: American Schools of Oriental Research, 2008.

Kramer, S. N. "The Sumerian Deluge Myth." *Anatolian Studies* 33 (1983): 115–21.

Kvanvig, H. S. "Gen 6,1–4 as an Antediluvian Event," *SJOT* (2002): 95–98.

Lambert, W. G. "The Theology of Death." In *Death in Mesopotamia*, edited by B. Alster, 53–66. Mesopotamia 8. Copenhagen: Akademisk Forlag, 1980.

"The Relationship of Sumerian and Babylonian Myth as Seen in Accounts of Creation." In *La circulation des biens, des personnes et des idées dans le Proch-Orient ancient, XXXVIIIe R.A.I.*, edited by

D. Charpin and F. Joannès, 129–35. Paris: Éditions Recherche sur les Civilisations, 1992.

Lambert, W. G., and A. R. Millard. *Atra-ḫasīs: The Babylonian Story of the Flood*. Oxford: The Clarendon Press, 1969.

Landsberger, B. "Ḫabiru and Lulaḫḫu." *Kleinasiatische Forschungen* 1 (1927–30): 321–34.

Lapinkivi, P. *The Neo-Assyrian Myth of Ištar's Descent and Resurrection* (State Archives of Assyrian Cuneiform Texts VI). Helsinki: The Neo-Assyrian Text Corpus project, 1992.

Machinist, P. "Rest and Violence in the Poem of Erra." *JAOS* 103 (1983): 221–35.

Michalowski, P. "Presence at the Creation." In *Lingering over Words: Studies in Near Eastern Literature in Honor of William L. Moran*, edited by T. Abusch et al., 381–96. HSS 37. Atlanta, Ga.: Scholars Press, 1990.

Millard, A. R. "A New Babylonian 'Genesis' Story." In *I Studied Inscriptions from before the Flood: Ancient Near Eastern, Literary and Linguistic Approaches to Genesis 1–11*, Vol. 4, edited by Richard S. Hess and David Toshio Tsumura, 114–28. Winona Lake, Ind.: Eisenbrauns, 1994.

Moran, W. L. "Atrahasis: The Babylonian Story of the Flood." *Biblica* 52 (1971): 51–61.

"Some Considerations of Form and Interpretation in *Atra-ḫasīs*." In *Language, Literature and History: Philological and Historical Studies Presented to Erica Reiner*, edited by F. Rochberg-Halton, 245–55. American Oriental Series 67. New Haven, Conn., 1987.

"The Gilgamesh Epic: A Masterpiece from Ancient Mesopotamia." In *Civilizations of the Ancient Near East*, edited by Jack Sasson, 2327–36. London: Charles Scribner's Sons, 1995.

Müller, H.-P. "Das Motiv für die Sintflut." *ZAW* 97 (1985): 295–316.

Oden, R. A. "Divine Aspirations in Atrahasis and in Genesis 1–11." *ZAW* 93 (1981): 197–216.

Oppenheim, A. L. "Mesopotamian Mythology I." *Or*NS 16 (1947): 207–8.

Pettinato, G. "Die Bestrafung des Menschengeslechts durch die Sintflut." *Or*NS 37 (1968): 165–200.

Poebel, A. *Historical Texts*. PBS 4/1. Philadelphia, Pa.: Publications of the Babylonian Section, 1914.

Schott, A. *Das Gilgamesch-Epos*. Stuttgart: Reclam, 1958.

Shaviv, S. "The Polytheistic Origins of the Biblical Flood Narrative." *VT* 54 (2004): 527–48.

Shifra, Sh., and J. Klein. *In Those Distant Days: Anthology of Ancient Near Eastern Poetry in Hebrew* (in Hebrew). Tel Aviv: Am-Oved, 1996, 88–130.

Skinner, John. *A Critical and Exegetical Commentary on Genesis*. 2nd Edition. ICC. Edinburgh: T & T Clark, 1930.

Speiser, E. A. "Atrahasis." In *Ancient Near Eastern Texts Relating to the Old Testament*, edited by James B. Pritchard, 104–6. Princeton, N.J.: Princeton University Press, 1950.

Steinkeller, P. "An Ur III Manuscript of the Sumerian Kinglist." In *Literatur, Politik und Recht in Mesopotamien: Festschrift für Claus Wilcke*, 267–92. Orientalia Biblica et Christiana 14. Wiesbaden: Harrassowitz, 2003.

Talon, Ph. *The Standard Babylonian Creation Myth Enūma Eliš*. SAACT 4. Helsinki: The Neo-Assyrian Text Corpus Project, 2005.

Tsumura, D. T. "Genesis and Ancient Near Eastern Stories of Creation and Flood: An Introduction." In *I Studied Inscriptions from before the Flood: Ancient Near Eastern, Literary and Linguistic Approaches to Genesis 1–11*, Vol. 4, edited by Richard S. Hess and David Toshio Tsumura, 27–57. Winona Lake, Ind.: Eisenbrauns, 1994.

von Soden, W. "Religion und Sittlichkeit nach den Anschauungen der Babylonier." *ZDMG* 89 (1935): 143–69.

"Der altbabylonische Atramchasis-Mythos." In *Texte aus der Umwelt des Alten Testaments* III/4, edited by O. Keiser, 612–45. Gütersloh: Gütersloher Verlagshaus, 1994.

Westermann, C. *Genesis 1–11*. Translated by John J. Scullion. Minneapolis, Minn.: SPCK, 1984. 395–98.

AIN'T NOTHING BUT A HOUND DOG?

THE MEANING OF THE NOUN *klb* IN NORTHWEST SEMITIC LANGUAGES IN LIGHT OF BT ROSH HASHANAH 4A*

MOSHE SIMON-SHOSHAN
ROTHBERG INTERNATIONAL SCHOOL, HEBREW UNIVERSITY

Barry Eichler's contributions to the study of both the Ancient Near East and the Bible, as testified to by the title of this volume, need no introduction here. Perhaps less well known is Professor Eichler's abiding interest in rabbinic literature and its relationship to his two primary areas of specialization. In this paper, I bring together these three fields by presenting a reading of a talmudic text that advances our understanding of the meaning of the term *klb* in the Bible and in Northwest Semitic languages in general.

Since the nineteenth century, scholars have speculated that the noun *klb*, the common Semitic word for "dog," might also have a secondary meaning of "prostitute" in Northwest Semitic languages. Various Semitists have claimed to have found such usages of *klb* in numerous Northwest Semitic languages. One Northwest Semitic language that has not yet been cited in this discussion is the Aramaic of the Babylonian Talmud. However, it is precisely in the Babylonian Talmud, Rosh Hashanna 4a, that we find a statement that presents the best evidence to date that *klb* can mean "prostitute" in Northwest Semitic languages.

Keleb *in Deuteronomy 23:19*

The central locus of the discussion concerning the possibility that the word *klb* may refer to something other than a canine is Deut 23:19:

> לֹא־תָבִיא אֶתְנַן זוֹנָה וּמְחִיר כֶּלֶב בֵּית ה' אֱלֹהֶיךָ לְכָל־נֶדֶר
> כִּי תוֹעֲבַת ה' אֱלֹהֶיךָ גַּם־שְׁנֵיהֶם.
>
> You shall not bring the fee of a whore or the pay of a *keleb* into the house of the LORD in fulfillment of any vow, for both are abhorrent to the LORD your God.

* I would like to thank Peggy Guinan, Shalom Holtz, Adina Moshavi, David Prebor, James Rosenblum, David Rothstein, and, as always, my wife Bracha, for their help with this article.

The ancient commentaries and translations understood the Hebrew word *keleb* in its common meaning of "dog."[1] This remained the standard interpretation until the modern period. Since the nineteenth century, many biblical scholars have proposed that the term *klb* be under-stood here as referring to a male prostitute.[2] This reading has the advantage of replacing the seemingly incongruous pairing of the fee for a prostitute's services with the proceeds of the sale of a dog with a clear parallelism between the female and male prostitute. This interpretation is further strengthened by the context established by the immediately preceding verse:

> לֹא־תִהְיֶה קְדֵשָׁה מִבְּנוֹת יִשְׂרָאֵל וְלֹא־יִהְיֶה קָדֵשׁ מִבְּנֵי יִשְׂרָאֵל
>
> No Israelite woman shall be a cult prostitute,
> nor shall an Israelite man be a cult prostitute

This verse also discusses a prohibited connection between prostitution and the Temple. It too makes use of a clear parallelism in the two halves of the verse between a female and male prostitute.

Some interpreters have gone even further and suggested that verse 19, like verse 18 before it, refers specifically to cultic prostitution. The supposition that *keleb* in Deut 23:19 refers not only to a male prostitute but to a sacred male prostitute underlies the oft-cited explanation as to how it is that a word for "dog" came to mean "prostitute." D. Winston Thomas draws attention to the use of dog as a term for a "faithful servant" in Akkadian. He argues that the word *keleb* here similarly refers, like *qadesh*, to a temple functionary, in general, and a sacred prostitute, in particular.[3]

Still others have argued that *keleb* in this verse needs to be interpreted simply as a type of temple functionary without any sexual connotations.[4] This reading comes in light of the fact that in the past twenty years, several scholars have challenged the very existence of ritual pros-

---

1 See LXX, Vulgate, Josephus *Antiquities* 2.8.9, Sifrei 261, Mishnah Temurah 6:3 and Rashi, Ramban, et al., ad loc.

2 See the following commentaries on our verse: Luzzato, *Perush shadal*; Driver, *Deuteronomy*; von Rad, *Deuteronomy*; Thomson, *Deuteronomy*; Phillips, *Deuteronomy*; Mayes, *Deuteronomy*. See also BDB s.v. *keleb*; *Interpreters Dictionary of the Bible* s.v. "Dog"; *HALOT* s.v. *keleb* and Rudolf, "Präparierte Jungfrauen?," 66.

3 Thomas, "*Kelebh* 'Dog.'"

4 See *Anchor Bible Dictionary* 6, 1144 and Nelson, *Deuteronomy*, ad loc.

titution in ancient Israel.[5] These scholars argue that the term *qadesh* refers simply to a temple functionary and, as such, so must *keleb*.[6]

The Use of klb *in Other Northwest Semitic Languages*

The argument on the basis of Deut 23:19 that the word *klb* can mean something other than "dog" remains speculative. It is based on the assumption that the meaning of this word in this particular context must closely parallel those of the terms in the first part of the verse and at the end of the preceding verse. In principle however, there is no reason the word could not in fact mean "dog," even if it produces less than perfect parallelism. The case for *klb* meaning either "prostitute," "temple functionary," or some combination of the two would be greatly bolstered if other examples of such usage could be proffered. While no such cases exist in biblical Hebrew, several such examples have been suggested for *keleb*'s cognates in other Northwest Semitic languages.

The most commonly cited example of *klb* used to refer to a prostitute in Northwest Semitic is from a Phoenician inscription that was found on a stone near Larnaka, Cyprus in 1869, at a site believed to be the ancient city of Kition.[7] The reverse of the stone records payments made to the personnel of the temple of the god Mukol, apparently the principle god of Kition.[8] Line ten of the reverse inscription reads: "*lklbm wlgrm qr3 wp' 3.*" This translates literally as "For the dogs and for the puppies[9] 3 *qr* and 3 *p'*." *qr* and *p'* are both types of coins.[10] Many scholars have suggested that, in light of Deut 23:19, *klbm* in the Kition inscription might also refer to temple prostitutes.[11] There is no internal evidence to suggest *klbm* might refer to prostitutes in the inscription. As such, other scholars have taken a more conservative approach. Since the context of the Kition inscription tells us only that the *klbm* are somehow affiliated

5 For discussion of this trend see Goodfriend, "Could *keleb* in Deuteronomy 23:19," 384 n. 13. To this list should be added Weiser, *Mikra ve-lashon*, 154–56.

6 See especially Gruber, "The Qādēš," 167–76, and Gruber, "Hebrew *Qedeshah*," 133–48.

7 CIS I, Vol. 1, 99, no. 86b.

8 See Peckam, "Notes on a Fifth-Century Phoenician Inscription," 324.

9 We have translated *grm* as "puppies" according to the suggestion of Stager, "Deities and Dogs," 41.

10 See Hoftijzer and Jongeling, *Dictionary of Northwest Semitic Inscriptions*, s.v. p'_1 and qr'_2.

11 CIS I, Vol. 1 no. 86b; Cooke, *Text Book of North-Semitic Inscriptions*, 67–68; Donner and Röllig, *Kanaanäische und aramäische Inschriften*, 54; Gibson, *Text Book of Syrian Semitic Inscriptions*, 130; Hoftijzer and Jongeling, *Dictionary of Northwest Semitic Inscriptions*, 509.

with the temple, these scholars favor the previously mentioned theory that *klb*, both in Deuteronomy and in the inscription, is a term for a temple functionary whose duties do not necessarily include sacred prostitution.[12] Yet, here too, there is no internal evidence that *klb* might bear this meaning. In both cases, it seems that the interpretation of *klb* as either "prostitute" or "temple functionary" was influenced by earlier readings of the Deuteronomy verse. This inscription thus cannot be used as an example in support of the claim that *keleb* means either "prostitute" or "temple functionary" in Deuteronomy.

Several lexicographers have claimed that *klb* can mean prostitute in still other Northwest Semitic languages. Payne-Smith in his *Thesaurus Syriacus* lists *cinaedus*, "sodomite," as a meaning of *klab*. Similarly, Sokoloff, in his *Dictionary of Jewish Palestinian Aramaic*, lists "male prostitute" as a meaning of *kelab*.[13] However, both authors cite as their proofs Aramaic translations of Deut 23:19. These sources do little more than show that the translators rendered the Hebrew *keleb* with its exact Aramaic cognate. Even if the word *keleb* does mean "male prostitute" in the verse, there is no evidence that the translators understood it as such.

Finally, Aistleitner, in his *Wörterbuch der Ugaritsche Sprache*, lists "prostituierter" as a possible meaning for *klb* in Ugaritic.[14] He cites as an example *KTU* 4.54.[15] This text presents a list of proper names, between two of which we find the phrase *ṯlṯ klbm*, "three dogs." It is not clear why Aistleitner interprets this phrase as referring to male prostitutes. On the basis of the first line, this text is described as a list of "royal guards on duty."[16] It makes sense that dogs might be listed among the names of soldiers in such a list. Furthermore, elsewhere in his lexicon, Aistleitner appears to concur that this text refers to a group of soldiers.[17]

The Use of κύων *in New Testament Greek*

Payne Smith further supplements his case with similarly problematic citations of Syriac translations of New Testament verses in which the Greek word for dog, κύων, is alleged to refer to prostitutes. Other schol-

---

12 Slouschz, *Otzar ketovot ha-fenikiot*, 80; Peckam, "Notes on a Fifth-Century Phoenician Inscription," 317; Delcor, "Le personnel du temple d'Astarte a Kition," 161–63.

13 Smith, *Thesaurus Syriacus*, Vol. 1 s.v. *klab*; Sokoloff, *A Dictionary of Jewish Palestinian Aramaic* s.v. *kelab*.

14 Aisleitner, *Wörterbuch der Ugaritische Sprache* s.v. *klb*.

15 First published in Virolleaud, "Textes administratifs," 21.

16 Dietrich, Loretz, and Sanmartin, *The Cuneiform Alphabetic Texts*, 223.

17 See Aisleitner, *Wörterbuch*, entry 1702, 197.

ars have made similar claims.[18] Given the Judaic background of the New Testament, such a text would be potentially relevant to our discussion, despite the fact that it is written in a non-Semitic language. However, on examination, these verses do not fulfill their promise. The most commonly cited text is Revelation 22:15:

> ἔζω οἱ κύνες καὶ οἱ φάρμακα καί οἱ πόρνοι καί οἱ φονεῖς καί οἱ εἰδωλολάτραι καί πᾶς φιλῶν καί ποιῶν ψεῦδος.
>
> Outside are the dogs and sorcerers and fornicators and murders and idolaters, and everyone who loves and practices falsehood.

Payne-Smith also cites Philippians 3:2:

> βλέπετε τοὺς κύνας, βλέπετε τοὺς κακοὺς ἐργάτας, βλέπετε τὴν κατατομήν.
>
> Beware of the dogs, beware of the evil works, beware of those who mutilate the flesh!

In both of these instances the various forms of κύων are clearly used in a metaphorical manner as a pejorative description of some group of people. There is, however, no contextual evidence that the individuals referred to are prostitutes. Once again the reading of these texts as referring to prostitutes appears to be driven by the assumption that Deut 23:19 uses the word *keleb* to mean "male prostitute." If we cannot establish this meaning in Deuteronomy, then we must reject such a reading of the New Testament texts as well.

Does keleb *Mean "Dog" Exclusively?*

As we have seen, most of the alleged examples of *klb* meaning "prostitute" in Northwest Semitic languages do not hold up under scrutiny. The examples cited by scholars do not stand on their own, relying on the assumption that such a meaning has already been attested to in Deuteronomy. However, as we have seen, the claim that Deut 23:19 refers to a male prostitute, or to anything besides a common *canis lupis familiaris*, is itself speculative. In light of this, both Lawrence Stager and Elaine Adler Goodfriend have recently argued that *klb* has no meanings other than "dog" in any Northwest Semitic language.[19] They see no reason to reject the traditional reading of Deut 23:19 as prohibiting pro-

---

18 Ford, *Revelation*, 345, Cooke, *Text-Book of North-Semitic Inscriptions*, 68 and Goodfriend, "Could *keleb* in Deuteronomy 23:19," 387.

19 See Goodfriend, "Could *keleb* in Deuteronomy 23:19," and Stager, "Deities and Dogs."

ceeds from the sale of a dog from the Temple. Stager similarly interprets the *klbm* and *grm* of the Kition inscription as describing sacred dogs used in healing cults.

Stager and Goodfriend legitimately call attention to the paucity of documented sources, in which *klb* describes a prostitute or, indeed, any other human being. However, it would be imprudent to altogether dismiss the possibility that *klb* might sometimes refer to something non-canine. The parallel between *zona* and *keleb* in Deut 23:19 remains most tantalizing. We still do not have a satisfactory explanation as to why the Bible would single out dogs as particularly abominable creatures in a cultic context.[20] It would certainly make more sense if, like the *zona* and most probably the *qadesh/qedesha* as well, the *keleb* here was a human being and a sexually promiscuous one at that.

The Use of klb *in Jewish Babylonian Aramaic: Rav's Statement on Rosh Hashanah 4a*

Support for this position may be adduced from a talmudic statement attributed to the great third-century rabbi known as Rav. As we shall see, it makes most sense to understand this statement as making use of the Babylonian Aramaic word for a female dog, *kalbeta*, as a term for a prostitute.[21]

Rav's statement comes in the context of a much larger exegetical discussion that begins on 3a. In light of the Mishnah's treatment of various calendrical systems, the Talmud embarks on an attempt to reconstruct the chronology and calendar of the Persian Empire, based on biblical sources. On 3b, the Talmud comes to the rather startling conclusion that Cyrus, Darius, and Artaxerxes are all names of a single king. Furthermore, the Talmud asserts that this king began as a righteous king but in the end "went bad" and became a sinner. The Talmud then demands evidence from the biblical text that this king did indeed turn to evil later in his career. The Talmud provides several possible answers, the third of which contains the relevant statement of Rav:[22]

---

20 To be sure, the Bible as a whole hardly projects a positive attitude toward dogs, see Schwartz, "Dogs in Jewish Society," 246–49.

21 Note that *HALOT* mentions Babylonian Jewish Aramaic as a source for *klb* meaning "prostitute," but does not supply a source.

22 Text is that of the standard Vilna printing, checked against MSS as recorded on the Lieberman project CD-ROM. Only major variants have been noted.

1

(אמר) רב יוסף ואיתימא חבי יצחק[23]:

מנלן דאחמיץ?

(a) מהכא: "ויאמר לי המלך והשגל יושבת אצלו"

(b) מאי שגל? אמר רבה[24] בר לימא משמיה דרב, כלבתא.

2

(a) [25]אלא מעתה הא דכתיב:

"ועל מרא שמיא התרוממת ולמאנייא די ביתיה היתיו קדמך ואנת ורברבניך שגלתך ולחנתך חמרא שתין בהון."

ואי שגל [כלבתא היא][26] כלבתא בת משתיא חמרא היא?

הא לא קשיא דמלפא לה ושתייא.

(b) אלא מעתה דכתיב

"בנות מלכים ביקרותיך נצבה שגל לימינך בכתם אופיר"

ואי שגל כלבתא היא מאי קא מבשר להו (נביא)[27] לישראל?

הכי קאמר בשכר שחביבה תורה לישראל כשגל לעובדי כוכבים זכיתם לכתם אופיר.

ואיבעית אימא לעולם שגל מלכתא היא

ורבה בר לימא גמרא גמיר לה.

ואמאי קרי לה שגל?

שהיתה חביבה עליו כשגל אי נמי שהושיבה במקום שגל.

1

R. Joseph or, as some say, R. Isaac said:

Whence do we know that [the king morally] deteriorated?

(a) "And the king said unto me, the *shegal* also sitting by him" (Neh 2:6)

(b) What is *shegal?* Rabbah b. Lema said in the name of Rav, a she-dog (*kalbita*).

---

23 MS Munich 95 reads אמ' רב יצחק ואיתימ' רב נחמן. MS Oxford Opp. Add. Fol. 23 has a conflation of the two readings.

24 MS Munich 95 and JTS Rab. 218 (EMC 270) read רבא.

25 MS New York - JTS Rab. 1608 (ENA 850) reads here אמ' ליה אביי.

26 Found in almost all MSS. Probably dropped in printed edition due to haplography.

27 Missing from most MSS.

2
(a) But if that is so, what are we to make of the verse,
"But hast lifted up thyself against the Lord of heaven, and they have brought the vessels of His house before thee, and thou and thy lords, the *shegalot* and thy concubines have drunk wine in them" (Dan 5:23)?
Now how can a *shegal* here be a dog? Do dogs drink wine?
This is no difficulty, as [we can suppose that] it was taught to drink.
(b) But what of the verse where it is written,
"King's daughters are among thy favorites, at thy right hand doth stand the *shegal* in gold of Ofir" (Ps 45:10)?
Now if *shegal* is a dog, what promise is the prophet bringing to Israel?
Because the Torah is dear to Israel as a *shegal* to the heathens, you have earned as your reward the gold of Ofir.
Alternatively, I may say that *shegal* as a rule does mean "queen,"
but in this case Rabbah b. Lemma had a tradition [that it means 'dog']
and the reason why it is called [in the text] *shegal* is because it was as dear to him as a queen, or possibly because he put it on the queen's seat.

This passage consists of two sections. The first is the answer to the Talmud's question "How do we know he degenerated?" which is quoted in the name of either by R. Joseph or R. Isaac. This answer itself consists of two citations: one of a biblical verse from Nehemiah (a) and one of a gloss on the word *shegal* in the verse (b). This gloss is presented by Rabbah b. Lema in the name of Rav.

The second part of this passage is Stammaitic in nature. The "Stam" is the anonymous voice of the Talmud. Contemporary scholarship tends to assume that the "Stammaim" who composed this aspect of the Talmud text were active following the period of Amoraim, the named rabbis of the Talmud.[28] This section also consists of two parts. In each section a biblical verse is cited as a counter-text to challenge Rav's interpretation of the word *shegal*. Each time, the Stammaim offer a response in Rav's name, which is meant to maintain the viability of his interpretation.

The passage as whole can thus be seen as an effort to determine the exact meaning of the biblical Hebrew noun *shegal*. *Shegal* appears only

---

[28] On the Stammaim and their role in the aggadic passages of the Bavli, see Rubenstein, *Creation and Composition*, esp. 1–10.

twice in the biblical Hebrew corpus, in the Nehemiah and Psalms verses cited above. Additionally the word appears in biblical Aramaic three times in the book of Daniel, in the verse cited, and in 5:2 and 3. This talmudic passage might thus be described as an effort to determine the meaning of the word *shegal*. Using methods not unlike those of modern lexicographers, the Talmud gathers together and examines the various occurrences of the word and attempts to find a meaning that takes into account the different contexts in which the word appears.

The Talmud starts with the Nehemiah verse, "And the king said unto me, the *shegal* also sitting by him." This verse tells us very little about the meaning of *shegal*. Based on the verb *yoshevet*, "sitting" (feminine participle) we can deduce that *shegal* is a female being that is capable of sitting. The prepositional clause, "by him" further tells us that this being might sometimes be found sitting next to a king. The most likely guess for the meaning of the word based on this evidence might be "queen" or "royal consort." However, Rav's proposal of "she-dog" remains possible and cannot be disproved on the strength of this verse alone.

We then proceed to the verse from Daniel: "But hast lifted up thyself against the Lord of Heaven, and they have brought the vessels of His house before thee, and thou and thy lords, the *shegalot* and thy concubines have drunk wine in them." This verse once again presents the *shegal* as a part of a king's court, bolstering the case for the word meaning some thing like "queen." The Stammaim, however, focus on a more fundamental point. Since the *shegalot* are described as drinking wine, they must be human beings and not animals. The response in favor of Rav is that, technically, it is possible to train dogs to drink wine, so the verse *could* still refer to dogs.

Finally we have the Psalms verse: "King's daughters are among thy favorites, at thy right hand doth stand the *shegal* in gold of Ofir." In this verse the word *shegal* is placed in poetic parallelism with the phrase "king's daughters." The meaning of *shegal* thus must be within the same semantic range as "princess." "Royal consort" is thus possible, but "she-dog" seems like it must finally be eliminated. The Stammaim, however, feel duty bound to defend Rav and his statement. They offer two possible responses. First, interpreting the verse as referring to the Torah, the Stammaim suggest that perhaps it means that Israel loves the Torah and as much as a heathen loves his dog. Second, it is possible that in general *shegal* does indeed mean queen, as we have been arguing all along. However, in Nehemiah the verse refers to the king's dog as his "queen" because the king loved her and treated her like a queen.

At this point, it is quite clear that while the Stammaim have made Herculean efforts to defend Rav's glossing of the word *shegal* as "she-dog," the interpretation of the word that best fits its appearances in the Bible is clearly something along the lines of "queen." This interpretation is shared by modern scholars, who suggest that *shegal* derives from the Akkadian *sa ekalli*, which means queen or royal consort.[29]

I would like to propose a different interpretation of Rav's gloss than that assumed by the Stammaim. We must ask ourselves, what could possibly have motivated Rav to interpret the word *shegal* as meaning "she-dog"? It seems almost nonsensical. The assumption that *kalbeta* in this case refers to a dog becomes even more problematic if we subject the first, Amoraic section of the passage to close reading. In this section an Amora, variously identified, presents the Nehemiah verse with Rav's gloss as an answer to the question "How do we know that the king became a sinner?" However we understand Rav's interpretation of the verse, it must provide a satisfactory answer to this question. In other words, it must portray the king as a sinner. But what sin could there be in sitting next to a dog? Rashi explains that the king used this dog for sexual relations. This fits in with the Stammaitic section of the passage, which repeatedly compares men's love for dogs and for women. However, within the Amoraic section itself, which presumably existed independently prior to work of the Stammaim, there is no indication that this dog is anything but a common pet. Furthermore, what would be Rav's basis for the extraordinary claim the king had an ongoing sexual relationship with his dog? The verse does not appear to provide even the germ out of which such a midrash might be developed.

It seems that we must seek a new understanding of Rav's statement, one in which *kalbeta* and *shegal* share a meaning that is neither "dog" nor "queen." Let us go back to the linguistic evidence for *shegal* and see if we can find another possible meaning for the word that would have been compelling to a rabbinic reader if not necessarily to a contemporary one. As we have said, the noun *shegal* appears only twice in biblical Hebrew and three times in biblical Aramaic and these texts all seem to point to meaning like "queen" or "royal consort." There is also however, a biblical Hebrew verb root *shagal*. While it is not clear to modern scholars that *shagal* is related to *shegal*,[30] the rabbis would have had no reason to question the relationship. *Shagal* appears four times in the Bible.[31] In each of these cases it refers to a promiscuous act of sexual intercourse.

---

29 See *HALOT*, BDB, and the new JPS translation and NRSV on the relevant verses.

30 See *HALOT* s.v. *shagal*.

31 Deut 28:30, Is 13:16, Jer 3:2, Zech 14:2.

Three times it refers to rape at the hands of the enemy. In the fourth case, Jer 3:2, it refers to harlotry:

> שְׂאִי־עֵינַיִךְ עַל־שְׁפָיִם וּרְאִי
> אֵיפֹה לֹא שגלת (שֻׁכַּבְתְּ)
> עַל-דְּרָכִים יָשַׁבְתְּ לָהֶם, כַּעֲרָבִי בַּמִּדְבָּר
> וַתַּחֲנִיפִי אֶרֶץ, בִּזְנוּתַיִךְ וּבְרָעָתֵךְ.

> Look up to bare heights, and see:
> Where have they not lain (*shugalt*-[*ketiv*]) with you?
> You waited for them on the roadside like a bandit in
> the wilderness.
> And you defiled the land with your debauchery.

The sense that the verb *shagal* refers to sexual acts that are obscene is reinforced by the fact that in the Massoretic text this verb is always replaced with a *qeri* of the equivalent form of the verb *shakhav*, which is the common term for sexual intercourse. The Massoretes apparently saw *shagal* as an obscene term that should not be read and replaced it with an acceptable substitution.[32] This *ketiv/qere* pair is mentioned in the Talmud and was almost certainly widely accepted already in rabbinic times.

If *shagal* refers to illicit sexual acts, it would have been very reasonable for a rabbinic reader to have understood *shegal* as the noun form of the verb *shagal* and hence read it as referring to a person who engages in illicit sexual activities, i.e., something like a prostitute.

A similar conclusion as to the meaning of *shegal* might be reached if we investigate the evidence provided by rabbinic Hebrew.[33] Neither the verb *shagal* nor the noun *shegal* appears in the corpus of rabbinic literature outside of citations of the biblical verses mentioned above. However the word *shiglonot* does appear once, in BT Sanhedrin 95b:

> אמר רב יהודה אמר רב
> בא עליהם סנחביר הרשע
> בארבעים וחמשה אלף איש בני מלכים
> יושבים בקרונות של זהב ועמהן שגלונות וזונות.

32 See BDB s.v. *shagal*.

33 While modern scholars see rabbinic Hebrew as distinct from biblical Hebrew and might hesitate to draw a conclusion about the meaning of a word from one to the other, the rabbis did not generally recognize such a distinction.

> R. Judah said in the name of Rav:
> The wicked Sennacherib advanced against them
> with a force consisting of forty-five thousand princes,
> each in a golden chariot, and with them *shiglonot* and prostitutes.

The fact that this text juxtaposes the term *shiglonot* with *zonot* "prostitutes" gives credence to the supposition that *shiglonot* similarly refers to some sort of woman of easy virtue. Koehler and Baumgartner (*HALOT*), in their entry for *shegal*, give as a definition for *shiglonot*: "Women who sleep around."[34] If so, it is a small jump from the rabbinic perspective to interpret the biblical *shegal* as prostitute as well. It is perhaps not coincidental that the only rabbinic statement to make use of the word *shiglonot* is cited in the name of Rav, the very same tradent who proposes our problematic gloss on the word *shegal.*

Finally, the medieval midrashic compendium *Yalkut Shimoni* contains a passage that implicitly interprets *shegal* as "prostitute." In the *Yalkut*'s comments on Ps 45:10 (section 750) we read:

1
(a) בנות מלכים ביקרותיך נצבה שגל לימינך בכתם אופיר
בשכר שחביבה תורה לישראל כשגל זו לעובדי אלילים,
זכו לכתם אופיר.
2
(b) רבא אמטי קרבנא לבר ששך ביום חגו,
אמר קים ליה ביה דלא פלי לאלילים,
אזל אשכחיה דיתיב עד צואריה במיא דוורדא
וזונות ערומות קיימות קמיה.
אמר ליה אית לכו כהאי גוונא לעלמא דאתי
אמר ליה לדידן אית לן עדיף מהאי.[35]

[34] This definition is given in the Hebrew section of the dictionary. See, however, the *shegal* entry in the Aramaic section of the dictionary. Dalman, *Aramäisch-neuhebräisches Handwörterbuch*, defines *shiglonot* as "Beischlaeferin." Note, however, that Sokoloff, Review, 106, vigorously rejects these readings, citing Rashi's rendering of the word as "queens." Rashi, however, was clearly influenced by our *sugya* in Rosh Hashanah and is not providing a contextual interpretation of the word.

[35] Text taken from the Bar-Ilan Response Project CD-ROM.

1

"King's daughters are among thy favorites, at thy right hand doth stand the *shegal* in gold of Ofir" (Ps 45:10).

Because the Torah is dear to Israel as a *shegal* to the heathens, you have earned as your reward the gold of Ofir.

2

Raba once sent a present to Bar-Sheshak (a gentile friend) on a heathen feast-day,

saying "I know that he does not worship idols."

But on paying him a visit, he found him sitting up to his neck in rose water while naked harlots were standing before him.

[Bar-Sheshak] said to him, "have you Israelites have anything like this in the World to Come?"

He replied, 'we have much finer than this'.

This passage consists of citations of two talmudic sources. The first (1) is a slightly edited line from our own passage in BT Rosh Hashanah. As it appears there, it comes as an explanation of how Rav could read the Psalm's usage of *shegal* as referring to a dog. The Stam replies that he could understand the verse as comparing Israel's love of Torah to the gentile's love of a *shegal*. In its original talmudic context it is quite clear that this means that Rav could read the verse as referring to gentiles' passion for their dogs, a theme that appears throughout this passage. However, in the *Yalkut* this line is brought without its context. Furthermore, the line that appears in the talmudic version intervening between the verse and the exegesis, which defines *shegal* as a dog, has been eliminated in the *Yalkut*. Read independently of its talmudic parallel, there is no reason to suppose *shegal* is intended to mean "dog" here.[36]

In fact, the version found in the *Yalkut* appears to have a different definition of *shegal* in mind. The *Yalkut*, or some earlier source on which it drew, re-contextualized this statement by following it up with a citation of a rather piquant story (2) taken from BT Avodah Zara 65a. This story once again compares and contrasts gentile desires to those of the Jews. Here the gentile desires prostitutes. It would seem that this passage assumes that the word *shegal* means "prostitute" and brings this story to illustrate the gentile's love of the *shegal*=prostitute mentioned in the first citation. Thus, at least in the Middle Ages there existed an interpretive tradition that *shegal* meant prostitute.

---

[36] This line is similarly quoted out of context in *Midrash Tehillim* (Buber), Psalm 45, section 6.

In light of all of this, I would like to propose that Rav understood the biblical word *shegal* to mean "prostitute" and that the term *kalbeta* that he uses to gloss *shegal* means in this context not "she-dog," but rather serves as an alternate term for prostitute. If this is correct, we can now understand how Rav's comments fit into the Amoraic argument that Neh 2:6 is evidence for the fact that the Persian king became a sinner. If Rav understood the Nehemiah verse as describing the king as having a prostitute sitting at his side, it is clear why one would cite this verse with his gloss as proof that the king descended into profligacy.

My understanding of the development of the passage in BT Rosh Hashanah may be summarized as follows: Rav understood the biblical word *shegal* as referring to a "prostitute." This was apparently based on the usage of the biblical verb *shagal* to refer to illicit or obscene sexual activity and perhaps on the existence of a rabbinic Hebrew term *shiglonot* that meant prostitutes. Rav thus glossed the word *shegal* in Neh 2:6 with the Aramaic word *kalbeta*, a term referring to a prostitute. Next, later Amoriam, understanding that *kalbeta* here means "prostitute" and not "she-dog," used Rav's understanding of the Nehemiah verse to prove that the Persian king fell into a life of sin. Finally, the Stammaim understood Rav's use of the word *kalbeta* as referring to a dog and attempted to reconcile this interpretation of *shegal* with evidence of biblical usage. There are two possible interpretations of the Stammaitic understanding of Rav's gloss. One is that they were genuinely unaware of the possibility that *kalbeta* might mean prostitute and hence misunderstood Rav's interpretation. Such a usage, which given its lack of broad attestation was likely rare to begin with, may have fallen from use in the centuries intervening between Rav and the redactors of the latest strata of the Talmud. Furthermore, given Rav's Palestinian origins, this may have been an expression of western provenance that was never well known in Babylonia. However, it is also possible that the Stammaim were aware of the usage of *kalbeta* to mean "prostitute" but midrashically misread Rav's gloss in order to create a pretext for presenting their own theory that *shegal* means "queen." This Stammaitic passage might also be seen as a sort of satiric discussion of gentiles' excessive love of dogs.[37]

Having made the case for *klb* meaning "prostitute" in the Talmud, and thereby potentially in the Bible as well, we now must reconsider the

---

37 This passage may particularly take aim at the high status of dogs in the Persian culture of the time. Dogs were revered and protected in Zoroastrianism. See Moazami, "The Dog in Zoroastrian Religion," 127–49. Dogs were also well regarded in the Greco-Roman world. See Schwartz, "Dogs in Jewish Society," 250–53.

origins of this usage. Since we have rejected the possibility that *klb* refers specifically to a temple prostitute, we can no longer argue that the term emerges from a perception of dogs as "loyal servants." It is likely that the word *klb* came to be associated with human prostitutes because dogs were known for their excessive sexuality.[38] Dogs are known to copulate in public and the female of the species is known for her prodigious sexual appetite when in heat. The rabbis duly noted both of these phenomena.[39] Lane reports that in Arabic *kalba* can be used as a pejorative term for a woman.[40] This usage may be based upon a similar conception of the sexuality of female dogs. In English we find a parallel use of the word "bitch."[41]

If this reasoning is correct, it is primarily the female forms of the word *klb* that refer to prostitutes in Northwest Semitic languages. The Bible's use of the word *keleb* for a male prostitute would thus be a back formation from the feminine form. It should hardly surprise us that the feminine form is primary in this case. In most societies, female prostitution is a far more common phenomenon than male prostitution. We have already seen, in the previous verse, how the term *qadesh* may be a term for male prostitute that derives from *qedesha*. Similarly, in English, the unmodified word "prostitute" refers to a female of the profession. To refer to a man of similar occupation one must modify the basic term and say "male prostitute."

In sum, the case for *klb* referring to a prostitute in *BT Rosh Hashanah* 4b is not conclusive. As in the case of Deut 23:19, the argument rests on the fact that reading *klb* as referring to a prostitute would make the text read more smoothly. We cannot discount the possibility that in both of these instances *klb* simply means "dog." However, these two readings each increase the plausibility of the other and, in turn, of the likelihood other usages of *klb* in Northwest Semitic languages refer to prostitutes.

---

38 This has previously been suggested in *The Jewish Encyclopedia* IV, 63.

39 Bereishit Rabba 36:7, Eicha Rabba 1:30.

40 Lane, *Arabic English Lexicon*, 2625.

41 As the term is used today, "bitch" does not necessarily have overt sexual connotations. However, the *Oxford English Dictionary* writes with regard to "bitch": "applied opprobriously to a woman, strictly a lewd and sensual woman."

Note:

After completing this piece and submitting it for publication in this volume, I was contacted by R. Yaakov Jaffe of the Maimonides School in Boston, who had heard about my work. He wanted to suggest an alternative explanation for Rav's glossing of the word *shegal* with *kalbeta*. He called attention to the Persian word *sheghal*, meaning "jackal," suggesting that Rav simply explained a rare biblical word using a Persian homophone. This suggestion requires further investigation and may well be an equal or superior solution to the problem than the one that I have suggested here.

Works Cited

Aisleitner, Joseph. *Wörterbuch der ugaritischen Sprache*. Berlin: Akademie-Verlag, 1963.

Brown, F., S. R. Driver, and C.A. Briggs (BDB). *A Hebrew and English Lexicon of the Old Testament with an Appendix Containing the Biblical Aramaic*. Corrected Edition. Oxford: Clarendon Press, 1951.

Buttrick, G. A. et al (eds.). *Interpreter's Dictionary of the Bible*. New York: Abingdon Press, 1962.

Cooke, G. A. *A Text-Book of North-Semitic Inscriptions: Moabite, Hebrew, Phoenician, Aramaic, Nabataean, Palmyrene, Jewish*. Oxford: Clarendon Press, 1903.

Dalman, Gustaf H. *Aramäisch-neuhebräisches Handwörterbuch zu Targum, Talmud and Midrash*. Hildesheim: Gg. Olms, 1967.

Delcor, M. "Le personnel du temple d'Astarte a Kition d'apres une Tablette phénicienne (CIS 86A et B)." *Ugarit-Forschungen* 11 (1979): 147–64.

Dietrich, Manfried, Oswald Loretz, and Joaquin Sanmartin. *The Cuneiform Alphabetic Texts from Ugarit, Ras Ibn Hani and Other Places (KTU)*. Second, Enlarged Edition. Münster: Ugarit-Verlag, 1995.

Donner, H., and W. Röllig. *Kanaanäische und aramäische Inschriften*, Vol. 1. Wiesbaden: Harrassowitz, 1962.

Driver, S. R. *A Critical and Exegetical Commentary on Deuteronomy*. Edinburgh: T & T Clark, 1895.

Ford, J. Massyngberde. *Revelation*. The Anchor Bible 38. Garden City, N.Y.: Doubleday, 1975.

Freedman, David Noel et al (eds.). *The Anchor Bible Dictionary*. New York: Doubleday, 1992.

Gibson, J. C. L. *Textbook of Syrian Semitic Inscriptions*, Vol. 3. Oxford, 1982.

Goodfriend, E. A. "Could *keleb* in Deuteronomy 23:19 Actually Refer to a Canine?" In *Pomegranates and Golden Bells: Studies in Biblical, Jewish and Near Eastern Ritual Law and Literature in Honor of Jacob Milgrom*, edited by David P. Wright, David Noel Freedman, and Avi Hurvitz, 381–397. Winona Lake, Ind.: Eisenbrauns, 1995.

Gruber, M. I. "The Qādēš in the Book of Kings and in Other Sources." *Tarbiz* 52 (1982/3): 162–76.

"Hebrew *qēdēšāh* and Her Canaanite and Akkadian Cognates." *Ugarit-Forschungen* 18 (1986): 133–48.

Hoftijzer, J., and K. Jongeling. *Dictionary of Northwest Semitic Inscriptions*. Leiden: E. J. Brill, 1995.

Koehler, L., and W. Baumgartner. *The Hebrew and Aramaic Lexicon of the Old Testament*. Leiden: E. J. Brill, 1994–.

Lane, E. W. *Arabic English Lexicon*, Book. 1, Part 8. New York: F. Ungar Publishing Co., 1957.

Luzzatto, S. D. *Perush Shadal al Hamishah Humshei Torah* (Shadal's Exegesis on the Five Books of the Pentateuch). Tel Aviv: Devir, 1966.

Mayes, A. D. H. *Deuteronomy*. Greenwood: Attic Press, 1979.

Moazami, M. "The Dog in Zoroastrian Religion: *Vidēvdād* Chapter XIII." *Indo-Iranian Journal* 49.1–2 (March, 2006): 127–49.

Nelson, Richard D. *Deuteronomy: A Commentary*. Louisville, Ky.: Westminster John Knox Press, 2002.

Peckam, J. B. "Notes on a Fifth-Century Phoenician Inscription from Kition, Cyprus (CIS 86)." *Or*NS 37 (1968): 457–68.

Phillips, Anthony. *Deuteronomy*. Cambridge: University Press, 1973.

Rubenstein, Jeffrey L., ed. *Creation and Composition: The Contribution of the Bavli Redactors (Stammaim) to the Aggada*, Tübingen: Mohr Siebeck, 2005.

Rudolf, W. "Präparierte Jungfrauen? (zu Hosea 1)." *ZAW* 75 (1963): 65–73.

Schwartz, Joshua J. "Dogs in Jewish Society in the Second Temple Period and in the Time of the Mishnah and Talmud." *Journal of Jewish Studies* 55.2 (2004): 246–77.

Slouschz, N. *Otzar ketovot ha-fenikiot*. Tel Aviv: Mosad Bialiḳ, 1942.

Smith, R. Payne. *Thesaurus Syriacus*, Vol. 1. Oxford: Clarendon Press, 1879.

Sokoloff, Michael. *A Dictionary of Jewish Palestinian Aramaic of the Byzantine Period*. Ramat-Gan: Bar Ilan University Press, 1992.

Review of *Hebräisches und aramäisches Lexikon, zum Alten Testament* by Ludwig Koehler and Walter Baumgartner. *Dead Sea Discoveries* 7.1 (2000): 74–109.

Stager, L. "Deities and Dogs – Their Sacred Rites." *Biblical Archaeology Review* 17.3 (1991): 40–42.

Thomas, D. Winton. "*Kelebh* 'Dog': Its Origin and Some Usages of It in the Old Testament." *Vetus Testamentum* 10 (1960): 410–27.

Thomson, J. A. *Deuteronomy: An Introduction and Commentary*. Tyndale Old Testament Commentary. London: Inter-Varsity Press, 1974.

Virolleaud, C. "Textes administratifs de Ras-Shamra en cunéiforme alphabetique." *Revue d'Assyriologie et d'Archéologie orientale* 37 (1940–41): 11–44.

von Rad, G. *Deuteronomy: A Commentary*. London: SCM Press, 1966.

Weiser, Asher. *mikra ve-lashon*. Tel Aviv: Niv, 1965.

Ḫ > Ḥ IN ASSYRIA AND BABYLONIA*

RICHARD C. STEINER
YESHIVA UNIVERSITY

What is it about Mesopotamia that continues to hold West Semites like my distinguished friend and colleague, Prof. Barry Eichler, in thrall so many centuries after the Assyrian and Babylonian captivities? Only Barry can answer that question, and I suspect he will do so in his remarks. I wish to address a more modest question. How should Barry pronounce the word that to this day is used to refer to the devastation visited by the East Semites on his ancient homeland—the Yiddish word *khurbn*?

Semitic originally had a contrast between the voiceless pharyngeal fricative **ḥ* and the voiceless uvular fricative **ḫ*; a minimal pair that can be reconstructed for Proto-West-Semitic is **ḥālum* "sand" ≠ **ḫālum* "maternal uncle." Until two or three decades ago, most Semitists assumed that uvular **ḫ* was lost already in Old Aramaic, as the result of a merger with pharyngeal **ḥ*.[1] Today, thanks to papyrus Amherst 63 (the Aramaic text in Demotic script), there is a new conventional wisdom. That text, probably dictated to an Egyptian scribe at the beginning of the third century BCE, consistently distinguishes **ḫ* from **ḥ*.[2] Thus, Aram. חמר "wine" is transcribed with Demotic *ḫ* in four places (cf. Ug. *ḫmr* "wine"), while Aram. חמת "venom" is transcribed with Demotic *ḥ* in three places (cf. Ug. *ḥmt* "venom").[3] Similarly, Aram. -מנחר "nostril" and -נחרת "snorts" are transcribed in the text with *ḫ* (cf. Arab. *manḫar* "nostril" and *naḫīr* "snort"), while Aram. נחש "copper, bronze" is transcribed with *ḥ* in two places (cf. Arab. *nuḥās* "copper").[4]

---

* I am greatly indebted to P.-A. Beaulieu and S. Shaked for their patient guidance and to G. Frame for his very generous assistance prior to the conference at which this paper was delivered.

1 See, for example, Degen, *Altaramäische Grammatik*, 37; and Segert, *Altaramäische Grammatik*, 88.

2 So already Nims and Steiner, "A Paganized Version," 263: "the Proto-Semitic contrast of *ḥ* with *ḫ* is perfectly preserved." See now Steiner, "On the Dating," 235–37.

3 Steiner and Moshavi, "A Selective Glossary," 1256, 1257.

4 Steiner and Moshavi, "A Selective Glossary," 1260–61.

During the past two decades, this discovery has made its way into the handbooks.[5] However, it would be hasty to conclude that the earlier assumption was completely wrong. After all, Amherst 63 comes from Egypt. What about the other areas where Aramaic was spoken, especially Mesopotamia? How long was uvular *ḫ preserved there?

In this article I shall attempt to answer that question. I shall argue that Amherst 63 sheds light on the fate of *ḫ in Mesopotamia as well as Egypt—and perhaps even in Akkadian as well as Aramaic. Examination of the evidence will suggest that the shift ḫ > ḥ occurred in Assyria before it occurred in Egypt and before it occurred in Babylonia.

Aramaic Renderings of Akkadian Ḫ

Amherst 63 contains several Akkadian loanwords relevant to our problem, loanwords that exhibit inconsistency in the treatment of Akk. ḫ. In one of them, נחתם "baker" (V/5 *nḫ.t*ᵐ *m.k.*ᵐ "your baker") < *nuḫatimmu* "cook/baker,"[6] Akk. ḫ is rendered with Aram. ḫ (written with Dem. ẖ in this instance). This is the usual rendering of Akk. ḫ in West Semitic both earlier and later. Thus, from Akk. *maḫīru* "purchase, purchase price" in the second millennium BCE, we find Ug. *mḫr* "price" with ḫ.[7] Much later, in Arabic, we find four renderings with ḫ: *faḫḫār* "(baked) pottery" < *paḫāru* "potter," *ḫazaf* "(unbaked) pottery" < *ḫaṣbu* "clay, sherd, pot" (cf. Dan 2:41 חסף די פחר), *ḫābiya* "a large jar" < *ḫabû* "earthenware jug," and *nusḫah* "copy" < *nisḫu* "copy."[8]

In another loanword, פחה "governor" (XVIII/4 *pḫ*ᵐ, XIX/2 *pḫ.*ᵐ) < *paḫatu* "governor," Akk. ḫ shows up rendered with a pharyngeal ḥ.[9] This is not due to mishearing; the same Akkadian word appears as *fḥt* in

---

5 Beyer, *Die aramäischen Texte*, 101–2; Hug, *Altaramäische Grammatik*, 51; Segert, "Old Aramaic Phonology," 118–19; Muraoka and Porten, *A Grammar of Egyptian Aramaic*, 10 nn. 36–37.

6 P.-A. Beaulieu informs me (email communication, March 16, 2009) that "in LB temple archives, it seems that the *nuḫatimmu* is the baker, as he is responsible for preparing cakes, sweets, and bread."

7 *CAD* M/1, 97; Del Olmo Lete and Sanmartin, *A Dictionary of the Ugaritic Language*, 539–40. Cf. Hoch, *Semitic Words in Egyptian Texts*, 150–51.

8 Kaufman, *Akkadian Influences*, 53, 54, 78, 79. Note that most of these words do not seem to be scholastic borrowings, borrowed from a dead or dying language; four of them relate to everyday occupations such as baking and pottery. They must have been borrowed by Babylonian Aramaic before the Late Babylonian period (from 625 BCE until the disappearance of cuneiform documents). At that period, Akkadian was "an imperfectly learned, dying language" (ibid., 169).

9 Steiner and Nims, "Ashurbanipal and Shamash-shum-ukin," 71, 73, as corrected in Steiner, "The Aramaic Text in Demotic Script," 323, 324.

a Liḥyanite inscription of the Persian period (mid-fifth century BCE).[10] We may also note the absence of χ in the Septuagint's rendering of three names of Akkadian origin: (1) Ασορ(αδ)δαν = אסר חדן Kgs 19:37, Isa 37:38) < *Aššur-aḫ-iddina*, (2) Αλαε = חלח (2 Kgs 17:6, 18:11) < *Ḫalaḫḫu*, and (3) Αβωρ = חבור (2 Kgs 17:6, 18:11) < *Ḫābūr*.[11] In all three names, there is a zero-rendering of Hebrew ח; in חלח, there is also a rendering with ε. Both are normal renderings of pharyngeal *ḥ* in the LXX; for uvular *ḫ*, the LXX uses χ.[12]

Why do פחה "governor" and אסר חדן "Esarhaddon" differ from נחתם "baker" and חבית "jar" in their treatment of Akk. *ḫ*? The first explanation that comes to mind is chronological: we might assume that נחתם and חבית (with Aram. *ḫ* for Akk. *ḫ*) were exported from Mesopotamia earlier than פחה and אסר חדן (with Aram. *ḥ* for Akk. *ḫ*), i.e., before the sound [ḫ] was lost in Akkadian and/or Aramaic. This is hardly likely, however, since פחה and אסר חדן are attested already in early passages of Isaiah and Kings, whereas נחתם is first attested in Amherst 63 (beginning of the third century BCE)[13] and חבית is not attested until the Nisa ostraca (first century BCE).[14] A more likely explanation is geographical: the forms with pharyngeal *ḥ* come from Assyria rather than from Babylonia.

---

10 For the dating of the Liḥyanite inscription, see Winnett, *A Study of the Lihyanite and Thamudic Inscriptions*, 50–51; Grimme, "Neubearbeitung," 311; Albright, "Dedan," 4; Winnett and Reed, *Ancient Records from North Arabia*, 115–16; Eph'al, *The Ancient Arabs*, 212; and id., "Syria-Palestine under Achaemenid Rule," 163. The later dating of Caskel (*Lihyan und Lihyanisch*, 101–2) is part of a downward revision of Liḥyanite chronology that has not been accepted; see Müller, "Das Frühnordarabische," 21, 22. Note also LXX φααθμωαβ for the name פחת מואב, but the absence of χ proves little here, since the Greek translation of Ezra-Nehemiah, in which this transcription appears, reflects a stage of Hebrew in which *ḫ has already merged with *ḥ*; see Blau, *On Polyphony*, 65–67; and Steiner, "On the Dating," 261. Blau (*On Polyphony*, 67) adds that the word פחה "could have reached Hebrew by the mediation of a dialect in which *x* had already shifted to *ḥ*," thereby anticipating our conclusion.

11 See Blau, *On Polyphony*, 44–45, 48; cf. also Wutz, *Die Transkriptionen von der Septuaginta*, 139.

12 Blau, *On Polyphony*; Steiner, "On the Dating"; id., "*A*-Coloring Consonants."

13 Also from the third century BCE is an Egyptian ostracon in which a man is identified as נחתמא; see Porten and Yardeni, *TAD*, 4.202–3, RÉS 1301 l. 7.

14 Hoftijzer and Jongeling, *Dictionary*, 357 s.v. *ḥwt*.

Ḫ *and* Ḥ *in Assyria*

Let us look first at Assyria. According to P. V. Mankowski, "the BH and Aramaic forms [of פחה] are certain loans from Assyrian."[15] This seems plausible: the loanword derives from an Akkadian term that came to be widely used at the time of the Neo-Assyrian empire,[16] and two of its literary occurrences are in speeches of Assyrians (an Assyrian official in 2 Kgs 18:17 and an Assyrian king in Amherst 63, XIX/2). An Assyrian origin is even more likely for the examples from the Septuagint; one, Ασορ(αδ)δαν, is the name of an Assyrian king and the other two, Αλαε and Αβωρ, are toponyms mentioned in connection with Assyrian kings. The evidence suggests that there was a shift *ḫ* > *ḥ* in Assyria before the fall of Nineveh in 612 BCE. However, from the evidence presented thus far, it is not clear whether this shift took place in Aramaic (with phonemic merger) or Akkadian (without phonemic merger) or both. Any one of these scenarios would account for the *ḥ* in *pḥ*ᵐ / *pḥ.*ᵐ and *fḥt* and for the absence of χ in Ασορ(αδ)δαν, Αλαε, and Αβωρ.

Evidence that seems to bear on this question comes from a Neo-Assyrian inscription of Esarhaddon in which the Median name **Xšaθrita-* appears with an initial *k*: *Ka-áš-ta-ri-ti, Kaš-ta-ri-ti.*[17] Assuming that the Median name was really pronounced with an initial [x],[18] it is difficult to understand why *k* would be used to render it. Why not use *ḫ* as in *Ḫa-šá-at-ri-tu*$_4$, the Late Babylonian (Darius I) rendering of the same name?[19] This evidence suggests that the shift affected the Akkadian spoken in Assyria, at the very least. I came to this conclusion before I knew that the shift had already been posited, on independent grounds, for that dialect. According to J. Hämeen-Anttila, "*h* (velar [*ḫ*]) has probably been changed in Neo-Assyrian to pharyngeal *ḥ* or even to laryngeal *h*."[20] Since two pieces of evidence for the shift involve Esarhaddon, we may conclude that it probably occurred during his reign (681–669 BCE) at the latest.

What about the *Aramaic* spoken in Assyria? We cannot rule out the possibility that the shift occurred only in the Assyrian dialect of Akka-

---

15 Mankowski, *Akkadian Loanwords*, 128.

16 See, for example, Henshaw, "The Office of Šaknu," 465, 479–83; Mankowski, *Akkadian Loanwords*, 128–29; and the literature cited in these sources.

17 Zadok, *The Ethno-linguistic Character*, 66 (§6.10); Borger, "Kas/štarita," 476. The Assyrian form is probably to be read *Kastarita* rather than *Kaštarita*.

18 See n. 41 below.

19 Malbran-Labat, *La version akkadienne*, 103 (§41); Hinz, "Kyaxares," 399.

20 Hämeen-Anttila, *A Sketch of Neo-Assyrian Grammar*, 15.

dian, leaving *$\underset{\smile}{h}$ unchanged in the Assyrian dialect of Aramaic. That scenario would suffice to account for the appearance of the Akkadian loanword פחה with a pharyngeal ḥ in Egypt and Arabia. Nevertheless, since the entire population of Assyria spoke Aramaic by the beginning of the seventh century BCE, the speakers of Akkadian being bilingual,[21] it seems more likely that the two languages would have changed their pronunciation in tandem. Moreover, the shift would have been far more natural in Aramaic, since it already possessed the rare and difficult pharyngeal sound [ḥ].

The evidence for the loss of *$\underset{\smile}{h}$ in Assyria is surprisingly inconsistent. In the Septuagint to 2 Kings, one verse before Ασορ(αδ)δαν = אסר חדן (19:37) < *Aššur-aḫ-iddina*, we find Σενναχηριμ = סנחריב (19:36) < *Sin-aḫḫē-erība*.[22] Sennacherib appears with χ in other sources, as well: Herodotus' *Histories* (2.141.2 Σαναχαριβος) and Josephus' *Antiquities* (10.1.1 §1, etc. Σεναχειριμος). Similarly, Esarhaddon appears with χ in Tobit (1:21 Σαχερδονος) and in Josephus' *Antiquities* (10.1.5 §23 Ασαραχοδδας). Finally, the Habor River appears with χ in the Septuagint to 1 Chronicles (5:26 Χαβωρ) and in Ptolemy's *Geography* (5.18 §3 Χαβωρας), with *ch* in Pliny's *Natural History* (31.22, 32.7 *Chabura*), and with $\underset{\smile}{h}$ in Arabic sources (*al-Ḫābūr*).[23] A similar inconsistency is found in Amherst 63, which contains another Akkadian loanword whose form and meaning point to Neo-Assyrian as its source: לחן "temple servitor" (VII/12 *r.*⌈$\underset{\smile}{h}$⌉*.n.n*^{m} "temple servitors") < NA *laḫḫinu* "temple official."[24] The $\underset{\smile}{h}$ in this Demotic rendering of לחן contrasts with the ḥ in the Demotic rendering of פחה. Assyrian renderings of velar fricatives in foreign names also exhibit inconsistency. In some foreign names, the Assyrians use $\underset{\smile}{h}$ rather

---

21 See Parpola, "National and Ethnic Identity," 5–49 and the literature cited there. We might add that, already in the late eighth century BCE, Sargon II was fighting a losing battle against Aramaic. In one letter, he chastises his correspondent for writing to him "on an Aramaic document," asking: "Why did you not write on an Akkadian tablet?" (*CAD* S s.v. *sepēru*). Nine hundred years later we find R. Judah the Prince fighting a similar battle and asking a similar question: "Why (use) the Syrian language in the Land of Israel?" (Soṭa 49b, BQ 83a).

22 This form is the only evidence cited by Mankowski (*Akkadian Loanwords*, 157) in support of his claim that "Akkadian PNs containing *x* that are attested in BH show χ in the LXX."

23 For medieval attestations of the Arabic name, see Lassner, "Khābūr," 897–98.

24 Steiner and Moshavi, "A Selective Glossary," 1259; *AHw* 528; *CAD* A/1, 294; Porten, *Archives from Elephantine*, 200–1; Kaufman, *Akkadian Influences*, 66 n. 176.

than *k* to render initial velar fricatives, e.g, *Ḫi-lak/la-ak/-ku/i* = ח(י)לך "Cilicia."[25]

What are we to make of this inconsistency? It is possible that *ḫ was not completely lost in Assyria—that some speakers in that ethnically heterogeneous land[26] never carried out the shift.[27] It is also possible that the shift took place (at least in part) during Esarhaddon's reign and that his name made its way to the West in two forms: with *ḫ* before the shift and with *ḥ* after it.

Ḫ and Ḥ in Babylonia

In Babylonia, there were apparently three mergers involving Aramaic ח. First, *ḫ merged with *ḥ, as in Assyria and Palestine. Subsequently, *ḥ* lost its pharyngeal constriction, merging with *h*. Finally, *h* became silent in at least some positions, merging with zero. Evidence of the second and third mergers in Mandaic and Jewish Babylonian Aramaic texts, including the magic bowls (ca. 5th–7th centuries CE), has frequently been noted.[28] The second merger is reflected already in the Hebrew pronunciation of R. Ḥiyya (late second century CE), a Babylonian disciple of R. Judah the Prince. The latter once suggested to his son that he tease R. Ḥiyya about his inability to distinguish ח from ה, with the claim that it led him to commit blasphemy when, instead of וחכיתי לה׳ "I shall wait for the Lord" (Isa 8:17), he read והכיתי לה׳ "I shall smite the Lord" (Megilla 24b)! The evidence for the second merger is also, indirectly, evidence for the first, since it affected ח from both *ḫ (e.g., Mandaic *haila* "force, army"; cf. Amherst 63, passim *ḫyr*^{m} "force, troop") and *ḥ (e.g., Mandaic *hiia* "life"; cf. Amherst 63, XVII/7 *ḥ.yn*^{m} "life").[29]

The first merger seems to have occurred later in Babylonia than it did in Assyria. One piece of evidence comes from the Aramaic version of Darius's Bisitun inscription (ca. 510 BCE), in which the scribe uses the Aramaic letter ח to render Iranian *x* in the toponym רחא, corresponding

---

[25] For חילכיא / חלכין "Cilicians" in the Arsham letters, see Driver, *Aramaic Documents*, 25–28 (5:1*, 5:2, 6:4), 61; Porten and Yardeni, *TAD*, 1.110–11, 114–15; cf. חילך "Cilicia" in Ezek 27:11.

[26] See Postgate, "Ancient Assyria," and Parpola, "National and Ethnic Identity."

[27] One might speculate that Assyrians of Anatolian and Iranian origin did not carry out the shift because they realized /ḥ/ as [x] in their Aramaic speech.

[28] For discussion and literature, see Macuch, *Handbook of Classical and Modern Mandaic*, 79–88; Morgenstern, הארמית הבבלית היהודית, 60–61, 64–65; id., "On some Non-Standard Spellings," 251–54.

[29] Drower and Macuch, *A Mandaic Dictionary*, 120, 143; Steiner and Moshavi, "A Selective Glossary," 1256–57.

to *Raxā* in the Old Persian version.[30] This transcription suggests that uvular **ḫ* still existed in Babylonian Aramaic in ca. 510 BCE. If the letter ח represented only pharyngeal *ḥ* at the time, the scribe should have used כ, which, as I have shown elsewhere, already had the value [x] in postvocalic position in Babylonian Aramaic.[31] Indeed, the Akkadian version of the Bisitun inscription uses cuneiform *k* for the presumed Iranian [x] in the name *Ú-ma-ku-iš-tar*,[32] corresponding to *Huvaxštra* "Cyaxares" in the Old Persian version. Thus, the Aramaic version of the Bisitun inscription seems to provide a late-sixth-century terminus post quem for the loss of uvular *ḫ* in Babylonian Aramaic.

When we attempt to fix the date of the change more precisely, we find that the evidence is contradictory. One possible terminus ante quem comes from Arsham letter 11, written in Babylon in the late fifth century BCE.[33] There we find the name of one of the addressees is written once as חנדסירם and once as כנדסירם.[34] Driver wrote that "no satisfactory derivation has been proposed" for the name,[35] but it is now believed to be Luwian, with the first three consonants representing Common Anatolian **ḫant-* "before" (cognate to Latin *ante*) and the last three consonants representing a divine name.[36] If so, we have here hesitation between two Aramaic renderings of Luwian *ḫ* in the same name and the same document. This hesitation could be a result of the loss of the uvular fricative. After the loss, when speakers of Babylonian Aramaic needed to transcribe an initial velar fricative, they might well have used either the velar stop כ (to capture the *place* of articulation)[37] or the pha-

---

30 Greenfield and Porten, *The Bisitun Inscription*, 38–39, 60. Similarly, in the Persepolis texts (Bowman, *Aramaic Ritual Texts*, 64, 115), we find the personal name סחררת rendering an otherwise unattested *Suxra-raθa* in a document dated to year 13 of Artaxerxes I (452/51 BCE).

31 Steiner, "Variation, Simplifying Assumptions," *60–*65. It seems unlikely that the use of ח to write Iranian *x* was a historical spelling already in 510 BCE.

32 Malbran-Labat, *La version akkadienne*, 97, 99, 103; however, see n. 41 below.

33 Driver, *Aramaic Documents*, 10–11.

34 Driver, *Aramaic Documents*, 34 (11:1*, 11:2), 61; Porten and Yardeni, *TAD*, 1.124.

35 Driver, *Aramaic Documents*, 67.

36 See Grelot, *Documents araméens*, 476; Kornfeld, *Onomastica aramaica*, 34; Muraoka and Porten, *A Grammar of Egyptian Aramaic*, 19; cf. Houwink ten Cate, *The Luwian Population Groups*, 149–50.

37 It was a stop in initial position, but the fact that it was a fricative in postvocalic position may have promoted its use even in initial position.

ryngeal fricative ח (to capture the *manner* of articulation).[38] If this is correct, the change would seem to have occurred before the late fifth century BCE. When we combine this terminus ante quem with the terminus post quem suggested above, we are left with the early/mid-fifth century BCE as the date of the change.

Unfortunately, this argument is weakened by the fact that the Luwian name happens to have a prefixed ו– in Arsham letter 11; thus, strictly speaking, we are dealing with a postvocalic כ. Moreover, it is not certain that the evidence from that letter reflects the linguistic situation in Babylonia; the spellings of the Luwian name could derive also from Cilicia or northern Syria. Indeed, we find a very similar hesitation between ח and כ in the coins of Pharnabazus, the Persian satrap of Cilicia in ca. 379–374 BCE. Some of these have חלך for Cilicia, while others have כלך.[39] On the other hand, the use of initial כ to render [x] is not limited to Cilician names. The same rendering is found in the word כרוזא "herald" (Dan 3:4), derived from Iranian **xrausa* "herald."[40] Although we cannot exclude the possibility that the explanation of this rendering is to be found in Iranian dialectal variation,[41] it gives some legitimacy to our use of Arsham letter 11 to assign a late-fifth-century terminus ante quem to the sound change.

The evidence of Arsham letter 11 is contradicted by evidence from Greek transcriptions of Akkadian, which seem to suggest a later date. Westenholz has pointed to the rendering of Akk. *ḫ* with χ in two examples: Αδαδναδιναχης = **Adad-nādin-aḫḫē* and Σεχες (for *Σεχετ) = *šiḫṭu* "Mercury."[42] The so-called "Graeco-Babyloniaca" texts use Greek ξ to render Babylonian *ḫ* with one exception.[43] In one tablet, we find γισιμαρ

---

38 It is also possible that, by the late fifth century, the use of ח to write Luwian *ḫ* was a historical spelling.

39 Cooke, *A Text-Book of North-Semitic Inscriptions*, 343–44 (cf. 346).

40 This etymology, proposed by M. Schaeder, is universally accepted today. The existence in BA (Dan 5:29) of a denominative verb from the same root shows that the borrowing was not a recent one.

41 S. Shaked informs me (email communication, July 15, 2003) that "in *xrausa-* the initial *x* is etymologically a *k* realized as a fricative because it forms a cluster with the following consonant. This is true, incidentally, of most other cases of *x* in Iranian.... It is arguable that in one of the Iranian dialects Iranian *k* was not pronounced *x* in the case of **krausa-* (and possibly in other cases as well), and that it was from this dialect that Aramaic borrowed the word."

42 Westenholz, "Graeco-Babyloniaca," 283.

43 Knudsen, "Akkadian in Greek Orthography," 73, 75; Geller, "Last Wedge," 67; Westenholz, "Graeco-Babyloniaca," 282. This rendering is unique. Elsewhere we find ξ used for *ṣ* or *š*; see Steiner, *Affricated Ṣade*," 69.

Μηλω Μηλ⸢ω⸣ = gišimmar Meluḫḫa Meluḫḫū "date-palm of Meluḫḫa" and σοος = *suḫuššu* "young date-palm."[44] Here we see Sumerian and Akkadian ḫ rendered by zero, even when geminated.[45] If these exceptional renderings are the result of a sound change in Babylonian *Aramaic*, we might have to date that sound change to the first century BCE or CE, around the time that it occurred in Palestinian Aramaic.

Conclusions

The available evidence suggests that ḫ > ḥ occurred later in Babylonia than in Assyria, in both Akkadian and Aramaic. In Assyria, it seems to have occurred—for some speakers, at least—before 669 BCE; in Babylonia it seems to have occurred after 510—with some evidence pointing to the early/mid-fifth century BCE and other evidence pointing to the first century BCE or CE. The geographic difference is reflected in two Akkadian loanwords in Amherst 63: Aram. פחה from Assyria written with Demotic ḥ and Aram. נחתם from Babylonia written with Demotic ẖ.

WORKS CITED

Albright, W. F. "Dedan." In *Geschichte und Altes Testament*. Tübingen: J. C. B. Mohr, 1953, 1–12.

Beyer, K. *Die aramäischen Texte vom Toten Meer: samt den Inschriften aus Palästina, dem Testament Levis aus der Kairoer Genisa, der Fastenrolle und den alten talmudischen Zitaten*, Vol. 1. Göttingen: Vandenhoeck & Ruprecht, 1984.

Blau, J. *On Polyphony in Biblical Hebrew*. Jerusalem: Israel Academy of Sciences and Humanities, 1982.

---

44 Sollberger, "Graeco-Babyloniaca," 66; Geller, "Last Wedge," 70.

45 It is difficult to accept the view of Westenholz ("Graeco-Babyloniaca," 291) that the zero-rendering is found with Sumerian ḫ but not Akkadian ḫ, because it is difficult to understand how Sumerian phonology could have escaped the influence of Akkadian phonology once Sumerian became a dead language, and how both of them could have escaped the influence of Aramaic phonology once Akkadian became a dead language. The influence of spoken languages on dead languages is well known from Latin and Hebrew. For Latin in France, see Smith, "The English Language," 168: "Every change in the vernacular extended simultaneously to the pronunciation of Latin." For Latin in England, see Brittain, *Latin in Church*, 55: "Since the time of Erasmus, it has followed the changes in English phonetics step by step." For Hebrew examples, see Steiner, "Variation, Simplifying Assumptions," *60 n. 30.

Bowman, R. A. *Aramaic Ritual Texts from Persepolis*. Chicago, Ill.: University of Chicago Press, 1970.

Brittain, F. *Latin in Church: The History of its Pronunciation*. 2nd ed. London: A. R. Mowbray, 1955.

Caskel W. *Lihyan und Lihyanisch*. Köln: Westdeutscher Verlag, 1954.

Cooke, G. A. *A Text-Book of North-Semitic Inscriptions: Moabite, Hebrew, Phoenician, Aramaic, Nabataean, Palmyrene, Jewish*. Oxford: Clarendon Press, 1903.

Degen, R. *Altaramäische Grammatik der Inschriften des 10.–8. Jh. V. Chr.* Abhandlungen für die Kunde des Morgenlandes 38,3. Mainz: Deutsche Morgenländische Gesellschaft, 1969.

Del Olmo Lete, G., and J. Sanmartin, *A Dictionary of the Ugaritic Language in the Alphabetic Tradition*. Leiden: E.J. Brill, 2003.

Driver, G. R. *Aramaic Documents of the Fifth Century B.C.* Oxford: Clarendon Press, 1957.

Drower, E. S., and R. Macuch. *A Mandaic Dictionary*. Oxford: Clarendon Press, 1963.

Eph'al, I. *The Ancient Arabs: Nomads on the Borders of the Fertile Crescent, 9th to 5th century B.C.* Leiden: E. J. Brill, 1982.

"Syria-Palestine under Achaemenid Rule." In *Cambridge Ancient History*, Vol. 4, *Persia, Greece, and the Western Mediterranean c. 525–479*, edited by John Boardman et al., 139–64. Cambridge: Cambridge University Press, 1988.

Greenfield, J. C., and B. Porten. *The Bisitun Inscription of Darius the Great: Aramaic Version*. London: Published on behalf of Corpus Inscriptionum Iranicarum by Lund Humphries, 1982.

Grelot, P. *Documents araméens d'Égypte*. Paris: Éditions du Cerf, 1972.

Grimme, H. "Neubearbeitung der wichtigeren Dedanischen und Lihjanischen Inschriften." *Le Muséon* 50 (1937): 269–320.

Hoch, J. E. *Semitic Words in Egyptian Texts of the New Kingdom and Third Intermediate Period*. Princeton, N.J.: Princeton University Press, 1994.

Houwink ten Cate, P. H. J. *The Luwian Population Groups of Lycia and Cilicia Aspera During the Hellenistic Period*. Leiden: E. J. Brill, 1961.

Hug, V. *Altaramäische Grammatik der Texte des 7. und 6. Jh.s v.Chr.* Heidelberger Studien zum Alten Orient 4. Heidelberg: Heidelberger Orientverlag, 1993.

Kaufman, S. A. *The Akkadian Influences on Aramaic*. Chicago, Ill.: University of Chicago Press, 1974.

Knudsen, E. E. "Akkadian in Greek Orthography: Evidence of Sound Change in an Ancient Traditional Pronunciation." *Orientalia Suecana* 38–39 (1989–90): 71–80.

Kornfeld, W. *Onomastica aramaica aus Ägypten*. Vienna: Verlag der Österreichischen Akademie der Wissenschaften, 1978.

Lassner, J. "Khābūr." In *The Encyclopaedia of Islam*, Vol. 4, 897–98. New Edition. Leiden, E.J. Brill, 1960–.

Macuch, R. *Handbook of Classical and Modern Mandaic*. Berlin: Walter de Gruyter, 1965.

Malbran-Labat, F. *La version akkadienne de l'inscription trilingue de Darius à Behistun*. Rome: GEI, 1994.

Mankowski, Paul V. *Akkadian Loanwords in Biblical Hebrew*. Winona Lake, Ind.: Eisenbrauns, 2000.

Morgenstern, M. הארמִית הבבלִית היהודִית בתשובות הגאונים — עיונים בתורת ההגה, בתצורת הפועל, בכינויים ובסגנון. PhD Dissertation, Hebrew University, 2002.

"On some Non-Standard Spellings in the Aramaic Magic Bowls and their Linguistic Significance." *JSS* 52 (2007): 245–77.

Müller, W. W. "Das Frühnordarabische." In *Grundriss der arabischen Philologie*, Vol. 1, edited by W. Fischer, 17–29. Wiesbaden: Reichert, 1982.

Muraoka, T., and B. Porten. *A Grammar of Egyptian Aramaic*. Leiden: Brill, 1998.

Nims, C. F., and R. C. Steiner, "A Paganized Version of Ps 20:2–6 from the Aramaic Text in Demotic Script." *JAOS* 103 (1983): 261–74.

Parpola, S. "National and Ethnic Identity in the Neo-Assyrian Empire and Assyrian Identity in Post-Empire Times." *Journal of Assyrian Academic Studies* 18 (2004): 5–22.

Porten, B. *Archives from Elephantine: The Life of an Ancient Jewish Military Colony*. Berkeley: University of California Press, 1968.

Porten, B., and A. Yardeni. *Textbook of Aramaic Documents from Ancient Egypt*. 4 vols. Winona Lake, Ind.: Eisenbrauns, 1986–1999.

Postgate, N. "Ancient Assyria—A Multi-Racial State." *Aram* 1 (1989): 1–10.

Segert, S. *Altaramäische Grammatik: mit Bibliographie, Chrestomathie u. Glossar*. Leipzig: VEB Verlag Enzyklopädie, 1986.

"Old Aramaic Phonology." In *Phonologies of Asia and Africa*, Vol. 1, edited by A. S. Kaye, 115–25. Winona Lake, Ind.: Eisenbrauns, 1997.

Smith, G. C. Moore. "The English Language and the 'Restored' Pronunciation of Latin." In *A Grammatical Miscellany Offered to Otto Jespersen on his Seventieth Birthday*, edited by Niels Bøgholm, Aage Brusendorff, and Carl Adolf Bodelsen, 167–78. Copenhagen: Levin & Munksgaard, 1930.

Sollberger, E. "Graeco-Babyloniaca." *Iraq* 24 (1962): 63–72.

Steiner, R. C. *Affricated Ṣade in the Semitic Languages*. New York: American Academy for Jewish Research, 1982.

"The Aramaic Text in Demotic Script." In *The Context of Scripture*, Vol. 1, edited by W. W. Hallo and K. L. Younger, Jr., 309–27. Leiden: E.J. Brill, 1997.

"On the Dating of Hebrew Sound Changes (*Ḫ > Ḥ and *Ġ > ʿ) and Greek Translations (2 Esdras and Judith)." *JBL* 124 (2005): 229–67.

"Variation, Simplifying Assumptions and the History of Spirantization in Aramaic and Hebrew." In *Shaʿarei Lashon: Studies in Hebrew, Aramaic and Jewish Languages Presented to Moshe Bar-Asher*, Vol. 1, edited by A. Maman et al., *52–*65. Jerusalem: Bialik Institute, 2007.

"*A*-coloring Consonants and Furtive *Pataḥ* in Biblical Hebrew and Aramaic According to the Tiberian Masorah." In *Zaphenath-Paneah: Linguistic Studies Presented to Elisha Qimron on the Occasion of his Sixty-Fifth Birthday*, edited by D. Sivan et al., *143–*155. Beer Sheva: Ben-Gurion University of the Negev Press, 2009.

Steiner, R. C., and A. Moshavi. "A Selective Glossary of Northwest Semitic Texts in Egyptian Script." In *Dictionary of the North-West Semitic Inscriptions*, edited by J. Hoftijzer and K. Jongeling, 1249–66. Leiden: E. J. Brill, 1995.

Steiner, R. C., and C. F. Nims. "Ashurbanipal and Shamash-shum-ukin: A Tale of Two Brothers from the Aramaic Text in Demotic Script." *Revue Biblique* 92 (1985): 60–81.

Westenholz, A. "The Graeco-Babyloniaca Once Again." *ZA* 97 (2007): 262–313.

Winnett, F. V. *A Study of the Lihyanite and Thamudic Inscriptions*. Toronto: University of Toronto Press, 1937.

Winnett, F. V., and W. L. Reed, *Ancient Records from North Arabia*. Toronto: University of Toronto Press, 1970.

Wutz, *Die Transkriptionen von der Septuaginta bis zu Hieronymus*. Stuttgart: W. Kohlhammer, 1925.

TRACING THE COURSE OF THE ARRAPḪA-ASSYRIA WAR: A PROPOSAL*

MAYNARD P. MAIDMAN
YORK UNIVERSITY

Barry Eichler is that rare individual, a true blessing to his students. His concern, both intellectual and personal, has touched us all, often repeatedly and throughout the years. It is a privilege, a precious gift, to be able to offer a paper in homage to Barry, in the presence of our teacher. Barry's skill in teaching Akkadian is famous. Only after we left Barry's classroom did we discover how supposedly arcane and intractable was the knowledge we had acquired and how deeply was it ingrained. At least as influential was what Barry insists we do with that knowledge. The beginning of all our Assyriological pursuits, whether historical, literary, or anthropological, was the text. The text *is* privileged, and its clarity, the understanding of its *pᵉšaṭ*—its plain sense—is the foundation of all subsequent intellectual pursuit. The edifice of intellectual structure and historical reconstruction ultimately rests on the foundation stone of comprehension of the text. This afternoon I am presenting a paper I hope does some justice to those lessons wonderfully and wisely imparted.

The study of Nuzi has focused mainly on its internal history, especially the agrarian regime so richly documented. Family law and law in general, to which our honoree has contributed so substantially, and regional administration and production, as well as production of, and trade in, commodities, have also been treated at some length. Such attention has not been lavished on the foreign relations of the kingdom of Arrapḫa of which Nuzi was, it turns out, a surprisingly important component. I propose to identify in the Nuzi texts traces of Assyria's relations with Nuzi, mostly in the last year or so of Arrapḫa's existence, and to suggest an outline of the course of events that transpired during that period. If this reconstruction lacks precision and certitude, it definitely is characterized by substantial verisimilitude. Something like what I am about to describe must certainly have taken place.

To set the stage of the Assyrian campaign against the kingdom of Arrapḫa and to supply the needed context for the descriptions the texts

* This paper derives from research first undertaken for Maidman, *Nuzi Texts*.

give, let us first enumerate the extant data regarding both the regional toponymy and the time frame of the documentation. In short, what do we know of the space and time of the events we are considering?

First, space. The Nuzi texts supply hundreds of toponyms of all sorts. Indeed, the Nuzi texts merit a separate volume in the *Répertoire géographique*,[1] quite apart from, and even larger (by over 100 pages) than, the volume on the rest of Middle Assyrian and Middle Babylonian GNs with which the Nuzi data would naturally belong.[2] And yet, of the place names appearing in the Nuzi texts, only four may be located with certainty: Aššur (Qal'at Širqat), Natmani (Tell 'Ali), Nuzi (Yorghan Tepe), and the city of Arrapḫa (Kirkuk). Three other place names may be located with reasonable certainty: Turša (at or near Tel Māḫūz), Kurruḫanni (Tell el-Faḫḫar *may* be Kurruḫanni), and Lubti (at or near Tāwūq / Dāqūq). From west to east these seven places are: Aššur, Natmani (not important for our purposes), Turša, Kurruḫanni (like Natmani, Kurruḫanni is also not important), Nuzi, Arrapḫa (the city), and Lubti. These are the fixed points in the toponymy. In addition to place names, there is a plethora of data linking places together. These come mostly in the form of descriptions of roads. They are identified as "road to GN," and, often, such descriptions are embedded in contexts such that we know the other terminus of the road. So, in effect, route descriptors result in a series of linkages of pairs of towns. What is of note here is that it appears these linkages identify towns that are relatively close to each other. Leaving aside Aššur, since it is not part of Arrapḫa anyway, there is, for example, no attested linkage of Turša at the western limit of the country to Nuzi or to Arrapḫa in the center, much less to Lubti in the east. Lubti is also not linked to any of the other fixed toponyms. But there *is* an attested route connection between Nuzi and Arrapḫa, both located in central Arrapḫa.[3] Nuzi is connected to many towns (presumably all nearby), but two in particular, as we shall see, claim our attention in the present context: Zizza and Apena.[4] These two

1 Fincke, *Orts- und Gewässernamen der Nuzi-Texte.*

2 Nashef, *Orts- und Gewässernamen der mittelbabylonischen und mittelassyrischen Zeit*. Recall that this volume includes the texts from Nippur, Aššur, and all the other major Mesopotamian sites from the Late Bronze Age. Pedersén, *Archives and Libraries*, 15-29 and 237–282, esp. 275, confirms that the number of Nuzi texts dwarfs that of each of its Mesopotamian contemporaries.

3 *EN* 9/1 25, recognizing that the Āl-ilāni mentioned there is to be located in the city of Arrapḫa.

4 For the connections between these towns, see, for example, *JEN* 324 (Nuzi-Zizza) and *JEN* 152 (Nuzi-Apena).

are amongst the most frequently mentioned neighbors of Nuzi and each lay at the center of an agriculturally active hinterland. In short, as far as space is concerned, there are six fixed or nearly fixed points, three in the west, Aššur, Turša, and Natmani, two clustered in the center, Arrapḫa and Nuzi, and one in the southeast, Lubti. In addition, routes are described implying that Zizza and Apena lie in the central region near Nuzi.

Such is the situation vis-à-vis space. The situation regarding time is less precise. The Nuzi texts lack a coherent, widely used dating system, although some texts are dated to particular occasions. This chronological weakness renders the writing of history a very difficult matter. Fortunately, the loss is not complete. Family archives, especially those in which real estate title looms large, continue for as long as five generations. Thus, the chronological horizon of the Nuzi texts extends some 125–150 years. Prosopographical juxtaposition allows us to date many Nuzi texts, if only approximately. But administrative archives, and even much of the non-real estate material from at least some family archives, date only to the last generation, and probably only to the last five or ten years of the last generation. This is demonstrated prosopographically: the named members of multi-generational families cluster to the last generation of those families. Furthermore, it is almost a truism that government archives in Mesopotamia weigh heavily to the last years of a given institution.

Thus—and this also verges on a truism—the military activity attested in the Nuzi texts corresponds to that which put a violent end to stratum II, that is, Late Bronze Age Nuzi. Equally obvious, but equally worthy of note, whatever is described in the Nuzi texts takes place before Nuzi's destruction. Thus, to anticipate our results, Turša, to the northwest, is captured, and Lubti, to the southeast, is taken, before Nuzi is destroyed. On the other hand, Nuzi was probably destroyed before the fall of Arrapḫa, since the Nuzi texts fail to mention it, as they do mention other places under attack.[5]

As for any absolute dates for these events, the best we can come up with is a surmise. But the surmise is fairly convincing: Nuzi's destruction and the fall of the state of Arrapḫa should be assigned to the predatory activity of Aššur-uballiṭ I, sometime around 1350 BCE or shortly thereafter. Such are the chronological data available for our study.[6]

5 Texts from Arrapḫa *may* hint at an impending struggle but the evidence is indirect at best. See von Dassow, "Sealed Troop Rosters." Kurruḫanni texts do not intimate that a crisis was looming. That is no surprise. It was a small outpost, having no administrative centrality.

6 I justify these assertions in *Kaskal* 8 (2010) as part of a larger study on Nuzi,

And now we approach the Arrapḫa-Assyria confrontation.[7] The relations between Assyria and Arrapḫa were dominated by hostility, apparently at first sporadic, ultimately both regular and inexorable. But, it must not be imagined that confrontation alone marked the relations between the two states. Earlier, peaceful relations are attested, and not rarely at that. For at least two generations before Nuzi's downfall, there existed normal diplomatic, commercial, and other relations between Assyria and Arrapḫa. Assyrians are described as engaged in peaceful pursuits in Arrapḫan territory in texts from the Nuzi horizon. Chariots from the Nuzi region may have been exported to Assyria.[8] Assyrians are present in Arrapḫan territory as diplomats[9] and, once, a scribe makes an appearance.[10] Assyrians as legally unattached aliens even show up as slaves for Nuzians.[11] All these men sell themselves into slavery. Thus our texts recognize Assyrians in Nuzi. Contemporary, analogous texts from Assyria, if such were recoverable, would likely attest to Nuzians and other Arrapḫans in Assyria.

But during Nuzi's last generation, there is clear evidence that the political climate turned ominous and, ultimately, catastrophic. This was not a sudden turn of events, however. The Arrapḫan military infrastructure and planning seem to have developed in an orderly fashion to judge from a large number of government administrative texts and from their matter-of-fact tone. The presence and apparently orderly integration of Mittannian military contingents into the Arrapḫan army also imply sustained and gradual planning. Even the well-attested Assyrian attack on the Turša region in the west[12] cannot have taken place in the last days of Nuzi, since normal economic activity continued elsewhere in the Arrapḫa state perhaps for months, if not years, after the clash.[13] It is possible, though, that the military planning was stepped up as a result of the Assyrian Turša campaign.

But decisive hostilities were looming indeed. A directive issued from the main administrative center in the capital, Arrapḫa, is crucial as

---

Arrapḫa, the war with Assyria, and international developments in the fourteenth century.

7 Some of the following material is adapted from my *Nuzi Texts*, 15–20.

8 AASOR 16 84.

9 HSS 14 48, 50; and *EN* 9/3 284.

10 *JEN* 613.

11 *JEN* 446, 458 and 613.

12 See further, below.

13 See Maidman, "Peace and War at Nuzi," 207–8, n. 37.

a pivotal piece of evidence for this historical reconstruction.[14] It orders those mayors in the border areas of the kingdom[15] to quell raids and other manifestations of disquiet in those areas, emphasizing mayoral culpability for failure to do so. There are musters of archers,[16] clearly a preparation for armed conflict. Such musters (and there is a variety of such texts) must have taken place toward the start of these battles. Also to be discerned, probably at this stage, is the involvement of the Mittannian army. An inventory of bronze scales, taken for fashioning armor, notes the different types or styles of armor used by Arrapḫans and their Mittannian overlords.[17] Such records frequently show that actual hostilities had taken place. Texts note that some military equipment was lost and some used up in battle.[18] Other texts describe chariotry of the left and right wings that did not return from battle.[19]

Another pivotal text[20] in the schema describes an actual battle, among the first, if not the very first, of the military confrontations. The record is a very lengthy catalogue of the losses in men, real property, and mobilia inflicted on the region of Turša, on this western frontier of Arrapḫa. Captured property, that is, war booty, here is described by its geographical origin in the vicinity of Turša and by its destination in Assyria and occupied Arrapḫa. The attackers are identified as Assyrians. Four further texts derive from this same attack, each cataloguing property taken[21] or, in one case, identifying the leadership of the places to which property was delivered.[22] The Assyrian capital, Aššur, is explicitly mentioned twice as a place where slaves from Arrapḫa now live.[23] Some of the names of the enemy leaders are conspicuously Assyrian. In sum, five texts deal directly with a successful attack on Turša. And of these, three mention Assyrians or Aššur explicitly,[24] while the other two implicitly implicate the Assyrians as the aggressors.

---

14 HSS 15 1.

15 That is, the Assyrian border, the only one from which danger could have emanated, as is shown below.

16 For example, HSS 15 22.

17 HSS 15 5.

18 For example, HSS 13 195.

19 For example, HSS 15 99.

20 Actually two virtually identical texts, *JEN* 525 and 670.

21 HSS 13 383; HSS 16 393; and *EN* 9/3 472.

22 HSS 16 328 + *EN* 10/2 136.

23 HSS 16 391 (probably a slave [the text is not from the cluster under study at this point]) and 393.

24 *JEN* 525/670; *EN* 9/3 472; and HSS 16 393.

A digression is required at this point. Assyria, and no other power, appears as Arrapḫa's enemy and, therefore, ultimately its destroyer. This point deserves emphasis because it has been asserted that, not Assyria, but Babylon, "the land of Akkad" in the Nuzi texts, was the destroyer of Nuzi. But this is most unlikely because there are so many mentions of Assyria in this context and because perusal of the war documents reveals only one possible text in which Babylon even appears.[25] Assyria appears in the same text, and the context is too laconic and obscure to bear the burden of such a far-reaching conclusion. If Babylon was involved at all (and I doubt this), it was probably in a skirmish with Assyria as Assyria marched through Arrapḫa on its way to the Babylonian border. This conclusion is borne out through further consideration.

The improbability of Babylonian aggression against territory bordering on Assyria increases greatly when considering the evidence of the larger international political picture. In precisely the period of our texts, Babylonia whines to Egypt that Assyria no longer recognizes its inferior position to Babylonia.[26] Shortly thereafter, an Assyrian-Babylonian dynastic marriage places an Assyrian royal grandson on the Babylonian throne. The overthrow of this dynast results in an immediate and successful Assyrian attack on Babylonia.[27] This is not a picture of Babylonia consistent with an attack on Assyria in Arrapḫan territory. Much less is this picture consistent with Babylonian designs on Arrapḫa itself. Not only is evidence lacking, such a proposition is itself illogical.

What would Babylonia gain by destroying Nuzi, Kurruḫanni (presumably), and possibly Arrapḫa, only to abandon these sites? This would just clear the way for Assyria, unless we assume a subsequent Assyrian battle with Babylonia in Arrapḫa for which there is no evidence either. Such hypothesizing violates the principle of Ockham's Razor. Babylonian opposition to Assyria would have been better served by *occupying* Arrapḫan sites. There is, of course, no evidence for this.

Contrast with this the situation whereby Mittanni opposes Assyria, not by attacking Arrapḫa, but rather by helping Arrapḫa. It is possible, of course, to claim that Mittanni and Arrapḫa are allied because Arrapḫa is a continuing vassal of Mittanni. But this alliance would have been called for even if the vassal relationship were no longer in place.

---

25 HSS 13 63.

26 *EA* 9.

27 Grayson, *Chronicles*, nos. 21 ("Synchronistic History") and 22 ("Chronicle P"); see also Glassner, *Mesopotamian Chronicles*, nos. 10 ("Synchronistic History") and 45 ("Chronicle of the Kassite Kings" [=Chronicle P]).

Babylonia's alleged destruction of Arrapḫa and subsequent abandonment of the field could only have helped Assyria and further have weakened Mittanni. And *that* would not have been in Babylonia's best interests.

To resume the account of the Arrapḫa-Assyria war, the Battle of Turša took place at or near the start of hostilities with Arrapḫa. This is so because, as noted above, its outcome did not signal Nuzi's (or Arrapḫa's) end. That took place only later. Furthermore, the Turša region is located close to Assyrian territory. And so it would have been attacked first.

Before continuing with this description, let us step back a moment and consider what kinds of texts describe the military clashes with Turša, on the one hand, and with central and eastern Arrapḫa, on the other.

We learn of the Assyrian success in the west mostly through detailed accounts of losses in goods and persons, as well as damage to real property. The losses are in private property. Our main sources come from private archives, including texts from those victimized by the raid.[28] Other texts come from government sources and closely echo the private texts. These latter records may have served to document claims for restitution for losses suffered. "Official" military records are lacking.

By contrast, our knowledge of military activity in the central and eastern marches derives mostly from government archives. Those documents are typically bureaucratic lists: armor fashioned, personnel deployed, men and equipment lost, and so on. Some otherwise irrelevant bureaucratic texts are dated by reference to one clash or another. All these records are important as logistical indicators for military administrators, especially quartermasters.

Thus, the kind of knowledge we get regarding the two phases of the Arrapḫa-Assyria War differs as the kinds of documents and their purposes differ from each other.[29] Not only does this difference sensitize us as to what kind of knowledge we may expect regarding these happenings, it alerts us to the role of Nuzi in these events. There is no indication at all that the government at Nuzi played any role in the lead-up-to or

---

28 *JEN* 525, 670; HSS 13 383; and, possibly, HSS 16 328 + *EN* 10/2 136.

29 Unless government records regarding the Turša battle were written so much earlier than the others that they were destroyed already in antiquity as being outdated. In that case, the battle would have left no trace among the bureaucratic lists for modern students to find.

in the aftermath of the initial Assyrian aggression. Perhaps that key role was played by the capital at Arrapḫa City.[30]

In contrast to Nuzi's relative passivity in the Turša campaign, the rest of the conflict must have been directed primarily from Nuzi. Not only is the deployment and fate of Arrapḫan forces minutely described in a host of Nuzi documents, but the integration and participation of Mittanni military contingents, reinforcements from outside Arrapḫa, seem at least partly directed from Nuzi. This is to be deduced because that is where the texts were found! And so, Nuzi emerges not as a middling town, as I once considered it,[31] but as an important center in the defense of the kingdom of Arrapḫa.

Resuming our description of the campaigns, which started at Turša, we turn to the second phase of activities. Other towns mentioned in Nuzi texts in connection with military activity are Apena, Zizza, Arn-apu, and Arwa in the central sector and Lubti and Ṣilliya in the east. Of these, only the location of Lubti is known, more or less. It is at the eastern limit of the Arrapḫan state in the direction of Babylonia. If Assyrian activity has been perceived correctly, then the following description is a logical interpretation. Assyria attacked and captured the area of Turša in western Arrapḫa, on the Assyrian border. Eventually, from that base, Assyrian forces advanced southeast, attacking Zizza and Apena, and probably Arn-apu and Arwa as well, somewhere in south central Arrapḫa, south of the city of Arrapḫa and more immediately south of Nuzi. Apena and Zizza, in any case, were the loci of Arrapḫan forces. Zizza especially seems to have been the site of considerable activity. Three records describe men, horses, and equipment that did not return from battle there.[32] A dolorous account informs that 38 soldiers (possibly from Nuzi) were captured in Zizza when the enemy occupied that town, as were an additional ten or more from the neighboring town of Apena.[33]

Apena was also defended, at least in part, by soldiers from Mittanni. This is described in a very interesting and, in fact, unique text:[34] the Mittannians have PNs bearing little resemblance to the Nuzi onomasticon.

---

30 In passing, perhaps the failure of the capital to repulse the Assyrians led to the promulgation of the well-known directive to mayors, HSS 15 1, imposing on them the responsibility for defense of the borderlands in their respective regions.

31 Maidman, "Nuzi: Portrait," 931.

32 HSS 15 29 (men and horses), 40 (men), and 14 (equipment).

33 HSS 15 43.

34 HSS 15 32.

This was, it appears, a largely non-Ḫurrian Mittanni contingent. Mittannian chariotry, furthermore, was stationed in the towns of Arn-apu and Arwa.[35] Arwa, at least, has been identified as being in the neighborhoods of Zizza and, indirectly, of Apena as well.[36]

Heading southeast from Zizza and Apena the Assyrian army would have reached the vicinity of Lubti. And there, battles appear to have been fought at Lubti itself and at Ṣilliya. One text links the two towns as sites of chariot confrontations.[37] Charioteers from Nuzi were also dispatched to Temtena in the vicinity of Lubti.[38] The charioteers actually arrive in the towns of Irḫaḫḫe and Teliperra. These places, therefore, must be near Temtena—and therefore near Lubti. A further document again refers to the town of Teliperra.[39] The enemy, it is implied, controls that settlement and may be threatening to inflict (additional) damage unless persuaded to abstain from further action. A seemingly only marginally interesting text notes that a man from Lubti, a prisoner of war probably, surfaces in the Assyrian capital of Aššur.[40] This text is most telling. Part of the rationale for assigning the responsibility for Nuzi's destruction to the Babylonians is the site of this battle: the southeastern location of the battle allegedly demanded a Babylonian foe rather than an Assyrian enemy. Here, it is made explicit that a man of Lubti (probably more than one) was sent to the Assyrian capital of Aššur before disappearing altogether. In other words, Assyrian forces reached the farthest reaches of Arrapḫa, the area closest to Babylonia.

In attacking southeast from Zizza and Apena, the Assyrians would have bypassed Nuzi, possibly because of its military concentration as implied above, and the capital city itself, prizes to be collected once the rest of Arrapḫa was captured.[41] Thus, the military progress of Assyrian forces would be complete, from Turša in the northwest to Lubti in the southeast. One recalls here the words of Tiglath-Pileser I, claiming, some two and a half centuries later: "I marched to Karduniaš [Akkad in the Nuzi texts]. I conquered from the city Turšan on the other [that is, the eastern] side of the Lower Zab [River], the city of Arman[42] of

---

35 HSS 14 171.

36 See Fincke, *Orts- und Gewässernamen der Nuzi-Texte*, 30.

37 HSS 14 249.

38 HSS 14 238.

39 HSS 14 248.

40 HSS 16 391.

41 Compare Sennacherib's strategy in Judah.

42 It is plausible that this could be the town of Arwa (in central Arrapḫa) of the Nuzi texts.

Ugarsallu, as far as the city Lubdu. I crossed over the river….."[43] In other words, the proposed route of Assyrian forces deduced from the Nuzi texts corresponds to an actual later Assyrian military campaign. Thus, logic and analogy combine to make reasonable sense of the inchoate data at our disposal.

One presumes that, only then, Nuzi (which yields these data up to this stage) would have been mopped up and finally Arrapḫa presumably captured or destroyed. Unfortunately, it is only by an argument from silence (and archaeological inference in the case of Nuzi) that one can deduce this last stage—at least so far.

WORKS CITED

Fincke, J. *Die Orts- und Gewässernamen der Nuzi-Texte*. Répertoire géographique des textes cunéiformes 10. Beihefte zum Tübingen Atlas der Vorderen Orients, Reihe B (Geisteswissenschaften), 7/10. Wiesbaden: Ludwig Reichert, 1993.

Glassner J.-J. *Mesopotamian Chronicles*. Edited by B. R. Foster. Writings from the Ancient World 19. Atlanta, Ga.: Society of Biblical Literature, 2004.

Grayson, A. K. *Assyrian and Babylonian Chronicles*. Texts from Cuneiform Sources 5. Locust Valley, N.Y.: J. J. Augustin, 1975.

Assyrian Rulers of the Early First Millennium BC I (1114–859 BC). RIMA 2. Toronto: University of Toronto Press, 1991.

Maidman, M. P. "Nuzi: Portrait of an Ancient Mesopotamian Provincial Town." In *Civilizations of the Ancient Near East*, vol. 2, edited by J. M. Sasson, 931–947. New York: Charles Scribner's Sons, 1995.

"Peace and War at Nuzi: A Prosopographical Foray." In *Treasures on Camels' Humps: Historical and Literary Studies Presented to Israel Eph'al*, edited by M. Cogan and D. Kahn, 199–220. Jerusalem: The Hebrew University Magnes Press, 2008.

Nuzi Texts and Their Uses as Historical Sources. Edited by A. K. Guinan. Writings from the Ancient World 18. Atlanta, Ga.: Society of Biblical Literature, 2010.

---

43 Grayson, RIMA 2, 53 A.0.87.10 (lines 36–38).

Nashef, K. *Die Orts- und Gewässernamen der mittelbabylonischen und mittelassyrischen Zeit*. Répertoire géographique des textes cunéiformes 5. Beihefte zum Tübingen Atlas der Vorderen Orients, Reihe B (Geisteswissenschaften), 7/5. Wiesbaden: Ludwig Reichert, 1982.

Pedersén, O. *Archives and Libraries in the Ancient Near East, 1500–300 B.C.* Bethesda, Md.: CDL Press, 1998.

von Dassow, E. "Sealed Troop Rosters from the City of Arrapḫe." In *General Studies and Excavations at Nuzi 11/2 in Honor of David I. Owen on the occasion of his 65th Birthday*, edited by G. Wilhelm, 605–636. SCCNH 18. Bethesda, Md.: CDL Press, 2009.

IMAGES, TRADITION, AND MEANING

THE SAMARIA AND OTHER LEVANTINE IVORIES OF THE IRON AGE

CLAUDIA E. SUTER
BASEL

The ivory carvings from Samaria, Israel, were products of the large-scale manufacture of luxurious ivory objects that flourished in the Levant of the early Iron Age. This manufacture continued a tradition of the Late Bronze Age, which evinces influences from surrounding cultures, especially Mesopotamia and Egypt. In the following, I will explore the imagery carved on Iron Age Levantine ivories with the goal of elucidating its overall theme and its indebtedness to the Mesopotamian and Egyptian visual traditions. It is with the greatest pleasure that I offer this slice of current research to Barry Eichler, a marvelous teacher and a wonderful human being.

The Samaria Ivories

The Samaria ivories were discovered in the pioneer times of Near Eastern archaeology. While the Harvard Expedition found a handful in 1909–1910, the Joint Expedition unearthed "hundreds of fragments" between 1932 and 1935.[1] All ivories came from the area of the palace, but were found in disturbed contexts of Hellenistic and Roman debris.[2] By comparison with other Levantine ivories, they are generally dated from the ninth to eighth century BCE, a time coinciding with the Israelite kingdom. Their discovery was regarded as so important that they were published before all other excavation reports. The monograph from 1938, however, includes only 197 pieces and lacks a proper catalogue.

The Samaria ivories are significant for both the classification of Levantine ivories and the cultural history of Israel. Nevertheless, they have been neglected in discussions of these topics, notwithstanding that single pieces are frequently illustrated. One reason lies in the paradox that Iron Age ivories are studied by Mesopotamian rather than

1 Reisner et al., *Harvard Excavations*, 368; Crowfoot and Crowfoot, *Ivories from Samaria*.

2 Tappy, *Archaeology of Israelite Samaria II*, 443–95; Tappy, "The Provenance of the Unpublished Ivories."

Syro-Palestinian specialists, because the vast majority came to light at Nimrud, the Assyrian capital from the ninth to eighth centuries BCE. Moreover, scholarship has been prejudiced by the Bible in the assessment of material remains from Israel. The eminent ivory specialist Richard Barnett, for example, proposed that the Samaria ivories "formed part of the pagan cult material of ivory which she (Jezebel) is known to have introduced."[3] Although he assumed that Iron Age ivory workshops existed in "all the richest cities of Syria, Phoenicia and Palestine,"[4] he could not conceive of local production in Israel.

The industrious excavation activity in Israel, which has led to a revision of Israel's cultural history, and the publication of many more Iron Age ivories have made the time ripe for a reassessment of the Samaria ivories. This is the aim of a project, which has already made an astounding discovery: instead of a total of c. 500 pieces assumed in literature,[5] I have found approximately 12,000 pieces. My visit to Jerusalem and London prompted "excavations" in storerooms. Many fragments of the Joint Expedition were still full of dust in attractive cigarette boxes of the time. Even if mostly small fragments, the extent of the largest assemblage of Iron Age ivories found in the Levant is much larger than has hitherto been assumed.[6]

Like smaller collections from other Levantine sites, the Samaria ivories do not form a distinct assemblage in terms of object types, technique, imagery, or style. They cannot be separated from other Levantine ivories and have parallels in material mainly from Nimrud, Khorsabad, and Arslan Tash.[7] In some cases, the correspondences are so close as to suggest that pieces found at different sites originated in the same workshop or even belonged to the same set of furniture.[8] If Georgina

---

3 Barnett, *Ancient Ivories*, 49.

4 Barnett, *Ancient Ivories*, 55.

5 Winter, review of *Ivories from Nimrud III*, 203; Barnett, *Ancient Ivories*, 49.

6 The incentive for the Samaria Ivories project came from Christoph Uehlinger. My study, including the first comprehensive catalogue, analyses, and re-assessment of the material will be published in a forthcoming OBO volume.

7 Winter, "South Syrian Style," esp. 109–15; Herrmann, *Ivories from Nimrud IV*, 33–35.

8 Compare, for example, Crowfoot and Crowfoot, *Ivories from Samaria*, pl. II:1 with Herrmann, *Ivories from Nimrud IV*, no. 1032; Crowfoot and Crowfoot, *Ivories from Samaria*, pl. XIV:2 with Herrmann, *Ivories from Nimrud IV*, nos. 1177–78; Crowfoot and Crowfoot, *Ivories from Samaria*, pl. XVII:4 with Herrmann, *Ivories from Nimrud IV*, no. 769; Crowfoot and Crowfoot, *Ivories from Samaria*, pl. XXI:6 with Herrmann, *Ivories from*

Herrmann's assumption is correct that the ivories from room SW 37 of Fort Shalmaneser at Nimrud came from Sargon's western campaign in 720,[9] which brought the final blow for Israel,[10] then it is indeed possible that parts of the same set were found both at Samaria and Nimrud.

Iron Age ivories remain difficult to classify for various reasons I cannot develop here.[11] It is clear, however, that, except for a small group from Nimrud depicting images of Assyrian royal representation, they were products of the Levant. The Samaria ivories reinforce Irene Winter's general distinction of three regional groups: Phoenician, North Syrian, and South Syrian.[12] They comprise mainly South Syrian pieces, a substantial number of Phoenician ivories, but hardly any North Syrian ones. Phoenician ivories betray strong Egyptian influence; North Syrian ivories are more at home in the Syro-Hittite sphere; and the South Syrian group adopted elements from both of them and developed its own particularities.

Iconography and Contexts of Use

Because research on Iron Age ivories centers on the still problematic classification of the material, the imagery has received little attention since Barnett's monumental catalogue of Nimrud ivories from 1957. Although single motifs have been discussed in different places,[13] no comprehensive study of the repertoire and its thematic context is extant. Barnett's approach of seeking myth and ritual in the images lacks sound methodology and cannot be substantiated.[14] Nor can an

---

Nimrud V, no. 361; Crowfoot and Crowfoot, *Ivories from Samaria*, pl. V:3 with Herrmann, *Ivories from Nimrud IV*, no. 599.

9 Herrmann, *Ivories from Nimrud IV*, 53.

10 Becking, *Fall of Samaria*.

11 On the problems in classifying Iron Age ivories, see Suter, "Frau am Fenster," 12–20; Herrmann, "Naming, Defining, Explaining"; Winter, "Establishing Group Boundaries"; Suter, "Luxury Goods in Ancient Israel."

12 Winter, "South Syrian Style."

13 E.g., Suter, "Frau am Fenster"; Ciafaloni, *Eburnea Syrophoenicia*; Rehm, "Abschied," 487–519; Gubel and Cecchini in Suter and Uehlinger, *Crafts and Images*.

14 Many of his interpretations are outdated. Hardly anyone today would endorse, for example, the idea that the lion hunt depicts divine events in the realm of solar myths (Barnett, *Catalogue*, 70–72) or that the woman at the window was a symbol of "religious sacrifice of virginity" (ibid., 145–51). On the former, see below; on the latter, see Suter, "Frau am Fenster," and Rehm, "Abschied."

overemphasis on religious symbolism[15] or the recent trend of an apotropaic-beneficent explanation do justice to the images.[16] Luxuriously inlaid furniture, precious treasure chests, cosmetic boxes, fly whisks, and goblet stands were hardly made for protecting their users from evil or bringing them luck. We cannot interpret images without scrutinizing their carriers: What functions and purposes did they serve? Who used them? What were the circumstances of their production?[17]

Unfortunately, Iron Age ivories were rarely excavated in primary contexts of use. Tens of thousands of pieces were carried off to Nimrud. The second largest assemblage is Samaria, while other sites stretching from Iran in the east to Spain in the west produced smaller collections or

---

15 Keel and Uehlinger, *Göttinnen, Götter und Gottessymbole*, approached the visual arts of Israel/Palestine with the goal of elucidating the history of religions in this region. Although the inclusion of the material record in the reconstruction of history presents an important contribution, the authors' use and interpretation of images lack sound methodology (see Kletter, review of *Göttinnen, Götter und Gottessymbole*), and their focus on the divine world is too narrow. Egyptianizing images related to the solar cycle, for example, cannot be confined to the divine world, since solar symbolism was an essential component of royal ideology not only in Egypt, but also in Anatolia and Mesopotamia (Fauth, *Helios Megistos*), 191–202). See also Oggiano, *Dal terreno al divino*, 87, who understands the images carved on the Samaria and other Levantine ivories as representations of power and prestige rather than as an expression of the religiosity of the court.

16 Rehm, *Kykladen und Alter Orient*, 124; Rehm, "Abschied"; Braun-Holzinger and Rehm, *Orientalischer Import*, 135–36; Busch and Wicke, "Alles nur Kopie," 52–53. Rehm, *Kykladen und Alter Orient*, 124, based this interpretation on the assumption that adopted Egyptian motifs were not understood in the Levant. Several studies (see note 59 below), however, demonstrate to the contrary that Egyptian motifs were adapted to Levantine ideas and concepts. While I would not exclude an apotropaic function in some cases, e.g., the Udjat-Eye on horse blinkers, the interpretation of the entire repertoire according to this one aspect is simplistic and ignores the primary function of the image carriers.

17 These questions are rarely addressed. The attempt of Gubel, "Multicultural and Multimedial Aspects," 206–9, to define user groups of Phoenician art based on iconography is methodologically problematic. Beach ("The Samaria Ivories," and "Transforming Goddess Iconography") suggested that a small group of ivory furniture panels belonged to couches of the Marzeah institution. Although I would not exclude the possibility that this institution owned ivory furniture, a thesis already proposed by Barnett, *Ancient Ivories*, 47, her argumentation is flawed, including artificial clusters, erroneous interpretations of find spots, and the wrongly assumed funerary nature of the Marzeah; on the latter, see McLaughlin, *The Marzeah in the Prophetic Literature*, 70–79.

scattered finds.[18] This wide distribution, together with the biblical and Homeric descriptions of the Phoenicians as merchants *par excellence*, has led to the assumption that Iron Age ivories were made for trade.[19] Another common assumption is that Assyrian kings acquired Levantine ivories for their own use.[20] Both assumptions can be disproved.[21] Luxury goods made of exotic material imported from far away tend to be produced for proper consumption.[22] Herrmann and Millard have shown that the Levantine ivories found in Assyria were shut away in treasuries and that the Assyrians had no particular liking for this material.[23] Moreover, their imagery was hardly suited for Assyrian royalty, whose official art differed from that of the Levant. The small number of Levantine ivories found in Iran, Anatolia, and the Mediterranean, excluding derived local styles, does not allow us to speak of an industry made for export. They are best explained in terms of occasional gifts that Levantine merchants presented to the local elite in order to establish trade routes and encourage bulk trade in raw materials.[24]

---

18 More than thirty years ago, Winter, "Phoenician and North Syrian Ivory Carving," 12–13, mapped out the then known find spots of North Syrian and Phoenician ivories with relative amounts in the ancient world, excluding the western Mediterranean. Her useful maps have only very partially been updated by one confined to the Levant and Assyria without indicating amounts or distinguishing styles: Herrmann, "The Ivories from Nimrud," 229.

19 E.g., Barnett, *Catalogue*, 129; ibid., *Ancient Ivories*, 53–55; Sommer, *Die Phoenizier*, 84–102.

20 More recently, Ciafaloni, *Eburnea Syrophoenicia*, 111–22; Thomason, *Luxury and Legitimation*, 120–50.

21 So also Busch and Wicke, "Alles nur Kopie," 53, yet without going into any detail.

22 Helms, *Craft and the Kingly Ideal.*

23 Herrmann and Millard. "Who Used Ivories," 377–402. See also Rehm, "Assyrische Möbel," who showed convincingly that Assurbanipal's couch was an Assyrian rather than Levantine piece of furniture.

24 So already Frankenstein, "The Phoenicians in the Far West," 273–78; Markoe, "L'art du métal phénicien," 171–72, reached the same conclusion for Levantine precious metal vessels. However, when he suggests that decorated cups were made exclusively for gift exchange because hardly any have been found in the Phoenician homeland, he underestimates the chance of archaeological finds. If they were made for foreign destinations only, this would be reflected in their iconography. For a good discussion of this question with regard to metal cauldrons, see Muscarella, "Greek and Oriental Cauldron Attachments," 40–45. On Levantine luxury goods in Greece, see also Braun-Holzinger and Rehm, *Orientalischer Import*, esp. 181–83.

Levantine ivories were thus fashioned for the Levantine elite, consisting of small-state royalty and a merchant oligarchy.[25] Given that in the Iron Age elephant tusk was in all likelihood imported from Africa,[26] the ivories were probably commissioned by patrons who provided the artisans with the raw material. The principle function of such luxury goods can be defined as "rhetorical and social."[27] They were status symbols that added to the social prestige of their owners. Assyrian kings seized them precisely for this reason: by stripping subjugated rulers of their status symbols, they gained control over them also on a symbolic level.[28] Based on these observations, I propose as a working hypothesis that the images carved on Levantine ivories reflect ideology with which the Levantine elite identified.

The Repertoire of Motifs: In Search of a Theme

Rather than mere mythology or apotropaic symbolism, I perceive in the repertoire of motifs carved on Iron Age ivories an assembly of images from various visual traditions that center on royal ideology. Notwithstanding cultural differences, Egypt, as well as Western Asiatic states, considered kingship the very basis of civilization.[29] The king formed the link between the human and divine worlds. Chosen by the gods, he was their representative on earth. His responsibilities were to maintain the cult, provide justice, and prevail over wilderness, as well as foreign enemies. In return for his services, the gods granted him a long rule and prosperity for his people. As provider and protector of his people, the king was the prototype of the ideal male; through his link with the divine world he became god-like.

---

25 This is corroborated by owner inscriptions on ivories (Röllig, "Alte und neue Elfenbeininschriften," nos. I 1, II 6, 7, and 8?), as well as by the contexts, in which ivory carvings came to light in the Levant: mainly royal palaces (Samaria, Zincirli) or rich residences (Hamath, Arslan Tash, Til Barsip), some burials (Tell Halaf), rarely sanctuaries (Carchemish, Sarepta); see Herrmann, *Ivories from Nimrud IV*, 32–35; Herrmann and Millard, "Who Used Ivories," 388–89.

26 Caubet and Poplin, "La place des ivoires," 95.

27 Appadurai, "Introduction," 38.

28 In a talk held in September 2008 at the Oriental Institute of Chicago, Marian Feldman, to whom I am grateful for sharing the manuscript with me, came to the same conclusion. She goes even a step further, arguing that by acquiring North Syrian ivories, the Assyrian kings sought to erase the memories of the North Syrian elite.

29 The topic of kingship has received renewed interest in recent years, see Erkens (ed.), *Die Sakralität von Herrschaft*; chapter II in Beckman and Lewis (eds.), *Text, Artifact, and Image*, 346; Brisch (ed.), *Religion and Power*.

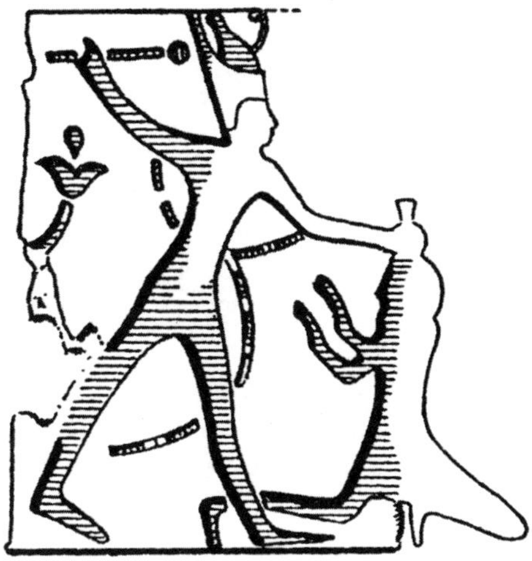

Fig. 1
Smiting pharaoh on champlevé plaque from Samaria
(Crowfoot and Crowfoot 1938: pl. XIV: 1)

In contrast to monumental royal art, luxurious small arts focus, not surprisingly, more on the provider and protector aspects of the king than on the warrior. Nevertheless, the latter is also visualized. A cloisonné stand from Nimrud[30] and a champlevé plaque from Samaria (Fig. 1) depict the smiting pharaoh, a motif with roots in pre-Dynastic Egypt (e.g., the Narmer Palette). An Egyptianizing soldier is seen on a horse frontlet from Nimrud.[31]

Another war-related motif, which goes back to Egypt's Old Kingdom, depicts the king in the shape of a sphinx stepping over a defeated enemy. This motif occurs on a number of Phoenician and South Syrian ivories from Nimrud and Samaria;[32] among the latter is a cloisonné panel, the pieces of which are spread over different institutions in Jerusalem, London, and Cambridge, Mass. (Fig. 2). Also the beautiful series

30 Safar and al Iraqi, *Ivories from Nimrud*, no. 12.

31 Safar and al Iraqi, *Ivories from Nimrud*, no. 73a.

32 E.g., Safar and al Iraqi, *Ivories from Nimrud*, nos. 60–66; Barnett, *Catalogue*, no. S.163; Herrmann, *Ivories from Nimrud IV*, nos. 87–97, 656, and 1111–16; Crowfoot and Crowfoot, *Ivories from Samaria*, pls. VII:8, X:3–5, and XIV:7.

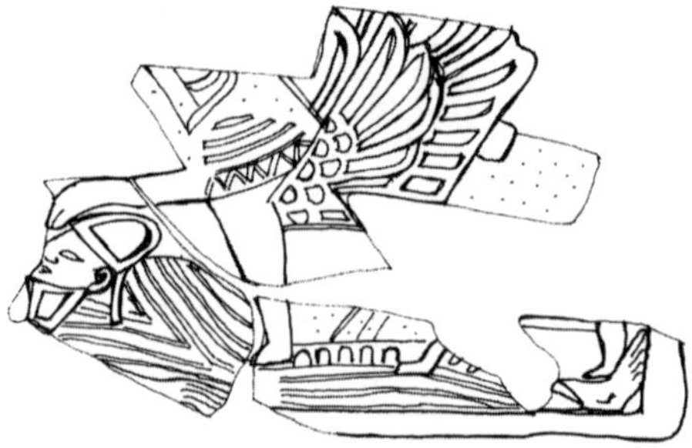

Fig. 2
Sphinx stepping over defeated enemy on cloisonné panel from Samaria (drawing by author)

of statuettes representing Egyptianizing tributaries belongs to the war theme.[33]

The royal hunt can be traced back to the beginning of urban society and recurs in many different civilizations. It manifests not only the king's prowess and chief status, but also his aspect as protector of the civilized world. This is evident, for example, in Šulgi Hymn B (71–76): "In the sheepfold and the cattle-pen, where heads are laid to rest (?), I put the shepherd tribesmen at ease. Let no one ever at any time say about me, 'Could he really subdue them all on his own?' The number of lions that I have dispatched with my weapons is limitless; their total is unknown."

Iron Age ivories depict the royal hunt in two forms: chariot hunt and close combat with a lion or griffin. The former is confined to North Syrian ivories, which stand in the tradition of the Late Bronze Age International Style;[34] the latter occurs mainly on Phoenician and South Syrian ivories (Fig. 3),[35] which, although also inspired by Late Bronze Age prototypes,[36]

---

33 Herrmann, *Ivories from Nimrud V*, nos. 298–303.

34 Compare, for example, a furniture panel and a pyxis from Nimrud (Mallowan and Herrmann, *Ivories from Nimrud III*, no. 1:9; Wicke, *Vorderasiatische Pyxiden*, no. Nim.35) with a golden fan from Tutankhamun's tomb or an ivory game board from Enkomi, Cyprus (Feldman, *Diplomacy by Design*, pl. 12, fig. 42). Even details, such as the dog under the chariot, were faithfully transmitted on Iron Age ivories. Although the chariot hunt is best known from New Kingdom Egypt, the horse-drawn chariot was introduced into Egypt by the Hyksos from Western Asia in the Second Intermediate Period.

35 Examples of the lion slayer are: Herrmann, *Ivories from Nimrud IV*, nos. 73–78, 80, 254, and 1179; Herrmann, *Ivories from Nimrud V*, nos. 293–94 and 297.

go back to different traditions. The griffin slayer is of Aegean origin and was introduced into the Levant in the Late Bronze Age through Cyprus,[37] while the close combat with a lion is a much older Mesopotamian motif.[38] In contrast to the unmistakably royal protagonist of the chariot hunt, ruler

Fig. 3
Lion and griffin slayer on stand from Nimrud
(Herrmann 1986: nos. 78–79)

Examples of the griffin slayer are: Herrmann, *Ivories from Nimrud IV*, nos. 79, 81–86, 316–18, 1051, and 1117–20; Herrmann, *Ivories from Nimrud V*, nos. 141–42, 240–41, and 328. For North Syrian versions of close combats, see Barnett, *Catalogue*, nos. S.2, S.4, S.20, and S.30.

36 For example, mirror handles from Palaepaphos, see Orthmann (ed.), *Alte Orient*, fig. 473b, and from Enkomi, see Scigliuzzo, "Un nuovo motivo," fig. 3.

37 Scigliuzzo, "Un nuovo motivo," 92.

38 It is first depicted on the Uruk Stela (Feldman, *Diplomacy by Design*, 78 fig. 47), occurs in minor arts across millennia (Matthäus, "Toreutik und Vasenmalerei," 306–17), and finds a new expression in Neo-Assyrian royal art (Winter, "Le Palais Imaginaire," 54–60).

and hero are interchangeable in close combat.[39] Since kings likened themselves to heroes in literary texts, the hero figure must have called the king to mind. Iron Age ivories reflect this ambiguity: lion and griffin slayers are represented both with and without an Egyptianizing crown.

The king not only subdues potent wild beasts, but is also equated with them. Šulgi boasts (A 1–3): "I, the king, was a hero already in the womb; I, Šulgi, was born to be a mighty man. I am a fierce-looking lion, begotten by a dragon." Or (Ca 1–2): "I am the king, a wild bull of acknowledged strength, a lion with wide-open jaws!" On a symbolic level, animal combat scenes, which have an old tradition in Mesopotamia, can then be associated with the king's role as hunter and protector against the chaotic forces of nature. Animal combats are frequent on North and South Syrian ivories (Fig. 4).[40] Their closest parallels are again examples of the Late Bronze Age International Style.[41] The exquisite cloisonné panel from Nimrud with a lion cub tearing a Nubian

Fig. 4
Animal combat on openwork panel from Samaria (Collection of the Israel Antiquities Authority, exhibited at the Israel Museum, Jerusalem, photo by author; reduced to 81%)

39 While the Uruk Stela and Assyrian art depict a royal protagonist, the hero figure prevails in other minor arts.

40 Crowfoot and Crowfoot, *Ivories from Samaria*, pls. VIII, X:1, 2, and XII:7; Buhl and Riis, *Hama*, nos. 995, 997, and 1002; Safar and al-Iraqi, *Ivories from Nimrud*, nos. 6, 15, and 31; Mallowan and Herrmann, *Ivories from Nimrud III*, no. 105; Herrmann, *Ivories from Nimrud IV*, nos. 667–700; Herrmann, *Ivories from Nimrud V*, nos. 195 and 308–9.

41 Compare, for example, Fig. 4 with Feldman, *Diplomacy by Design*, pl. 10, and Safar and al Iraqi, *Ivories from Nimrud*, no. 15 with Feldman, *Diplomacy by Design*, pl. 2.

youth belongs in the same context:[42] it conveys the king's victory over a traditional enemy.

Several pyxides from Nimrud depict banquet scenes.[43] The banqueter sits on a sphinx throne or an elaborate armchair, brings a cup to his mouth, and faces a table laden with food while attendants whisk away flies, servants bring food, and musicians perform. A fragmentary openwork panel from Samaria with an enthroned figure and a solid panel from Til Barsip depicting servants carrying food and musicians must have belonged to such scenes.[44] Banquets were held on a variety of occasions.[45] They formed part of regular festivals, manifesting the king's maintenance of the cult, or celebrated a specific event, such as a military victory as depicted on a Late Bronze Age panel from Megiddo[46] on which the banqueting king receives war captives. The unique sarcophagus of Ahirom of Byblos, which was inspired by Late Bronze Age scenes, like that on the Megiddo panel, seems to collapse an audience of the king with the ceremony for his funeral. Syro-Hittite funerary stelae then depict a repast of the deceased.[47] Like the Ahirom sarcophagus, the ivories are modeled on Late Bronze Age prototypes, yet probably render a royal banquet.[48] Regardless of their occasion, such banquets formed part of a symbolic system of ceremonies that cemented the recognition of authority and hierarchy.[49]

The aspect of the king as provider of prosperity through divine favor is implied on countless ivories depicting ornamental bands of plants or grazing animals and antithetical scenes of animals, sphinxes, or genies flanking a stylized tree (Figs. 5–7).[50] These motifs are predominant in the South Syrian group and occur also on North Syrian and Phoenician ivories.[51] While the ruler's association with grazing animals

---

42 Barnett, *Catalogue*, no. O.1.

43 Wicke, *Vorderasiatische Pyxiden*, nos. Nim.19–24.

44 Crowfoot and Crowfoot, *Ivories from Samaria*, pl. XI:1; Bunnens, "Ivories from Til Barsib," no. 4.

45 Collon, "Banquets in the Art of the Ancient Near East."

46 Barnett, *Ancient Ivories*, pl. 19a.

47 Bonatz, *Das syro-hethitische Grabdenkmal.*

48 Wicke, *Vorderasiatische Pyxiden*, 86–87.

49 Michalowski, "The Drinking Gods," 36–37.

50 On the association of these motifs with the ruler, see Winter, "Ornament and the 'Rhetoric of Abundance' in Assyria."

51 To give just a few examples, see Thureau-Dangin et al., *Arslan-Tash*, pl. XXVII:22; Bunnens, "Ivories from Til Barsib," no. 5; Mallowan and Herrmann, *Ivories from Nimrud III*, no. 104; Herrmann, *Ivories from Nimrud*

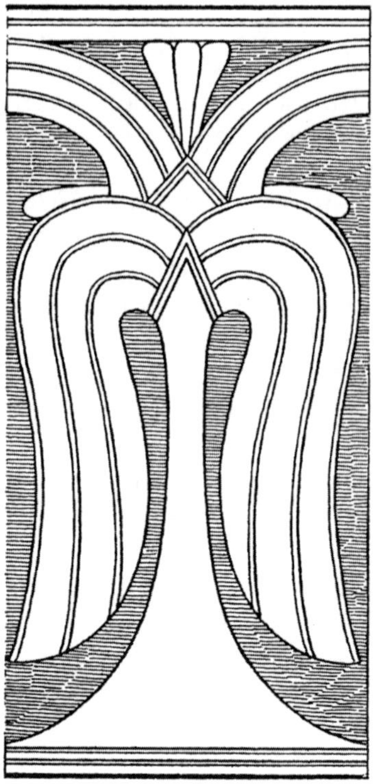

Fig. 5
Palmette on openwork panel from Samaria
(Crowfoot and Crowfoot 1938: fig. 7)

Fig. 6
Grazing ibex on openwork panel from Nimrud

Fig. 7
Sphinxes flanking stylized tree on panel from Nimrud
(Herrmann 1986: no. 619; reduced to 75%)

goes back to the earliest phases of urban society in Mesopotamia, as, for example, on a famous Uruk-period seal,[52] his association with the stylized tree is best illustrated on reliefs from the palace of Assurnasirpal II at Nimrud, which depict winged genies artificially pollinating a stylized tree with the king interposed between them and the tree, a visual metaphor for his role as intermediary in the divine creation of agricultural abundance.[53] The prototypes for the ivories are found again on Late Bronze Age luxury goods.[54]

Both in Egyptian and Western Asian royal ideology, kings were nurtured by goddesses. This topos was visualized not only in the concrete image of an Egyptianizing breast-feeding goddess,[55] a motif with

---

IV, nos. 4, 527, 583, 586, 602–3, 617, 619, 719, 1107, and 1254; Herrmann, *Ivories from Nimrud V*, nos. 331, 368, 454, 456, and 459. For examples from Samaria, see Crowfoot and Crowfoot, *Ivories from Samaria*, pls. V–VI, X:8, XIV:4–6, and XVII.

52 Orthmann, ed., *Alte Orient*, fig. 126a.

53 On the latter, see Porter, *Trees, Kings, and Politics*, 11–37. Among the anthropomorphic figures flanking a stylized tree are not only winged genies, which I understand as providers more than protectors of agricultural abundance, but also royal figures (e.g., Herrmann, "Ivories from Nimrud," 227 fig. 27c; Herrmann, *Ivories from Nimrud IV*, no. 617; Rehm, *Kykladen und Alter Orient*, pl. XVI). Moreover, the sphinx, which is the predominant figure associated with the stylized tree, can be understood as a manifestation of the king.

54 E.g., Feldman, *Diplomacy by Design*, pls. 6–7 and 9, and fig. 40.

55 Herrmann, *Ivories from Nimrud IV*, no. 1019, which depicts Isis suckling the infant Horus.

Fig. 8
Cow suckling calf on panel from Arslan Tash
(Thureau-Dangin et al. 1931: pl. XLI: 75)

Fig. 9
Isis and Nephtys guarding Djed-column on cloisonné panel from Samaria
(Collection of the Israel Antiquities Authority,
exhibited at the Israel Museum, Jerusalem,
photo by author; reduced to 78%)

Bronze Age antecedents in the Levant,[56] but more often in the visual metaphor of a mother animal suckling her young (Fig. 8).[57] The cow-suckling-calf motif, which also has its origins in Egypt, was especially popular on South Syrian ivories.

The best-preserved panels from Samaria belong to the Phoenician group that depicts Egyptianizing scenes (Fig. 9).[58] The often un-Egyptian compositions of these scenes reveal that the Phoenicians adapted Egyptian motifs to their own ends and that they were familiar with their meaning.[59] Some Egyptian motifs entered the Levant already in the early Bronze Age,[60] while others have prototypes in the New Kingdom or the Third Intermediate Period.[61]

The Egyptianizing scenes conveyed both religious concepts and royal ideology. One does not exclude the other, since the king played an important role in cosmic order. The representation of Horus as an infant on the lotus flower, a symbol of regeneration, also implied the king's rebirth, since the pharaoh was a manifestation of Horus on earth; the *Djed*-column guarded by Isis and Nephthys evoked Osiris' revival; at the same time, it was a symbol of stability with respect to the king's reign; the god *Heh* holding a notched palm rib personified eternity, which is usually associated with a long reign.[62] Also, the all-pervasive solar symbolism evoked not only the daily cycle but also referred to the king, since he was closely associated with the Sun in titulary and also addressed as such by his subjects.[63]

Meaningless Designs or Collective Memory?

The preceding review of motifs and themes, even if not exhaustive, is sufficient to demonstrate that the diverse imagery carved on Iron Age ivories revived Late Bronze Age royal iconography, which, in turn, was indebted mainly to Mesopotamian and Egyptian visual traditions. The

---

56 Orthmann (ed.), *Alte Orient*, fig. 427.

57 Herrmann, *Ivories from Nimrud IV*, nos. 701–8 and 1014–16; Herrmann, *Ivories from Nimrud V*, 132, 381, and 479; Thureau-Dangin et al., *Arslan-Tash*, pls. XXXVII:63 and XLII:80.

58 Crowfoot and Crowfoot, *Ivories from Samaria*, pls. I–III; Herrmann, *Ivories from Nimrud IV*, nos. 984–1043.

59 Hölbl, "Ägyptische Kunstelemente"; Busch and Wicke, "Alles nur Kopie."

60 Eder, *Die ägyptischen Motive*."

61 Ciafaloni, *Eburnea Syrophoenicia*, 19–30 and 41–46.

62 On ancient Egyptian symbolism, see Lurker, *Lexikon der Götter*," and Goff, *Symbols of Ancient Egypt*.

63 Redford, "The Concept of Kingship," 169–72.

most popular motifs can be traced to Marian Feldman's *International Koiné*, a group of Late Bronze Age luxury goods that is characterized by the hybrid iconography of an international kingship.[64] Hybridity allowed for a universalized meaning in the supraregional royal community of Egypt, Mesopotamia, Anatolia, the Levant, and the eastern Mediterranean. Feldman showed how the objects of this group mediated political relations, intercultural interactions, and economic negotiations within the international exchange of the Late Bronze Age, in which trade and crafts were largely monopolized by a small community of "great" kings.

What did this imagery signify in the geo-politically and socially changed landscape of the early Iron Age Levant? The rigid palace-centered system was long gone and had made way for a new order, a decentralized and entrepreneurial system in which politics and commerce were in the hands of local kings and diverse private or semi-private groups.[65] Rather than assuming meaningless decorative or merely protective designs, I subscribe to Feldman's suspicion that the persistence of the Koiné imagery has to do with a collective memory, evident also in the Homeric epics.[66]

The Homeric epics were put in writing in the same epoch as the Levantine ivories were produced, and they hark back to the same Late Bronze Age. Jan Assmann posed the question of why eighth-century Greece harked back to events 500 years past.[67] He argued that the aristocratic society of the ninth and eighth centuries BCE adopted the until-then orally transmitted stories of the Mycenaean age and heroized this age in order to construct continuity over the breach between the Mycenaean age and archaic Greece. The Mycenaean past served as a platform for the self-representation and self-definition of the early Iron Age elite, whose members traced their genealogy to Late Bronze Age heroes and established cult places at Bronze Age tombs and palatial ruins.[68]

Iron Age Levantine ivories are best understood along these lines. By adopting imagery of heroized kings of the past for objects that served primarily as status symbols, the Levantine elite of the Iron Age constructed a fictitious continuity over the shift from the palace-centered system of the Late Bronze Age to the new order of their own time with the goal of legitimizing their status, as well as the new order. In a world

---

64 Feldman, *Diplomacy by Design*.

65 Liverani, "The Influence of Political Institutions on Trade."

66 Feldman, *Diplomacy by Design*, 195.

67 Assmann, *Das kulturelle Gedächtnis*, 274.

68 For the latter, see Brent, "Glories of the Past."

governed by a new type of profit-seeking commerce, which entailed many insecurities, both local kings with restricted power and fluctuating spheres of influence and the new merchant oligarchy without a past idealized the much more structured, albeit rigid world of legendary "great" kings with a glorious past. They intentionally emulated these long gone kings, whose role they had taken on in trade. Even if not every single detail of the adopted designs was fully grasped, the message was clear: it was the link with the past that created prestige.

WORKS CITED

Appadurai, Arjun. "Introduction: Commodities and the Politics of Value." In *The Social Life of Things: Commodities in Cultural Perspective*, edited by Arjun Appadurai, 3–63. Cambridge: Cambridge University Press, 1986.

Assmann, Jan. *Das kulturelle Gedächtnis: Schrift, Erinnerung und politische Identität in frühen Hochkulturen*. München: C. H. Beck, 1992.

Barnett, Richard D. *A Catalogue of the Nimrud Ivories in the British Museum*. London: British Museum, 1957.

Ancient Ivories in the Middle East. Qedem 14. Jerusalem: Institute of Archaeology, 1982.

Beach, Eleanor Ferris. "The Samaria Ivories, Marzeah, and Biblical Text." *BiAr* 56 (1993): 94–104.

"Transforming Goddess Iconography in Hebrew Narrative." In *Women and Goddess Traditions*, edited by Karen L. King, 239–63. Minneapolis, Minn.: Fortress Press, 1997.

Becking, Bob. *The Fall of Samaria: An Historical and Archaeological Study*. Leiden: Brill, 1992.

Beckman, Gary M. and Theodore J. Lewis, eds. *Text, Artifact, and Image: Revealing Ancient Israelite Religion*. Brown Judaic Studies 346. Providence, R.I.: Brown University, 2006.

Bonatz, Dominik. *Das syro-hethitische Grabdenkmal: Untersuchungen zur Entstehung einer neuen Bildgattung in der Eisenzeit im nordsyrisch-südostanatolischen Raum*. Mainz: von Zabern, 2000.

Braun-Holzinger, Eva A., and Ellen Rehm. *Orientalischer Import in Griechenland im frühen 1. Jahrtausend v. Chr.* AOAT 328. Münster: Ugarit-Verlag, 2005.

Brent, Mieke. "Glories of the Past in the Past: Ritual Activities at Palatial Ruins in Early Iron Age Crete." In *Archaeologies of Memory*, edited by Ruth M. van Dyke and Susan E. Alcock, 81–103. Malden, Mass.: Blackwell, 2003.

Brisch, Nicole M., ed. *Religion and Power: Divine Kingship in the Ancient World and Beyond*. Oriental Institute Seminars 4. Chicago, Ill.: University of Chicago, 2008.

Buhl, Marie-Louise, and Poul J. Riis. Hama, *Fouilles et Recherches de la Fondation Carlsberg 1931–1938, II, 2: Les Objets de la Periode dite Syro-Hittite (Age du Fer)*. Copenhagen: Gyldendalske Boghandel, 1990.

Bunnens, Guy. "Carved Ivories from Til Barsib." *AJA* 101 (1997): 435–50.

Busch, Angela, and Dirk Wicke. "Alles nur Kopie? Elfenbeinarbeiten aus Nimrud illustrieren die phönikische Interpretation ägyptischer Motive." *Antike Welt* 5 (2005): 47–54.

Caubet, Annie, and François Poplin. "La place des ivoires d'Ougarit dans la production du Proche Orient ancien." In *Ivory in Greece and the Eastern Mediterranean from the Bronze Age to the Hellenistic Period*, edited by J. Lesley Fitton, 91–100. British Museum Occasional Paper 85. London: British Museum, 1992.

Ciafaloni, Davide. *Eburnea Syrophoenicia*. Studia Punica 9. Roma: Universita degli studi Tor Vergata, 1992.

Collon, Dominique. "Banquets in the Art of the Ancient Near East." *Res Orientales* 4 (1992): 23–29.

Crowfoot, John W., and Grace M. Crowfoot. *Samaria-Sebaste 2: Early Ivories from Samaria*. London: Palestine Exploration Fund, 1938.

Eder, Christian. *Die ägyptischen Motive in der Glyptik des östlichen Mittelmeerraums zu Anfang des 2. Jts. v. Chr.* Orientalia Lovaniensia Analecta 71. Leuven: Peeters, 1995.

Erkens, Franz-Reiner, ed. *Die Sakralität von Herrschaft: Herrschaftslegitimierung im Wechsel der Zeiten und Räume*. Berlin: Akademie Verlag, 2002.

Fauth, Wolfgang. *Helios Megistos: Zur synkretischen Theologie der Spätantike*. Leiden: Brill, 1995.

Feldman, Marian H. *Diplomacy by Design: Luxury Arts and an "International Style" in the Ancient Near East, 1400–1200 BCE*. Chicago and London: University of Chicago Press, 2006.

Frankenstein, Susan. "The Phoenicians in the Far West: A Function of Neo-Assyrian Imperialism." In *Power and Propaganda: A Symposium on Ancient Empires*, edited by Mogens Trolle Larsen, 263–94. Mesopotamia 7. Copenhagen: Akademisk Forlag, 1979.

Goff, Beatrice L. *Symbols of Ancient Egypt in the Late Period: The Twenty-First Dynasty*. The Hague: Mouton Publishers, 1979.

Gubel, Eric. "Multicultural and Multimedial Aspects of Early Phoenician Art, c. 1200–675 BCE." In *Images as Media: Sources for the Cultural History of the Near East and the Eastern Mediterranean (1st millennium BCE)*, edited by Christoph Uehlinger. 185–214. OBO 175. Fribourg: University Press, 2000.

Helms, Mary W. *Craft and the Kingly Ideal: Art, Trade, and Power*. Austin, Tex.: University of Texas Press, 1993.

Herrmann, Georgina. *Ivories from Nimrud IV: Ivories from Room SW 37, Fort Shalmaneser*. London: British School of Archaeology in Iraq, 1986.

Ivories from Nimrud V: The Small Collections from Fort Shalmaneser. London: British School of Archaeology in Iraq, 1992.

"Naming, Defining, Explaining: A View from Nimrud." In *Crafts and Images in Contact: Studies on Eastern Mediterranean Art of the First Millennium BCE*, edited by Claudia E. Suter and Christoph Uehlinger, 11–21 and pls. I–VI. OBO 210. Fribourg: Academic Press, 2005.

"The Ivories from Nimrud." In *New Light on Nimrud: Proceedings of the Nimrud Conference 11th–13th March 2002*, edited by John E. Curtis, Henrietta McCall, Dominique Collon, and Lamia al-Gailani Werr, 225–32. London: British Museum, 2008.

Herrmann, Georgina and Allan Millard. "Who Used Ivories in the Early First Millennium BC?" In *Culture through Objects: Ancient Near Eastern Studies in Honour of P. R. S. Moorey*, edited by Timothy Potts, Michael Roaf, and Diane Stein, 377–402. Oxford: Griffith Institute, 2003.

Hölbl, Günther. "Ägyptische Kunstelemente im phönikischen Kulturkreis des 1. Jahrtausends v. Chr.: Zur Methodik ihrer Verwendung." *Or*NS 58 (1989): 318–25.

Keel, Othmar, and Christoph Uehlinger. *Göttinnen, Götter und Gottessymbole: Neue Erkenntnisse zur Religionsgeschichte Kanaans und Israels aufgrund bislang unerschlossener ikonographischer Quellen*. Quaestiones disputatae 134. Freiburg: Herder, 1992.

Kletter, Raz. Review of *Göttinnen, Götter und Gottessymbole*, by Othmar Keel and Christoph Uehlinger. *RBL*, October 15, 1999.

Liverani, Mario. "The Influence of Political Institutions on Trade in the Ancient Near East (Late Bronze Age to Early Iron Age)." In *Mer-*

canti e politica nel mondo antico, edited by Carlo Zaccagnini, 119–63. Roma: Bretschneider, 2003.

Lurker, Manfred. *Lexikon der Götter und Symbole der alten Ägypter: Handbuch der mystischen und magischen Welt Ägyptens*. Bern: Scherz, 2002.

Mallowan, Max E. L., and Georgina Herrmann. *Ivories from Nimrud III: Furniture from SW 7, Fort Shalmaneser*. London: British School of Archaeology in Iraq, 1974.

Markoe, Glenn E. "L'art du métal phénicien: Les coupes décorées." In *La Méditerranée des Phéniciens de Tyr à Carthage*, edited by Elisabeth Fontan and Hélène Le Meaux, 167–73. Paris: Institut du monde arabe, 2007.

Matthäus, Hartmut. "Toreutik und Vasenmalerei im früheisenzeitlichen Kreta: Minoisches Erbe, lokale Traditionen und Fremdeinflüsse." In *Crafts and Images in Contact: Studies on Eastern Mediterranean Art of the First Millennium BCE*, edited by Claudia E. Suter and Christoph Uehlinger, 291–350. OBO 210. Fribourg: Academic Press, 2005.

McLaughlin, John L. *The Marzeah in the Prophetic Literature: References and Allusions in Light of Extra-Biblical Evidence*. Vetus Testamentum Supplement 68. Leiden: Brill, 2001.

Michalowski, Piotr. "The Drinking Gods: Alcohol in Mesopotamian Ritual and Mythology." In *Drinking in Ancient Societies: History and Culture of Drinks in the Ancient Near East*, edited by Lucio Milano, 27–44. Padova: Sargon srl, 1994.

Muscarella, Oscar W. "Greek and Oriental Cauldron Attachments: A Review." In *Greece between East and West: 10th–8th Centuries BC*, edited by Günther Kopcke and Isabella Tokumaru, 16–45. Mainz: von Zabern, 1992.

Oggiano, Ida. *Dal terreno al divino: Archaeologia del culto nella Palestina del primo millennio*. Roma: Carocci, 2005.

Orchard, J. J. *Ivories from Nimrud I, 2: Equestrian Bridle Harness Ornaments*. London: British School of Archaeology in Iraq, 1967.

Orthmann, Winfried, ed. *Der Alte Orient*. Propyläen Kunstgeschichte 14. Berlin: Propyläenverlag, 1975.

Porter, Barbara N. *Trees, Kings, and Politics: Studies in Assyrian Iconography*. OBO 197. Fribourg: Academic Press, 2003.

Redford, Donald B. "The Concept of Kingship during the Eighteenth Dynasty." In *Ancient Egyptian Kingship*, edited by David O'Connor and David P. Silverman, 157–84. Leiden: Brill, 1995.

Rehm, Ellen. *Kykladen und Alter Orient: Bestandskatalog des Badischen Landesmuseums Karlsruhe*. Karlsruhe: Badischen Landesmuseums, 1997.

"Abschied von der Heiligen Hure: Zum Bildmotiv der 'Frau am Fenster' in der phönizisch-nordsyrischen Elfenbeinschnitzkunst." *UF* 35 (2003): 487–519.

"Assyrische Möbel für den assyrischen Herrscher!" In *Crafts and Images in Contact: Studies on Eastern Mediterranean Art of the First Millennium BCE*, edited by Claudia E. Suter and Christoph Uehlinger, 187–206. OBO 210. Fribourg: Academic Press, 2005.

Reisner, George A., Clarence S. Fisher, and David G. Lyon. *Harvard Excavations at Samaria, 1908–1910*. Cambridge, MA: Harvard University Press, 1924.

Röllig, Wolfgang. "Alte und neue Elfenbeininschriften." In *Neue Ephemeris für semitische Epigraphik*, Vol. 2, edited by Rainer Degen, Walter Müller, and Wolfgang Röllig, 37–64. Wiesbaden: Harrassowitz, 1974.

Safar, Fuad, and Muyasser S. al Iraqi. *Ivories from Nimrud*. Baghdad: Republic of Iraq, 1987.

Scigliuzzo, Elena. "Un nuovo motivo iconografico egeo negli avori di Nimrud." *EVO* 26 (2003): 91–98.

Sommer, Michael. *Die Phoenizier: Handelsherren zwischen Orient und Okzident*. Stuttgart: Kröner Verlag, 2005.

Suter, Claudia E. "Die Frau am Fenster in der orientalischen Elfenbeinschnitzkunst des frühen 1. Jahrtausends v. Chr." *Jahrbuch der Staatlichen Kunstsammlungen in Baden-Württemberg* 29 (1992): 7–28.

"Luxury Goods in Ancient Israel: Questions of Consumption and Production." In *Proceedings of the 6th International Congress on the Archaeology of the Ancient Near East (Rome, 5–10 May 2008)*, edited by Paolo Matthiae et al., 994–1002. Wiesbaden: Harrassowitz, 2010.

Suter, Claudia E., and Christoph Uehlinger, eds. *Crafts and Images in Contact: Studies on Eastern Mediterranean Art of the First Millennium BCE*. OBO 210. Fribourg: Academic Press, 2005.

Tappy, Ron E. *The Archaeology of Israelite Samaria II: The Eighth Century BCE*. HSS 50. Winona Lake, Ind.: Eisenbrauns, 2001.

"The Provenance of the Unpublished Ivories from Samaria." In *'I Will Speak the Riddles of Ancient Times:' Archaeological and Historical Studies in Honor of Amihai Mazar*, edited by Aren M. Maeir and Pierre de Miroschedji, 637–56. Winona Lake, Ind.: Eisenbrauns, 2006.

Thomason, Allison K. *Luxury and Legitimation: Royal Collecting in Ancient Mesopotamia*. Aldershot: Ashgate, 2005.

Thureau-Dangin, François, A. Barrois, G. Dossin, and Maurice Dunand. *Arslan-Tash*. Paris: Paul Geuthner, 1931.

Wicke, Dirk. *Vorderasiatische Pyxiden der Spätbronzezeit und der Früheisenzeit*. AOAT 45. Münster: Ugarit-Verlag, 2008.

Winter, Irene J. "Phoenician and North Syrian Ivory Carving in Historical Context: Questions of Style and Distribution." *Iraq* 38 (1976): 1–22.

Review of Max E. L. Mallowan and Georgina Herrmann, *Ivories from Nimrud III*, 1974. *AJA* 80 (1976): 201–3.

"Is there a South Syrian Style of Ivory Carving in the Early First Millennium BC?" *Iraq* 43 (1981): 101–30.

"Le Palais Imaginaire: Scale and Meaning in the Iconography of Neo-Assyrian Cylinder Seals." In *Images as Media: Sources for the Cultural History of the Near East and the Eastern Mediterranean (1st Millennium BCE)*, edited by Christoph Uehlinger. 51–87. OBO 175. Fribourg: University Press, 2000.

"Ornament and the 'Rhetoric of Abundance' in Assyria." *Eretz-Israel* 27 (2003): 252–64.

"Establishing Group Boundaries" In *Crafts and Images in Contact: Studies on Eastern Mediterranean Art of the First Millennium BCE*, edited by Claudia E. Suter and Christoph Uehlinger, 23–42 and pls. VII–X. OBO 210. Fribourg: Academic Press, 2005.

NOTES ON THE MEDES AND THEIR "EMPIRE" FROM JER 25:25 TO HDT 1.134*

MATTHEW WATERS
UNIVERSITY OF WISCONSIN, EAU CLAIRE

The 2003 publication of *Continuity of Empire (?): Assyria, Media, Persia* (ed. G. Lanfranchi, M. Roaf, and R. Rollinger) heralds a renewed focus on the traditional view of the Median Empire in ancient Near Eastern history. The contributions to that volume revisit the central place that the Medes have traditionally held in modern scholarship as an integral component in a continuum of ancient Near Eastern empires from the Neo-Assyrian to the Persian. From that volume's impetus, here are offered observations on some relevant biblical and Herodotean evidence for the history of the critical, yet poorly understood, period c. 650–550 BCE—from the denouement of the Assyrian Empire to the rise of the Persian Empire under Cyrus, i.e., the apparent zenith of Median power. The traditional view of the Median Empire, dependent primarily upon Herodotus' account of the dynasty founded by Deioces (1.96–107), is a retrojection of Greek conceptions, often stereotypical, of the Achaemenid Persian Empire at its height. In other words, for Greeks writing in the fifth and fourth centuries, it was reconstruction of the past based on a (mis)understanding of the contemporary.

Mario Liverani's contribution to *Continuity of Empire* highlights the use of the plural "kings" of the Medes in Jer 25:25, 51:11, and 51:27–28 in the historical context of the late seventh and early sixth centuries.[1] In

* It is my pleasure to offer these brief notes in a volume honoring my esteemed teacher, Prof. Barry Eichler. This paper is a significantly modified version of a presentation given at the conference in Barry's honor, "Tablet and Torah: Mesopotamia and the Biblical World," in March 2009.

1 Liverani, "Rise and Fall of Media." Note especially his remarks (8–9) on the switch to the singular "king" in the Septuagint (influenced by Greek historiography); the translation followed herein is that of the NRSV, available via several online resources. Compare Tuplin, "Medes in Media," 234–35. Note also Diakonoff, "The Near East on the Eve of Achaemenian Rule," 223–30, though Diakonoff's focus is different from that of Liverani and that presented here. The rhetorical and stylized language of these passages must be acknowledged.

conjunction with the Assyrian and Babylonian evidence these passages provide a comprehensible depiction of the geopolitical situation across northern Iran: a plurality of kings, rather than one singular king, ruling a unified, centralized, organizational empire. In an inscription of Nabonidus from the Eḫulḫul temple in Sippar, for example, the king of the *umman-manda* (i.e., the Medes) is accompanied by additional "kings going at his side" (LUGAL.MEŠ *ālik idišu*).[2] This description fits well with other evidence describing the Medes of this period and will be revisited below.

In Assyrian sources there are, with two potential exceptions, no named Median kings. The first Mede attested by name, a certain Ḫanaṣiruka, occurs in an inscription dated c. 820 (reign of Šamši-Adad V). Ḫanaṣiruka is associated with a royal city, Sagbita, from which it may be extrapolated that he was a king, though he is not explicitly labeled as such.[3] The other prospective exception is manifest in an inscribed bronze plaque attributed to a certain Šilisruḫ. There are a number of problems with this intriguing inscription: its reading, its interpretation, its provenience, its date, and thus its historical context.[4] It was found near Hamadan; based on internal evidence, Diakonoff (followed by Radner) associates it with Bīt-Ištar, the ruler of which is labeled a city-lord in the royal inscriptions of Tiglath-pileser III and Sargon.

The Šilisruḫ plaque contains reference to a king (obv. 2 and 8), though it is not evident that the king mentioned in the inscription is the Šilisruḫ who apparently commissioned it. The word "king" does not accompany Šilisruḫ's name as a title. Unless one assumes that the king referenced is the Assyrian king, an assumption that would lead to other questions, it is unclear to whom else it could refer. The assumption that Šilisruḫ was an authority figure seems straightforward enough, but he

---

2 Schaudig, *Die Inschriften Nabonids*, 416–17 i 7–29 (l. 25 for LUGAL.MEŠ *ālik idišu*). For the use of the pejorative *umman-manda*, see Reade, "Why Did the Medes Invade Assyria?" 153 and Rollinger, "The Western Expansion," 297–305. Note also Zawadzki, *The Fall of Assyria and Median-Babylonian Relations*, chapter VI.

3 Grayson, *RIMA* 3, 185–86 A.0.103.1 iii 27–36; Radner, "Assyrian View," 41. Whether or not Ḫanaṣiruka was considered a king by the Assyrians, it is impossible to determine whether Assyrian labels matched Median usage.

4 The superabundance of qualifications in this section reflects the uncertain interpretation of this inscription, which is treated only in brief here. See for discussion Radner, "Median Sanctuary," 119–30. The inscription was (re-) published by Diakonoff, "Cuneiform Charter," 51–59; see Diakonoff's comments on the original find (and publication) by E. Herzfeld, with references. Note also Muscarella, *Bronze and Iron*, 238–40.

is otherwise unattested and thus his position cannot be corroborated. Locating Bīt-Ištar—if that is the correct attribution—in Median territory and, by extension, assuming that Šilisruḫ (king or not) was also Median is a sensible, but certainly not ineluctable, progression.[5] Radner also notes a city-lord of Bīt-Ištar named Burburazu during Sargon II's reign. If Burburazu is correctly identified as a Kassite name and if the name reflects its bearer's ethnicity, its etymology testifies to the apparently not uncommon (nor surprising) phenomenon of city lords of varying ethnicities in the Zagros region.[6]

Appellatives of the Medes vary, and it is not clear what defines particular groups of people as Median. The Assyrians generally and consistently, however, label Medes as living in settlements ruled by *bēl ālāni* ("city lords"). There are dozens of these city lords in the Zagros region mentioned in the extant documentation from Tiglath-pileser III's and Sargon II's reigns.[7] In the case of the Median *bēl ālāni* in the eighth and seventh centuries, their official position appears to be on par with tributary kings in the Assyrian organizational structure, as evinced, *inter alia*, by their occurrence in *adê*-agreements. A key component observed with the title *bēl āli* is its hereditary, i.e., dynastic, nature. This ought to be considered when modeling the confluence of Median power in conjunction with the overthrow of Assyria and its aftermath in northern Iran. The coalescence of broader authoritative power presumably had its origins in the interpersonal relationships among these Median *bēl ālāni*.

The transition from a collection of independent (at least from each other) Median city-lords to the force arrayed against Assyria in the 610s

---

5 Radner, "Median Sanctuary," 122–23 asserts that the name Šilisruḫ is neither Indo-European nor Semitic and that the "king" in this inscription is Šilisruḫ. Note Diakonoff, "Cuneiform Charter," 61: "We suppose that Šilisruḫ is a name belonging to an aboriginal language, perhaps akin to Elamite."

6 For Burburazu, see Radner, "Median Sanctuary," 123 and R. Schmitt (*PNA* 1/2, 353). Another example of this phenomenon is Humbareš, the city lord of Median Naḫšimarti (see Radner, "Assyrian View," 60). That an Elamite—inferred from the apparently Elamite name (see *PNA* 2/1, 478)—held a position of authority in a Median area poses many questions about Assyrian administration and Median-Elamite connections, if this instance is not simply anomalous.

7 See especially Lanfranchi, "Assyrian Expansion," 87–89, 94–96, and 112–16 on *bēl āli* (especially 95 for its shifting use over time in the Neo-Assyrian period) and Radner, "Assyrian View," 49–50. Use and alteration of labels in these cases and others in the Neo-Assyrian period is a topic far beyond the scope of this paper and one in need of attention.

under Umakištar/Cyaxeres remains unclear. Liverani has argued that the traditional view, so heavily influenced by Herodotus and the Greek tradition, is not only skewed but wholly inaccurate.[8] In Liverani's view there was no transition per se—i.e., an evolution from city lords to regional rulers (or kings) in some sort of hierarchical rubric—but simply a short-term unification under a primary Median king to strike at a vulnerable Assyria in the 610s and, thereafter, a rapid return to the status quo as pertained during the eighth and early seventh centuries.

Yet such a reconstruction does not allow for a Median entity that appears to have been a major force in the late seventh and early sixth centuries through the rise of Cyrus. The deconstruction of the Median "Empire" has yet to be reconciled not only with the Medes' prominent role in Assyria's downfall but also with their function as a significant power on Babylonia's eastern frontier well into the sixth century—considered as such in both Babylonian and Greek sources—as well as the Medes' distinctive positions in the military and administration of the Persian Empire subsequently. It is one thing to attribute Median involvement in Assyria's overthrow to a short-term coalition of Median (and other Iranian?) kings; it is another to extrapolate from such a coalition to a significant force—however labeled, even if many now would hesitate to term it an "empire"[9]—that appears to have played a major role in the ancient Near Eastern calculus of power for at least sixty years before Cyrus' conquest. There is much that remains opaque, both in the interpretation of the extant source material itself and in its application to historical reconstruction.

To approach this question from another perspective, one must also consider the Persians' geographically proximate forerunners in Elam.

---

8 See Liverani, "Rise and Fall of Media," 9 for just such an assessment, with which he concludes: "Once the exasperated tribes decided to put an end to the aggressive [i.e., Assyrian] empire, in the same time they put an end to their own political formations and reverted to the stage of tribal pastoralism." Note Radner, "Assyrian View," 61–62 on the significance of the lack of extant references to the Medes in documentation from the reign of Ashurbanipal; see also Lanfranchi, "Assyrian Expansion," 116–17, and Reade, "Why Did the Medes Invade Assyria?"

9 Rollinger's emphasis, "The Western Expansion," 296–305, on the Medes' stereotypical place in Nabonidus' inscriptions is appropriate; note also Jursa, "Observations on the Problem of the 'Median Empire'," 169–79. For a classic treatment on defining empire, see Doyle's perspective on informal vs. formal and annexation vs. control, *Empires*, 30–47 (esp. 32). Note also Parker, *The Mechanics of Empire*, esp. 8–13 and 253–60 on such questions with regard to Assyria's northern frontier.

Our knowledge of Elam at this period is also fraught with uncertainties. No less than six (at a minimalist counting) kings and rulers may be identified circa 650–550 BCE; their relationships, chronology, and extent of rule are all poorly understood, if at all traceable. Anchoring these individuals in a historical framework, within a wider rubric termed "Elamite-Persian ethnogenesis" or the like, has proven a frustrating task, despite its clear import for understanding the Persians' rise.[10] That Jer 25:25's "kings of Elam" (emphasis on the plural) describes the geo-political situation in southwestern Iran well enough does not mean, of course, that the passage's corollary "kings of the Medes" for northern Iran is necessarily accurate.[11] But when greater primacy is given to the Near Eastern sources than to the Greek, it strikes a more consistent chord.

Cyrus' conquest of Astyages and the Medes is, again, known to us mainly from Herodotus and the Greek tradition. How does one correlate Cyrus' conquests of the Medes, the Lydians, the Babylonians, and, further, much of the rest of the Near East as well as tracts of south central

10 As a geo-political term, "Elam" in this period is essentially indeterminate and is applied herein mainly as a cultural and geographic term. For an excellent overview and discussion of the relevant issues, see Henkelman, *Other Gods*, chapter 1, with references. Note also the contributions to Alvarez-Mon and Garrison, eds., *Elam and Persia*. This rough accounting does not include the seemingly innumerable tribal groups of varying ethnicities in these areas; see the remarks of Henkelman, *Other Gods*, 36–37.

One example of such groups is the Martenians ([LÚ]*mar-te-na-a-a*) of *ABL* 879 obv. 3 and 9, whom one is tempted to connect with Herodotus' Persian tribe, the Mardians (1.125). Such facile etymological bridges are always to be approached warily, of course, and this is no exception—not least among the difficulties is the geographic assignment of these groups. See Briant, *History of the Persian Empire*, 728–29 for discussion of the Mardians in classical sources and also Briant, *État et pasteurs*, 61–62, as well as Weissbach, "Μάρδοι," 1647–51 and Kaletsch, "Mardoi," 876. To illustrate the problem of etymologically based links—independent of the attendant, historical questions—note the attested *Martenoi* of the Arabian desert (Grohmann, "Martenoi," 2000).

11 To recall the rhetorical character of some of these passages, cf. Jer 49:38, where the singular "king of Elam" is used, but in conjunction with plural "officials" (so the NRSV translation); contrast, e.g., May and Metzger (eds.), *The New Oxford Annotated Bible with Apocrypha*, 981, which translates "princes" for *sârîm*. It is difficult to ascertain what significance, if any, such interchange may imply with respect to biblical (or, at least, Jeremiah's) perspective on Elam. See, e.g., Holladay, *Jeremiah I*, 387–89. I thank Prof. Clyde C. Smith for sharing his insights on this passage.

Asia?[12] The ancient Near Eastern sources (primarily Babylonian royal inscriptions and chronicles) present their own obstacles, but they offer critical chronology and perspective to balance the Greek tradition. What resounds through the sources, in varying degrees, is the prominent place afforded to the Medes both during Cyrus' conquests (e.g., Mazares and Harpagus in Asia Minor; Hdt 1.156–177) and during the flourishing empire, in context of the Achaemenid military and administration (e.g., the Medes' prominent place alongside the Persians on the Apadana reliefs).

The majority weight of *Continuity of Empire* may thus be said to have stripped the Medes of much of their "empire," though contrarian voices therein still maintain a case, especially for that nebulous but critical period under discussion here.[13] Herodotus needs revisiting in this context, especially his description of Median rule at 1.134.3:

> Ἐπὶ δὲ Μήδων ἀρχόντων καὶ ἦρχε τὰ ἔθνεα ἀλλήλων,
> συναπάντων μὲν Μῆδοι καὶ τῶν ἄγχιστα οἰκεόντων σφίσι,
> οὗτοι δὲ αὖ τῶν ὁμούρων, οἱ δὲ μάλα τῶν ἐχομένων,
> κατὰ τὸν αὐτὸν δὴ λόγον καὶ οἱ Πέρσαι τιμῶσι.
> προέβαινε γὰρ δὴ τὸ ἔθνος ἄρχον τε καὶ ἐπιτροπεῦον.
>
> When the Medes held dominion, likewise[14] did the nations rule each other. The Medes ruled all together and (directly) those living nearest; and these, further, ruled their neighbors and so again, in turn, they theirs, according to the very same principle whereby the Persians esteem others. So indeed it proceeded, each nation both ruling and governing (its neighbor).

---

12 Only the conquest of Babylon may be firmly dated, i.e., October, 539. The conquest of Astyages may be dated to 553 or 550, with the latter (based on the Chronicle) typically given greater credence. The date of the conquest of Lydia may, formally, be considered wide open; a date in the 540s (though no longer 547/546) is typically applied. See Briant, *History of the Persian Empire*, 35–38 and Kuhrt, *Persian Empire* 1, 53 n. 5 (and all her chap. 3 for text excerpts, discussion, and references). With regard to the Lydian conquest in particular note also Stronach, "Campaign of Cyrus the Great," 163–73 and Rollinger, "The Median 'Empire'," 51–65.

13 Roaf, "The Median Dark Age" and Stronach, "Independent Media"; cf. Genito, "Archaeology of the Median Period," 317–26.

14 This "likewise" (or perhaps better, "similarly"—rendering Greek καὶ here) refers to the immediately preceding, parallel point, i.e., how the Persians valued peoples relative to how far removed from the Persians they lived. Greek text from the online Thesaurus Linguae Graecae.

Despite the compressed Greek—and the acknowledged problems with its translation and interpretation (especially the last sentence[15])—Herodotus' depiction contains possibilities for reconciling the Medes' prominence during and after the fall of Assyria with their previously thin record. If one leaves aside the search for a formal, organizational structure of a Median "empire," since one seems unlikely to be found, a more productive approach converges upon questions of influence or authority, and the exercise thereof.[16]

Envisaging Median "domination" via a system of hierarchical, informal (but de facto) rule provides a model with which to work. Ctesias' *Persica*, the extant parts of which exhibit no shortage of interpretive difficulties,[17] supports such a perspective. Ctesias presupposes a close relationship between the Medes and northeastern Iran; Cyrus' victory over Astyages resulted in the subsequent submission of the Hyrcanians, Parthians, Scythians, and Bactrians, who were subject to Astyages previously.[18] If this report has any basis in historical reality, it provides a rubric for expansion of Persian authority into northeastern

---

15 See in particular Tuplin, "Medes in Media," 227–28 and 243–45 for discussion of this passage and its problems. Tuplin argues that the last nine words (προέβαινε γαρ δὴ τὸ ἔθνος ἄρχον τε καὶ ἐπιτροπεῦον) "should either be obelised or deleted as a gloss" (ibid., 245). My translation follows the sense of How and Wells, *A Commentary on Herodotus*, 116, taking ἔθνος ("people, nation") as distributive; they translate: "each nation took its place in order as ruler and administrator"; similarly Liddell-Scott, *A Greek-English Lexicon*, προβαίνω 1470 mng. 3. The verb προέβαινε is here rendered impersonally.

16 Tuplin, "Medes in Media," 234 and 242–43 argues for use of the word "domination" rather than "empire" or "hegemony" or the like. Note also Vogelsang, *Rise and Organisation of the Achaemenid Empire*, esp. 177. Accepting, even with all appropriate caveats, Herodotus' description here does not necessitate endorsement of his story of the foundation of Deioces' power (1.96–107), whatever historical elements may be couched within. Those difficulties, including the infamous Scythian interlude, have been treated extensively elsewhere; see, e.g., Kuhrt, *Persian Empire* 1, chap. 2 for discussion and references.

17 For text and commentary, see Lenfant, *Ctésias de Cnide*, and note Lanfranchi's remarks, "Assyrian Expansion," 118.

18 Lenfant, *Ctésias de Cnide*, 108–9 (text) and lxi (discussion) with notes; Ctesias uses the more generic term *archōn* ("ruler"). See also Briant, *L'Asie centrale*, chapter 3 and Vogelsang, *Rise and Organisation of the Achaemenid Empire*, 210–11. The voluntary submission of these regions may be seen as parallel to those of the Trans-Jordan regions of the Neo-Babylonian Empire as relayed in the Cyrus Cylinder (lines 28–30; Schaudig, *Die Inschriften Nabonids*, 553 and 556); see Briant, *L'Asie centrale*, 36.

Iran. By extension, it offers specific (and expected) names that one may associate with Herodotus' generic description of Median power at 1.134.3, as quoted above.

Based simply on brief passages in Herodotus and Ctesias, it may be precipitous to assume that Median authority extended to such points eastward. But, at the risk of unwarranted conflation of the source material, one may suggest that the rulers of the Hyrcanian, Parthian, Scythian, and/or Bactrian *ethnea* (to use the Greek term) were the "kings going at his side"—of the king of the *umman-manda* in Nabonidus' Sippar Cylinder—i.e., those who rode in support of, and presumably at the behest of, the Median king. The plurality of kings mentioned in Jeremiah ("kings of the Medes") fits such a reconstruction: Median domination over multiple, neighboring peoples, each of whom owed allegiance, directly or indirectly to a Median overlord, chief, or king, however the Median ruler styled himself.

It must be emphasized that there is no record, and it should not be presumed, that the Median kings ever used the title "king of kings."[19] However, the relationships described in Babylonian and Greek sources imply subordination to a Median ruler, regardless of which specific titles are applied. The phenomenon as it related to a period of Median primacy finds echoes in classical sources via acknowledgment of other kings, for example, of Armenia, Cappadocia, and Cilicia.[20] One does not need to attribute a "Cyrus-sized" king to conceptualize the phenomenon at work nor does one need to insist upon consistency of specific titulary in the varied source material.

The testimony for multiple kings of the Medes—in Jer 25:25 and other passages, biblical or otherwise—may be accepted at face value, if with qualification. In conjunction, Herodotus' description of Median dominion at 1.134.3 is more credible than his account of Deioces' dynasty. The evidence from Ctesias discussed above may also be read in support of a Median king holding authority over other regions without the structure of an organizational empire. Such a construct preserves Median reputation as a major power and concurrently explains why the trap-

---

19 I demur from the question of the Median origin, let alone use, of that title, regardless of purported etymological indications from Old Persian royal inscriptions; see Tuplin, "Medes in Media," 230–31 with references. Note Seux, *Épithètes royales akkadiennes et sumériennes*, 318–20 for the long history of the title *šar šarrāni* in Akkadian texts.

20 Xenophon, *Cyropaedia* 3.1.31; 3.2.1–43; and 4.2.31. See Liverani, "Rise and Fall of Media," 8 and note also Petit, *Satrapes et satrapies*, 20–66 and Radner, "Assyrian View," 49–50 for the phenomenon in Neo-Assyrian times (e.g., kings in Cilicia and Cyprus).

pings of a centralized empire have not been found. For reasons that we may only speculate, the Medes did not (or could not) impose a centralized, bureaucratic structure on their dominion. That throws into greater relief the achievements of Cyrus, Cambyses, and Darius in having done so with the Persian Empire, and it confirms the opinions expressed so forcefully in many contributions to *Continuity of Empire:* that continuity in the workings of empire into the Persian period should be sought mainly via the Assyrians, Babylonians, and Elamites.

WORKS CITED

Alvarez-Mon, J., and M. Garrison, eds. *Elam and Persia*. Winona Lake, Ind.: Eisenbrauns, 2011.

Briant, P. *État et pasteurs au Moyen-Orient ancient*. Cambridge: Cambridge University Press, 1982.

L'Asie centrale et les royaumes proche-orientaux du premier millénaire. Paris: Editions Recherche sur les Civilisations, 1984.

History of the Persian Empire. Translated by P. Daniels. Winona Lake, IN: Eisenbrauns, 2002.

Diakonoff, I. "A Cuneiform Charter from Western Iran (The Metropolitan Museum, Rogers Fund 1052, No. 52.119.12)." In *Festschrift Lubor Matous,* vol. 1, edited by B. Hruska and G. Komoróczy, 51–68. Budapest: Eötvös Loránd Tudományegyetem, 1978.

"The Near East on the Eve of Achaemenian Rule (Jeremiah 25)." In *Variatio Delectat: Iran und der Westen. Gedenkschrift für Peter Calmeyer*, edited by R. Dittman et al., 223–30. Münster: Ugarit-Verlag, 2000.

Doyle, M. *Empires*. Ithaca, N.Y.: Cornell University Press, 1986.

Genito, B. "The Archaeology of the Median Period: An Outline and a Research Perspective." *Iranica Antiqua* XL (2005): 315–40.

Grayson, A. K. *Assyrian Rulers of the Early First Millennium BC II (858–745 BC)*. RIMA 3. Toronto: University of Toronto Press, 1996.

Grohmann, A. "Martenoi." *RE* 14/2 (1930): 2000.

Henkelman, W. *The Other Gods Who Are: Studies in Elamite-Iranian Acculturation Based on the Persepolis Fortification Texts*. Achaemenid History 14. Leiden: Nederlands Instituut voor Het Nabije Oosten, 2008.

Holladay, W. *Jeremiah I: A Commentary on the Book of the Prophet Jeremiah, Chapters 1–25*. Philadelphia: Fortress Press, 1986.

How, W. W., and J. Wells. *A Commentary on Herodotus* I. Oxford: Oxford University Press, 1912.

Jursa, M. "Observations on the Problem of the 'Median Empire' on the Basis of Babylonian Sources." In *Continuity of Empire (?): Assyria, Media, Persia*, edited by G. B. Lafranchi et al., 169–79. Padova: Sargon Editrice e Libreria, 2003.

Kaletsch, H. "Mardoi." *Der Neue Pauly* 7 (1999): 876.

Kuhrt, A. *The Persian Empire*, vol. 1. London: Routledge, 2007.

Lanfranchi, G. "The Assyrian Expansion in the Zagros and the Local Ruling Elites." In *Continuity of Empire (?): Assyria, Media, Persia*, edited by G. B. Lafranchi et al., 79–118. Padova: Sargon Editrice e Libreria, 2003.

Lenfant, D. *Ctésias de Cnide: la Perse, l'Inde, autres fragments*. Paris: Les Belles Lettres, 2004.

Liddell, H. G., and R. Scott. *A Greek-English Lexicon*. Revised Edition with Supplement. Oxford: Oxford University Press, 1968.

Liverani, M. "Rise and Fall of Media," in *Continuity of Empire (?): Assyria, Media, Persia*, edited by G. B. Lafranchi et al., 1–12. Padova: Sargon Editrice e Libreria, 2003.

May, H., and B. Metzger, eds. *The New Oxford Annotated Bible with Apocrypha*. Oxford: Oxford University Press, 1962.

Muscarella, O. *Bronze and Iron: Ancient Near Eastern Artifacts in the Metropolitan Museum of Art*. New York: The Museum, 1988.

Parker, B. *The Mechanics of Empire*. Helsinki: Neo-Assyrian Text Corpus Project, 2001.

Petit, T. *Satrapes et satrapies dans l'empire achéménide de Cyrus le Grand à Xerxes Ier*. Liège: Bibliothèque de la Faculté de Philosophie Lettres de l'Université de Liège, 1990.

Radner, K. "A Median Sanctuary at Bīt-Ištar." In *Continuity of Empire (?): Assyria, Media, Persia*, edited by G. B. Lafranchi et al., 119–30. Padova: Sargon Editrice e Libreria, 2003.

"An Assyrian View on the Medes." In *Continuity of Empire (?): Assyria, Media, Persia*, edited by G. B. Lafranchi et al., 37–64. Padova: Sargon Editrice e Libreria, 2003.

Reade, J. "Why Did the Medes Invade Assyria?" In *Continuity of Empire (?): Assyria, Media, Persia*, edited by G. B. Lafranchi et al., 149–56. Padova: Sargon Editrice e Libreria, 2003.

Roaf, M. "The Median Dark Age," in *Continuity of Empire (?): Assyria, Media, Persia*, edited by G. B. Lafranchi et al., 13–22. Padova: Sargon Editrice e Libreria, 2003.

Rollinger, R. "The Western Expansion of the Median 'Empire': A Re-Examination," in *Continuity of Empire (?): Assyria, Media, Persia*, edited by G. B. Lafranchi et al., 289–318. Padova: Sargon Editrice e Libreria, 2003.

"The Median 'Empire,' the End of Urartu, and Cyrus the Great's Campaign in 547 BC (Nabonidus Chronicle II 16)." *Ancient West & East* 7 (2008): 51–65.

Schaudig, H. *Die Inschriften Nabonids von Babylon und Kyros' des Großen samt den in ihrem Umfeld entstandenen Tendenzschriften: Textausgabe und Grammatik*. AOAT 256. Münster: Ugarit-Verlag, 2001.

Seux, M.-J. *Épithètes royales akkadiennes et sumériennes*. Paris: Letouzey et Ané, 1967.

Stronach, D. "Independent Media: Archaeological Notes from the Homeland." In *Continuity of Empire (?): Assyria, Media, Persia*, edited by G. B. Lafranchi et al., 233–48. Padova: Sargon Editrice e Libreria, 2003.

"The Campaign of Cyrus the Great in 547 BC. A Hitherto Unrecognized Source for the Early History of Armenia?" *Aramazd: Armenian Journal of Near-Eastern Studies* 2 (2007): 163–73.

Tuplin, C. "Medes in Media, Mesopotamia, and Anatolia: Empire, Hegemony, Domination or Illusion." *Ancient West & East*, 3/2 (2004): 223–51.

Vogelsang, W. J. *Rise and Organisation of the Achaemenid Empire*. Studies in the History of the Ancient Near East 3. Leiden: Brill, 1992.

Weissbach, F. H. "Μάρδοι." *RE* 14/2 (1930): 1647–51.

Zawadzki, S. *The Fall of Assyria and Median-Babylonia Relations in Light of the Nabopolassar Chronicle*. Poznan: Adam Mickiewicz University Press, 1988.

OBSERVATIONS ON THE FESTIVALS AND RITUALS OF DUMUZI/TAMMUZ

MARK E. COHEN
UNIVERSITY OF MARYLAND

There exists but a handful of textual references to the term "festival of Dumuzi," all of which date before the Old Babylonian period. However, throughout all historical periods there were calendars with a month named for Dumuzi or Tammuz, presumably a reflection of a past or current cultic event involving the god during that month. And, texts from the first millennium BCE discuss or allude to rituals for the month Tammuz in which Dumuzi/Tammuz was the major figure. This paper will attempt to identify possible bases for at least some of these festivals or rituals.

In the late third and early second millennia BCE Dumuzi's main associations were with shepherding and the sprouting of spring vegetation. A few remarks on the annual cycle of sheep-herding are, therefore, germane.

Fall marks the beginning of the sheep-breeding season. In many breeds of sheep the decrease in daylight and increase in darkness causes the ram to have increased sperm production and to secrete a pheromone onto his wool that attracts the female. The gestation period for sheep is approximately five months; thus spring is the time of most lambing. Wool can be shorn any time during the year, but it is best to do so in the early spring, before the heavy coat becomes burdensome for the animal in the hot weather. Also, once a lamb is born and lactation begins, the ewe's wool becomes sticky and dirty from the lactation. Thus, the wool is optimally shorn in the spring, just before lambing occurs. The period of suckling lasts two months and is followed by the weaning, which takes another two months.

Within a herd, the optimal ratio of ewes to rams can differ based upon the breed and size of the herd, but generally a ratio between 35:1 and 50:1 is best. A ram can service, on average, three ewes per day. And

---

Barry and I share some ancient history: he was my first teacher of cuneiform languages and I was in his first class after his appointment to the faculty of Oriental Studies at the University of Pennsylvania. Barry, to quote from "The Godfather," "is a man of his word; he is a modest man; he will always listen to reason."

lastly, a male lamb reaches puberty in about five months, when he first attempts to mate with the ewes. Herders discourage such contact, since the newly maturing male lambs are often sexually ineffective at this early stage and, more importantly, they interfere with the mature rams mating with the ewes. Therefore, during the weaning season, before the male lambs consume much of the pasturage that will be needed to sustain the female lambs, the ewes, and the rams, many of the male lambs are culled from the herd. Presumably, in ancient times they were slaughtered for their meat, offered up for cultic activities, or sold to other herders in need of rams to build up their herds. Some male lambs surely were not killed at this time, but were slaughtered throughout the year as a continuous source of meat for the community.

Below is a matrix populated with the festivals of Dumuzi and the months named for Dumuzi in the third and early second millennia BCE against the twelve months of the year, the locality or time period in which the occasion occurred, and the annual sheep-herding cycle.[1]

	ED	*Ur*	*Umma*	*Girsu*	*Uruk*	*Adab*	*Amorite*	*Sippar*
xii	**f**		**m**	**f**				
i			**f** (Sarg.)					
ii								
iii	**f**	**m**					**m**	
iv					**f**			**m**
v								***ūm kimīt***
vi				**f/m**				
vii								
viii								
ix								
x	**f**							
xi								

f = festival of Dumuzi; **m** = month named for Dumuzi

Shearing/Lambing //// Weaning/Culling Breeding

1 For the textual references upon which these data points are based, see the appropriate city and month in Cohen, *Cultic Calendars*. The Sargonic attestation in month 12 at Umma might easily be the same as during the Ur III period, a result, perhaps, of a one-month calendar shift. Although the

Note the absence of Dumuzi events during the breeding season. Of course, the fact that no month or festival for Dumuzi is known to have occurred during the breeding season in no way excludes the likelihood that there were rituals to ensure its success. After all, this is a culture in which just about every liminal event was marked by ritual. It is possible, however, that the festival of Dumuzi in month 6 at Girsu may have marked the onset of breeding and the Early Dynastic festival in month 10 was a celebration of its successful conclusion.

Th. Jacobsen had suggested that the festival of Dumuzi in Umma, during the twelfth month, celebrated the sacred marriage with Inana in the form of the *entu*-priestess. Jacobsen cites a text from AS5: "3 grass-fed sheep and 3 male goats for Dumuzi going to the priestess."[2] Other Umma texts dated to the twelfth month record expenditures for Dumuzi's wedding gifts (níĝ-mí-ús-sá), presumably to Inana.[3]

There does not appear to be any direct correlation between this union of Inana and Dumuzi in month 12 and the herding-cycle. Were there a connection, I would expect the festival to have occurred at the beginning of the breeding season, not once the flock's sexual-union phase had been completed. More likely this celebration with sexual overtones at Umma, and perhaps at Girsu (and in the Early Dynastic period), was, as Jacobsen suggests, more general in nature, a union to ensure the overall prosperity for the coming year and was related to herding only in so far as the herds were part of the overall resources and wealth of the community. This celebration probably reflected, as well, Dumuzi's aspect as the force behind the upcoming spring vegetation.

There is one Early Dynastic, two Ur III, and two Old Babylonian festivals or cultic events during months 3 and 4. If there is a connection to herding, then I suggest that the event being marked was the onset of the culling and the slaughter of the male lambs, an event that would have elicited an emotional response in most anyone who viewed it or took part in it. The scene of a lamb forcibly separated from its mother and then killed, of course, resonates with the tale of Dumuzi: his mother, Duttur, the ewe, searching for her missing child, her missing lamb,

---

provenances of the ED tablets with references to a festival of Dumuzi are unknown, most probably each is from one of the four cities Umma, Girsu, Zabalam, and KI.AN, the cities mentioned elsewhere in the mu-iti texts published by S. Monaco in *Early Dynastic mu-iti Cereal Texts in the Cornell University Cuneiform Collections*, CUSAS 14, 2011.

2 Jacobsen, "Religious Drama in Ancient Mesopotamia," 78 n. 6.

3 For a fuller discussion of month 12 at Umma see Cohen, *Cultic Calendars*, 86–188.

bleating, crying out for her "5 breads," her "10 breads,"[4] and then the chase and capture of Dumuzi by the *gallu*-demons—the herdsmen running after the male lambs, dragging them away from the ewes to be killed, perhaps clubbing them to death right there in the pasture. I, therefore, suggest the possibility that this Dumuzi narrative reflects the culling and slaughter of the male lambs and that this culling served as the basis of the Dumuzi-related cultic events during months 3 and 4.

Of course, we must acknowledge the possibility that some or all of the Dumuzi festivals in months 3 and 4 may, instead, reflect Dumuzi as the force behind the growth of spring vegetation.

In summary, then, in the third millennium BCE and into the Old Babylonian period, the Dumuzi rites of month 12 seem designed to ensure general prosperity and are not directly related to herding events, whereas the rites of months 3 and 4 may be a response to the herding-cycle, to the onset of the culling of the male lambs. The festival of Dumuzi in month 6 at Girsu and month 10 in the Early Dynastic period may have marked, respectively, the onset and conclusion of the breeding cycle.[5]

The other major attested event involving Dumuzi/Tammuz is from the first millennium BCE. The occasion lasted three days, the 26th through the 28th, or the 27th through the 29th, of the month Tammuz, depending on the city, during which the image of Tammuz was on display. The first day was called "the screaming" (*ikkillu*); the second day "the release" (*pašāru*); and the third simply "Dumuzi." A hemerology records that the second day was also called *ūm tarbaṣi*, "day of the animal pen."[6] This occasion had, by the Neo-Assyrian period at least, become more than merely some sort of commemoration of Dumuzi and his fate. It apparently had evolved into a time when the entire community confronted the cycle of life and death, with implications far greater than just the Dumuzi narrative. It was a time of ghosts, of the spirits of the dead, as well as the appropriate moment for rituals against life-threatening conditions[7] and may well have been the background to the

---

4 Alster, *Dumuzi's Dream*, 9–11. "My mother, my Duttur, will call. My mother will call for the five breads. My mother will call for the ten breads," Alster, *Dumuzi's Dream*, 53.

5 For the possible significance of *ūm Dumuzi* at Sippar in the fifth month, see below, note 20.

6 For references see Livingstone, *Mystical and Mythological Explanatory Works*, 139.

7 For detail on the various aspects and rituals associated with this festival, as well as an analysis of the healing ritual associated with it, see Scurlock, "K 164," 53–67.

reference in Ezek 8:14, to women at the temple in Jerusalem wailing for Tammuz, a practice presumably introduced during Assyrian domination of that area.

The following is a translation by A. Livingstone of the ritual for Dumuzi during the festival in the Egašankalamma temple, which, according to the text, was to be performed as it had been in Nippur.[8] I have removed the esoteric Assyrian commentary from Livingstone's edition so that all that remains is the ritual instruction.

> [When the ordinances of] Egašankalamma are enacted, like those of Nippur let them be enacted.
> [In Tammuz,] when Ištar wept in lamentation for Ištarān, her brother,[9]
> they carry his [....]. and they go into the temple of Ištar.
> Let him beat the corpse of Ištarān and [let] the blood [go down] to the underworld.
> He prepares her [...].
> He prepares bundles of reeds for her.
> The chariots which they dispatch from the steppe, and they enter Aššur.
> The cult dancer and equerry who bathe together, and the equerry sprinkles Bēl.
> He prepares her goblet.
> He prepares her bread.
> The women roasted .[grain]. They carry stones and they lift the stones up among the women.
> [The ... which] comes out and keeps giving its cry.[10]
> [....]
> The fox which comes out and keeps giving its cry.
> They carry the woman of the city on their heads and necks and go to a field and scatter seed.
> They scatter seed in handfuls when they fill to the brim.
> They call .. a well.
> [.] ....

8 Translation is according to Livingstone, *Mystical and Mythological Explanatory Works*, 117.

9 For Ištarān being identified with Dumuzi and for the possible reason for Ištarān, not Dumuzi, being named in this ritual, see Livingstone, *Mystical and Mythological Explanatory Works*, 137.

10 Perhaps *būṣu*, "hyena," should be restored here (see note 23 below), although hyenas merely yelp and don't have the striking call of the fox.

It is put on a table. The women cut the [..] upper parts. …they strip them off. They take out [the lower] parts onto their laps and carry . and above ....

[...]. they threw in front of themselves 7 ....[.....].. which they throw .. [.......]

[...] which they throw.

Jacobsen understood this festival as originally marking the movement of the flocks to winter pastures and, in a similar vein, Livingstone, trying to identify the original basis of this festival, suggests "that the death of the provider of the sheep, the shepherd Dumuzi, was a mythical metaphor for the withering and death of the sun-parched vegetation on which the livelihood of the sheep depended."[11] However, I offer an interpretation that has nothing at all to do with sheep, shepherds, or withering pasture land, but something, I believe, to be more central to the Near Eastern psyche than the seasonal movement from one pasturage to another.

Three other texts, I suggest, provide the clue as to the underlying phenomenon reflected in this ritual and, thereby, the original significance of this three-day festival of Dumuzi.

The first text is Assyrian Astrolabe B, which describes the month Tammuz as: "the month to pile up the grain and put out the early seed...month in which the shepherd Dumuzi is bound."[12] The other two texts mention burning. According to a temple list, the temple of Tammuz in Babylon is where the "burning" occurred.[13] The second text states more fully for the fourth month "Libation of water: descending into the grave. Burning of the shepherd: opening of the grave."[14]

Why, as we find in these two texts, was Dumuzi burned? The Sumerian literary texts relate that Dumuzi was beaten, not burned.

As has been documented and written about over and over again, all societies mark liminal events. I suggest that what is being ritualized here is one of the most important liminal moments in any agrarian society. This festival of Dumuzi, *at least originally*, marked the end of one harvest cycle and the beginning of the next. As Astrolabe B informs us, in the month Tammuz was the beginning of the sowing for the next harvest.

11 Livingstone, *Mystical and Mythological Explanatory Works*, 138.

12 See Livingstone, *Mystical and Mythological Explanatory Works*, 138.

13 Landsberger, "Bemerkungen," 289 (see Livingstone, *Mystical and Mythological Explanatory Works*, 137).

14 See Livingstone, *Mystical and Mythological Explanatory Works*, 137.

Although there is no definitive evidence of Dumuzi's having been a god of grain or the harvest, there are several indicators that suggest that this identification probably was valid at some point. The syncretizing of Dumuzi, a god of vegetation and a young, dying god, with Amaušumgalanna, Ningišzida, Ištarān, and Damu may have been a major step in the evolution.

Th. Jacobsen maintained that at some point Dumuzi/Tammuz became the embodiment of the power of the grain.[15] Jacobsen surmised that a medieval rite called "the rattle," in which the body or bones of Tammuz were understood to be the grain ground at the mill, must have evolved from a tradition of Tammuz being the power of the grain from a time when the cult of Tammuz was fairly active.[16]

F.A.M. Wiggerman comments on Dumuzi as a god of vegetation who is depicted with grain growing from his body:

> ...the once absent and now returning god with grain growing from his body can be recognized as a dying and resurrecting god of vegetation, and indeed, Frankfort, *Cylinder Seals*, 115 (ad Pl. XXe) and Moortgat, *Tammuz*, 87 detected a Tammuz here. The acceptance of this figure as both a shepherd and a dying/resurrecting god of vegetation would establish his identity independent of the later material. It would also vindicate much of Moortgat's Tammuz.[17]

And lastly, Dina Katz cites two texts that may allude to Dumuzi having been identified with the harvested grain by the Old Babylonian period. The first text is the harvest ritual CT 58 21. Katz, summarizing the text, writes: "They harvest the crop, collecting and arranging it in the reed huts of *arali*. Immediately following, with no dividing line, is a reference to the young dying god....Since the text dates to the Old Babylonian period, and at that time Dumuzi remained the only incarnation of the young dying god, these lines probably describe the performance of Dumuzi's annual lamentation ritual."[18]

---

15 Jacobsen, *Toward the Image of Tammuz*, discussing the forms of Dumuzi, refers to one of Dumuzi's aspects as "Dumuzi of the Grain" and states "Tammuz as the power in the grain dies when the grain is crushed between the millstones, floats dead with the malt in the mash tun" (ibid., 75). However, Jacobsen cites no evidence for his assertion.

16 Jacobsen states: "The rite generally survived into Medieval times, when, we are told, the women of Harran celebrated a rite called 'the rattle' at which they wept for Ta'uz, i.e., Tammuz or Dumuzi, whose master cruelly ground his bones in a mill. The women during this celebration also abstain from all milled foods" ("Religious Drama in Ancient Mesopotamia," 72).

17 Wiggermann, "Image of Tammuz," 336.

18 Katz, *Netherworld*, 162.

The second text noted by Katz is a letter from Mari (AO 1146) in which "a connection between the killing of Dumuzi and the harvest is made":[19]

> Now, why [am I not] like Dumuzi? At the end of the year they kill him, [in the spring] he keeps returning to the temple of Annunitum. Myself, I always do so: i[n the grain/harvest?] whatever I do, I do not store, and [ ].

Before the new harvest can be planted, the fields must be cleared of the remains of the old harvest. Note the process that occurs in many agrarian, non-industrialized societies for the removal of the stubble, of the straw—of the remains of Dumuzi—after the harvest. I base these observations on practices found in many agrarian societies even today, wherein four post-harvest phases are performed in the fields, which must be cleared before the next harvest cycle can begin with the seeding.

(*a*) In the first phase, the stubble or straw of the last harvest that is easiest to collect is bound into sheaves or loaded onto wagons, so that it can be used for animal fodder, as bedding for humans and animals, as organic material in construction work, and so on.

(*b*) The second phase is the pasturing of animals to eat the stubble that had not been removed in the first phase. Even today stubble-grazing is one of the major food sources for herding animals.

(*c*) The third phase is the complete elimination of all stubble not consumed by the animals. The fields are set ablaze. This still continues throughout the world today, including in Iraq. There have been worldwide efforts to stop this practice because of the danger of the fires spreading, as well as the air pollution.

(*d*) The final fourth phase is the manual removal of all material, such as stones, that was not consumed by the fire.

Thus, before the seeding for the upcoming harvest can commence, four events occur to clear the stubble, the remains of Dumuzi, the power of the grain: (*a*) the gathering of the straw, (*b*) the grazing of animals, (*c*) the burning of the field, (*d*) and the manual removal of all debris not consumed by the fire, such as stones. Now let us again consider our ritual and note the phrases in bold.

---

19 Katz, *Netherworld*, 165.

[When the ordinances of] Egašankalamma are enacted, like those of Nippur let them be enacted.
[In Tammuz,] when Ištar wept in lamentation for Ištarān, her brother,
they carry his [....]. and they go into the temple of Ishtar.
Let him beat the corpse of Ištarān and [let] the blood [go down] to the underworld.
He prepares her [..]. .
(*a*) He prepares **bundles of reeds** for her.
(*b*) The **chariots** which they dispatch from the steppe, and they enter Aššur.
(*b*) The cult dancer and **equerry** who bathe together, and the equerry sprinkles Bēl.
He prepares her goblet.
He prepares her bread.
(*c, d*) The women **roasted** .[**grain**]. They carry **stones** and they lift the stones up among the women.
[The ... which] comes out and keeps giving its cry.
[....]
The **fox** which comes out and keeps giving its cry.
They carry the woman of the city on their heads and necks and go to a field and **scatter seed**.
They **scatter seed** in handfuls when they fill to the brim.
They call .. a well.
[.] ....
It is put on a table. The women cut the [..] upper parts. ...they strip them off. They take out [the lower] parts onto their laps and carry . and above ....
[...]. they threw in front of themselves 7 ....[.....].. which they throw .. [.......]
[...] which they throw.

Note that the order of the terms in bold matches the order of events that occur in the post-harvest process of preparing the fields for the upcoming sowing.

(*a*) Sheaves

The binding of sheaves was the first step in stubble removal. Perhaps this is what is alluded to by *ūm kimīt Dumuzi* in the fifth month at Old Babylonian Sippar and should be understood as "when (or the day) Dumuzi was bound," referring to the binding of sheaves. So too this may be the "binding of Dumuzi" mentioned for the month in Assyrian Astrolabe B.

(*b*) Horses

The Assyrians had large numbers of horses and it is inconceivable that they were not led onto the stubble-laden fields to graze. The chariot coming to Ashur from the plain and the otherwise puzzling participation of an equerry may symbolize the movement of horses from their stables, presumably near where the chariot equipment was stored, to the fields, where they could graze upon the stubble. This may also well explain why the second day was called *ūm tarbaṣi*, "day of the pen." "Day of the pen" may have noted either that phase in which the animals of the *tarbaṣu* (horses, cattle, goats, and sheep) grazed on Dumuzi's remains or, I think more likely, the time when the grazing animals were brought back from the fields, to their pens, out of harm's way, so that the field with its remaining stubble could be set ablaze.[20]

(*c*) Burning

The roasting or burning of grain represents the third phase in the stubble-clearing process: the burning of Dumuzi's body. I draw attention to the two aforementioned texts that refer to the burning of Dumuzi during the festival.[21]

(*d*) Stones

The lifting of stones would refer to the removal of those hindrances to plowing and seeding that were not consumed by the fire, thus the clearing of stones in the fields.

Fox

The fox was a symbol of desolation, of an area so empty that only the fox could survive under such conditions. Desolation is described in some texts by "the fox drags his tail through it."[22] Another texts states "the hyena and the fox make their lairs (in the ruins)."[23] In other words, after the final removal of the stubble, after the field burning, after the stones had been removed, the land was so barren that only a fox could inhabit it. Dumuzi could live there no more; the last trace of grain was gone.

---

20 Protection of the grazing animals that had returned from the field at the conclusion of the second phase, out of the fire's reach, may have been the reason for the ritual circumambulation of the pen on the second day, *ūm tarbaṣi* (for reference to this circumambulation, see Scurlock, "K 164," 62).

21 See notes 13 and 14 above.

22 See, e.g., Cohen, *Canonical Lamentations*, 104: a+223.

23 *CAD* Š/2, 268 s.v. *šēlebu* 1a: *šēlabu u būṣu iqnunu qinnu*.

Sowing

Last occurred the symbolic strewing of the first seed of the next harvest-cycle, performed by the women, who were carried out to the fields.

In conclusion, I suggest that the *original* festival, as reflected in this ritual, marked the transition from one harvest cycle, with the clearing of the stubble (the dead Dumuzi), to the beginning of the next, with the sowing (the reborn Dumuzi). Apparently this liminal event evolved to embrace a wider significance than just the harvest-cycle, the cycle of the life and death of the grain, of Dumuzi. It eventually became a time to confront the human cycle of life and death, as reflected in other first-millennium texts concerning these three days.

WORKS CITED

Alster, B. *Dumuzi's Dream.* Mesopotamia 1. Copenhagen: Akademisk Forlag, 1972.

Cohen, M. E. *The Canonical Lamentations of Ancient Mesopotamia.*" Potomac, Md.: Capital Decisions, 1988.

The Cultic Calendars of the Ancient Near East. Bethesda, Md.: CDL Press, 1993.

Jacobsen, Th. *Toward the Image of Tammuz*. Cambridge, Mass.: Harvard University Press, 1970.

"Religious Drama in Ancient Mesopotamia." In *Unity and Diversity: Essays in the History, Literature, and Religion of the Ancient Near East*, edited by H. Goedicke and J. J. M. Roberts, 65–97. Baltimore, Md.: Johns Hopkins University Press, 1975.

Katz, D. *The Image of the Netherworld.* Bethesda, Md. CDL Press 2003.

Landsberger, B. "Bemerkungen zu einigen in Ungers Babylon übersetzten Texten." *ZA* 41 (1933): 287–99.

Livingstone, A. *Mystical and Mythological Explanatory Works of Assyrian and Babylonian Scholars*. Winona Lake, Ind.: Eisenbrauns, 2007.

Scurlock, J. A. "K 164 (BA 2, P. 635): New Light on the Mourning Rites for Dumuzi." *RA* 86 (1992): 53–67.

Wiggermann, F. A. M. "The Image of Dumuzi: A Diachronic Analysis." In *Gazing on the Deep*, edited by J. Stackert et al., 327–50. Bethesda, Md.: CDL Press, 2010.

MARKED FOR SERVITUDE
MESOPOTAMIA AND THE BIBLE*

NILI S. FOX
HEBREW UNION COLLEGE

Corporal Marks of Culture

It seems that humans have always been intrigued with the canvas of the natural body, utilizing body marking as one way of altering its appearance. While clothing can express personal and social identity, and religious and secular values, it constitutes only temporary bodily transformation. In contrast, branding, tattooing, and piercing usually serve to permanently alter the body. Notably, these modes of body manipulation, attested worldwide from earliest antiquity to modern times, have been practiced to convey a broad range of cultural information. That information, communicated non-verbally to both the wearer and viewer of an in-group, is transmitted by way of symbols, which in turn represent meaningful ideas. Interpreting those corporal markings, however, especially from the ancient world, is complicated for modern researchers by fragmentary data and the fact that culturally they are in the out-group. Still, the existence of the practice in the ancient Near East, seemingly in diverse contexts, begs for scholarly explication. The present study focuses on aspects of body marking that relate to servitude in Mesopotamia and biblical Israel.

Body Marking in Mesopotamia

Practices of body marking in Mesopotamia may have originated as early as the Neolithic period. Uncertainties lie in the nature of the evidence, which consists of figurines bearing various types of markings, such as painted or incised dots and lines that may mirror marks placed on actual human bodies.[1] In Egypt such markings on figurines did reflect those

* It is a privilege to contribute to this conference volume in honor of Prof. Barry Eichler—my teacher, colleague, and friend. This paper is an attempt to explicate one aspect of a complex cultural phenomenon prevalent in the ancient Near East: servitude. I wish to acknowledge my colleague Prof. Samuel Greengus for sharing his insights with me on this difficult topic.

[1] Dominique Collon, *Ancient Near Eastern Art*, 46 fig. 25. Two clay female

on humans, as verified by tattooed mummies.[2] Textual evidence from Mesopotamia suggests techniques involving branding, tattooing, and piercing. Branding, a common method of marking ownership of herd animals and beasts of burden, appears to have been used to mark persons bound in servitude to human masters or dedicated to a deity. While ample texts mention corporal marking, the method of marking is not always made explicit. For example, the verb *šamātu* and nominal forms *šimtu/šindu* are non-specific and could actually indicate marking with dye, as was practiced on herd animals in the Old Babylonian period. In later periods, as in the Middle Babylonian and Neo-Babylonian, animals and people were marked with their owner's sign or name.[3] The expression *šimtu/šindu parzilli*, "iron stamp," indicates the instrument employed, which could have been a branding iron or an iron-tattooing stylus.[4] However, when the term *šaṭāru* or *eṣēru*, "to write, incise, draw," is used, the method likely refers to tattooing: incising with a sharp instrument and inserting indelible ink.[5]

Not all slaves in Mesopotamia, especially household servants, were marked. Even those who were often bore temporary marks. The Old Babylonian *abbuttu*, for example, seems to be characterized by a curl or lock of hair growing from a specific part of the scalp, the remaining hair having been shaved.[6] Shaving the hair in itself was a sign of shame, add-

figurines from the Ubaid period (4500) are illustrated. Similar figurines are attested from later historical periods, as a male and female figurine from the Old Babylonian period displayed in the Museum of Archaeology in Istanbul.

2 Keimer, *Remarques sur le Tatouage*, 8–15; figs. 6, 8–11; pl. 12.

3 For textual examples see *CAD* Š/1, 307–8; Š/3, 9–11.

4 Muhammad Dandamaev, *Slavery in Babylonia*, 232, 488; *CAD* Š/3, 9–11; *CAD* P, 214. Dandamaev (*Slavery in Babylonia*, 229) is incorrect in calling marking with a hot iron "tattooing"; that is, rather, the process of branding.

5 Some later texts use the term *uṣṣuru* (*Dar.* 492:2; *CAD* E, 348; *AHw* 3, 1439). Mendelsohn, *Slavery in the Ancient Near East*, 44–47.

6 *CAD* A/1, 48–49. Defining the *abbuttu* from textual contexts is sometimes difficult. For example, one Old Babylonian literary text notes that the *simat* on the face of an imprisoned slave "should be/is surely" an *abbuttu* (KBo 12). Probably, the text indicates that the slave's "visage/appearance" (see *CAD* S, 283, *simat pani*) is marked by an *abbuttu*. In contrast, Hurowitz ("His Master Shall Pierce His Ear," 58) translates *simat* as "brand," suggesting that the slave had an additional mark. For a detailed discussion of this text, the *abbuttu* more generally and other slave marking, see Hurowitz, "His Master Shall Pierce His Ear," 54–61. Certain earlier theories have been laid to rest, for example, Mendelsohn's suggestion that the *abbuttu* was a tag

ing the *abbuttu* slave mark rendered a person's status public.[7] In the case of the *abbuttu,* however, the mark could be removed if the slave was manumitted.[8] Fugitive slaves, especially those known to be runaways, could have an additional, permanent sign incised on their face in clear view. "This one is an escapee, capture him"[9] is an example of an inscription borne by one slave on his forehead. Clearly, marking state or private slaves, whether by shaving, branding, or tattooing, held a pejorative meaning in society and could function as both a visible sign of slave status and evidence of punishment for a disobedient slave.

Notably, also young slave children could be marked with their owners' names. One Neo-Babylonian document concerning a six-year-old slave girl named Nana-silim states that she bore the names of mul-

---

worn by the slave (*Slavery in the Ancient Near East,* 45). Another, that it was a mark incised in the flesh, is based in part on a misreading of a text from Nuzi originally understood as citing an *abbuttu* gash placed on the feet of disobedient sons (HSS 5 73:22; Driver and Miles, *Babylonian Laws,* 307–8). The term in the text, however, is *abbūtu,* "a father's legal power," not *abbuttu* the mark (*CAD* A/1, 50). The correct reading also solves the enigma behind a slave mark on the feet.

7 Bakir identifies the shorn heads with pigtails of imported Asiatic female slaves (*ꜥꜣmt*) on a Middle Kingdom Egyptian stele with this Babylonian practice (*Slavery in Pharaonic Egypt,* 68). However, it is more likely that the hairstyle pictured is in keeping with Egyptian styles for teen girls, especially performers, as illustrated in a number of Egyptian works of art. It is noteworthy that these Asiatic slaves don Egyptian body ornaments (otherwise they appear naked) and bear Egyptian names. For a detailed description, see *Cairo* 20549e in Lange and Schäfer, *Grab und Denksteine,* vol. 2, 179; for hairstyle depictions, see Lange and Schäfer, *Grab und Denksteine,* vol. 4, pls. 67–68. One could perhaps argue that marking slavery in Mesopotamia by a hairstyle known to designate childhood robbed the slave of adult/independent status. That conjecture, however, assumes both the knowledge and significance of a foreign custom.

8 Erica Reiner questions whether the *abbuttu* was a hair lock or actually a tattoo. She suggests that perhaps the expression *abbutta gullubu,* "to shave the *abbuttu,*" refers to removing the tattoo on the head of a slave who was being freed ("Runaway—Seize Him," 479–80). That interpretation, however, raises certain problems. First, *gullubu* seems to be the wrong verb to mean effacing a tattoo; when referring to humans it is used in regard to cutting or shaving body and head hair (*CAD* G, 129–30). Second, removing a tattoo (or a brand) requires delicate surgery. The assumption that in antiquity a barber was also skilled as a surgeon (so implied by Driver and Miles, *Babylonian Laws,* 308) is questionable.

9 Akkadian *ḫalaq ṣabat*. Hurowitz ("His Master Shall Pierce His Ear," 61–63) cites the example from the lexical text Ai II = *ana ittišu*.

tiple owners.[10] In the case of children, however, we should not assume the same rationale for marking. While it is possible that also youngsters were in the habit of fleeing from their masters, it is equally likely that they were easily abducted and required proof of their owner's identity in order to be retrieved.

Another category of marked slaves is that of temple servants, usually marked with symbols of their temple's deity. These servants, however, did not seem to bear the same low status of other slaves. The *širkûtu* of the Neo-Babylonian and Persian periods, one class of temple officials, were men and women dedicated to the service of particular deities.[11] That these persons were not necessarily slaves in the normal sense can be deduced from texts attesting to stratification within the group, their commercial dealings, and their right to own property—even slaves.[12] Still, some had been slaves previously, dedicated to temple service by their owners.[13] In the case of children, they were often dedicated by a parent, as in the example of a desperate widow who marked her two young sons with Ishtar's star (*kakkabu*) for a lifetime of *širkûtu* service to the goddess.[14] Generally, in the Neo-Babylonian period temple slaves dedicated to Ishtar were marked by her star and by another mark of uncertain shape, called *arrātu.* While the type of neither mark is certain—brand or tattoo—some scholars favor the brand, deriving *arrātu* from the verb *arāru*, which in rare usages means "to burn."[15] Ishtar's star, also used to mark animals owned by her temple, likely involved branding as well, since animals would not be tattooed. But regardless of the type of mark, the dedicatory divine symbols on humans should not be equated to the marks of punitive slavery. Although these persons were indeed bound to temple estates, their marks very possibly indicated a special relationship between the bearer and

---

10 *Nbn* 693 in Dandamaev, *Slavery in Babylonia,* 680 no. 38.

11 See Dougherty, *Shirkûtu.*

12 Dougherty includes texts from various collections that testify to the status of *širkûtu* (*Shirkûtu*, 13–32). For a *širku* slave-owner see YBT VII 114 (=YOS 7 114) in Dougherty, *Shirkûtu,* 71–72.

13 YBT VII 17 (=YOS 7 17) and REN 2 (=YOS 6 2) in Dougherty, *Shirkûtu,* 40–42.

14 REN 154 (=YOS 6 154) in Dougherty, *Shirkûtu,* 33.

15 Mendelsohn (*Slavery in the Ancient Near East,* 46–47) considers the stars tattoos whereas Oppenheim ("Assyriological Gleanings II," 15–16) identifies them as branding (also Dougherty, *Shirkûtu,* 82). Dandamaev (*Slavery in Babylonia,* 488) defines the mark as a "tattoo," as does von Soden (*AHw* 1, 71); *CAD* has "brand" (A/2, 305). Both identifications are speculative.

the patron deity. Comparable examples from Egypt feature tattooed priestesses and palace performers marked with symbols of the divinities they served.[16]

Regarding the difficulty in accurately defining some of the above Akkadian terms, we should consider a semantic range with usage determined mainly by context. An Egyptian example of the discrepancy between text and illustration supports such an approach. Although tattooing was undoubtedly practiced in Egypt, no term with that meaning is known from Egyptian texts. What does exist from the written record is a term for branding, *ȝbw/t*, identified by its hieroglyph determinative: a firebrand. The term appears in records of Rameses II and of his grandson Rameses III in the pharaohs' boastings that they had branded captives with their royal names.[17] Curiously, an artistic depiction from Medinet Habu, the mortuary temple of Rameses III, shows Sea People prisoners being marked by Egyptian scribes with stylus-type instruments indicative of tattooing, not branding.[18] One way to explain the discrepancy is to suppose that the term for branding could also denote tattooing.

Another form of bodily manipulation practiced in Mesopotamia involved piercing or more severe mutilation of the ears, nose, lips, tongue, or jaw. Simple piercing was common for the purpose of inserting nose rings and earrings of a decorative nature to display the wearer's ornaments and status. But piercing also functioned to designate legal status in terms of punitive signs. Perforating the ears by piercing (*palāšu*), mutilating (*ḫapû*, to crush), or actually severing them (*nakāsu*) is mentioned in various laws. MAL A40, for example, stipulates that a slave woman who was caught veiled, thus dressing in a manner not befitting her class, would have her ear cut off. Anyone who shielded her from the authorities would have his ears pierced and tied back, thereby marking him as an accomplice by mimicking the punishment. Laws A4, A5, A24, A44, and A59 indicate that mutilating the ears, including severing them, was an acceptable punishment that a master could inflict on his servant or a husband on his wife.[19] Such drastic measures are also

---

16 Keimer, *Remarques sur le Tatouage*, 8–15; figs. 6, 8–11, 39.

17 The record of Rameses II is from the Blessing of Ptah on a stela in the Abu Simbel temple: *ARE* 3, 414. The one from Rameses III is from his war against the Libyans: Papyrus Harris I, 77:4–6; ARE 4, 405. See the discussion in Bakir, *Slavery in Pharaonic Egypt*, 110–12.

18 Breasted, ed., *Medinet Habu I*, pl. 42.

19 For MAL and LH see Roth, *Law Collections*, 122, 132, 156, 161–62, 167–68, 170, and 175–76. Practices of mutilating a slave's ears and nose are attested also in the Hittite Laws 95 & 99 (229).

found in the earlier LH 205 and 282 for dealing with disobedient slaves. Similar practices of disfiguring a slave's ear continue to be attested in first-millennium texts. For example, a text from the Persian period claims that the ear was split, *letû*, perhaps meaning that it was slit.[20] Clearly, we should not equate any of these punitive methods to the piercings made to hold ornamental nose or ear rings.

Additional cases from Mesopotamia demonstrate that various crimes were punished by disfiguring parts of the face.[21] One case concerns an Old Babylonian litigation over inheritance in which the contender filed a wrongful claim.[22] To prevent him from bringing a future suit, he was marched around town with his arms bound before him, his head half-shaved, and his nose pierced. He was to remain a marked man—the pierced (mutilated) nose presumably functioning as a permanent sign. Similarly, a palace record from the reign of Tukulti-Ninurta reports that a harem woman who cursed the king's son was sentenced to 30 lashes and nose piercing. While the lashing was punitive in the short term, the nose piercing marked her more permanently to the outside world as insubordinate.

More extreme examples are portrayed in depictions of captive kings led by cords tied to rings pierced through their nose, lips, or jaw. An example is a relief on a stele of Esarhaddon showing the Assyrian king holding two royal captives by ropes attached to a ring piercing their lips.[23] In an inscription of Ashurbanipal, the king claims to have made jest of Uate' the Qedarean by piercing his cheeks, placing a ring through his jaw, and collaring him like a dog.[24] Apparently in some cases, the symbolic marks were as significant as the corporal punishments, or even more so. In his study on the subject, Victor Hurowitz suggests that the act of piercing is related to one in which a peg is driven into the

---

20 See *Camb.* 290:3–5; Dandamaev, *Slavery in Babylonia*, 229 and 232–33; Meissner, *Babylonien und Assyrien*, 382. Josef Klíma states that in the Neo-Assyrian period slaves had their ears pierced; however, he does not cite textual examples ("Zur Stellung," 24).

21 Samuel Greengus maintains that there is no observable correlation between the type of crime and the punishment of mutilation ("A Textbook Case of Adultery," 41–43). Shalom Paul discusses various crimes for which the punishment is dismemberment of the nose and ears according to Mesopotamian, Hittite, and Egyptian sources ("Biblical Analogues to Middle Assyrian Law," 344–46).

22 CT 45 18; Pritchard, *ANET*, 543–44.

23 One of the king's captives may be Tirhakah of Egypt (Pritchard, *ANEP*, fig. 447; 300–1).

24 Pritchard, *ANET*, 300.

mouth of a person denying his master and another ceremony in which the same is done symbolically to a figurine representing a run-away slave. In each case the act symbolizes the master's ownership, being comparable to driving a peg into one's property.[25]

Body Marking in Biblical Israel

As in Mesopotamia, body marking in the region of Syria-Palestine seems to have a long history. While the earliest examples derived from marked figurines are inconclusive,[26] jewelry uncovered in excavations from prehistoric and historical sites confirms practices of ear and/or nose piercing. Biblical evidence also attests to the popularity of piercing for the purpose of attaching ornaments (e.g., Gen 24:30, 47; 35:4; Exod 32:2–3; Judg 8:24–26). Other biblical references, however, indicate that ear and nose piercing was practiced to mark wearers with recognizable derisive symbols.

Marking the legal status of a person on his or her face, that part of the body most visible to the outside world, is simple and effective. Just as ornaments enhance the appearance and function to display wealth and status, so too markings can signify the opposite. As in Mesopotamia, nose and ear perforation was employed in biblical Israel as a punitive measure and to signify a person's lowly status. Several prophetic texts mention such examples: Isaiah prophesies that God will drag Sennacherib away from Judah and back to Assyria by a nose hook (2 Kgs 19:28; Isa 37:29), a well-known image from Assyrian depictions of captive rulers;[27] the prophet Ezekiel, in more brutal terms, states that Judah's enemies will cut off the nose and ears of Israelite war prisoners (Ezek 23:25).[28] Clearly these practices were not merely punitive acts but served to permanently mark the subservient victims.

Most informative for Israelite practices are the biblical laws in the Covenant Code and Deuteronomy that describe the marking of perpetual Hebrew slaves (Exod 21:5–6, males only; Deut 15:16–17, males and females). They stipulate that if an indentured servant at the end of his

---

25 Hurowitz, "His Master Shall Pierce His Ear," 68–77. He discusses the cuneiform text *LKA* 135 in detail.

26 Two female figures from 'Ain Ghazal Jordan dated to the PPNB (ca. 7000) bear marks on their bodies that have been identified as rocker-stamped stippled tattooing. Rollefson and Simmons, "The Early Neolithic Village," 40–42; figs. 3 and 4.

27 See note 23.

28 The sense is that Judah is punished for adultery by her foreign lovers according to their laws, for example MAL A15.

seven-year term waves his right to emancipation, thus committing to permanent servitude, his master is to mark the servant's ear in a ceremony confirming the servant's new status. The ritual is to take place in a religious/legal context: the door or doorpost "before God/gods," *el hāĕlōhîm* (Exod 21:6).[29] While not explicit that the door is that of the master's house, rather than the entrance of a communal shrine, one can argue that the slave's bond to his now permanent home is the more powerful symbol.[30] In that case, *el hāĕlōhîm* can refer to household deities or the Israelite god, whose name(s) may have been inscribed on the doorpost.[31] The ritual culminates with the boring of the slave's ear with a tool commonly taken to be an awl. According to Deuteronomy, the awl is to penetrate through the ear into the door, *bĕ'oznô ûbaddelet* (15:17).

Not surprisingly, this ritual has elicited much discussion among early exegetes and modern scholars.[32] Several issues are at stake: the ear as the body part of choice, the type of mark, and the purpose of the mark. While the choice of the ear may be related to its symbol as the organ of "hearing/obeying," key too is its visibility and the ease with which it can be deformed. Since the status of permanent servitude had legal implications, a person in that social position needed to be identifiable for the rest of his life. The fact that the ceremony was performed before the deity(s) made it binding and irreversible. But what about the type of mark?

Notably, neither biblical passage mentions the insertion of an earring or other object in the slave's ear. As Jeffrey Tigay notes, that is an

---

[29] The translation "judges" for *hāĕlōhîm* is unacceptable (see Hurowitz, "His Master Shall Pierce His Ear," 48–49).

[30] So Cornelius Houtman who argues convincingly for the powerful symbolism of the master's doorway (*Exodus*, 116–19). William Propp, too, discusses a variety of symbols attached to the doorway of a home but presents the pros and cons of other possibilities as well (*Exodus 19–40*, 192–94).

[31] Deut 6:9; 11:20. At the Iron Age II site of Kuntillet Ajrud in the Sinai, inscriptions of cultic significance (blessings invoking YHWH and Ba`al) were found on plaster fragments from a wall and an entrance post; a drawing of a head accompanies one inscription (Meshel, *Kuntillet Ajrud*, 12–13). Jeffrey Tigay assumes that the specification *el hāĕlōhîm* is absent from the law in Deuteronomy because the removal of local sanctuaries transformed the ceremony into a secular one (Tigay, *Deuteronomy*, 150). However, since Deuteronomy's law of centralization (12:4–7) applied only to sacrificial sites, it would not necessarily have eliminated household divine symbols or even communal ones.

[32] See the discussion in Hurowitz, "His Master Shall Pierce His Ear," 47–53; 74–77; Tigay, *Deuteronomy*, 147–50.

unlikely omission of a crucial detail if so intended.[33] Thus, if the mark was a simple piercing it would have healed and eventually disappeared. Thereby, although the slave's ear was to be pierced in a ritual, the ritual was to leave no lasting sign.[34] Such a scenario raises a number of problems. In the case of the absence of a document, what proof does the master have of the servant's lifetime commitment? Conversely, can the slave count on the master's provisions for the duration? Socially, does the slave hold the same status as a short-term Israelite indentured servant?

The answer to what type of mark was inflicted on the slave depends in part on our understanding of the text's terminology, specifically the noun *marṣeʿ* and the verb *raṣaʿ*. First, it should be noted that the key terms in this law, *marṣeʿ*, "awl," and *raṣaʿ*, "pierce," appear in the Bible only in these verses and so cannot be further elucidated from wider usage.[35] The translation of *marṣeʿ* as an awl-type tool used to penetrate the ear into the doorway (Deut 15:17) likely indicates that we are dealing with a more severe mutilation than a simple piercing; consequently *raṣaʿ* should be understood accordingly. Notably, William Propp in his reading and comments on Exod 21:6 translates *marṣeʿ* and *raṣaʿ* as "drill," concurring that the ritual entailed an act closer to boring than piercing.[36]

In conclusion, I propose that when considering the meaning of *raṣaʿ* the biblical practice in question should be viewed in light of the Mesopotamian facial mutilations discussed above, especially those inflicted on the ears of slaves.[37] Essential too for understanding the biblical law is gauging its societal implications. Since the ritual and its aftermath labeled certain Israelites as perpetual servants, only a permanent mark could identify them as such to the outside world. Therefore, it seems reasonable to redefine the verb *raṣaʿ* as the infliction of a substantial, permanent perforation that in some way disfigured the ear.[38]

---

33 Tigay, *Deuteronomy*, 150.

34 Propp suggests that in that case the ritual functioned to remind the slave of the day he entered lifelong bondage (*Exodus 19–40*, 194).

35 The noun *marṣeʿ* appears in Exod 21:6 and Deut 15:17; the verb *raṣaʿ* appears only in Exodus. Akkadian *marṣāʿu* is rarely attested and does not provide clarification. In other biblical passages "to pierce" is rendered by the widely attested terms *naqab* (e.g. 2 Kgs 12:10; Job 40:24–26) and *naqar* (e.g. Judg 16:21; 1 Sam 11:2).

36 Propp, *Exodus 19–40*, 5, 194–95.

37 Hurowitz's suggestion that the ritual is comparable to the act of driving a peg into the mouth of a disobedient servant is one option ("His Master," 72–77), though others that involve marking the ear are also comparable.

38 Probably we are speaking of the main portion of the ear, that part that can

As far as other methods of corporal marking, such as tattooing or branding, those are not mentioned in the Bible in conjunction with slave marks as they are in Mesopotamian sources. Lev 19:28, in fact, is a law prohibiting tattooing, although it does not specify the reason for the ban or whether all types of tattoos are affected. Still, several biblical texts (Gen 4:15; Isa 44:5; 49:16; Ezek 9:4) do refer to special markings that can be interpreted as brands or tattoos. Interestingly, those marks are presented in a positive light, as signs of God's protection of the bearer and the bearer's devotion to God.[39] According to the Bible, then, it appears that only Israelites who voluntarily committed themselves to perpetually serve other Israelites bore a derisive slave mark, one consisting of mutilation of the ear. Seemingly, it identified these Israelites as socially of lesser rank, as members of a class that chose not to be free or, more likely, were forced into that arrangement by life's circumstances.[40] Whether this biblical picture accurately reflects the scope of Israelite practices associated with slavery is open for debate. Seemingly, only the discovery of extra-biblical sources on the subject could further elucidate cultural links and distinctions between Mesopotamian and Israelite conventions.

---

be punctured by resting it against the door frame (Deut 15:17). Maneuvering the earlobe against the doorpost would be physically difficult if not impossible.

39 In Genesis Cain is marked with a sign on his forehead to signal God's protection; in Isaiah and Ezekiel it is the devotees of YHWH whose bodies are marked as a sign of their allegiance to God. Even if these examples are only literary metaphors, their authors must have drawn on customs from neighboring cultures. One can also argue that the persons devoted to God in these biblical examples are actually in service to him, although they are not servants of a temple comparable to the *širkûtu* discussed above. For a detailed discussion on tattooing and branding, see Fox, *On the Ancient Catwalk* (forthcoming).

40 Later priestly legal material redefines Israelite servitude. Lev 25:41–42 states that lifetime slavery extends only until the jubilee year; since Israelites are God's servants they cannot really be sold to anyone else. Jacob Milgrom proposes a connection between this priestly ideology and the tattoo prohibition. He claims that the ban on tattoos also banned puncturing the ear of servants and abolished lifetime slavery among Israelites (*Leviticus 17–22*, 1694–95). The attribution of the ban on tattooing to the abolition of slavery, however, is not convincing especially in light of the positive view of corporeal marking expressed by the prophets Second Isaiah and Ezekiel, both exilic writings.

WORKS CITED

Bakir, Abd El-Mohsen. *Slavery in Pharaonic Egypt*. Cairo: l'Institut français d'archéologie orientale, 1952.

Breasted, J. H., ed. *Medinet Habu I: Earlier Historical Records of Ramses III*. OIP 8. Chicago, Ill.: University of Chicago Press, 1930.

Chiera, E. *Texts of Varied Contents*. Excavations at Nuzi 1. HSS 5. Cambridge, Mass.: Harvard University Press, 1929.

Collon, D. *Ancient Near Eastern Art*. Berkeley, Calif.: University of California Press, 1995.

Dandamaev, M. A. *Slavery in Babylonia from Nabopolassar to Alexander the Great (626–331 BC)*. Rev. ed. Translated by V. A. Powell and edited by M. A. Powell and D. B. Weisberg. Dekalb, Ill.: Northern Illinois University Press, 1984.

Dougherty, Raymond P. *The Shirkûtu of Babylonian Deities*. YOR 5/2. New Haven, Conn.: Yale University Press, 1923.

Driver, G. R. and J. C. Miles. *The Babylonian Laws*, vol. 1. Oxford: Clarendon Press, 1952.

Fox, N. *On the Ancient Catwalk: Studies on Dress and Identity in Israelite and Neighboring Cultures*. Forthcoming.

Greengus, S. "A Textbook Case of Adultery in Ancient Mesopotamia." *HUCA* 40–41 (1969–1970): 41–43.

Houtman, C. *Exodus*, vol. 3. Leuven: Peeters, 2000.

Hurowitz, V. "His Master Shall Pierce His Ear with an Awl" (Exodus 21:6)—Marking Slaves in the Bible in Light of Akkadian Sources." *Proceedings of the American Academy for Jewish Research* 58 (1992): 54–61.

Keimer, L. *Remarques sur le tatouage dans l'Égypte ancienne*. Cairo: l'Institut français d'archéologie orientale, 1948.

Klíma, J. "Zur Stellung der mesopotamischen Sklaven." In *Neue Beiträge zur Geschichte der alten Welt* I, edited by E. C. Welskopf, 19–29. Berlin: Akademie-Verlag, 1964.

Lange, H. O., and H. Schäfer, *Grab und Denksteine des mittleren Reichs*. 4 vols. Berlin: Reichsdruckerei, 1908.

Meissner, B. *Babylonien und Assyrien*. Heidelberg: Carl Winters Universitätsbuchhandlung, 1920.

Mendelsohn, I. *Slavery in the Ancient Near East*. New York: Oxford University Press, 1949.

Meshel, Z. *Kuntillet Ajrud: A Religious Centre from the Time of the Judaean Monarchy on the Border of Sinai*. Jerusalem: Israel Museum, 1978.

Milgrom, J. *Leviticus 17–22*. Anchor Bible 3A. New York: Doubleday, 2000.

Oppenheim, A. L. "Assyriological Gleanings II." *BASOR* 93 (1944): 14–17.

Paul, S. "Biblical Analogues to Middle Assyrian Law." In *Religion and Law: Biblical-Judaic and Islamic Perspectives*, edited by E. Firmage et al., 333–350. Winona Lake, Ind.: Eisenbrauns, 1990.

Propp, W. *Exodus 19–40*. Anchor Bible 2A. New York: Doubleday, 2006.

Reiner, E. "Runaway—Seize Him." In *Assyria and Beyond: Studies Presented to Mogens Trolle Larsen*, edited by J. G. Dercksen, 475–82. PIHANS 100. Leiden: Netherlands Institut voor het Nabije Oosten, 2004.

Rollefson, G., and A. Simmons. "The Early Neolithic Village of 'Ain Ghazāl, Jordan." In *Preliminary Reports of ASOR-Sponsored Excavations 1981–83*, edited by Walter Rast, 35–52. Winona Lake, Ind.: Eisenbrauns, 1985.

Roth, M. *Law Collections from Mesopotamia and Asia Minor*. 2nd ed. Writings from the Ancient World 6. Atlanta: Scholars Press, 1997.

Strassmaier, J. N. *Inschriften von Cambyses, König von Babylon (529–521 v. Chr.)*. Babylonische Texte 9. Leipzig: E. Pfeiffer, 1890.

Inschriften von Darius, König von Babylon (521–485 v. Chr.). Babylonische Texte 10. Leipzig: E. Pfeiffer, 1892.

Tigay, Jeffrey. *Deuteronomy*. JPS Torah Commentary 5. Philadelphia, Pa.: The Jewish Publication Society, 1996.

DIVINE CAUSALITY AND BABYLONIAN DIVINATION

FRANCESCA ROCHBERG
UNIVERSITY OF CALIFORNIA, BERKELEY

When Cicero, in his treatise *De Fato*, focused on the nature of propositions, particularly those that "make a statement about a future event and about something that may happen or may not" (*De Fato* I 1), a two-thousand-year-long tradition of such propositional statements about future events in the form of Babylonian omen texts stood in the background and was well known to him (*De Divinatione* I 1, cf. 19). We are fortunate to have Cicero's works on divination because of his engagement with other thinkers, especially Stoics such as Diogenes of Babylon[1] and Chrysippus, whose works are not otherwise preserved. Consequently we know the terms of a certain portion of the ancient discourse on divination, the Greco-Roman portion, some of which was contemporary with the late, i.e., third century and later, continuation of Babylonian divination, especially astrology. Because some of the philosophical argument among Greeks and Romans interested in prognostication from signs has an underlying polemic attached, i.e., does divination really work and if so how, their discussion touches upon the subject of causality and how signs and their portents are thought to be connected. I would like to redirect the question of causality to the other portion of ancient divination, that is, of the ancient Near East. Of interest to me here are the questions as to how in ancient Mesopotamia signs and portents were thought to be connected, and whether there was anything viewed as causal in these connections.

The difficulty of accounting for causality has had a long and distinguished career, made particularly acute in the eighteenth century by David Hume. "The problem," quoting Wesley Salmon, "is that we seem unable to identify the *connection* between cause and effect, or to find the *secret power* by which the cause brings about the effect. Hume is able to find certain *constant conjunctions*—for instance, between fire and heat—but he is unable to find the connection. He is able to see the spatial contiguity of events we identify as cause and effect, and the temporal pri-

[1] Cicero, *De Divinatione*, I 3, II 43.

ority of the cause to the effect—as in collisions of billiard balls, for instance—but still no *necessary connection*. In the end he locates the connection in the human imagination—in the psychological expectation we feel with regard to the effect when we observe the cause."[2]

The way connections between things are conceived in cuneiform omen texts is unlike that of fire and heat or the collisions of billiard balls. Nonetheless, sources for Mesopotamian divination are, if nothing else, a reflection of the imagination, of culturally particular ways of imagining the connections between events, between phenomena in nature and society, and how phenomena bear meaning for human beings who observe or know them. Omen texts, therefore, seem to me to be a prime body of evidence for our consideration of ancient Mesopotamian thinking about causality, at least among the scribal intellectuals of the Neo-Assyrian period, from which most of the sources come. But as long as we seek from our own physical perspective the connection between sign and portent it remains difficult to meet the Assyrian and Babylonian scholars on their own terms.

The first significant difference is that the events paired in the "if P then Q" statements of cuneiform omens appear to represent a series of inferences not causes.[3] In the vast corpus of such omens, inference from P to Q is made on the basis of a variety of relations construed between them. For example, analogies are used to relate or connect P and Q in ways analyzable in terms of Mesopotamian cultural norms. Other techniques of encoding meaning in the elements of omens are also utilized, but let us for the moment consider that of analogy, for instance in omens concerning a star standing in the halo of the moon. One such omen pairs an unnamed star trapped inside the moon's halo with the situation of the king and his troops being besieged (SAA 8 376:4–5). This seems to be a connection based on a visual analogy. Another concerns a particular star, the King Star, standing in the lunar halo, paired with the birth of male children. Why the sign of the King Star inside the halo is not taken to signal the king's being besieged, in accordance with the visual analogy of the other omen, we cannot know. We can explain the prediction of male children perhaps by the star enclosed in a halo being analogous to an unborn child inside the womb, and the King Star, which is male,

---

2 Salmon, *Philosophy of Science*, 35 and see Hume, *An Enquiry concerning Human Understanding*, sect. VII, parts I and II, paragraphs 48–61, edition of 1777 reprinted in Selby-Bigge, *Enquiries concerning Human Understanding*, 60–79.

3 See my discussion of the inferential nature of omens in Rochberg, "Inference, Conditionals, and Possibility," 4–25.

means the birth of boys (SAA 278:1–4).[4] There is also an omen for Sipazianna, *True Shepherd of Anu* (Orion), standing in the lunar halo, which portends the exercise of world rule for the king of Assyria (SAA 8 302 rev. 4–5) on the basis, one might suggest, of the analogy between the king and a shepherd or protector of his people, a metaphor common throughout cuneiform royal inscriptions.[5] Finally, in another fairly obvious association, the omen for the Bow Star in the halo of the moon is connected to violence among men (GURUŠ.MEŠ *innaddarūma*) (SAA 8 378:1–2). Each of these omens presents a star appearing inside a lunar halo, yet each has its own particular way of employing analogy to yield a different consequent.

Connections made by analogies between some aspect of the sign and its consequent lack the dimension of necessity that connects cause to effect according to our way of thinking. We, therefore, would rather say the omens reflect a system of correlation not causation. But this is because we define a "cause" as something that directly and necessarily produces an effect, that is, that the antecedent should be directly, physically, and necessarily responsible for the consequent. Elizabeth Anscombe said, "It is often declared or evidently assumed that causality is some kind of necessary connection, or alternatively, that being caused is—non-trivially—instancing some exceptionless generalization saying that such an event always follows such antecedents."[6] In such cases, an event Q is related to its antecedent or sign P, as in the gopher hole signifying the presence of gophers because gophers cause gopher holes. This, however, is clearly not the kind of sign relationship the cuneiform scribes used in constructing omen texts.

In the realm of Mesopotamian divination, the idea of "exceptionless generalization," from a mechanical-causal standpoint, is clearly not found, but in consideration of the schemata and patterns of association, such as in the analogies just illustrated, a certain resonance can be noted. Inherent in analogies is a generalizing force, in the sense that similar things behave in similar ways. And although the aim of interpreting signs, seemingly, was not to generalize but to relate a sign of a partic-

---

4 The same apodosis is found in SAA 8 5 rev. 2 but paired with the Pleiades in the halo of the moon. D. Brown noted that a celestial body within the halo of the moon could have been "thought to represent a foetus in the womb," clearly another kind of analogy and entirely possible. See Brown, *Mesopotamian Planetary Astronomy-Astrology*, 135.

5 Kings, like gods, are called shepherd of their people, for example Hammurapi, "the shepherd called by Enlil (to rule)," Codex Hammurabi i 51, and other references in *CAD* R, 310 s. v. *rē'û* usage 2b.

6 Anscombe, "Causality and Determination," 88.

ular character to a particular portent, the connections established in the omen texts were, in fact, held generally. If they were not, the utility of the omen list for future reference and guide to the interpretation of signs would have been nil, and the fact that the lists continued to be copied and cited by the scribes in letters and reports concerning observed signs plainly testifies to their general application.

If we are not concerned with exceptionless general physical causality, or with causality in a mechanical way, is there a place for causal thinking within the Mesopotamian divinatory system? Perhaps the signification of phenomena and the causality of phenomena are not mutually exclusive, but operate on different and not incompatible levels. That we can identify the techniques by which an omen signifies should not mean that the system is reducible to the mere manipulation of words, symbols, analogies, or any of the other linguistic devices that create meaning. Divination, for those who divine, is fundamentally a technique of communication with divinities. It is perhaps in terms of this that we can see the emergence of a causal language, revealing where causality is located in the framework of thought and experience to which divination belongs.

That the gods do speak to human beings within the Mesopotamian divinatory system is expressed in a variety of ways, for example, in constructions with verbs performed by gods, such as *parāsu*, "to decide (a decision)" or "make a judgment (as in a legal case)"; *dânu*, "to make a judgment (in court)"; *šâmu*, "to decree (as in fate)"; *wamā'u* or *amû* / *awû*, "to speak"; *tamû*, "to swear an oath"; or *ṭêmu*, "to inform, give orders, command"; and their related nouns, the objects of the gods' performative speech: *purussû*, "decision, judgment, verdict"; *dīnu*, "judgment"; *šīmtu*, "fate"; *tamītu*, "speech, oath"; *tāmītu*, "oracle query"; and *ṭēmu*, "report, decision, counsel." T. Abusch has shown the parallelism between *ṭēmu* and *alaktu* in the meaning "decision," "decree," or "oracle,"[7] suggesting specifically that this oracular decision is conveyed through ominous celestial signs, as the request for such a divine pronouncement is addressed to the gods of the night, or to specifically named astral deities. In the opening lines of *Maqlû*, Abusch translates *dīni dīna alaktī limdā*, "judge my case, grant me an (oracular) decision."[8] The synonymy of *alaktu* with *dīnu*, *ṭēmu*, and *purussû* also extends the legal metaphor in play within the semantics of divination.

---

[7] Note the lexical equivalents *ṭēmu* and *alaktu* for a.rá, see Abusch, "*Alaktu*," 19, and further discussion, 18–23.

[8] Abusch, "*Alaktu*," 17.

Omen divination, therefore, evinces a fundamental anthropomorphism, where what we call nature is perceived as divine speech, matter turned expressive, meaning materialized in the world of phenomena. In an omen, celestial bodies (or other phenomena) function as parts of divine speech, elements of meaning that can be "read" and interpreted in accordance with a grammar of repeating structures of sense. Focusing on the ancient metaphor of divine speech is one way in which we might understand how divination by omens from the phenomena of nature, surely one of the primary vehicles for what we think of as Babylonian science, fits within a broader religious view of the connections between observed or imagined phenomena and human social life.[9]

The crux of the omens lies in the relation between the antecedent P and the consequent Q. The grammar of the conditionals that form omen statements, with the verb of the *šumma*-clause in the preterite and the verb of the apodosis in the durative, suggests that P is temporally antecedent to Q. This implies that whatever is given in the second clause is expected to occur after or in some sense "as a result of" the phenomenon in the first clause. But this is a matter of logic, specifically conditional logic, not physics, and so does not constitute a causal relationship from a mechanical-causal point of view. In semantic terms, the conditional mode of the antecedent infects the meaning of the consequent: Should P occur, Q (should also) occur. The linguistic modality of these conditional statements—if, were, should P happen, then Q—is balanced by the use of magical means in the form of ritual and incantation, that is, by verbal appeal to the gods, who will hear human speech and respond.[10] That magic was thought to be efficacious by virtue of divine-human communication further suggests that Babylonian omens functioned as defeasible conditionals, that is, P implies Q unless something else obtains, such as an apotropaic ritual appealing to the divine to undo the consequent, again pointing away from a mechanical-causal connection between P and Q.[11]

---

9 Consider the following aphorism of Aviad Kleinberg ("Apophthegmata," 711), on the painful transcendence of the sacred and its remoteness from the (profane) world of human beings: "Human beings cannot bear the sound of God's utter silence. They need noise to calm down. They seek to make God speak."

10 For further discussion, see Maul, "How the Babylonians Protected Themselves," 123–29 and also Niek Veldhuis on the nature of magical language in "The Poetry of Magic," 35–48.

11 Hankinson, *Cause and Explanation*, 371, pointed out that astrology, "deals in defeasible conditionals...rather than adamantine categoricals."

One of the more telling indications of the force of divine agency in the antecedent/consequent relation is that the Akkadian term for the consequent is *purussû*, "(divine) decision" or "verdict."[12] *Enūma Anu Enlil* Tablet 20 includes an instruction to the diviner at the close of each omen to observe the moon-god's eclipse and to "hold wind such-and-such in your hand"; thereby a decision (*purussû*) is given for such-and-such land and the king of that land.[13] Indeed, many comparable references to the apodosis clause, the consequent, as a divine decision or verdict (*purussû*) are to be found in omen commentaries, reports, and letters from scholars concerning omen texts, as well as other genres. It occurs in Neo-Assyrian divinatory magical texts, e.g., *STT* 73 passim, as discussed by Reiner.[14] There the conjurations and rituals are for the purpose of "seeing a divine decision," the subscripts to the prayers ending with the statement that "if you do such-and-such, you will see a divine decision" (*purussâ tammar* / EŠ.BAR IGI.TUḪ). It is still found in this usage in the subscript to a late astronomical text from Uruk, which reads BE-*ma* EŠ.BAR 3,20 *ana* IGI-*ka*, "In order for you to see a divine decision concerning the king" (TCL 6 11 rev. 37).[15]

The depiction of Mesopotamian gods as judges whose decrees establish the way things are is well known. Divine epithets, such as "the ones who judge the law of the land," "who determine the nature of things," "who draw the cosmic designs," and "who decree the destinies,"[16] all exemplify the gods' ultimate power to decide, control, and command. Considering that written omens and written laws in cuneiform culture share the same casuistic "if...then" formulation, this suggests that in dealing with omens we are not only in the realm of signification but, conceptually speaking, of case judgment as well, and that, in the manner of the so-called law codes, the omen compendia represent a kind of codification of divine judgments. In this sense the omens in the cuneiform texts reflect a written record of what has been promulgated through divine speech. But before the omens were codified on cunei-

---

12 See E. Reiner's discussion of *purussâ* / *parāsu* as a technical term in divination in "Fortune-Telling in Mesopotamia," 25. See also my discussion in *The Heavenly Writing*, 194–96 and 266–67, and Fincke, "Omina," 131–47.

13 See *ABCD*, chapter 10 passim. See also *ACh* Suppl. I 1:1–8, and the discussion in Rochberg, "Lunar Data in Babylonian Horoscopes," 36 and n. 7.

14 See note 10.

15 See Brack-Bernsen and Hunger, "TU 11," 12.

16 *LKA* 109:1–8.

form tablets, the signs themselves had an explicitly literate character, being an inscriptional record of divine will in the natural world. Thus communication between god and human was made possible. Natural phenomena, by this reasoning, not only represented the divine written word, but also embodied the further notion that the future is written by the gods on the physical world.

The conception of ominous phenomena themselves as a written language is well attested in first-millennium scholarship. Whether it goes back to the third millennium, to the description of the goddess Nisaba's tablet, the dub mul-an, attested both in the Gudea Cylinder[17] and in the Sumerian composition *The Blessing of Nisaba*, is another question.[18] The meaning of dub mul-an, literally "tablet of the 'star of heaven'," can be read as employing a complex metaphor. The reading of mul not simply as "star" but also as "script" can be made on the basis of an Old Babylonian lexical correspondence between mul and *siṭirtum*, thus "the tablet of heavenly writing,"[19] or "the tablet of the star (which is) the writing of heaven." It is tempting to read the metaphor back even further and extend it to the "tablet of the 'star of heaven'" itself, in which case dub is metaphoric for the sky as its script is for the stars. The metaphor of the celestial bodies as signs written on the heavens extends itself as far as Neo-Babylonian royal inscriptions,[20] and beyond the cul-

---

17 Gudea Cyl. A iv 26 and v 23, see Edzard, *Gudea and His Dynasty*, 72.

18 For *The Blessing of Nisaba*, see Hallo, "Cultic Setting," 125 lines 29–31, and see also Sjöberg and Bergmann, *Sumerian Temple Hymns*, 49:538–39, also cited in Horowitz, *Mesopotamian Cosmic Geography*, 166–167. For MUL = *šiṭirtum*, see *CAD* Š/3, 144 s. v. lexical section.

19 Sjöberg and Bergmann, *Sumerian Temple Hymns*, 138b, citing MSL 2, 132 VI 57 mul = *šiṭirtum*. Nisaba holds the "holy tablet of the heavenly star/ writing (dub-mul-an-kù)" as well in the composition *Nisaba and Enki* lines 29–33, see Hallo, "Cultic Setting," 125, 129, and 131. In their discussion of the term *lumāšu* "constellation," used in the sense of a form of writing with astral pictographs or "astroglyphs," as they have been called, Roaf and Zgoll note that Sumerian mul "star" (or mul-an "heavenly star") "can refer both to a star in the sky and to a cuneiform sign on a tablet." Roaf and Zgoll, "Assyrian Astroglyphs," 289. The notion of the god (often Šamaš) "writing" the signs on the exta of sheep is well known; see for example *ina libbi immeri tašaṭṭar šērē tašakkan dīnu*, "you (Šamaš) write upon the flesh inside the sheep (i.e., the entrails), you establish (there) an oracular decision" OECT 6 pl. 30 K. 2824:12.

20 In the following inscriptions of Nebuchadnezzar: VAB 4 187 i 39, also 74 ii 2, YOS 1 44 i 21; cf. *BBSt* 5 ii 28. Also in the form *šiṭir burūmê*, literally "writing of the firmament," for which, see *CAD* B, 345 s. v. *burūmû* usage b, predominantly in Neo-Assyrian royal inscriptions, but also in a hymn

tural boundaries of Mesopotamia in the magical and religious-philosophical literature of late Hellenism. The divinity of script, in Greek and Late Antiquity, seen as the letters of the alphabet (*stoicheia*), was projected onto the heavenly cosmos in much the same way. Notably, in a passage arguing for a linguistic signification through analogy, reminiscent of what has been defined above as the antecedent-consequent relation in Babylonian omen texts, rather than for a causal nature of the heavenly phenomena, Plotinus said:

> Those who know how to read this sort of writing can, by looking at them as if they were letters, read the future from their patterns, discovering what is signified by the systematic use of analogy.[21]

Omens and divinatory texts support an even more general Mesopotamian conceptualization of the cosmic order of things as being the result of divine command and utterance. Illustrative of this broader conception, that the world order is produced by the creative power of divine word, is a passage from *Enūma Eliš*: "By your (meaning Marduk's) utterance let the star be destroyed, command again and let the star be restored."[22] And in a prayer accompanying an interrogatory divination, a request for an oracular consultation in a Sultantepe text, the diviner says "The gods, your fathers, listen to your sublime words ...Since you have been so kind (before) as to let me know your divine decision (*ṭēmu*), so (again) send me your decision (*ṭēmu*) and let my mouth pronounce it!"[23]

Further reference to divine speech is found in the oracle queries, called *tāmītu*. In a prayer to Sîn the great gods ask the moon-god to "give the divine answers to the oracular questions (*tāmītu*)," specifying the day of the disappearance of the moon on the 29th as the day of Sîn's responses. As Lambert points out in his edition of the *tāmītu* texts, the various usages of the term *tāmītu* have in common the basic root mean-

---

to Aššur (see Livingstone, *Court Poetry and Literary Miscellanea*, 4 no. 1:21). See also Horowitz, *Mesopotamian Cosmic Geography*, 15 n. 25 and 226.

21 See Armstrong, *Plotinus Ennead III*, no. 434. See also the remarks of Miller, that "astrologers...found more and more correspondences between human writing and heavenly phenomena; when they contemplated the skies, they saw what one modern scholar has called 'Himmelsschrift,' a celestial text whose lights formed the moving script of divine order." See Miller, "In Praise of Nonsense," 497.

22 *Enūma Eliš* IV 23f.

23 *ṭēm ilūtiki rabīti*, "your great divine decision," *STT* 73:19, 33 and 41; see Reiner, "Fortune-Telling in Mesopotamia," 32.

ing of "formal speech or judicial utterance."[24] The linguistic underpinning of what we might call the Babylonian theory of divination seems also to be reflected in the use of the term *pišru* (from *pašāru* "to release, undo, or solve") by the scholars to refer to interpretive elements of an omen, including the quotation of an omen (preceded by the phrase *anniu piširšu* "this is its interpretation") for the purpose of elucidating an observed sign.[25] The verb has a number of usages, including "to recount" as of a dream and "to explain or report" what someone said.[26] The root has the force of releasing or revealing, in this case, one form of speech by means of another. The noun *pišru*, used in the scholars' reports overwhelmingly with reference to celestial omens, is defined in the *CAD* as "interpretation" or "hidden meaning." In a letter from the scholar Balasî, the meanings, or interpretations (*pišru*), of monthly omens—*šume ša urḫāni* (ITI.MEŠ) are said to be "not comparable" (*la mušul*) and that each goes its own way. Each omen having its own interpretation, if that is what this means, affirms the importance not of generality but of particularity in the system. How causality figures in the scribes' language with regard to divination is supplied in the statement from the same letter that "the one who 'made' (*epēšu* 'caused') the earthquake also made the *namburbi* against it." The responsible party is Ea: "Ea has done/caused (*epēšu*), Ea has undone/solved (*pašāru*)." Both the sign and the ritual are thought to come from the same divine source. The connection between the sign P and its portent Q, so we may then infer, is attributable to divine intent, presumably actualized by divine verbal pronouncement.

There seems to be little meeting ground between what we can extract from Balasî's letter or other evidence of Assyro-Babylonian divination and more familiar parts of the history of the investigation of causality. In Greco-Roman antiquity the discussion about causality was often tied to various commitments regarding necessity.[27] But the classical philosophical tradition is rife with ambiguity on the question of whether the relation between the antecedent and consequent of astro-

---

24 Lambert, *Babylonian Oracle Questions*, 6.

25 The relationship between the specifically divinatory hermeneutical practice denoted by Akkadian *pišru* and the practice of pesharim in the Qumran community has been noted and discussed by Martti Nissinen in "Pesharim as Divination."

26 *CAD* P, 241–242 s. v. *pašāru*, mng 8. Cf. the interpretation of Zgoll, *Traum und Welterleben*, 383–96 in which *pašāru* means to be released from rather than to recount a dream.

27 See for example in Cicero, *De Divinatione* I 125–27, *De Fato* 13–14, and Sextus Empiricus, *Adversus mathematicos* VIII.

logical divination involved necessity and its implied determinism. Cicero, in his literary dialogue with the Stoic Chrysippus, discusses the deterministic implication of the omen about Fabius' birth at the rising of the Dogstar, namely, that he will not die at sea. Having already occurred in the past, Cicero argues, Fabius' birth at the rising of the Dogstar cannot be changed and so is necessary (on the grounds that "what is past cannot turn from true into false" and "all things true in the past are necessary" [*De Fato* VII 14]). But the necessity of the occurrence of the second proposition, that he will not die at sea, depends on whether one thinks (as Cicero claims the Stoic Diodorus does) that there is a correspondence between the necessity of the antecedent and the inevitability of the consequent.[28]

These are not concerns of the Assyro-Babylonian scholars. In the absence of grounds for seeing any interest in determinism or necessity with respect to the signs and portents, the Mesopotamian theory of the connections between the sign and portent is closer to the Humean idea of constant conjunction, though Hume referred to conjunctions between physical things, not as in the omen texts, physical and social phenomena. In Richard Sorabji's words, the Humean idea is that "If A causes B on a particular occasion, this implies that events like A are constantly conjoined with events like B,"[29] and he draws the distinction between deterministic laws and constant conjunctions, where A's causing B implies that a deterministic law relates A to B. The deterministic law is the equivalent of the "covering law model of explanation" associated with philosopher Carl Hempel.[30] This model consists of three elements, the universal generalization (law statement) in the form of "whenever an event of type b happens, an event of type a happens,"[31] the initial conditions or occurrence of event of type b, and the consequent, which is the occurrence of an event of type a.[32] On the surface this model bears formal resemblance to the reconstruction of how an omen works, though one would be reluctant to see the pairing of the events in the omen statement as the equivalent to the "law statement," if the basis of the universally general law is physical. But it also bears resemblance to the Stoic "first undemonstrated inference scheme," which takes the form of the argument 'if the first, then the second. The first, therefore the

28 Sorabji, *Necessity, Cause, and Blame*, chapter 4 "Stoic Embarrassment over Necessity."

29 Sorabji, *Necessity, Cause and Blame*, 37.

30 Hempel, *Aspects of Scientific Explanation*, ch. 12.

31 See Taylor, *Explanation and Meaning*, 8.

32 Again, see Taylor, *Explanation and Meaning*, 8.

second.' It is interesting, however, given the Assyro-Babylonian legalistic terminology of divine "verdict," to think about the resemblance to a "law" given by divine command. The "law-like" nature of Babylonian omens also derives from the fact that the signs and portents seem to imply a connection between specific sign and specific portent occurring repeatedly. In his study of causality in Greek philosophy, Sorabji concluded that the idea of a cause as a necessitating condition, or part of one, is original to the Stoics, but had substantial longevity after Hellenistic antiquity.[33] If we focus on necessity, the "theory" of omens (strictly in terms of the content of omen texts themselves) does not appear entirely continuous with Greek ideas. Babylonian omens bear a formal resemblance to later Greek formulations of the relation of two events by logic, determinism, necessity, or law, but do not share the philosophy, physics, or cosmology that underpin them. Both do share, however, a drive to create a rational system that can apply generally to a great many and various particulars.

If the idea of necessity is not a part of the Mesopotamian theory of divination, the notion of fate, attributed to the verbal decrees of gods, is. Fate is attached to divine will, which, when pronounced or decreed, is responsible for (causes) the signs and portents, as well as for the magical means to dispel them. Divine will trumps physical necessity and determinism. Even the omens can be changed by the gods, as in the line from a prayer to Nabû: "You (Nabû) are able to turn an untoward physiognomic omen into (one that is) propitious."[34] The scholars are equally unambiguous about the role of the gods in changing the interpretation of a sign, as in this statement from Nabû-nādin-šumi: "the king, my lord, should not be worried about this omen (*ittu*). Bēl and Nabû can make a portent (GISKIM) pass by. They will cause it to bypass the king, my lord. The king, my lord, should not be afraid."[35]

The question of fate and causality in Mesopotamian intellectual culture seems to have been attributed to the gods, specifically through their judicial decision-making role. Divine decisions were conceived of as being inscribed in or on the world and the learned elite scholars who were trained to read and interpret the divine script thereby had access to knowledge of future events. In his work on divination, Cicero (*De Div.* I 127) said: "since everything happens by fate...if there were a human being who could discern the connection of all causes with his mind, surely he would never err. For someone who grasps the causes of future things necessarily grasps

33 Sorabji, *Necessity, Cause, and Blame*, 39.

34 *STT* 1 71:20, and see Lambert, "The Sultantepe Tablets," 135.

35 SAA 10 278:12–rev. 7.

what the future thing will be. But as nobody can do this except god, it is left to human beings to gain their foreknowledge by means of signs which announce what will follow" (cf. *De Div.* I 12–13, 16, 23, 25, II 47).[36] I read this as fitting rather comfortably with the Babylonian omens and the cuneiform scholars' language of divine causality. Indeed, it is the idea that signs are not themselves causes but rather convey divine decisions about what will happen that makes for common ground.

Babylonian divination, and particularly celestial divination and astrology, was known to Hellenistic intellectuals. Although the texts are mostly no longer extant, titles of Greek works concerning the problem of signs, fate, and causality attest to the continuing interest in these subjects for at least four hundred years, beginning with Chrysippus in the third century BCE.[37] Evidence for the transmission to and influence on this tradition from Babylonian ideas about divination, fate, and divine causality is indirect but compelling. The idea of the linguistic character of ominous signs persisted into much later antiquity, as, for example, when St. Augustine, influenced by and echoing Plotinus,[38] said that the positions of stars are "some kind of speech that foretells the future." This comment is found in Augustine's argument against stellar influence, that is, against the idea of astrological signs as causes.[39]

It is significant that Babylonian scholars sought to formalize their understanding of the gods' judicial role in the cosmos in a vast system of conditional statements. The meaning of conditional statements can vary widely, from co-occurrences without an understood causal connection (Hume's "constant conjunctions," such as fire and heat) to certain events in the future necessarily following certain events in the past

---

36 Bobzien (*Determinism and Freedom*, 165) commented on this particular passage as follows, "We do not know how far this reflects early Stoic thought, but it comfortably fits with all we know about early Stoic theories of divination and causation."

37 Bobzien, *Determinism and Freedom*, 6.

38 See note 18.

39 Augustine, *Civ.* V 1, 191. 25–34, ed. Dombart and Kalb, apud Bobzien, *Determinism and Freedom*, 166: "Now it could be said that the stars indicate those <human actions> rather than bring them about, so that their position is *some kind of speech* which foretells the future, and not an active power...but the astrologers do not usually say, for example, 'Mars in this position indicates a murderer', but 'brings about a murderer'. However, let us concede that they do not express themselves as they should, and that they ought to take from the philosophers the rule of how to formulate their predictions of what they believe they find in the position of the stars" (my emphasis).

(Cicero's analysis of the omen of Fabius being born at the rising of the Dogstar[40]), to certain kinds of causal relations (where "if P, then Q" can mean Q occurred because P occurred, often taken as an explanation of the form "Q would not have occurred but for P," e.g., if he trips, then he will fall). We can look at the omen statements and say that P and Q are not causally related, since they bear no physical or mechanical relationship. But a different causal language can be derived, both from the omens and from related literature that draws another picture altogether, one of divine causality effected not only through speech in the form of judicial verdicts, but also through a kind of writing on the tablet of the world in the form of the ominous phenomena themselves. If divine causation, described in this way, subsumes all other forms of causal links between events, then Babylonian ideas about causality are simply a part of their metaphysics concerning the role and effect of the divine in the world, and distinctions between god, causality, and fate are not sharply drawn, but make possible the statements about future events and about what may happen that we find preserved in the textual record of cuneiform divination.[41]

WORKS CITED

Abusch, T. "*Alaktu* and *Halakhah*: Oracular Decision, Divine Revelation." *HTR* 80 (1987): 15–42.

Anscombe, G. E. M. "Causality and Determination." In *Causation*, edited by E. Sosa and M. Tooley, 88–104. Oxford: Oxford University Press, 1993, repr. 2005.

40 Cicero, *De Fato* VI 12–VII 14, and Sorabji, *Necessity, Cause and Blame*, 72–78.

41 See Sharples, "Soft Determinism and Freedom," 266–67, where he discusses the Stoic chain of causes and its various identification or distinction from the idea of god as *pneuma*, the active principle in the universe. And despite philosophical argument and polemics among later Greek or Greco-Roman philosophers on the nature and effect of causes, divine causality remained a principal and pervasive conception throughout the ancient world of West Asia and the Mediterranean. Dale Martin argues that the acceptance of divine causality did not end with Greek Hippocratic explorations of the "natural" (humoral) causes of disease and that this development only has, to modern eyes, the surface appearance of the repudiation of the irrational. The evidence, he shows, points not to the philosophers' disavowal of divine causality, but only of the claim that disease is caused by gods (or demons), who were causes of good and of blessings, not evil. See Martin, *Inventing Superstition*.

Armstrong, A. H. *Plotinus Ennead III*. Loeb Classical Library 434. Cambridge, Mass.: Harvard University Press, 1967.

Bobzien, S. *Determinism and Freedom in Stoic Philosophy*. Oxford: Clarendon Press, 1998.

Brack-Bernsen, L., and H. Hunger. "TU 11: A Collection of Rules for the Prediction of Lunar Phases and of Month Lengths." *SCIAMVS* 3 (2002): 3–90.

Brown, D. *Mesopotamian Planetary Astronomy-Astrology*. Cuneiform Monographs 18. Groningen: Styx, 2000.

Edzard, D.-O. *Gudea and His Dynasty*. Royal Inscriptions of Mesopotamia, Early Periods 3/1, Toronto: Toronto University Press, 1997.

Fincke, J. C. "Omina, die göttlichen 'Gesetze' der Divination." *JEOL* 40 (2006–2007): 131–47.

Hallo, W. W. "The Cultic Setting of Sumerian Poetry." In *Actes de la XVIIe Rencontre Assyriologique Internationale. Université Libre de Bruxelles 30 Juin–4 Juillet 1969*, edited by A. Finet, 117–34. Publications de Comité belge de recherches historiques, épigraphiques et archéologiques en Mésopotamie 1. Ham-sur-Heure: Comité belge de recherches en Mésopotamie, 1970.

Hankinson, R. J. *Cause and Explanation in Ancient Greek Thought*. Oxford: Oxford University Press, 1998.

Hempel, C. G. *Aspects of Scientific Explanation and Other Essays in the Philosophy of Science*. New York: Free Press, 1965.

Horowitz, W. *Mesopotamian Cosmic Geography*. Mesopotamian Civilizations 8. Winona Lake, Ind.: Eisenbrauns, 1998.

Kleinberg, A. "Apophthegmata." *Critical Inquiry* 35 (2009): 711–14.

Lambert, W. G. "The Sultantepe Tablets: A Review Article." *RA* 53 (1959): 119–38.

Babylonian Oracle Questions. Mesopotamian Civilizations 13. Winona Lake, Ind.: Eisenbrauns, 2007.

Livingstone, A. *Court Poetry and Literary Miscellanea*. SAA 3. Helsinki: University of Helsinki, 1989.

Martin, D. B. *Inventing Superstition: From the Hippocratics to the Christians*. Cambridge, Mass. and London: Harvard University Press, 2004.

Maul, S. M. "How the Babylonians Protected Themselves against Calamities Announced by Omens." In *Mesopotamian Magic: Textual, Historical, and Interpretative Perspectives*, edited by T.

Abusch and K. van der Toorn, 123–29. Studies in Ancient Magic and Divination 1. Groningen: Styx, 1999.

Miller, P. C. "In Praise of Nonsense." In *Classical Mediterranean Spirituality: Egyptian, Greek, Roman*, edited by A. H. Armstrong, 481–505. New York: The Crossroad Publishing Company, 1986.

Nissinen, M. "Pesharim as Divination: Qumran Exegesis, Omen Interpretation and Literary Prophecy." In *On Prophecy in the Dead Sea Scrolls and in the Hebrew Bible*, edited by K. de Troyer and A. Lange, 43-60. Leuven: Peeters, 2010.

Reiner, E. "Fortune-Telling in Mesopotamia." *JNES* 19 (1960): 23–35.

Roaf, M., and A. Zgoll. "Assyrian Astroglyphs: Lord Aberdeen's Black Stone and the Prisms of Esarhaddon." *ZA* 91 (2001): 264–95.

Rochberg-Halton, F. *Aspects of Babylonian Celestial Divination: The Lunar Eclipse Tablets of Enuma Anu Enlil*. Archiv für Orientforschung Beiheft 22. Horn: Ferdinand Berger und Söhne, 1988.

Rochberg, F. "Lunar Data in Babylonian Horoscopes." In *Astronomy and Astrology from the Babylonians to Kepler: Essays Presented to Bernard R. Goldstein on the Occasion of His 65th Birthday*, Pt. I, edited by P. Barker, A. C. Bowen, J. Chabas, G. Freudenthal, and T. Langermann. *Centaurus* 45 (2003): 32–45.

The Heavenly Writing: Divination, Horoscopy and Astronomy in Mesopotamian Culture. Cambridge: Cambridge University Press, 2004, 2007.

"Inference, Conditionals, and Possibility in Ancient Mesopotamian Science." *Science in Context* 22 (2009): 4–25.

Salmon, W. C. *Introduction to the Philosophy of Science*. Indianapolis, IN: Hackett Publishing Co., 1999.

Selby-Bigge, L. A., ed. *Enquiries Concerning Human Understanding and Concerning the Principles of Morals by David Hume*. 3rd edition revised by P. H. Nidditch. Oxford: Clarendon Press, 1975.

Sharples, R. W. "Soft Determinism and Freedom in Early Stoicism." *Phronesis* 31 (1986): 266–79.

Sjöberg, Å. W., and E. Bergmann. "The Collection of the Sumerian Temple Hymns." In *The Collection of the Sumerian Temple Hymns*, edited by Å. W. Sjöberg, E. Bergmann, and G. B. Gragg. Texts from Cuneiform Sources 3. Locust Valley, N.Y.: J. J. Augustin, 1969.

Sorabji, R. N. *Necessity, Cause, and Blame: Perspectives on Aristotle's Theory*. Chicago, Ill.: University of Chicago Press, 1980.

Taylor, D. M. *Explanation and Meaning: An Introduction to Philosophy*. London: Cambridge University Press, 1970.

Veldhuis, N. "The Poetry of Magic." In *Mesopotamian Magic: Textual, Historical, and Interpretative Perspectives*, edited by T. Abusch and K. van der Toorn, 35–48. Studies in Ancient Magic and Divination 1. Groningen: Styx, 1999.

Zgoll, A. *Traum und Welterleben im antiken Mesopotamien: Traumtheorie und Traumpraxis im 3.–1. Jahrtausend v. Chr. als Horizont einer Kulturgeschichte des Träumens*. AOAT 333. Münster: Ugarit-Verlag, 2006.